THE PREHISTORIC
FOUNDATIONS OF EUROPE

THE PREHISTORIC
FOUNDATIONS OF EUROPE
To the Mycenean Age

BY

C. F. C. HAWKES

*With twelve plates, six maps and many
text illustrations*

LONDON
METHUEN & CO LTD
BARNES & NOBLE BOOKS
NEW YORK

First published in 1940
This edition reprinted 1973 by
Methuen & Co Ltd
11 New Fetter Lane
London EC4P 4EE
and Barnes & Noble Books, New York
10 East 53rd Street
New York NY 10022
(a division of Harper & Row Inc.)
Printed in Great Britain by
Whitstable Litho, Straker Brothers Ltd

Methuen SBN 416 79020 8
Barnes & Noble SBN 06 472862 5

PREFACE

THIS book first took shape as a smaller volume, designed to interpret only the prehistoric collections of the British Museum and other museums in London, and I have to thank Sir George Hill and Dr. R. E. M. Wheeler both for its original inception and, together with the publishers, for the change of plan that has given it its present form.

My acknowledgements to the Trustees of the British Museum, and to those others who have generously allowed me to reproduce illustrations from various sources, will be found overleaf; here I should wish only to add my gratitude to the Director of the Museum and to the past and present Keepers of British Antiquities there, Mr. Reginald Smith and Mr. T. D. Kendrick, from whom I have learnt and received so much. For the rest, I have tried to see my subject as a whole, and to bring out the sense of a basic European unity which has been borne in upon me so strongly by the study of prehistory. I have tried to form my own judgement on the many issues of specialist controversy involved, and have not hesitated to interpret the story as I see it, rather than offer simply a compilation of the views of others. But, since one mind owes what it sees necessarily in the main to others' work, I wish above all to express my deep indebtedness to my masters and fellow-workers in prehistoric studies, not only in this country but throughout Europe. Something of this will appear from my bibliography, but it really goes much further than that. The feeling of solidarity and friendship between archaeologists of many nations has truly been, in the last twenty years, among the forces making for the intellectual harmony of our civilization, and I know that it will not be killed. Lastly, I owe more than I can say to the good counsel and long-sustained encouragement of my wife.

C. F. C. H.

BRITISH MUSEUM, LONDON, W.C. 1
December 1939

ACKNOWLEDGEMENTS

OF SOURCES OF ILLUSTRATIONS

I DESIRE to express my gratitude to Mr. T. D. Kendrick for Pl. I; to Dr. C. A. Nordman (National Museum of Finland, Helsinki) for Pl. VI, A; to Dr. J. G. D. Clark for Pl. VI, B ; to Dr. E. Sprockhoff (Römisch-Germanische Kommission) for Pl. VIII, 3 and Pl. IX, 2; and to Mr. S. Hazzledine Warren for Pl. IX, 5. All the other photographs used for the Plates are of originals or reproductions in the British Museum.

I am indebted to the Trustees of the British Museum for permission to reproduce the following illustrations from official publications:

From the *Stone Age Guide:* Fig. 1, 7-8; Fig. 2, 6; Fig. 3, ii-iv; Fig. 5, *i-k, n*; Fig. 13, 4-10; Fig. 15, 10, 13; Fig. 20, 6; Fig. 23, 8.

From *The Sturge Collection* (R. A. Smith): Fig. 1, 6, 12-13.

From the *Catalogue of Vases*, I, Pt. 1, *Prehistoric Aegean Pottery* (E. J. Forsdyke): Fig. 6, B 1-2, 4, C 1-3; Fig. 8, *d*; Fig. 21, 16-17.

From the *Bronze Age Guide:* Fig. 23, 1-3, 6-7, 12; Fig. 24, 2; Fig. 25, 1-3; Fig. 27, 2-5.

To the Council of the Society of Antiquaries of London I am indebted for Fig. 1, 2 from the *Antiquaries Journal*; to that of the Royal Anthropological Institute (with Mr. J. Reid Moir) for Fig. 1, 4, from the Institute's *Journal*; to that of the Prehistoric Society (with Prof. Dorothy Garrod) for Fig. 12, 13, (with Dr. J. G. D. Clark) for Fig. 22, 1-4, (with Mr. Stuart Piggott) for Fig. 25, D, and Fig. 27, from the Society's *Proceedings*; to Prof. George Grant MacCurdy, Director of the American School of Prehistoric Research, for Fig. 8, *a*, after Fewkes in the School's *Bulletin*; to Dr. E. Sprockhoff, as Director of the Römisch-Germanische Kommission, for Fig. 5, *m*, after *Germania*, and Fig. 2, 12, Fig. 21, 8-10, 13-15, and Fig. 27, *a* 5-8, after Hillebrand and Tompa in the Kommission's *Bericht, XXIV-V*;

and as Editor of the *Handbuch der Urgeschichte Deutschlands* for Figs. 9-10 and Fig. 11, 6-8, after Buttler; also to Dr. W. Unverzagt, Editor of the *Prähistorische Zeitschrift*, for Fig. 19, 5-8, after Jazdzewski. To Messrs. Methuen & Co. Ltd. and Dr. E. Cecil Curwen I am grateful for Fig. 12 and Fig. 13, 2, from Dr. Curwen's *The Archaeology of Sussex* (County Archaeologies series).

The following objects illustrated in line are in the British Museum: Fig. 1; Fig. 2, 1-2, 5-19 (11 a cast); Fig. 3, i-iv; Fig. 4, *g*, *x*; Fig. 5, *i-k*, *n*; Fig. 6, A 4, B 1-2, 4, C; Fig. 7, 1-3, 5; Fig. 8, *d*; Fig. 13, 1, 3-10; Fig. 14; Fig. 15, 1-2, 4-5, 10-13; Fig. 20, 1-4, 6, 16-17; Fig. 23, 1-3, 6-8, 12; Fig. 24, 2-3, 5-7; Fig. 25, A, B; Fig. 26, *b* 2-5. The remaining line-illustrations, for the most part simple sketches, are based on originals published in various places by various authors, among whom I am especially indebted for concurrence in respect of Figs. 4 and 5 to Dr. J. G. D. Clark.   C. F. C. H.

CONTENTS

PAGE

PREFACE v

ACKNOWLEDGEMENTS vii

Chapter One

PREHISTORY AND EUROPEAN FOUNDATIONS:
PROLOGUE I

Chapter Two

THE EPOCH OF FORMATION

1. ICE AND HUMANITY 7
2. THE PALAEOLITHIC AGE IN OUTLINE . . . 12
3. PALAEOLITHIC LIFE AND THE CREATION OF ART. . 35

Chapter Three

MESOLITHIC EUROPE AND THE DAWN
OF CIVILIZATION

1. THE MESOLITHIC AGE AND ITS BEGINNINGS . . 44
2. THE MESOLITHIC AGE AND ITS DEVELOPMENTS . . 54
3. THE DAWN OF CIVILIZATION 70

Chapter Four

THE SOUTH-EAST AND THE DANUBIAN
EXPANSION

1. AEGEAN CULTURES AND THE NEOLITHIC HINTERLAND . 87
2. THE SOUTH-EASTERN PEASANTRIES 92
3. THE SPREAD OF DANUBIAN CIVILIZATION . . . 109

Chapter Five

PAGE

THE WEST, THE SEA-WAYS, AND THE NORTH

1. THE WESTERN NEOLITHIC 125
2. TRADE, RELIGION, AND CIVILIZATION FROM THE MEDITER-
   RANEAN TO THE ATLANTIC 148
3. TRADE, RELIGION, AND CIVILIZATION FROM THE ATLANTIC
   TO THE BALTIC. 170

Chapter Six

MIGRATION, CONFLICT, AND CHANGE

1. THE NORTHERN NEOLITHIC AND THE WARRIOR CULTURES 200
2. PEOPLES, MOVEMENTS, AND METAL-WORKING . . 232
3. TOWARDS A BRONZE AGE EUROPE 257

Chapter Seven

THE BRONZE AGE AND THE EUROPEAN ACHIEVEMENT

1. THE MEANING OF THE AGE AND ITS INCEPTION IN
   CENTRAL EUROPE 284
2. THE WEST, THE NORTH, AND THE CHANNELS OF TRADE 303
3. ITALY, HUNGARY, AND THE BALANCE OF CULTURES:
   MYCENAE AND CRETE, EUROPE AND THE ORIENT . 332

Chapter Eight

PREHISTORY AND THE FOUNDATIONS OF EUROPE: EPILOGUE 357

BIBLIOGRAPHICAL NOTES 385
INDEX 398

PLATES

FACING PAGE

I. STONEHENGE: A VIEW SOUTH-EASTWARD FROM THE
CENTRE 80

II. THE 'VENUS OF WILLENDORF', AND TWO SMALLER
FEMALE FIGURES FROM THE GRIMALDI CAVES . 81

III. A. CYCLADIC MARBLE IDOL 112
B. FEMALE FIGURINES FROM ASIA MINOR AND S.E.
EUROPE 112

IV. A. POTTERY AND IMPLEMENTS FROM VINČA . . 113
B. BÜKK AND THEISS POTTERY FROM HUNGARY . 113
C. BOWL OF RÖSSEN POTTERY FROM NEAR MAINZ . 113

V. LIMESTONE STATUETTE FROM MALTA: CHALCOLITHIC
POTTERY, AXES, AND ARROWHEADS FROM MEDITER-
RANEAN AND ATLANTIC EUROPE . . . 208

VI. A. PERFORATED ELK - HEAD OF STONE, FROM
DWELLING-PLACE SITE, HVITTIS, SATAKUNTA,
FINLAND 209
B. ROCK-ENGRAVING OF ELKS AT EKEBERG, NEAR
OSLO, NORWAY 209

VII. NEOLITHIC POTTERY, AMBER, TOOLS, AND WEAPONS
FROM NORTHERN EUROPE 240

VIII. PAINTED POTTERY FROM KOSZYŁOWCE, GALICIA, AND
GUMELNITZA, RUMANIA 241

IX. BEAKER POTTERY FROM BRITAIN AND THE RHINE
AREA 304

FACING PAGE

X. 1. THE FOLKTON CHALK DRUMS 305

    2. FOOD-VESSELS OF YORKSHIRE AND IRISH TYPES . 305

XI. BRONZE AGE GOLD FROM BARROWS IN WILTSHIRE
    AND CORNWALL 336

XII. GOLD MASK AND INLAID DAGGER FROM SHAFT-
    GRAVE V, MYCENAE, AND LATE MINOAN I PAINTED
    VASE 337

ILLUSTRATIONS IN THE TEXT

FIG.   PAGE

1. LOWER AND MIDDLE PALAEOLITHIC FLINT IMPLEMENTS   19

2. UPPER PALAEOLITHIC FLINT AND BONE IMPLEMENTS.   29

3. ILLUSTRATIONS OF WEST-EUROPEAN UPPER PALAEO-
    LITHIC ART 42

4. MESOLITHIC IMPLEMENTS, I 49

5. MESOLITHIC IMPLEMENTS, II.   .   .   . 63

6. EARLY EGYPTIAN, SPANISH, MINOAN, CYCLADIC, AND
    HELLADIC POTTERY, AND FIRST-THESSALIAN POTTERY
    AND PAINTED DESIGNS   79

7. STONE AXES FROM THE NEAR EAST, SPAIN, THESSALY,
    AND THE DANUBE 81

8. EARLY PAINTED POTTERY AND DESIGNS FROM SOUTH-
    EAST EUROPE 101

9. DANUBIAN POTTERY FROM GERMANY   .   . 112

10. RECONSTRUCTIONS OF THE NEOLITHIC SETTLEMENTS AT
    AICHBÜHL AND KÖLN-LINDENTHAL   .   . 120

11. WESTERN NEOLITHIC POTTERY AND AXES.   .   . 135

12. (a) SECTION OF A FLINT-MINE AT HARROW HILL, SUSSEX   139
    (b) PLAN OF THE NEOLITHIC CAMP AT COOMBE HILL,
    JEVINGTON, SUSSEX   139

13. NEOLITHIC POTTERY AND IMPLEMENTS FROM BRITAIN   143

14. POTTERY AND SLATE IDOL-PLAQUE FROM MEGALITHIC
    TOMBS IN PORTUGAL   162

15. EARLY METAL DAGGERS, FLINT ARROWHEADS, ETC.,
    AND BEAKER POTTERY FROM MEDITERRANEAN AND
    ATLANTIC EUROPE 165

FIG.   PAGE

16. MEDITERRANEAN, ATLANTIC, AND NORTH-EUROPEAN
    CHAMBERED TOMBS, ETC.   171

17. ART-MOTIVES AND POTTERY ASSOCIATED WITH WESTERN
    MEGALITHS   183

18. CISTS, GALLERY-GRAVES, LONG BARROWS, AND DOLMENS
    OF WESTERN AND NORTHERN EUROPE .   .   .   195

19. NORTHERN NEOLITHIC AND RELATED POTTERY .   .   207

20. CORDED WARE AND OTHER POTTERY, STONE BATTLE-
    AXES, AND HAMMER-HEADED PIN   .   .   .   229

21. IMPLEMENTS AND POTTERY OF THE DANUBIAN COPPER
    AGE AND ITALY, AND MINYAN WARE FROM GREECE.   243

22. BRITISH 'HENGE' MONUMENTS; DUTCH PALISADE-
    BARROWS; ROCK-CUT TOMB AND LONG STONE CISTS   275

23. METAL AND FLINT AXES AND DAGGERS, ETC., OF
    WESTERN AND NORTHERN EUROPE   .   .   .   279

24. EARLY BRONZE AGE POTTERY AND ORNAMENTS FROM
    CENTRAL EUROPE   297

25. EARLY BRONZE AGE WEAPONS FROM SPAIN, THE RHÔNE
    VALLEY, ITALY, AND BRITTANY   313

26. GRAVE-GOODS OF THE EARLY BRONZE AGE IN WESSEX   331

27. SKETCHES OF ITALIAN AND HUNGARIAN BRONZE AGE
    POTTERY, BRONZE HALBERD FROM SHAFT-GRAVE AT
    MYCENAE, AND FAIENCE, STONE, AND GOLD TYPES
    FROM THE BRITISH ISLES   347

MAPS AND TABLES

(After page 414)

MAP I
TABLE I } LOWER AND MIDDLE PALAEOLITHIC

MAP II
TABLE II } UPPER PALAEOLITHIC AND MESOLITHIC

MAP III
TABLE III { THE SOUTH-EAST AND THE DANUBIAN EXPANSION: SOUTH-EASTERN AND DANUBIAN EUROPE, 3100-2100 B.C.

MAP IV
TABLE IV { THE WEST, THE SEA-WAYS, AND THE NORTH: MEDITERRANEAN, WESTERN, AND NORTHERN EUROPE, 3100-1900 B.C.

MAP V
TABLE V { THE ANTECEDENTS OF BRONZE AGE EUROPE: THE CHANGING PATTERN OF EUROPEAN CULTURES, 2300-1700 B.C.

MAP VI
TABLE VI } THE ACHIEVEMENT OF THE EUROPEAN BRONZE AGE, 1800-1400 B.C.

Chapter One

PREHISTORY AND EUROPEAN FOUNDATIONS:
PROLOGUE

THIS book is an attempt, based upon the findings of archaeology, to trace in outline the early foundations of human culture in Europe. The period so covered is there illumined by no written record of its own. In fact, whereas in its later phases such record begins to be available in the Near East, to which the West came to owe so much, the ages of European genesis are wholly prehistoric. But though, compared with the historian's, the prehistorian's task has its obvious disabilities, yet priority to historic time itself contains an ultimate advantage. For the significance of human doings and institutions does not begin with their written history, and 'he who thus considers things in their first growth and origin, whether a State or anything else, will obtain the clearest view of them'. That remark was made by Aristotle in introducing his treatise on Politics, and whether or no we can call prehistoric man a 'political animal', it at least brings out the vital importance of prehistory in the study of human kind. And there is no true cleavage between history and prehistory: the verbal distinction between them rests simply on the presence or absence of written material in our equipment for their pursuit. It is indeed often said that there are 'peoples which have no history'. But all peoples have culture which can be assessed and accounted for, and beyond the scope of history this is the business of archaeology, which thus carries out for the peoples of the past the work which anthropology does for those who have remained 'without history' until the present, in its critical sifting of not only diffusion among them, but 'functional' interlocking within them, of living elements of culture. And the further archaeology can go towards fixing events of the human past in definite order of time, the greater will be its contribution to the anthropologist's, no less than to the historian's, knowledge of humanity.

Ultimately prehistory has its natural place in the understanding of the evolution of life as a whole, the scientific appreciation of the adaptiveness which, as its surroundings change, alone offers opportunities for its survival. The sensitive vitality which can so respond supplies the momentum of evolution, by gradual increase of control over environment and its changes, from dependence towards dominance. And the biological climax of evolution has been in man. When, after the great sequences of Primary and Secondary geological age, the mammals began their decisive spread, the Tertiary world was entering upon a long-drawn crescendo of land-formation, which culminated in the Miocene mountain-building responsible for the main bulk of the Alpine-Himalayan backbone of Europe and Asia. It was a critical age in the earth's history, to which mammalian evolution was a biological response. Most mammals, like the lower forms of life then and before, tended to seek their appropriate dominance by developing a specialized bodily structure. Among them, the Primate group thus developed a bodily adaptation for a climbing life among forest trees, particularly in their hands and feet with more or less opposable thumb and digits. But within this group the anthropoid apes and man, favoured by their mechanism of reproduction, became unique in their further evolution. It was controlled not by more specialization of limb, but by the vital growth of the brain. The ancestors of man thus reached no physically fixed equation between their equipment and their opportunities. Their terms could be infinitely varied, if only the dominance of brain, through its perfected organs of sense and reaction, maintained its hold over the body's versatility. The ensuing Pliocene period was marked by a sharpening of contrasts in landscape. The Alpine-Himalayan chain was already cutting off the northern plains from the more varied regions running southward to the tropical forests. Its effect was to delimit the continuous extent of vegetation, while decreasing temperatures could in part replace forest by open country. Responding to such changes in the nature of their habitat, the forerunners of man could forsake tree life, and face their surroundings and their future erect upon the ground. Man's dawning intellect thus found a new diversity of opportunity. And his first characteristic act of which we have concrete evidence was to equip the body to its service in a new way of his own. He had done with the limits of self-sufficing limb and claw and tooth. He began to use tools, and in that beginning civilization was made possible. From the choosing of a stick or stone shaped suitably for his purpose, he took to breaking or bending a stick, or chipping one stone with another to produce a shape he could not find to hand. And from strata bequeathed by the Pliocene world to geology come the 'eoliths' which many archaeologists regard as the oldest palpable relics of his handiwork.

With the appearance of stone or flint tools we get our first glimpse of human material culture. True, it is a very incomplete one. The disappearance of perishable materials is the archaeologist's greatest handicap. And though geological deposits of a kind to make some preservation of them possible are scarcely to be hoped for even in the ensuing Pleistocene period, yet even from the residue of stone (and occasionally bone) implements that we have we can already learn something: we can recognize man serving his simple needs with tools of his own devising, and as they take on a more definite range of forms, we can perceive more clearly what their whole existence implies. These primitive human creatures, unique in this among their anthropoid kin, have created a crude but effective tradition of manual ability, of doing certain things in certain ways for certain purposes deliberately conceived. Such a tradition involves much more than the actual skill to make the tools and use them. Just as that skill would have been impossible without man's delicately adjusted stereoscopic vision, so, without the close correlation of nervous and muscular controls in his organs of hearing and utterance, neither it nor any other fund of higher experience could have been imparted to his fellows or to his dependent young. The faculty of even the simplest speech could substitute precept for mere example in the training of the singly born children whose slow-passing infancy kept them so long in need of it.

Thus the collective experience of a human group could become an inheritance handed down the generations by means of that human peculiarity, a spoken language. So the capacity to create and transmit the elements of culture is the direct outcome of man's organic evolution, and thereby that evolution in humanity has been exchanged for cultural progress. It is in this progress that the adaptive vitality of mankind is manifest, and the history of human culture will be its record of achievement.

What, then, of human culture in what we know as Europe? Its long-drawn-out genesis, however remote its inception, leads at last to our own civilization: its prehistory comes ultimately to lie directly behind the historic record of our own doings. How that has come to pass, and through what changes from within and influences from without, will be our theme throughout what follows. But first we have to realize that the whole story is indissolubly bound up with the physical character of Europe itself, the landscape and climate which have made the environment of human culture. And that character is unique. The mountain backbone of Asia, with that of America curving away behind it like a tail, runs westward to culminate in the European Alps and Pyrenees. Its wrinkled ridges may crowd together in the rugged clusters of Armenia or the Balkans, or swing apart to enclose high table-lands like those of Persia or Asia Minor. Between the Black Sea and East-Mediterranean depressions to north and south, Asia Minor stretches forward as a land-bridge into Europe, from a root fixed where the apex of Arabia divides the river-land of Babylonia from the causeway across to the answering river-land of Egypt. From the Nile mouths the North African coast runs on to meet in the ridges of the Atlas a sundered limb of the same mountain backbone, enclosing with the Apennine and Spanish highlands the further depression of the West Mediterranean. Here there have thus been land-bridges out of Africa, and if the Sahara behind them be watered by a favouring climate, the way lies open from the tropical forests to the south. Beyond again stretches only the western ocean, but beyond the eastern land-bridge of Asia Minor the Caucasus and Crimea form another sundered mountain limb whose foothills run past the Caspian depression, to give on to the great expanse of the steppe-land which marches with the whole length of Eurasiatic backbone out of Central Asia into the plains of Northern Europe. Between the Caspian and the Urals the steppe forms an open highway, and the plains to westward only narrow to their end, half drowned under the shallow northern waters, between the foreland of Carpathians or Alps and the upcast continental rim of Scandinavia and Highland Britain.

If the converging structures of Asia and Africa thus make of the whole Old World a giant L, Europe is its apex. It lies open to the great continents on east and south, to form the inevitable meeting-place of whatever each may bring forth. Furthermore, it lies away from the Tropics, and the Atlantic helps in the west to restrain its temperatures from permanent extremes of cold and heat. The diversity of altitude and structure between its Alpine spine and the Mediterranean and Baltic depressions to south and north give life and landscape a wide range of conditions for its relatively small size. In short, it is capable, under secular changes of land-form and climate, of forming a natural paradise for the play of adaptive vitality.

And we shall find that vitality a recurrent characteristic of its inhabitants. Initially we have to witness, in the Quaternary Age of geological time, very decided changes of land-form and climate alike, from which the Europe we have described received gradually its stamp. During the Pleistocene period, ending only some 14,000 years ago, the 'Ice Age' alternated its visitations with milder inter-glacial phases on the face of the Continent. And even in the Holocene or 'Recent' period which has followed, the gradual retreat of the ice to its present limits has been accompanied by fairly pronounced oscillations of climate, and the greater Pleistocene changes in land- and sea-levels have been succeeded by fluctuations which continue to affect our coast-lines to this day. The cosmic processes ultimately responsible did not, of course, confine their effect to Europe: answering glaciations may be studied along the Asiatic mountain chains, and in Africa there is a partly relatable sequence of 'Pluvial' periods, while changes in land-form, with continued mountain-building and faulting, are recognizable in both those continents. Thus everywhere the environment of life underwent many degrees of alteration, which were bound to affect the existence of mankind. For man in the Pleistocene was a food-gatherer and a hunter, dependent for his subsistence on what vegetation and fauna allowed him, and so in these ages when the Europe we know was as yet in formation, prehistory is concerned in a special degree with his physical surroundings. The configuration of Europe, and its position at the apex of the Old World, are in fact here of controlling importance. Indeed, the varied European scene of later times, and its situation as the neighbour of both Africa and Asia, will hereafter be found no less critically important to the course, itself no less varied, of the human activity upon it that we shall try to chronicle in subsequent chapters. It is in many ways equally so to-day. In approaching, then, first the distant Europe of the Pleistocene, we are introducing a secular process of interaction between man and his environment, wherein lies the genesis of all the doings and developments of later Europe. Continuing, we shall see the descendants of the last Pleistocene inhabitants finally reacting to something more than their physical surroundings, namely, to the light of the early-born civilization of the Near East, itself the product of a similar but more creatively fertile process, which brought the old geographical factors out into a new dawn of opportunity. Thereafter, in less than twenty centuries of the varied interplay of forces new and old, adaptive vitality achieved a truly European pattern of human culture, distinctive in feature and dynamic in effect. And on that as foundation the history of our continent is ultimately based.

Chapter Two

THE EPOCH OF FORMATION

I. ICE AND HUMANITY

(Map I and Table I: at end)

UNDERSTANDING of the physical environment of life in Pleistocene Europe is obviously bound up with some comprehension of the 'Ice Age'. The geologists Penck and Brückner established a sequence of four main Pleistocene glaciations in the Alps, named after appropriate Swiss valleys, the Günz, Mindel, Riss, and Würm. This sequence is now familiar in our literature, but more recent work in Central and North-Central Europe has amplified it not a little. Not only is it now said that three 'Danubian' cold phases preceded the standard four, but the Günz, Mindel, and Riss have by some geologists each been doubled, and the Würm actually trebled, thus taking in what had been treated as a subsequent phase under the name of Bühl. The geological record of these glaciations takes various forms. Not only may ice-action be visible in the shaping of hills and ridges, but the glaciers themselves will have deposited lateral and terminal moraines, and also wide sheets of bottom-moraine, such as in England are called boulder-clays—more or less clayey deposits containing erratic boulders or other ice-borne foreign matter, beyond which the outwash of glacial gravels may form plateau sheets of related drift. Further, outside a continuously glaciated area, seasonal thawing will cause surface deposits to sludge over more deeply frozen subsoil: this phenomenon is called solifluxion, and from the contorted material which it will have left along a summit line, its progress down a slope may be detected by a trail of drift, until in a valley-bottom it has deposited the materials of a basal river-gravel. River-deposits of gravel or other drift may themselves be interpreted in definable time-succession, and related to the main glacial sequence of their region.

7

The energy of a river in carving out its bed, varying with its volume and speed, will carry away the material thus denuded towards the sea. Obviously when the glaciation of water-supply reduces energy, the material will get very largely deposited on the way in the form of gravels, whereas a big volume of water from melting glaciers will effect erosion down the river's course. An alternation of glacial and warmer inter-glacial conditions will thus produce an alternation of deposit and erosion along a river, each erosion cutting down the bed and leaving the flanks of the previous deposit as a terrace on each side, so that in time a regular succession of such terraces is formed. Thus Penck and Brückner could base their Alpine glacial sequence on 'fluvio-glacial' terraces, and thus the river-deposits of Germany assist the correlation of Alpine with northern glaciations spreading from Scandinavia —the Mindel with that named the Elster, the Riss with the Saale, and the Würm with the Warthe and Weichsel or Vistula. But there was also a sequence of a different kind, that of changes in the base-level of land relative to sea, themselves referable to the disharmony between the slow oscillation of the land, caused by the alternation of depression under ice-load and recovery upon thaw, and the more rapid changes made by the same freezing and melting in the liquid volume of the sea. The raised or drowned sea-beaches around our modern coast-lines are not the only testimony to such changes; for clearly a river flowing at speed from high land to a low sea will erode its bed, while a sinkage of land, by checking it from the mouth upwards, will bring about an aggradation of deposits. Thus an alternation of these movements will of itself cause terrace-formation, and the interaction of this factor with that of the river's absolute volume may greatly complicate the geological record. In such cases the evidence of solifluxion for the periodic prevalence of glacial conditions can provide a key to the problems of correlation.

Another critically important form of deposit is that known as loess, the fine wind-borne material laid down over open country in the cold dry steppe conditions bordering a maximum of glaciation. Loess may, as on the Somme, be formed upon the terrace or solifluxion deposits along a river, and thus the relative ages of widespread loess-beds may be determined and their climatic significance assessed, while such phenomena as their surface weathering into loam have a corresponding further importance. River-drift itself, when deposited by a slow-moving current, may take the form of a loam or 'brick-earth', which will similarly form in the beds of lakes. And finally, the fossil flora and fauna of many Pleistocene deposits are naturally of essential value in determining their age and the climatic conditions of their formation. The appearance in them of new forms of life will be a critical factor, and climate may be established from the known attachment of various species to cold or warmth.

But the skill of the geologist can provide little more than a *relative* chronology for the Pleistocene, and neither he nor the geographer can confidently state why these great changes in conditions took place. It is astronomy that alone can offer a computation of absolute dates in years, and these are obtained through its newly divined capacity to explain the climatic succession in terms of the solar system. The eccentricity of the earth's orbit, the obliquity of the ecliptic, the helio-centric length of the perihelium—the cycles of change which these undergo are of closely calculable duration, and their correlated charting, first achieved by Milanković, presents a history for solar radiation, the major determinant of climates. The curve of its summer variation over measured time has been made to coincide successively, for a mean European latitude, with the climatic sequence determined by Pleistocene geology. With the successive minima of solar radiation correspond the successive maxima of terrestrial glaciation, and thus a great framework of natural chronology can be projected upon the archaeological record of the prehistory of man. It is safe to say that the progress of research will advance beyond the pioneer work of Koeppen, Wegener, and Soergel. But some already feel it possible tentatively to combine its findings with a table of the major known events of Pleistocene time in Europe. Extension southward across the Mediterranean, the Sahara, and Equatorial Africa involves, with change of latitude a skilful assessment of meteorology. For while a European glaciation should correspond to a

Pluvial period in Africa, a warm inter-glacial in Europe may not be automatically equated with the reverse; it appears that only the colder inter-glacials of our series can be answered by inter-pluvials in more southern latitudes, and in any case agreement has yet to harden over many of the issues concerned. Since our purpose is here to place human prehistory in the foreground, our essay in tabulation (Table 1) must necessarily do duty without close discussion of its features. But it will at least serve as a staging for our brief survey of the annals of humanity in the European Pleistocene.

We spoke in the first chapter of humanity's biological evolution, and it is obviously from discoveries of fossil man in Pleistocene deposits that the story of that evolution has to be documented down to the inception of recent times. But only in the period's later stages does that documentation even begin to be adequate, and what we know of it earlier is not only sparse, but must be studied as yet without direct knowledge of immediate antecedents. It is, however, at least now beginning to appear that both the Asiatic East and the African South of the Old World have each a different course of events to show from the converging regions of Western Asia and Northern Africa with their apex in Europe. It was formerly thought that modern or 'Neanthropic' man—*Homo sapiens*—was unrepresented in the European region until the final phases of the Pleistocene, when he superseded the very different human type commonly known as 'Neanderthal man'. But it is now thought that the 'Neanderthal man' of Europe belonged to a distinct, sometimes called 'Palaeo-anthropic' branch of the human stem, with no immediately ancestral relationship to the *Homo sapiens* before whose expansion he became extinct. And lately recognition has been won for the idea of a parallel ancestry for both 'Palaeo-anthropic' and 'Neanthropic' groupings of humanity, running probably right through the main stages of the Pleistocene from the unknown beyond. Just as the 'Heidelberg man' of the jaw from the Mauer Sands in Germany may thus be reckoned among the relatively early ancestry of the Neanderthal grouping, so *Homo sapiens* has his forbears likewise. This, whatever its exact geological age, is the context of the famous

Piltdown cranium, and the skull recently discovered at Swanscombe in Kent, in the Middle Gravel of the '100-foot' terrace of the Lower Thames, is, though incomplete, yet quite certainly a witness to the existence of the same strain, in a form already well within the type-range of modern man, in the inter-glacial epoch between the second and third, or probably Mindel and Riss, glaciations of the Pleistocene succession. One may add that, despite the cloud around the geological position of the jaw and skulls found not long before at Kanam and Kanjera in East Africa, their physical type should give them an analogous significance. And, wherever evidence is available, the industries of workmanship in stone associated with the two evolutionary series have been found constant in their differentiation one from the other.

This culminating fact, if it continues to recur in evidence, is of paramount importance for prehistory. For it bears out the notion, already here advanced, of man's creation of material culture as the outcome and counterpart of his organic evolution; if different evolutionary stocks may be recognized through correspondingly different traditions of material workmanship, then prehistory and the archaeological method can indeed be vindicated as the link between natural and human history. We shall, however, find as we proceed signs that the reality, as the Pleistocene ran on, is likely to be a good deal more complicated than the simple co-existence of two evolutionary stocks each with its own cultural tradition. Human genetics are not so straightforward, and elements of material culture can be interchanged between two or more groups without their physical alliance. In fact, it is precisely the geographical position of Europe, in connexion alike with Asia and with Africa, which, by making it the natural mixing-ground for the cultural traditions of different human groups, gives our continent the critical importance it has in prehistoric studies. So now that we are introduced to the idea of a long pedigree for modern man, running side by side with that of his now extinct cousins in a region of which our continent forms a pre-eminent part, and attested not only by a physical distinction of type, but by a cultural distinction of material equipment, we may embark on our outline of the Pleistocene record in human prehistory. That record is not too remote for the beginning of a study of European foundations.

2. THE PALAEOLITHIC AGE IN OUTLINE

(Maps I-II and Tables I-II: at end)

The Pleistocene comprises the Palaeolithic period, or Old Stone Age, of archaeology, and it has provided the prehistorian with stone and flint implements in great quantity. From the study of their technique and form they may be classified, and from their stratification in geological deposits of known age their relative antiquity may be determined. In former days Western Europe was thought to yield one continuous succession of Palaeolithic cultures, named after 'typical' French sites, Chellian, Acheulian, Mousterian, Aurignacian, Solutrian, and Magdalenian. That belief has served its purpose, and to-day a new pattern is taking its place, already clear in general outline. There are, first, two groupings of material culture in the Old Stone Age, with a third emerging later to join them. The first two are manifest in what are called core-industries and flake-industries, with blade-industries making the third. In a core-industry, man's object was to chip nodules or cores, or split pieces, of stone or flint directly into implements. In a flake-industry he made his implements from flakes struck off a parent core with a single primary blow. Blade-industries, theoretically classifiable with flake-industries, are in fact distinctive, and will be considered when we reach their time of dominance in Europe in the 'Upper', or latest main division of the Palaeolithic.

The eoliths introduced in our first chapter stand before and rather outside this system. Their recognition in the worn and ochre-stained specimens first collected by Benjamin Harrison over seventy years ago from the plateau-gravels capping the North Downs of Kent may still to-day be repudiated. They are formed of pieces of naturally tabular flint, with steep chipping round the edges, producing generally a sort of nosed shape ; this chipping is their only testimony to human workmanship, and some people believe it is purely natural. The gravels, being older than the hollowing-out of the Weald from the watershed whence they were spread, are perhaps Tertiary, and it can only be argued that the crudity of workmanship to be expected of man in so remote a period may be necessarily hard to distinguish from the product of natural agency. The debate on eoliths thus becomes a good deal a matter of opinion. A more definite introduction to the Palaeolithic is offered by the discoveries of the last thirty years, due to Mr. J. Reid Moir, in beds below the shelly deposits of East Anglia known as the 'Crag'. Though Pliocene from its fossil molluscs, the Crag's inclusion of elephant, horse, and ox remains should class it as Early Pleistocene, and in the basement-beds below it, formed of the strewage of older land-surfaces on the bottom of a cold northern sea, flints acceptable as of human shaping can be found, and furthermore divided into five groups, differing in wear, patina (exposure-condition revealed by colour), form, and workmanship. The three groups thus reckoned the oldest, mainly from the probable margins of the Crag Sea by Ipswich and Bramford, include tools like eoliths but made on deliberately struck flakes of flint, simply chipped pebble-nodule tools (Fig. 1, 1: as first recognized re-deposited in a later Suffolk formation at Darmsden), and the famous 'rostro-carinates' with their ridged or carinated back and terminal rostrum or beak.[1] The latter, most frequent beneath the Norwich Crag, are supported by kindred tool-forms which seem to culminate presently in the leading core-tool of the whole Palaeolithic, known as the hand-axe. Fairly convincing hand-axes, as well as flake-implements of quite good appearance [2] have been adduced in the fourth group, distinguishable as having suffered relatively little from wear before being covered by the marine deposit of the Shelly Crag, and in the midst of the Shelly Crag the shore-line 'floor' of Foxhall near Ipswich has produced the last group of the series. Thus the pre-Crag discoveries, though some strongly contest them, appear to introduce from yet more distant ages into the beginning of the Pleistocene a record of human material cultures embodied in both core-industries and flake-industries. The lower limit of their antiquity will be furnished by the age of the covering Crag,

[1] Fig. 1, 3.   [2] Fig. 1, 2.

and the Shelly ('Red') Crag of Suffolk and the latest or
Weybourne Crag of Norfolk are sea-floors laid down under
conditions of arctic cold, which calls for a place in the
recognized system of Pleistocene glaciations.

It is suggested that that place should be with the Günz
glaciation of the Continent, and this equation, though it has
its difficulties, seems confirmed by what follows. For the
next considerable deposit of East Anglia, following on the
shrinkage of the Crag Sea and ascribed to estuarine conditions,
is that called the Cromer Forest Bed, whose fossil fauna agrees
significantly with that of the Mauer Sands in South-West
Germany. And the Mauer Sands succeed directly to a Günz
horizon. We have already mentioned their famous fossil,
the jaw of 'Heidelberg man', and his kin may have been
responsible for some at least of the implements of Cromer,
which include a large-scale flake-industry of promising
significance.[1] But the estuarine gravel of the Forest Bed yet
contains passable core-tools and primitive hand-axes, and its
horizon has often been correlated with the first stage of hand-
axe core-culture in the old West European Palaeolithic
system, the Chellian. The 'type'-site of Chelles near Paris
has now been deprived of its honours, and the leadership
of the Abbé Breuil among contemporary prehistorians has
effected a re-christening under the name Abbevillian, since
at Abbeville Champ-de-Mars, on the Somme, a typical assemblage of implements has been found *in situ* overlying
what is probably a Günz solifluxion-gravel. The animal
remains here resemble those of Mauer and Cromer in including types of elephant, rhinoceros, hippopotamus and
other beasts indicating a warm climate. The Abbevillian hand-
axe (cf. Fig. 1, 3) is a massive implement worked on both
faces, probably by striking a big core against a stone anvil.
The blows of stone on stone produced deep abrupt flake-scars
whose alternation made a crude zigzag cutting-edge: the
most that is found by way of secondary work is some further
trimming, as a rule suggesting the use of a hammer-stone.
In France and South-East England these hand-axes are rare,
and usually found 'derived' in later deposits, but it was in

[1] Fig. 1, 4.

this warm period that their makers must chiefly have flourished, though some can have survived till after the land-recovery presently attested by erosion on the Somme, and change from estuarine to fresh-water conditions at Cromer, had been followed by the return of arctic cold. For what seems an unworn Late Abbevillian hand-axe has been found at Side-strand, close to Cromer, lying in the 'Till' deposited above the final, arctic beds of the Forest Bed series by the new glaciation in which this epoch culminated.

The Till contains erratics from Scandinavia, and should be equated with the ice-borne 'brick-earth' formation round Norwich known as the North Sea Drift, beyond whose limits this record of glaciation is carried on by the remains of the East Anglian Lower Boulder-Clay, and by the sands and gravels of the so-called Westleton series. The makers of Abbevillian hand-axes are believed to have retreated south-wards with the warm-climate animals towards Africa, where the hand-axe tradition lasts on to a much later ending in an unbroken continuity contrasting pointedly with the interrupted series of ice-invaded Europe. The North Sea Drift phase was followed by land-recovery and thaw, after which a considerable 'mid-glacial' interval or inter-glacial period ensued before the renewed glaciation which laid the East Anglian bottom-moraine now called the Middle Boulder-Clay. That, with its outwash sands and gravels, apparently represents the Alpine Riss, whereas its predecessor has long been connected with the Alpine Mindel. The Mindel is sometimes said to consist of two parts, each represented for example by a solifluxion on the Somme; in Germany it is to be equated with the Elster glaciation, which terminates the Mauer Sands as the Till terminates the Cromer Forest Bed. With this the Lower gives place to the Middle Pleistocene, and the return of the hand-axe people to Western Europe brings the superseding of the Abbevillian by the earliest European stages of its greater sequel, the Acheulian.

The name comes from the type-site of St. Acheul on the Somme. Early Acheulian hand-axes are rather more shapely than their predecessors, and were still made largely by the stone-striking method, but now a new technique of secondary trimming begins gradually to appear, the use of a softer striking-material, ultimately at least a bar of wood or bone, which by easing the blow's vibration produced flatter flake-scars and thus a straighter cutting-edge. When the hand-axe makers returned with the warm climate after the Mindel glaciation, the Early or 'Lower' stage of this Acheulian development of core-culture was fully formed. But we are now confronted by its co-existence with a wholly distinct development of flake-culture, which may, to judge by the worn state of its initial products, have first appeared earlier, but is anyhow found continued (e.g. on the Somme) directly after the final passing of the Mindel. This culture is the Clactonian, and in it we see the renewal, or even the continuation, of the old Cromer tradition of flake-industry. Its flake-tools (Fig. 1, 5) are struck on a stone anvil from the parent core, with a good breadth of the striking-plane allowed to each; the hard blow on the anvil brought off the flake at an obtuse angle, with a big and prominent bulb marking the point of percussion; the edges were then trimmed, in the culture's earlier stages, with a steep, 'nibbled' retouch. On the lower Thames, the Clactonian is first found *in situ* at Swanscombe, in the lowermost '100-foot terrace' gravel laid after the river had eroded the North Sea glacier-deposit, when temperate climate had brought into being well-wooded country, and a fauna including warmth-loving elephants (e.g. *antiquus*), rhinoceros, hippopotamus, ox, horse, and deer. Subsequent land-uplift caused the erosion of a deep channel, and this in its turn became filled with gravels and sands in which the Clactonian is again abundantly represented: in fact, it was in these that it was first discovered, on what is now the foreshore at Clacton-on-Sea in Essex. In ensuing phases of the inter-glacial it developed further: we shall meet its later stages shortly, and the finest expression of its workmanship was reached in that often called Clactonian III, best represented in the brick-earth formed above the Middle Boulder-Clay at High Lodge near Mildenhall in Suffolk. Here, as Fig. 1, 6 shows, the implements are well-made scrapers, points, etc., with edges beautifully trimmed in a technique close to that of the contemporary Acheulian.

On the lower Thames, tools already close to the High Lodge

type have occurred at Swanscombe in the middle series of '100-foot' gravels deposited after the channel had filled up again above the lower level, but this horizon is far richest in the finely worked hand-axes of the Middle Acheulian stages. The climate was consistently temperate, and the hunters of the abundant big game represented here and e.g. on the Somme show a greatly advanced skill in tool-making. These broadly triangular hand-axes with their even blades and heavy butts, and the delicate ovate implements [1] which subsequently appear, with their regular and often S-curved edges, show an admirable mastery of the 'wood-bar' technique. Flake-tools likewise achieve greater prominence, and the similarity of some of them to the Clactonian suggests a drawing together of the two cultures. In Southern France and Spain, where the material was often not flint but the native quartzitic rock, there is a greater prominence of work which reinforces the culture's similarity to its ever-continuing counterpart in Africa. And Africa's claim that the whole thing is the work of the ancestry of *Homo sapiens* (p. 11) has now been met by the indisputable fact of the Swanscombe skull's association with the Middle (strictly, early-Middle) Acheulian of Europe. The great Eurafrican core-culture province seems thus beginning to be attributable to the true forbears of modern man, with which the Steinheim skull from Württemberg may also be connected. On the other hand, east of the Rhine basin and away into Asia stretches the province of flake-cultures, which appear to demand a different attribution. At our apex of the two-limbed Old World in North-West Europe the two provinces overlap: while a northern continuation of the Clactonian is best represented (as in the Barnham gravels) in the East Anglian Breckland, a Southern outcome of it presently intrudes into the Acheulian country of South France as the Tayacian, and the same tradition in Belgium and beyond the Rhine lived on to produce a significant sequel in 'Middle' Palaeolithic times (p. 21). And before the onset of the Riss glaciation it seems to have given rise in Europe to what is really a new form of flake-culture altogether. This is called the Levallois, or Levalloisian, culture

[1] Fig. 1, 8.

after a site on the outskirts of Paris, and it first appears in the marginal lands of North-Western Europe late in the same period as the Middle Acheulian. Its tool-making technique, which seems to have originated within the Clactonian, is distinctive. Before any tool-flake was struck off, the parent core was itself first roughly hammer-trimmed all over into a sort of nearly plano-convex shape, comprehensibly called a tortoise-core. The butt-end of the tortoise-core was finely trimmed down to form a faceted platform, which was then struck against an anvil to detach the flake. By aiming his blow inwards, the maker got his flake off more or less at right angles to the platform, instead of the obtuse-angled slant of the Clactonian method, and thanks to the preparatory trimming, it was then at once a cutting-tool ready made without any further necessary work.

Like the Abbevillian, the earlier stages of the Levallois are rarely found *in situ* : on the Somme, for instance, their big broad flake-tools and blades mostly occur caught up in the solifluxion-deposits of the next glaciation, answering to the Alpine Riss. Remains of a cold-climate fauna attest the approach of this, and at the same time a rise of land-level brought about deep river-erosion; there were two stages of this on the middle Thames, which may prove to be related to the two stages of the 'older loess' which mark the duplication of the Riss, or Saale glaciation, in Germany. The late-Middle Acheulian workshop-site found by Commont at St. Acheul may fall in the temperate phase between them, and as regards the Levallois culture a Riss context has often been claimed for the well-known site of Baker's Hole at Northfleet on the Lower Thames. Here a group of Levallois people had a flint-work-shop, whose floor, covered with the remains of their distinctive industry (Fig. 1, 9), was overwhelmed by a mass of solifluxion-sludge, one of the so-called Coombe Rock deposits of the district. Unfortunately its identification is now disputed, and the recent contention that the Baker's Hole industry is really a rather late, and not an early Levallois, would equate it not with the Riss, but with the first of the three stages of the next glaciation, the Würm. In Germany the Levallois industry of Markkleeberg, near Leipzig, may have its claim to a Riss or

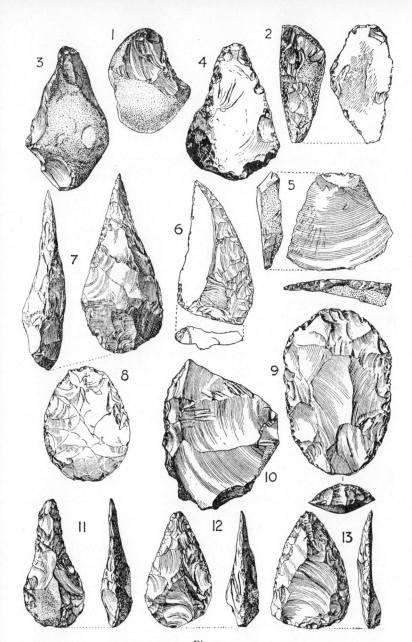

Fig. 1

LOWER AND MIDDLE PALAEOLITHIC FLINT IMPLEMENTS

Early types, East Anglia (pp. 13-14): 1, Darmsden pebble-tool; 2, Pre-Crag flake-tool; 3, Rostro-carinate, suggesting primitive hand-axe. Lower Palaeolithic flake-tools (pp. 14-18): 4, Cromer; 5, Clactonian of Swanscombe; 6, High Lodge; 9, Levallois of Baker's Hole, Northfleet. Acheulian (pp. 15-20): 7, Hand-axe, Hoxne; 8, Ovate, France; 11, Hand-axe, Lower Clapton (Thames 50-foot terrace). Middle Palaeolithic (pp. 20-22): 10, Side-scraper, Caddington, Beds.; 11, 12, Mousterian hand-axe and point, Le Moustier.

Scales : all $\frac{1}{3}$, except no. 7 ($\frac{1}{4}$).

Saale age likewise disputed, and the reader will easily guess that in these paragraphs we are necessarily passing by a good deal of such current controversy. At any rate, in East Anglia the Riss-Würm inter-glacial stage may be recognized in the famous lake-beds of Hoxne in Suffolk, lying as they do above the Middle Boulder-Clay that we have correlated with the Riss, and below the Upper Boulder-Clay or 'Upper Chalky Drift' laid by the ensuing glaciation, which should accordingly represent the Würm I of the Alps. The hand-axes of Hoxne (Fig. 1, 7) first discovered as long ago as 1797, are beautiful examples of the Late or 'Upper' phase of the Acheulian of Western Europe. A related industry is present in the contemporary deposits of the '50-foot terrace' or Taplow stage of aggradation on the Thames (Fig. 1, 11). The brick-earths of Crayford, with their fine specimens of the Middle Levallois culture now also developing, suggest by their fossils no more than a moderate climate, but on the Somme, e.g. at Montières near Amiens, a Middle Levallois industry is associated with a warm-climate fauna, which perhaps represents the height of this inter-glacial.

In fact, with the Upper Acheulian, and the developments of the Clactonian already noticed above, the West European region of overlap between eastern and southern connexions now begins its 'Middle' Palaeolithic with core-culture and flake-cultures in close contact. In fact, their respective products come to be found commingled, and in the technique of their flint-working there is evidence for interchange of ideas between the two traditions. An Acheulian industry will include regular Levallois flakes, often trimmed as scrapers in its traditional wood-bar technique, and conversely hand-axes will appear in a Levallois industry, trimmed in a now distinctive style of 'step-flaking'—controlled percussion-flaking bringing off small step-edged flakes. Such interaction led to the appearance of new forms of implements, and some students of the period have recognized in it not only side-scrapers like Fig. 1, 10, from an important site in the Chilterns, but actually backed knife-blades and even graving-tools foreshadowing the typical equipment of the blade-cultures of the ensuing 'Upper' Palaeolithic (p. 26). As we shall soon see, the Upper Palaeolithic blade-cultures have had their antecedents sought outside Europe, but this foregoing period is really only just beginning to be understood, and it seems probable that they contain a European element as well.

At present, it is enough to lay stress on the character of the European Middle Palaeolithic as a period of cultural interchange and fusion, and that not only between core-cultures and flake-cultures, but between one flake-culture and another. For the Levallois was not the only tradition of flake-industry present: the heritage earlier typified in the Clactonian was not dead, and the same cave of La Micoque which is the type-site for the Final stage of the Acheulian that followed the Würm I glaciation has yielded in its lowermost levels the Clactonian development industry already referred to as the Tayacian, which brings that heritage down to the opening of Middle Palaeolithic times. And the best known non-Levallois element of this period's flake-culture is that known as the Mousterian.

This name, long used to denote Middle Palaeolithic industries in general, comes from the cave of Le Moustier on the Vézère, a tributary of the Dordogne in Southern France, originally excavated in 1863. More scientific recent work here and in the cliff-shelter below has shown that in fact several Middle Palaeolithic occupations succeeded one another, with industries differing in important details. This same result, in varying forms, has been obtained elsewhere also, and it is now clear that no single 'Mousterian' culture embraces this period, but a number of cultures in which different traditions and their combinations are variously and distinctively apparent. In the true Mousterian, the non-Levallois tradition of flake-working without tortoise-cores survives pure, producing such tools (with unfaceted butts) as Fig. 1, 13: another form of it has incorporated hand-axes of Acheulian tradition (Fig. 1, 12), and such hand-axes made in the step-flaking Levallois technique, in evidence, e.g., at Combe-Capelle in the Dordogne, typify one of several apparent hybrid combinations of the Mousterian and the Levallois. The Tayacian form of the Clactonian tradition had also its contributions to make, and the true Levallois in its latest stages continued to flourish, and shows a wealth of thin blades together with triangular faceted-butt 'points', and varying degrees of hand-axe adoption as well.

In East Anglia the Final Acheulian is represented at Brundon in Suffolk, and there is a form of Combe-Capelle industry at Ipswich, likewise following the Würm I glaciation that laid the Upper Boulder-Clay. In Germany the first 'younger loess' equates this (as may now be held) with the northern Warthe: on the Thames the first stage of the upper 'flood-plain terrace' is marked by the peats formed by frigid marshes (as at Ponder's End), and the fauna is arctic both here and in the equivalent solifluxion-deposit on the Somme, which from a heightened base-level had eroded a new buried channel, flanked thereafter by successive deposits of 'younger loess' alternating with further solifluxion hill-washes. This series seems paralleled by the upper loams of the Ebbsfleet channel adjoining the Lower Thames, which alternate with solifluxion-deposits likewise: late and final Levallois flake-tools occur in connexion with both, and we seem here to have the north-westerly equivalents of the 'Mousterian' complex of the West European caves. Indeed, Mousterian cave-dwellers appear in this cold period at the Pin Hole Cave in the Creswell Crags of Derbyshire, and in the west the Cotte de St. Brelade in Jersey has yielded a Mousterian-influenced Late Levallois industry followed by a Levallois-influenced true Mousterian, both with a cold fauna and the latter with teeth of one of the human occupants. They show that he belonged to the stock which we have already noted as the final European representative of the 'Palaeoanthropic' or non-*sapiens* human groups, that usually known as Neanderthal man.

Wherever Middle Palaeolithic sites in Europe have produced fossil human remains, these have approximated more or less closely to the Neanderthal type, and the associated industries have been flake-cultures of one or other aspect of the 'Mousterian' complex. The original discoveries at Gibraltar and in the Neanderthal near Düsseldorf were solitary skeletons, but of all the associated finds made subsequently this equation has hitherto held good. Le Moustier itself has yielded a Neanderthal skeleton; the child's skull from the Gibraltar Devil's Tower accompanied a developed Mousterian industry

with Levallois contacts; at La Chapelle-aux-Saintes and La
Ferrassie in South France, and at Spy in Belgium, Neanderthal
types were associated with industries in general similar; and
at La Quina in the Charente one such skeleton lay with a
Mousterian which included hand-axes, and a rather later
skull with a pure Mousterian of a very uniform and developed
appearance.   The Neanderthal skull-type with its heavy
brow-ridging and retreating forehead, and therewith its
inferior brain-capacity, is very different from that of *Homo
sapiens*, and the distinction may be pursued in detail after
detail of skull and jaw, and in points such as the slouching
pose and gait required by the skeletal structure, in contrast
to the genuinely erect posture of modern man.   Earlier than
the Würm I glaciation there are remains of a slightly different,
higher-skulled type from Taubach-Ehringsdorf near Weimar,
with a 'Weimar culture' which is Levallois in its general
character, and to the same late period of the Riss-Würm
inter-glacial probably belong the finds at Krapina in Croatia,
where abundant but fragmentary remains of a rather peculiar
type were accompanied by a crude form of Mousterian;
despite the problems they raise, both these at least fall in
with our generalization that flake-industries and non-*sapiens*
men have an easterly bias in their distribution, as indeed do the
great discoveries of recent years outside Europe in Palestine.
The Neanderthal stock in its 'classic' form, in evidence by
the beginning of the Würm I glaciation and lasting through
it, supplements this with its wide distribution, together with
the mammoth, the reindeer, and other arctic animals, over
the bleak wastes surrounding the ice-bound mountains of
Western Europe; in recent years Italy has extended the picture
with the discovery of specimens near Rome, which closely
resemble those of Gibraltar.   But, though the old Acheulian
core-culture itself now no longer dominated the scene, it had
left quite evident legacies behind it among the material of the
'Mousterian complex', and it would be wrong to imagine that
that 'complex' must necessarily everywhere have been the
work of Neanderthal man.   The cultural admixtures of the
Middle Palaeolithic do not suggest a unitary population,
and the disappearance at this juncture of all descendants of

the Acheulian hand-axe makers is as improbable for Western Europe as it is for North Africa.   In fact, in Spain, along the old line of Eurafrican connexion, the industries of the 'Mousterian complex' are particularly varied, and the rich deposits of the Madrid district (e.g. at El Sotillo), though their stratification is not wholly evaluated, have shown not only an Acheulian hand-axe tradition present in its later as well as its earlier and middle stages, but a somehow contiguous range of the blade-tools and graving-tools already mentioned (p. 20) as answering to Upper Palaeolithic types.

It is true that there can now be no question of land-bridge connexion across the Straits of Gibraltar, for in the African equivalent of our Riss-Würm period there was intense volcanic activity which this cannot have survived.   But that will not have prevented originally related peoples from persisting on either side of the Straits, and in fact beyond the end of the Palaeolithic there was living in North Africa a stock with marked physical kinship to the 'Crô-Magnon' type now soon to meet us in Europe.   The unconformity that we shall note below between the material culture-histories of the two regions would seem only to emphasize that kinship's probable antiquity.   We ought therefore to be prepared to face the probability that survivals of Acheulian humanity lasted in Europe throughout the Middle Palaeolithic, with changing cultures, caught up in the 'Mousterian complex', from which the ensuing Upper Palaeolithic will have derived quite definite initial elements.   Perhaps this may be the context of the London skull found below the site of Lloyd's.   But this is not to say that the European blade-cultures of the new epoch do not include elements that are indisputably fresh; they do, and for the origins of these one must look outside Europe altogether.   The quest is one of outstanding importance; and, with Africa now cut off from its old connexion, our eyes must inevitably turn over to the Old World's Asiatic limb.

If, as we have divined, there is a primary connexion between *Homo sapiens* and a largely Eurafrican core-culture, and between his non-*sapiens* cousins and flake-cultures largely Eurasiatic, it by no means follows that his stock was a

Eurafrican monopoly excluded from Eurasia. On the contrary, it is widely believed that the core-culture peoples of Africa came there originally from Asia, where hand-axe industries more or less parallel to the African grew to flourish in large parts of India. And if northward of those latitudes Asia was a 'cradle' of non-*sapiens* types, this does not exclude—and, since there are presumably common roots in the background somewhere, may rather strengthen—the possibility of locating a *sapiens* 'cradle' there as well. In Western Asia, from the Siberian basin of the Ob to the southerly highlands of Iran, lie the historic breeding-grounds of many westward migrations, and the Eurasiatic mountain backbone, with the great corridor of steppe-land along its northern flank and the wide margins of Arabia to the south, makes a rugged midrib to the whole zone of connexion between Asia and Europe. Anthropologically, it may be attractively argued that those breeding-grounds are above all likely to have nurtured a major contribution to modern 'Europiform' humanity, while a 'Mongoliform' cradle lay to the east of them, a 'Negriform' to the south. And archaeologically, the distribution of Upper Palaeolithic blade-cultures seems to demand a main origin for their makers 'in some as yet unidentified Asiatic centre' whence North-Eastern Europe and East Africa could with the retreating of the ice alike become accessible. Pending that centre's identification, we can but outline the European culture-pattern that does so much to imply it.

'Classic' prehistory on the French model culminated over thirty years ago in the recognition that the 'Mousterian' had been succeeded by the blade-culture called the Aurignacian, after the typical cave-dwelling of Aurignac. Discoveries of its makers' remains, most notably at Crô-Magnon near by in the Dordogne, show them to be representatives of true *Homo sapiens*, and while they cannot possibly have evolved from the Neanderthal stock on the spot, the old idea of their immigration from North Africa has since fallen before the demonstration that the supposed prototype of their culture there, the so-called Capsian, belongs not to the beginning but only to the end of the Upper Palaeolithic. The problem of their origin thus posed can, however, be clarified by a reformed classification of the whole complex of blade-culture material, for this shows it to be no straightforward evolutionary sequence as in the old French theory. The hall-marks of true blade-cultures are, broadly speaking, two: the knife-blade, made on a relatively narrow flake, with one sharp cutting-edge and a back blunted by cross-flaking for the user's finger to press upon (Fig. 2, 1), and the graver or burin, which, whatever its precise form, is distinguished by a lengthwise facet, struck from the 'business' end so as to leave there a narrow transverse edge like that of a thick chisel or gouge (Fig. 2, 2). One has only to think for a moment of what these two forms of tool, the knife and the chisel, have meant to humanity ever since, to realize what an advance their invention made in prehistoric man's equipment. The starting-point of a proper account of the blade-cultures should obviously be the dating and localizing of their invention. But in the absence of so much Asiatic evidence this cannot yet be done with certainty.

It will be remembered that blades and gravers have been adduced here and there from Western Europe in the Riss-Würm period of cultural crossing between the Late Acheulian and the Middle Levallois (p. 20). The 'backed' blade (Fig. 2, 4, from a Levallois working-floor of the Taplow aggradation-stage (p. 20) on the Thames at Acton) would be a natural improvement on contemporary narrow flake-tools; and the successful making of gravers, normally on similar flakes (Fig. 2, 3, from the Mousterian shelter of Devil's Tower (p. 22) at Gibraltar), requires the wood-bar technique in which (p. 16) the Acheulian had long excelled. But both in Palestine and East Africa similar blades and gravers appear also in company with the Late Acheulian, and this points us back to the case for an origin of blade-culture outside Europe, in the 'as yet unidentified Asiatic centre' of which we have already spoken. This is the view most generally prevailing to-day. However, there is at present no means of connecting such a centre with Western Europe, either in the Riss-Würm period or on the morrow of the Würm 1 glaciation when the blade-cultures of the European Upper Palaeolithic really begin. The first of those cultures in France, traditionally called the 'Lower Aurignacian' but now better restricted to its type-site name of Châtelperron, used to be derived from the Mousterian, through a 'transition' typified at Abri Audi; numerous sites are now known in Moravia with broadly analogous industries, and it remains possible that this old view is at least partially right, if one combines it with the notion, already here adduced, of the presence of *Homo sapiens* as well as Neanderthal man in the European Mousterian complex. After the Würm I glaciation the Neanderthalers would have died out, while their *sapiens* neighbours remained to emerge into the Châtelperron blade-culture. This may even yet be true if the latter proves to have links binding it to Asia, for Asiatic immigrants and European survivors may in that case have mingled. The origin of the first blade-culture of Europe must then be left for the time being in doubt. Matters are clearer with the next, the true or 'Middle' Aurignacian, which presently intrudes upon the Châtelperron culture in the West: the Asiatic origin of this may be taken as certain, and the same is true of the 'Upper Aurignacian' which ensued in Eastern and Central Europe, whatever its relation to its Western contemporary of the same traditional name.

But the European possibility reappears with the culture which theoretically comes next after the Aurignacian trio. This is the Solutrian; its type-site of Solutré is in Central France, but it is known to have arrived there from the east. Formerly it too was ascribed to a mysterious Asiatic source, yet it now appears that the home of its initial stage was no further off than the mountain caves of Northern Hungary. Here the typical 'Proto-Solutrian' tool is not a blade-implement at all, but a rather roughly made almond-shaped affair trimmed on both faces like a small hand-axe (Fig. 2, 12). From it was perfected the true Solutrian 'laurel-leaf' which we shall shortly encounter when the culture spreads east and west from its Hungarian centre. It inevitably suggests a derivation from the hand-axes derived by the 'Mousterian complex' from the Acheulian, and while the Proto-Solutrian also contains blade-tools, it looks as though here too there must be in the background a European tradition of ultimate Acheulian descent. This would parallel the case of the African cultures which show similar 'laurel-leaf' developments. The Proto-

Solutrian of Hungary is usually made contemporary with the
'Upper Aurignacian' phase of Western Europe, but among
its blade-equipment are forms of steep-nosed scraping-tools
suggesting rather the Middle or Aurignacian proper, while the
Szeleta Cave has also produced one of the bone-implements
typical of that culture, a long point with a split base to facilitate
strong hafting.[1] The original blade-element in the Proto-
Solutrian may then be connected with the Aurignacian
proper, and this is the culture we have to consider next.

There seems absolutely no doubt of its origin in Western
Asia: its most primitive known industries are those which
succeed the initial blade-culture of Palestine and open the
Upper Palaeolithic in the caves of the Crimea. It is the
culture's fully grown form only which is spread westward
across Europe, and the original dispersal-centre cannot lie far
away, most probably, as Miss Garrod has suggested, on (or
near) the Iranian plateau. Attested not only in the Crimea
but also on the land-bridge of Asia Minor, the Aurignacian
travelled across Bulgaria, Rumania, Hungary, Austria, and so
to France, where it impinged upon the still developing
Châtelperron culture. M. Peyrony has maintained that the
two cultures flourished separately and side by side in the
Périgord, but they are probably better regarded as successive.
The distinction between their industries is a clear one: in
the first the Châtelperron knife-blade dominates, together
with thin-blade scrapers and gravers, while in the second the
scrapers are steep-nosed or keel-backed tools with 'fluted'
flaking (Fig. 2, 5); the gravers, with similar flaking, are thick
and 'busked' (Fig. 2, 7), and actual cores tend to be utilized
as well as blades. Also, a bone-tool series opens with the
split-base type of 'point' (Fig. 2, 6) already mentioned.
Typical Aurignacian cave-sites in South France are Aurignac
itself, and the cave of Crô-Magnon, where in 1868 human
remains were discovered of a peculiar type of *Homo sapiens*,
tall and strong, with a long head, a broad face, and a powerful
jaw. This must represent one of the leading human stocks
responsible for the culture, but it was by no means the only
type prevalent in Upper Palaeolithic Europe.

[1] Fig. 2, 6.

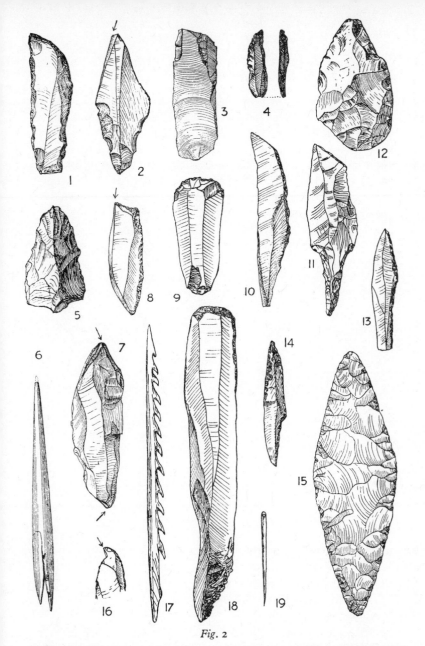

Fig. 2

UPPER PALAEOLITHIC (except 3-4) FLINT AND BONE IMPLEMENTS

Middle Palaeolithic (p. 26): 3, Mousterian graver, Gibraltar; 4, Backed blade, Acton. Upper Palaeolithic (pp. 26-34): 1, Châtelperron blade; 2, 'Screwdriver' graver; 5, 6, 7, Aurignacian keeled scraper, split-base bone point, and 'busked' graver; 8, Angle-graver; 9, End-scraper; 10, Gravette blade—all Dordogne; 11, Font-Robert point, Creswell Crags; 12, Proto-Solutrian implement, Szeleta Cave, Hungary; 13, 14, Shouldered points, Gagarino, S. Russia, and Les Eyzies, Dordogne; 15, Laurel-leaf, Solutré; 16, 17, 18, 19, Magdalenian 'parrot-beak' graver, bone harpoon, end-scraper on long blade, and bone needle—all Dordogne.

Scales: all $\frac{1}{2}$, except no. 10 ($\frac{1}{4}$), and no. 11 ($\frac{1}{3}$).

For the third of our original trio of blade-cultures remains to be described : the former Upper Aurignacian, now to be known as the Gravettian. Named after a type-site in the Périgord, its characteristic tool, the Gravette knife-blade (Fig. 2, 10), is a refined version of that of Châtelperron, and M. Peyrony has claimed, as has been indicated already, that the Périgord witnessed an unbroken succession from the older culture to the younger. But the sequence must be regarded against a wider background. We have seen that whatever European element may have been embodied in the Chatelperronian, a diffusion-centre for blade-culture in Asia seems none the less required, and the true Aurignacian need not be the only form of it with a West Asiatic home. The typical knife-blades of the Gravettian, and the forms of gravers and scrapers (e.g. Fig. 2, 8-9) which further characterize it, imply emergence from a Châtelperron or Châtelperron-like tradition. And whereas the mountain zone centred on Asia Minor, from Palestine to the Crimea, displays in its stead only the Aurignacian, the Gravettian is the first known blade-culture of the steppe-corridor out of Asia beyond it, in the loess-land sites of the South Russian plain. While the Aurignacian never ranges far from the Eurasiatic mountain spine, the Gravettian appears thus in the gateway from Asia across the frigid steppes, a hunting-culture with the mammoth and horse as its major quarry. In its earliest South Russian stage, at sites which, as at Kostienki and Gagarino, antedate the lower terraces of the rivers, there is, however, a new and distinctive tool, the 'shouldered point',[1] a blade with an offset tang for hafting, and further west in the loess-lands of the Danube basin the Gravettian reappears with typical knife-blades and just such tanged or shouldered points, at such sites as Vistonice in Moravia and Willendorf in Austria. At Vistonice Dr. Absolon's recent discoveries have revealed a wonderful range of implements in bone, mammoth-ivory, and antler, and the neighbouring site of Předmost has yielded another profusion of large-scale equipment in these materials. Předmost, furthermore, is one of several places in the neighbourhood of Brünn where human remains have been found

[1] Fig. 2, 13.

of a long-skulled physical type with well-ridged brows but a narrow face, in contrast to the more rugged, broad-faced Aurignacians of Crô-Magnon. Though this so-called 'Brünn race' need not be credited with an absolute monopoly of the Gravettian culture, it must at least have been prominent within it. The type is paralleled fairly closely at Combe-Capelle in South France, in an earlier, in fact a Chatelperronian, context, which deserves remembering in any assessment of the two cultures' genetic relationship. Actually, in the earlier Gravettian of France there are no shouldered points, and on the theory of Peyrony quoted above it will have been evolved directly from the local Chatelperronian, though drawing in part upon the Aurignacian also. There is no positive proof of this continuity, but the initial absence of shouldered points in the West is very distinctive, and seems to demand a division of the new culture into an East-Gravettian possessing shouldered points and wholly immigrant from Asia, and a West-Gravettian compounded with older local elements which excluded the use of these tanged implements until its later, so-called Font-Robert stage, when, amongst other features, they at last appear in a new, two-shouldered form (Fig. 2, 11). Though the Gravettian of North-West Europe is in the main undistinguished, a fine Font-Robert industry has been found in Derbyshire, at the Pin Hole Cave in Creswell Crags, where the culture, as will soon appear, had again a long survival.

The astronomical time-scale gives some 45,000 years as elapsing between the first maximum of the Würm glaciation and its second, and anyhow we have meanwhile witnessed the extinction of Neanderthal man in Europe and the rise of new populations, all of the stock of *Homo sapiens*, and all practising one form or another of blade-culture. Their importance to the prehistory of our continent cannot be over-emphasized. Though we have yet to chronicle the arrival of further groups of immigrants, there is every reason to believe that a fair proportion of the later inhabitants of Europe have drawn, in the network of their descent, upon the stocks of Upper Palaeolithic times. In particular, the sturdy tall Crô-Magnon group, with its long skull but big face, and the long-skulled but slighter group of Combe-Capelle or Brünn, stand as leading strains among the Aurignacian and Gravettian culture-groups, and were the ethnic complexion of those roving populations more widely known, we could probably recognize more than one set of components in the ancestry of the European 'races'—Nordic and Alpine at least, if not Mediterranean too—as later recognizable. The anthropologist of later Europe is wise, whatever knowledge he has yet to come by, to keep the Palaeolithic always in the background of his mind.

In view of the wide spread of the East-Gravettian in Central Europe, it is no surprise to find the early Solutrian strongly influenced by that culture, when it not only developed further in Hungary, but was borne thence eastward into Rumania and westward across Europe into France. Its industries have indeed in their blade-element much in common with the Gravettian, but the distinctive weapon is the 'laurel-leaf' of which we have already spoken. The finest examples are masterpieces of flint-work (Fig. 2, 15), and Solutrian craftsmanship was able to reach such heights above all through its perfecting of the technique of pressure-flaking, whereby very fine regular trimming could be carried out not by percussion but by the carefully applied pressure of a bone or wooden point. In the laurel-leaf this was done on both faces, but there are also narrower one-face 'willow-leaf' blades, and the hafting-tang already familiar in the East-Gravettian is again recognizable, especially in the later Solutrian of South-West France with its distinctive development of narrow single-shouldered blades or points (Fig. 2, 14). The penetration of Spain by Upper Palaeolithic cultures from across the Pyrenees has recently become more evident, and the Solutrian has been found not only in Catalonia but at the cave of Parpalló in Valencia, where it lived to elaborate remarkable forms of tanged and winged point. Britain, on the other hand, lay on the fringe of Solutrian influence only. At Solutré itself, a small open plateau-site in the Saône-et-Loire, the industry was associated with enormous accumulations of the bones of reindeer and also of the horse, which, though already present in the Font-Robert stage of the Gravettian, had evidently now arrived in Western Europe in great numbers, and was hunted intensively by Solutrian man. Human remains have been found at Solutré in considerable quantity, and these are of special interest as including, what we have not encountered in Europe before, several groups of distinctively broad skulls. Unfortunately the exact culture-associations of a number of them are uncertain, but in the more recent excavations several high and moderately broad specimens have been assigned to the preceding or Gravettian horizon; whatever the relation of the broadest to the Solutrian culture, it is in any case clear that now broad- as well as long-headed types of man were present in at least some parts of Europe. Thus the ancestry of some strands in the biological heritage of later European broad-headedness may also go back to the Palaeolithic, whatever their place in relation to the broad-headed 'Alpine race'-groups which we shall meet hereafter.

The cold steppe conditions in which the Solutrians lived their hunting-life were linked with the second oncoming of the Würm glaciation, the Weichsel or Vistula ice-phase of Northern Europe, responsible for the second 'younger loess' in Germany, and for corresponding deposits on rivers of both Eastern and Western Europe. To it belong probably the last or Brown Boulder-Clay of Norfolk and its equivalents further north, and certainly the final and least extensive moraines of France. Beyond the ice-margins in the west, the Gravettian tradition which the Solutrians penetrated and influenced yet maintained an essential continuity, and thence there emerged the consummation of the Palaeolithic known as the Magdalenian culture. It is so called after the Southern French cave of La Madeleine, and in its industries no less than six successive stages have been recognized, of which the first three, beginning while the climate was still of glacial severity, carry on the West-Gravettian tradition in flint-work, with bone lance-points either forked or bevel-ended for hafting. Then in the fourth stage appears the new device of the barbed throwing-harpoon, with a shaft at first merely notched, then barbed on one side (Fig. 2, 17), and finally on both. Therewith the later Magdalenian developed all its forms of hunting and domestic equipment to a remarkable degree: for example, there is a rich assortment of graver forms (e.g. the parrot-beak type of Fig. 2, 16); end-scrapers and blades were made on long sliver-like flakes of flint (Fig. 2, 18), and knife-blades could be refined to diminutive size; while the needles cunningly fashioned from bone splinters (Fig. 2, 19) imply the advancement of skin clothing. Occupations were evidently specialized, especially between the sexes, and the skill of the men's hunting-parties was balanced by the developed home-life to which so many caves bear witness. Of the art, which from already long-standing traditions now came to its most wonderful flowering, we shall say something in the next section. Its distribution is in the main restricted, with the culture in general, to France and North Spain: though the Magdalenian stretches by way of Switzerland across the Rhine into Bavaria, and appears also in Belgium, even just influencing England, it is essentially a specialized creation of the west of Europe. Spain south of the Cantabrian Mountains had its own humbler development from earlier traditions, distinctively Magdalenian only in the east. In Italy and the Riviera the Gravettian lived on as the Grimaldian, and Central and Eastern Europe witnessed parallel continuations of the East-Gravettian inheritance. In the north-west it is the same story: the English Upper Palaeolithic remained basically Gravettian, and the cave-deposits of Creswell Crags in Derbyshire, like those of the Grimaldi caves at Monaco, show the typical knife-blade ever diminishing in size, till what is called the Creswellian culture finally outlasts the Palaeolithic altogether. That there is more such survival awaiting recognition in the British Isles is suggested in particular by the distinctive culture of apparent Palaeolithic descent found established in later times in Northern Ireland (p. 67). These final phases are in fact everywhere marked by a growth of regional variations of culture.

In the North European plain the bleak tundra vegetation along the thawing margins of the ice supported a fauna dominated by the reindeer, and the men who came here for summer hunting from further south camped by the melt-water valleys that had emerged from under the ice-sheet. The reindeer-hunters' camp excavated at Meiendorf near Hamburg has provided a marvellous record of their culture, placed by geology, botany, and palaeontology together within this age of the last glacial retreat to fall within the North European Pleistocene, when the Weichsel ice-sheet, equated as we have seen with the Alpine Würm 2, shrank to the Pomeranian stage corresponding to Würm 3. The Hamburg culture, as it has been called, datable perhaps about 20,000 B.C., is thus the contemporary of the West European Magdalenian, not (as has been suggested) derivative from it, but an independent outgrowth, as shown by its use of a distinctive bone harpoon-type together with the tanged-point[1] tradition of flint-work, of the East-Gravettian of Central Europe. Its eastward range probably reached East Prussia, and westwards the North Sea may conceal connexions between it and the English Creswellian; in its central area, at any rate, it must be reckoned the starting-point of the whole subsequent prehistory of North Germany and Southern Scandinavia, as we shall see in the next chapter. In the far south the Upper Palaeolithic has been thought to close with new immigration of a different kind. The Capsian blade-culture of North Africa, rejected previously (p. 25) as an entrant into Europe at the beginning of the period, is accepted by some writers belatedly into Spain at its end. But it has also been argued that Spain can show no certain immigration out of Africa until after the end of Palaeolithic times. In any case, while the Pleistocene in the north was waning through its last millennia of glacial retreat, the south was only gradually maturing its contribution to the vital elements of European formation.

3. PALAEOLITHIC LIFE AND THE CREATION OF ART

The foregoing section has been an outline sketch of what strong imagination alone can bring into touch with human reality—the passage of perhaps over half a million years. The notion of twenty or twenty-five thousand generations of humanity passes easily enough as a matter of mere statistics, but is almost impossible to grasp as the multiplication of sentient men's and women's lifetimes. And if the astronomical time-scale to which we have drawn attention is accepted, it will make it impossible to reduce such figures without a

[1] Fig. 4, *k*.

wholesale revision of accepted correlations.   Though without insisting on that scale, we have, within barely twenty pages, brought culture after culture on to the scene, some of thousands of years' duration, and we have scarcely had time to pause and think of Palaeolithic man as a real and short-lived individual. Unconcerned as he was to look before and after, the tradition of his particular culture must have stood for him as part of an eternal order of things.   And yet with the lapse of time accumulated experience brought to birth new reactions of mind, new patterns of behaviour, new modes of material skill, whereby in due adaptation to surroundings the tradition achieved progress.   Over the greater part of Pleistocene time our archaeology can do no more than trace that progress in the skill devoted to tool-making in stone or flint.   That is of value not merely in default of other evidence, but inasmuch as it is tools that have made human civilization materially possible, and continuity of tool-craft that first bears objective witness to material culture in action.   With the contact and crossing of different tool-craft traditions, most evident in the Middle and Upper Palaeolithic, we get material culture in interaction, and with all that that implies of intelligent extension from the older range of single-group ideas we can measure in man's progress an effective increase of momentum.

While tool-finds of the Lower Palaeolithic only give us pin-points of human record in the immense annals of geological time, the disproportion between geology and the span of human life becomes less crushing when that life begins to concentrate in caves.   The chronology of Middle and Upper Palaeolithic times has in great part been built up from study of the super-position in which the cave-excavator finds his successive strata, following one another from the cave-floor upwards in the inevitable sequence wherein nature, man, or beast gradually accumulated their layers of débris, to preserve for the recording eye the leavings of hundreds of generations of coming and going human occupants.   Yet even here the total depth of the floor-beds may be impressive enough: the seventeen feet in the Pin Hole Cave is a very moderate figure—in the Tabun Cave in Palestine it was three times as great—and geology is still marching on a scale of thousands of years.

Actually, prehistoric man did not live in the depths of his caves, but rather in the mouth and on the terrace outside it, or even more frequently in places under overhanging cliffs where a natural shelter had been weathered in the rock-face. In such cave-mouths and rock-shelters a wind-break screening of boughs and skins, such as in previous ages must have sufficed for shelter in the open, could make habitation tolerable, even comfortable, for quite sizeable groups of human beings. They lived by food-gathering and the chase: hunting was the men's absorbing occupation, and the bones of hunted food-animals—mammoth, rhinoceros, cave-bear, antelope, reindeer, bison, horse, and the rest—came to lie in profusion in the floor-beds. In open country like the Moravian or South Russian loess-land, the dwellings of what archaeologists rather absurdly call an 'open station' were not necessarily mere flimsy wigwams: at Kostienki and Gagarino regular house-sites have been excavated by Russian prehistorians, with floors hollowed into the earth, and dug in them not only hearths and store-pits, but post-holes for the supports of a permanent roof, covered above with earth and sods. Here too the bones of food-animals were burnt as fuel, and the great accumulations of mammoth-bones explain such bone-heaps as we have already noticed at Solutré. In the surroundings of an arctic or sub-arctic world the group-life of communities was an inevitable response to material conditions of livelihood. Big game had to be hunted in organized parties: hearth and home and the tendance of children made women's work for all alike. Such a pattern of hunting-culture shows the adaptation of life to environment achieved on a communal scale.

Its material aspects alone reveal the human mind actively and intelligently at work,[1] in the tool-craft of flint and bone and the skilful employment of tool and weapon in the home and the chase, but self-conscious thought still lay below the level of the 'rational man's' cleavage between the material and spiritual worlds, and the same culture that embodied these practical activities embodied therewith, and no less naturally,

[1] The regular rows of notches on bones from Vistonice are claimed by Dr. Absolon as the earliest evidence for man's capacity to count, in a system of fives clearly suggested by the number of his fingers.

a vital concern with the mysteries of 'supernatural' experience. Primitive man, like the young child in all ages, knows but one all-embracing world: sense and imagination are for him on the same plane of reality. In all things he will see bodies endowed with forces answering to his own, able if it so be to outdo his own, but also perhaps to assist him in his needs and desires. From the remote past of human antiquity this heritage will have accumulated, and in the beliefs and practices therefrom engendered emerges the raw material of the study of primitive religion. That study is here not our direct concern, but it behoves the prehistorian never to forget the deep-seated inner inheritances, which in the long childhood of the mind were interwoven with the whole fabric of humanity's material existence.

In the Upper Palaeolithic their embodiment in the vital principle of magic has issued in creations which he cannot in any wise overlook. The pathetic mystery of death might call for the magical replacement of the departed life-force, which had seemed to reside in the warm vitality of the blood, and in the covering of the bones of the dead with red ochre we may see a rite created to assure them life and warmth renewed, as unseen but still no less powerful members of their tribe. Not a few such ochre-stained burials are attested from the Upper Palaeolithic, and it would seem that the first cave-burial to be discovered in modern times, the famous 'Red Lady' (really a youth) of the Paviland Cave in South Wales, is an example. Again, the dead would need (and perhaps grudge to their survivors) weapons and implements they had used in life: these were then buried with them, and in some cases, of which the most notable are the interments of the Grimaldi Caves, the corpses were fully attired in their clothes and rich ornaments of shell and bone. What manner of belief in 'after life' may therein be implied we need not here pause to enquire; it is enough that in magical observance the dead could be linked with the living, as reverence or fear of them found expression in the primitive mind. The answering mystery of birth evoked a like venera-tion. The earliest-known plastic representations of the human form are the statuettes made by people of the Gravettian culture, which are most usually female, and often apparently pregnant. Our illustrations (Pl. II) show how, no less than to the womb itself, emphasis was devoted to the full pendulous breasts, broad hips, and rotund buttocks; and even if it be going too far to see in these 'Venuses' evidence of a 'cult' of fertility, they show at least that the seeming miracle of generation was dwelt upon with an awe and desire which in this culture issued in the life-symbolism of a plastic art. The features of the face are normally ignored: the arms, often folded, play seldom more than a minor part in the sculptor's composition; but the main curves and masses of the woman's body are treated with a feeling for their line and exuberance which is manifest alike in more conventionalized and more naturalistic renderings

The distribution of these statuettes in Europe reinforces the notion of an eastern origin for the Gravettian. Of the Russian sites Kostienki has yielded one, Gagarino seven of them carved in mammoth ivory; and while others come from Malta in far-distant Siberia, Willendorf (Pl. II, 1) and Vistonice [1] by the Danube have been no less productive, and with Savignano in Emilia and the Grimaldi Caves (Pl. II, 2-3) their making reaches Western Europe. At Brassempouy and again at Sireuil in France the context was apparently not Gravettian but Aurignacian, perhaps evidence of contact between the cultures, for in and before the Aurignacian art had indeed appeared, but art of a different order. To the hunter vitally dependent upon his hunting, the magic of life and death concerned not his own kind alone, but above all the animal quarry whereon his own kind subsisted. As the Vistonice site has shown, the Gravettian could fashion talisman-figures of animal as well as human abundance, but the same inspiration of primary want had impelled his predecessors in Western Europe to what was an animal art essentially, the hunter's spontaneous imagery of the beasts it was his life to kill.

That this animal art had appeared already among the

[1] The extraordinary little portrait-head recently discovered at Vistonice by Dr. Absolon is an addition to our knowledge of Palaeolithic art which is at present unique.

Chatelperronian inhabitants of South-West France and Northern Spain seems to be shown at a number of sites where the simple line-engravings of its earliest phase have been found on cave-wall surfaces which the accumulation of later floor-beds put below standing height. Pair-non-Pair in the Gironde is a case in point, and the engraver's skill thereafter began to encompass perspective, showing, for instance, all four of an animal's legs. Single-colour painting went through the same early stages, and the still simple art-tradition lasted in these regions through the succeeding culture-periods until in the Early Magdalenian painters were dotting and shading in their outlines, and in the Middle filling their whole figures in in flat wash. The plastic sculpture of the Gravettians shows its influence in the combination of engraved outline with carving in relief, and at Laussel has been found a 'Venus'-figure so rendered, holding in her hand a bison's horn; in the Solutrian culture which followed, animal relief-sculpture could rise to real magnificence, as in the great beast-frieze of Le Roc in the Charente, so that the Magdalenian carver's art had behind it a long and blended tradition. In the maturity of the Magdalenian culture, carving and painting alike rose to their fullest mastery of design, and it is this age that has given us the wonderful animal portrayals of the Font-de-Gaume, Altamira, and so many other famous caves whose discovery has made the art of the ancient hunter universally renowned to-day. The subtle offsetting of naturalism by suggestion, the marvels of colour in the sensitive technique of polychrome painting—these and the whole multitude of such characters which have evoked modern admiration need not be rehearsed in these pages. There are now so many books, small as well as large, describing and illustrating cave art that no detailed appreciation is called for here. And it is scarcely less well known that the motive behind the art's production is now recognized as the deep-rooted principle of 'sympathetic magic' of which we have spoken above, crystallized not merely by the hunter for himself, but in the potency of generations of actual sorcerers, of whose mimetic ritual, practised in cavernous recesses often remote from inhabited places, these vivid animal-pictures were the figured instrument. The portrayal of the heart, the weapon shown mortally piercing the beast's flank, the outline of the trap around his body, are occasional features which leave no doubt of the reality of this tremendous hunting-magic, and the weird representation of the sorcerer himself, masked in animal motley and dancing the ceremonial dance of his wizardry, reveals it not only in the terrible masterpiece of Les Trois Frères, but even in the strange little bone-engraving from Creswell Crags (Fig. 3, i). For small-scale art as well as large reflects the same vital tradition through all its phases of creative achievement, and on pebble, bone, and antler there are engravings, like the bison and reindeer of our Fig. 3, ii and iii, which yield nothing to the bigger work on cave-walls in feeling and skill. The latter is on bone, from La Madeleine itself, the former on stone from the cave of Montastruc, Bruniquel, and both belong to a fairly early stage of the Magdalenian as does the lively glutton of Fig. 3, iv; thereafter relief-carving became more prominent, and the technique of sculpture in the round appears at its highest. The pair of reindeer, male following female, also from Montastruc, is a wonderful adaptation of animal realism to the form of the mammoth-tusk point on which it is carved; one might multiply examples, but it suffices to realize, when so many individual objects—from pebbles and slips of bone to antler rods and whole weapon-handles and spear-throwers—might be charged with this magical imagery, how all-pervading was the imaginative mysticism of the Magdalenian hunter's world.

In the course of centuries that world passed away. With the waning of the mountain-ice, open steppe and tundra began to give place to forest, and the big game of the glacial age slowly died out or moved away northward: the sorcerer lost the power of his magic, and the artist's inspiration ebbed. Throughout the Upper Palaeolithic a tradition of symbolic signs had persisted together with animal naturalism, and towards its end the animal forms themselves became more and more conventionalized, and portrayal was replaced by symbol. In the Azilian culture to which the Magdalenian eventually sank, the magic objects are just small pebbles painted with simple stripes and signs. But to see in this mere degeneration would be a mistake. To feel need of a

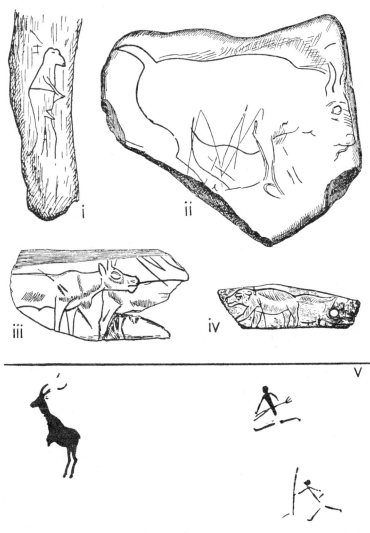

Fig. 3

ILLUSTRATIONS OF WEST-EUROPEAN UPPER PALAEOLITHIC
ART (p. 41)

    i, Human figure carved on bone, Pin Hole Cave, Creswell Crags.
    ii, Bison carved on stone, Bruniquel, Dordogne.
    iii, Reindeer carved on bone, La Madeleine, Dordogne.
    iv, Glutton carved on bone, Dordogne.
    v, EAST SPANISH ROCK-SHELTER PAINTING (p. 43), Roca del Lladoner,
      Valltorta.

Scales : i-iv, 2 : 3 ; v, about 1 : 8.

true portrayal in art-magic is elementary compared to belief in the efficacy of a symbol: a portrait is individual, a symbol collective or abstract. Thus with the passing of realism in art one may equate a rising of human intelligence towards abstract thought.

One province of Palaeolithic art yet awaits attention, in the south-east of Spain. Despite the Solutrian and Magdalenian penetrations to Parpalló in Valencia, and even the isolated group of Magdalenian paintings in the far south of Andalusia, this country remained, as we have already said, essentially a world of its own, with a long-lived but simple culture more or less of Chatelperronian type. And therewith the rock-shelters of the south-east display an entirely distinctive art. Occasional contacts with the sphere of the northern art are usually agreed to attest its like antiquity, but a glance at our Fig. 3, v, reveals the utterly different character of its 'shadow-picture' style, in which animals and abundant human figures appear together in lively scenes of hunting with the bow; or human forms alone, gaily caparisoned and plumed, gather in rite or festival. This East Spanish art has often been compared with art-groups of Stone Age Africa, as far south as Rhodesia and the Bushman country, but while there are rock-paintings in the Sahara which may come to show connexion, those of Mediterranean North Africa cannot be used to link on East Spain as the outlying province of a contemporary African art. For they have been shown to be of 'Neolithic' date, parallel in age to pre-dynastic and dynastic Egypt. Thus our Spanish art-group, if its Palaeolithic antiquity be accepted, still stands alone, though it seems impossible to dismiss its similarity of spirit to African as opposed to European creation. At all events, this was an essentially southern culture; it had a long survival, accompanied by a gradual conventionalizing of its art, and this takes us past the end of Palaeolithic times, and into a ew division of European prehistory.

Chapter Three

MESOLITHIC EUROPE AND THE DAWN OF CIVILIZATION

I. THE MESOLITHIC AGE AND ITS BEGINNINGS

(Map II and Table II: at end)

IN the early days of prehistoric studies a yawning gulf was thought to exist between the Upper Palaeolithic of the caves and the ensuing Neolithic period or New Stone Age. To fill this gap a 'hiatus' theory was put forward, postulating a period during which Europe was completely denuded of population. Very soon, however, as if in answer to the challenge, certain cultures were discovered which could be placed in neither the Palaeolithic nor the Neolithic periods, and a long series of subsequent discoveries has up to date revealed some seven main cultures with many local variants, intermediate in age between them. The term Mesolithic duly connotes this intermediate position, and while all the Mesolithic cultures are by descent connected with the Palaeolithic, they form a homogeneous whole, showing a clear separation from the ensuing Neolithic in which the arts fundamental to civilized life came into existence. The close of the Palaeolithic coincides with the passing of the great Pleistocene era, and the climatic changes which followed it combine with those of human industry and culture to give the new age its distinctive character. In these words, adapted from the Introduction to the first English book to take the Mesolithic for its subject, we may fittingly introduce it here. But at its outset there is a question to be encountered—that of the long-deferred Capsian invasion of Europe from North Africa by way of Spain, for which some writers have here found a new opportunity. It is, therefore, perhaps worth while devoting a few words, by way of preface, on the state of affairs in the North African quarter.

The European triad of Würm glaciations was there reflected in a pluvial period (p. 10), in which the rainfall, though fluctuating and gradually decreasing in amount, was yet able to maintain both animal and human life in the Saharan belt. But the human life was on a cultural level still essentially 'Middle Palaeolithic', displaying a varied complex of Levallois and Mousterian. This was in time partly succeeded by the peculiar culture known as the Aterian, in which Mousterian forms became modified especially by the appearance of tanged triangular points and also by 'laurel-leaves' recalling those of the Solutrian above discussed (p. 27). In the east this occurs at Kharga Oasis and elsewhere in Egyptian territory, but it is north-westwards that its habitat is most marked, along the whole stretch of French North Africa, and its domination there not only renders impossible any early or Chatelperronian movement over to Spain, but actually lasts out the best part of the Upper Palaeolithic. It is in fact only towards the very end of the pluvial period that the Capsian blade-culture appeared upon the scene.

Its immediate origin must lie to the south—very probably, as Miss Garrod has suggested, in the 'Upper Aurignacian' of Kenya, whither its ancestral form could have arrived from an original 'Asiatic centre' (p. 25) of blade-culture; but its North African distribution is distinctly restricted. The typical Capsian occurs no nearer Europe than behind the eastern end of the Atlas Mountain zone, that is, in the south of Constantine and Tunis, where lies Gafsa, the ancient Capsa, its name-site. Westward and along the coast towards Spain, it did no more than merge into a distinct form of blade-culture, called the Oranian, which succeeds to the long-standing Aterian tradition. Now if the Capsian is thereupon to issue in an invasion of Europe by way of Spain, it should do so through this Oranian culture, and with such an idea in mind the Oranian was for a long time called the 'Ibero-Maurusian', as supposedly common to Iberia and Morocco. But the best opinion is now quite satisfied that in Iberia the Oranian, with its suggestions of Aterian ancestry, is precisely what is nowhere to be found. Until, therefore, we can see a better archaeological bridge across the Straits of Gibraltar, North Africa and the question of its connexion with Spain may be left on one side, while we turn to the morrow of the Pleistocene in Europe itself.

The last phase of the Würm glaciation has been offered, in the system above noticed (p. 9), an astronomical date about 18,000 years ago, and the next known point in the northern ice retreat beyond its limiting moraines may be perhaps more firmly dated, in a manner shortly to be explained, soon after 12,000 B.C. in the terms of our time-reckoning. The shrinking of the European ice-sheets slowly drew northward from the Sahara and the Mediterranean the rain-giving storm-belt of Atlantic winds, and the pluvial conditions thus gave place there to a period of gradual desiccation. Into this period lasted the ancient and probably indigenous blade-culture of Southern Spain, which from the African invasion-theory has been normally called the Spanish Capsian. Like the Magdalenian to the north of it, it suffered with the change of climate and livelihood a decay of its old character. Its tools, from the stout angle-gravers and trimly made big knife-blades which distinguish its Upper Palaeolithic stage, become reduced to a comparative poverty of type, as is seen in a whole range of cave-sites from Malaga to Tarragona, and in a late example like Hoyo de la Mina in the former province the knife-blade form begins to appear shrunken in size to really small dimensions. We have already noticed such diminutive blade-forms in the late Magdalenian and its contemporaries to the east and north (p. 34), and they now come to confront us, under their generally current name of microliths, as a widespread characteristic of the Mesolithic cultures.[1] Their invention was the monopoly of no one cultural province; towards the close of Palaeolithic times there seems to have been a general tendency so to reduce the size of blades in relation to their hafts for certain purposes, and further, as well as using them individually, to mount a single haft with a whole row of such microlithic blades to make a 'composite tool'. How this might be done is shown in Fig. 4, *a* : the blunted back of the microlith, which could be crescentic or angular in form, was let into a slot in the haft; to sit there firmly without risk of splitting it, while the sharp

---

[1] Fig. 4, *e-f.*

untrimmed edge faced outwards, so that a row of them would form a continuous or a jagged composite cutting-instrument. It might furthermore be found better not to make each microlith out of a single little flake of its own, but to nibble a notch out of a relatively long blade-flake and then detach the microlith by a blow across the narrow bridge so left (Fig. 4, *b*, *c*). The detached half of the notch thus gave the microlith most of its back-blunting ready-made, while the other half was left, truncated by the slanting facet of the detaching blow, on the end of the original flake's remainder. The latter, with its slanting terminal facet, had the form of a little graving-tool or burin, and these objects are therefore known as micro-burins,[1] whether or no they were so utilized in any given case. Microliths thus made, with the accompanying micro-burins, occur in the Capsian within its easterly North African area, and still more in the 'Upper Capsian' form in which it spread during Mesolithic times rather nearer to the sea. They also occur, though at present more rarely, in the Oranian of the coast-lands opposite to Southern Spain. If such a technique can only have been invented in one place, one must then assume that the idea reached Spain from contact with the Oranians of the African side of the Straits, though their industry has been seen to be in other respects too dissimilar for certainty about an actual migration across into Europe. Otherwise, it must be believed a case of independent invention, accounted for by similarity of circumstances. In any event, notch or micro-burin technique remained restricted at this early date. But the production of microlithic blades without it was, as we have stated, a general feature of the outgoing Palaeolithic.

By the time the Magdalenian had reached its final stages in Cantabria and Southern France, both crescentic and angular microliths had become established side by side with larger flint tools, and their use was intensified in the Mesolithic culture to which its 'degeneration' led. This is known as the Azilian, from the cave of Mas d'Azil in the Ariège where its remains were first discovered fifty years ago, in a layer separated by a thick seam of flood-clay from a Late Magdalenian

[1] Fig. 4, *d*.

floor beneath. The layer contained many hearths, and bones no longer of the reindeer or other arctic animals of the Pleistocene, but the red deer and wild boar of the forest which with the waning of the old glacial climate had come to clothe the West European landscape. In bone and deer-horn there were only poor simple tools and flat rough barbed harpoons [1] contrasting with the fine hunting-equipment of Magdalenian times; in flint, graver and scraper types descended from the Magdalenian, but, above all, diminutive round-scrapers [2] and an abundance of microliths. Among them are evidences of the micro-burin technique, and as we have seen this to be foreign to Magdalenian descent, its presence may be ascribed to incomings from across the Pyrenees, which are indeed otherwise attested. For the strangest feature of the culture is the series of smooth round pebbles bearing simple signs in flat red paint,[3] which we have already mentioned as examples of the conventional symbols to which the magic art of the Palaeolithic had descended. This explanation of them is borne out by their constant occurrence in quantity on Azilian sites, and also by the character of the painted signs themselves. They have no prototypes in Magdalenian art, but find close parallels among the conventions which had been evolved from the distinctive art of Eastern Spain (p. 43). That evolution, it is thought, had gradually been proceeding meanwhile, and its progress may be minutely studied in the rock-paintings which in time spread over more and more of Spain. Eventually the culture they denote reached the Azilian belt in the north: in the Cantabrian caves two stages of the Azilian are distinguishable: the first of pure Magdalenian descent, and only the second including micro-burin technique and painted pebbles. Evidently, then, both the latter were introductions from the south, where, however, rock-painting populations continued much later in survival.

The Azilian itself was long-lived, and is found not only in Southern France but also further east, where it has been found near Basel, at the Falkenstein Cave in Hohenzollern, and locally developed in Bavaria. And where its Magdalenian

----

[1] Fig. 4, *i*.   [2] Fig. 4, *h*.
[3] Fig. 4, *g*.

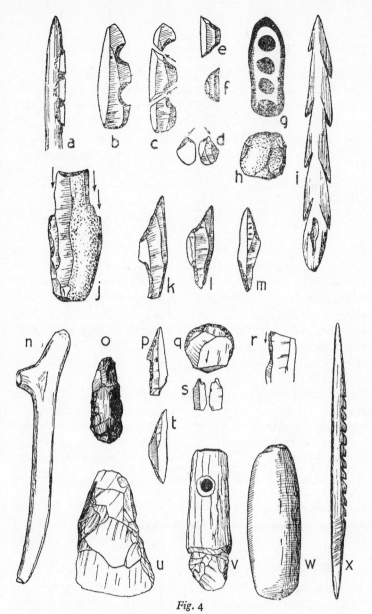

Fig. 4

MESOLITHIC IMPLEMENTS, I

a, Microliths mounted in slotted shaft, and *b*, *c*, Manufacture by notch technique of microliths as *e*, Trapeze ; *f*, Lunate ; with by-product micro-burin as *d* (p. 47) ; *g*, *h*, *i*, Azilian painted pebble, round scraper, and deer-antler harpoon (p. 48) ; *j*, Angle-graver, Hohle Stein, Westphalia ; *k*, Ham-burg, *l*, Swiderian, *m*, Ahrensburg tanged points (pp. 52-53) ; *n*, Lyngby reindeer-antler axe-haft (p. 53) ; *o*, core-axe, Klosterlund (p. 58) ; *p*, *q*, *r*, *s*, *t*, *u*, *v*, *w*, Maglemose tanged point, round scraper, micro-burin, angle-graver, microlith, flake-axe, core-axe in antler sleeve, and pebble-axe—all Denmark, Holstein, or Sweden (pp. 58-59) ; *x*, Maglemose antler harpoon, Hornsea, Yorks (p. 59).

Scales: $g, o, q, u, w, \frac{1}{3}$; h, i, j (just over), $k, l, m, r, s, t, \frac{1}{2}$; $n, \frac{1}{6}$; $p, x, \frac{1}{4}$; $v, \frac{2}{5}$.

parent had been excluded by the continuous survival of Gravettian cultures, these on their own account developed in a similar way into Mesolithic cultures with an abundant microlithic industry. The upper layers of the Grimaldi Caves show this well, as do such other sites in Italy as the Romanelli Cave near Otranto, and from the Creswellian culture and its like above remarked in the British Isles (p. 34) analogous developments proceeded (Fig. 5, *a*, from the Creswell Crags cave of Mother Grundy's Parlour). It is believed certain, though hard to prove in detail, that the rise of these Mesolithic cultures with their very uniform production of microliths was aided by northward and eastward migration from the south-western regions we have been surveying. Since in these earlier postglacial times Britain was not yet severed from the Continent, our country need be no exception, and for all the Creswellian survival the 'broad-blade' microlithic industries of the English Pennines, for instance, are so Continental in type as to make their immigrant origin really a certainty. Their close analogies are with the earlier Mesolithic of Northern France and Belgium, and the district of Liège has produced not only an early industry of this complexion,[1] but also a middle stage,[2] with the angular forms and micro-burin technique of the south distinctively developed, which in its turn was reflected in various parts of England. And in the Aisne country of North France is the region of Fère-en-Tardenois from which these non-Azilian microlithic cultures derive their common name of Tardenoisian. By the time these centuries of migration and slow development had so far advanced, indeed, it becomes impossible except in the vaguest way to distinguish Azilian from non-Azilian ancestry in the monotonous convention of microlithic work. What is usually called the Middle Tardenoisian might with equal justice be called the 'Azilio-Tardenoisian', but from such a clumsy name we may be saved by the excavation of a new type-site for this stage in France, Le Martinet at Sauveterre in the southern Périgord. We are here in the region of Azilian tradition, but the industry might almost equally well be a 'Middle Tardenoisian', with its crescentic and angular microliths and its moderate but not

[1] Fig. 5, *b*.   [2] Fig. 5, *c*.

excessive development of micro-burin technique, and the French now propose to call such industries in general Sauveterrian, reserving the name Tardenoisian in a strict sense for the later stage, to which we shall return below.

The spread of microlithic culture in general has been attributed to wide movements of migration, especially from the south-west of Europe northwards and eastwards. Uncertainty about Capsian immigrants into Southern Spain clouds the idea of a North African invasion, but there can be little doubt that from Iberia itself and from South-West Europe in general bands of Mesolithic hunters and fishers moved northward and into Central Europe, though it is difficult to say how far the physical type of the inhabitants was thereby more greatly diversified. Immigration from the east has also been claimed, since our central mountain zone is later found populated by the broad-headed, stocky, brunette type of the 'Alpine race', as yet ill-defined in the Palaeolithic, and Asia is regarded as the home of broad-headedness. At the cave of Ofnet in Bavaria an extraordinary deposit of skull-burials, showing the use of red ochre remarked on earlier (p. 38), and garnished with perforated shell and deer-tooth ornaments, displays not only long head-forms very possibly related to the 'Brünn race' of the Gravettian (p. 31), but also a range of broader types which look like early forms of 'Alpine'. The culture here is certainly Mesolithic and perhaps Azilian, but while such types occur elsewhere also at this time, the much earlier skulls of Solutré (p. 33) warn us against believing that broad-headedness was a Mesolithic novelty in Europe. The 'Dinaric' of South-Eastern Europe has indeed usually been reckoned a relatively late comer from a well-defined home in Anatolia, but the main Alpine block may cover elements of long-standing European formation. Thus it is not surprising that broad- as well as long-headed people should now have followed the retreating ice northward. Some indeed see here an origin for the Lapps, and in general, though the Mesolithic evidence is not very adequate, it seems fairly clear that the main constituents of 'Nordic' Europe must in this period have been moving together. Among them the dominant 'Teutonic' element, tall and long-skulled, is now certainly in evidence. Its exact antiquity in the north is not yet too firmly attested, but the general case for its distribution from the south-east, with an Asiatic centre in the remoter background, seems hard to reconcile with at all late dates. And archaeology points here no less than elsewhere to the Mesolithic as the main vital period in the setting-out of the human map of Europe.

In fact, the Mesolithic settlement of Northern Europe has in recent years come much more clearly into view. The hunting-camp at Meiendorf near Hamburg mentioned in the previous chapter (p. 34) is placed by its stratified natural associations towards the end of the last Pleistocene glaciation, before arctic tundra gave place to birch-wood, and the flint-work of this 'Hamburg culture' [1] belongs to the tanged-point tradition which we have seen widespread in the Upper Palaeolithic of Central and Eastern Europe. In East Germany, and above all in the dune country of Poland, that tradition likewise persisted thereafter, and in what is called (from the Polish site of Swidry) the Swiderian culture (Fig. 4, *l*) a long time-succession has begun to appear, from Central European precursors, by way of South Poland (Novy-Mlyn near Kielce) to a Swiderian I phase, running with the older dune-formations in the close of the Pleistocene, followed by a Swiderian II with the younger dunes in the full Early Mesolithic. Further west, caves in Westphalia show a Late Palaeolithic followed by an Early Mesolithic culture, which at Hohle Stein shows the tanged-point tradition developing microlithic forms like those of the Swiderian, and e.g. angle-gravers like Fig. 4, *j*; and while the Remouchamps Cave in Belgium displays a further aspect of the culture, it appears in the Hamburg area at Ahrensburg-Stellmoor (Fig. 4, *m*) in stratified succession, after the first birch-forest period and the promotion of pine-growth by a warmer sequel named the Allerød phase, to the older stage of it represented at Meiendorf. Thus from the south and south-east (for the Swiderian is reported as far away as the Ukraine) the transition to the Mesolithic saw a northward trend of peoples distinguished by their tanged flint implements; and the succession of their industries is carried

[1] Fig. 4, *k*.

further by the famous find of a large and fine tanged flint point in an early post-glacial sand at Nørre-Lyngby in the north of Jutland. But at this point there occurs something new.

Hitherto the Mesolithic peoples have appeared to us carrying on, as best they might, the Palaeolithic tradition of life. The changes they made in it were imposed on them by the post-glacial changes of European climate and the growth of forest, to which they had slowly had to adapt themselves, and this was in some respects at least a matter of impoverishment. The arctic game which had been hunted so intensively over the naked Pleistocene landscape had given place to forest animals, with no truly big game amongst them, able to take advantage of the cover and obstructions of growing vegetation. The forest of birch and pine indeed furnished wood, but to chop wood of any size something more than small flint cutting-tools are needed, and small flint cutting-tools are actually all we have encountered hitherto. There is just one material solution of this problem—the invention of the axe. And at Nørre-Lyngby, probably from the same horizon as the tanged flint just mentioned, has been found a haft of reindeer-antler (Fig. 4, *n*), with the stump of the brow tine hollowed to take something like an axe-head. Further, among the dozen or so similar stray finds from Northern Europe several have the brow tine obliquely cut to form an axe-head or adze-head of itself. Lastly, at Ahrensburg-Stellmoor the recent brilliant excavations of the Kiel Museum have brought to light no less than twenty-five of these 'Lyngby axes', associated with an enormous assemblage of flints of the tanged-point culture to which Ahrensburg now gives its name (Fig. 4, *m*). The 'Lyngby axe' type has been claimed as the oldest thing of its kind known in Europe, or indeed in the world—the first sign of a 'heavy industry' devised by man in response to a forest environment. Actually, these implements can scarcely in their own right be called true axes capable of really heavy work: the great Danish prehistorian Sophus Müller compared them to the sharp antler clubs used by some North American Indians for killing captured game, and this sort of club, though absent from the West European Magdalenian, occurs much earlier among the rich equipment of antler, ivory, and bone implements at the East-Gravettian site of Předmost in Moravia (p. 30).

Předmost even yields bone hafts perforated apparently for an axe-like head, and a deer-antler socket or 'sleeve' for a similar tool-head has been geologically dated, along with a human skull-cap, to the Würm 2-Würm 3 inter-glacial at Hengelo in Holland. It seems probable, then, that the Late Palaeolithic movements from Central towards Northern Europe brought them sufficient familiarity with large implements in antler to provide a context of tradition for the 'Lyngby axes'.

But in them the tradition reached a point from which the invention of a true 'heavy' axe was only a single step distant, and it is in fact within the Ahrensburg-Lyngby culture-area that the earliest true flint axe-heads soon appear. Therewith begins the tale of the so-called 'Forest Cultures' of Northern Europe. In them, Mesolithic man came to show the best of which he was capable in adaptation to a forested world. When all is said and done, despite the invention of the axe, the story is not one of dazzling cultural achievement. But what is of the first importance to prehistory is its setting by modern science in a coherent system of natural chronology, and this must now engage our attention.

2. THE MESOLITHIC AGE AND ITS DEVELOPMENTS

(Map II and Table II: at end)

In the last phase of the Würm glaciation, credited by some (p. 46) with a date some 18,000 years ago, the end-moraine of the northern ice-sheet stretched across Pomerania and on the west doubled back across the mouth of the Baltic to South Sweden. It is known as the Baltic end-moraine, and just as the preceding ice-retreat over North Germany and Denmark is called the Daniglacial phase, so the next stage of regression, from South Sweden northward over Gotaland, is called the Gotiglacial. The ensuing halt across Scandinavia and Finland is marked by the so-called Fenno-Scandian moraines, and thereafter the ice shrank again through a 'Finiglacial' retreat till in the valleys of Central

Scandinavia it divided into two, corresponding to the North Swedish and Norwegian mountain-masses. Now this gradual withdrawal of the ice-sheet left an annual deposit of sediment under its encircling melt-waters, the coarser material from each summer's thaw alternating with a finer band deposited in the winter. These layers of sediment, or 'varves', have thus been left by the retreating ice like 'a pack of playing-cards sprawling on a table, each card occurring in a definite relation to all the other cards'. And though at any given point only a limited number lie vertically upon one another, yet from the constant fluctuation of the amount of deposit between harder and milder years, the same series of varves can be recognized in sections taken a measured distance apart along the course of the retreat. Thus by proceeding from point to point the Swedish geologist Baron de Geer has been able to count the varves in unbroken sequence from South Sweden to the ice-sheet's point of bi-partition 500 miles further north. The total was some 5000, and subsequent work has added something like 8700 thereafter to the count to reach the present day. So it is that the retreat of the ice from South Sweden may be dated nearly fourteen thousand years ago, or approximately 12,000 B.C., the Fenno-Scandian moraines at 8300 B.C., and the final bi-partition at 6800 B.C. This 'geochronology', confirmed in its results in Finland and elsewhere, is the current basis of a natural time-scale for North European prehistory, and with its findings may be correlated those of two other departments of geology; the study of changes in land- and sea-levels, and the determination from plant and animal remains of the successive phases of the climate.

Land- and sea-level changes have already been noticed in the course of our second chapter, but here we may most fitly approach the fact of their connexion with the thawing of the ice, which naturally soon swelled the absolute volume of the sea, but more slowly also allowed the land to rise in response to the withdrawal of the huge weight of the ice-cap. Thus when the Gotiglacial ice-retreat ended on the Fenno-Scandian moraines, what had been an ice-dammed Baltic lake became at first an arm of the thaw-swollen open sea. It is known as the Yoldia Sea, from an arctic salt-water mollusc which throve in it.   Its outlet gulf flanked the ice-margin across Central Sweden, but south of this a slowly risen mass of ice-free land already stretched across unbroken from Denmark and the Continent.   Then as the ice drew off northwards in the Finiglacial retreat, more of such land-emergence encroached upon the gulf until it was at last bridged over, and turned the Yoldia Sea into what is called (from a distinctive fresh-water mollusc) the Ancylus Lake.

Geochronology gives this an initial date about 7800 B.C., and the Swedo-Danish land-mass then stretched away west-wards to limit the North Sea to a coast-line running straight over from North Jutland by the Dogger Bank to near Flam-borough Head in Yorkshire, while to the south the English Channel ended in a narrow bay off Beachy Head.   It was not until nearly three thousand geochronological years later, about 5000 B.C., that the further gradual rise of water-level flooded the Swedish land bridge at Lake Vänern and re-created the Baltic as the Litorina Sea, so named after the marine periwinkle (*Litorina litorea*) in which it soon abounded.   The corresponding 'Flandrian' sea-transgression which created our Narrow Seas had by then already separated Britain from the Continent, for botanical and zoological studies have recently combined to date this event about the middle of Boreal times, or not long after 6000; but it is safe to say that the separation was for long neither so deep nor so wide as it has since become. The Litorina maximum in Southern Scandinavia was reached by 4500-4000 B.C., and the shore-lines of that time may be traced as 'raised beaches' well above modern sea-level.   Thus from about 12,000 B.C. the Baltic area reveals four periods of alternating lake and sea.   Its climatic history, established from the remains of vegetation contained in peat-beds, and of geologically stratified fauna, falls into an answering sequence of periods.   During the ice-retreat from the Baltic end-moraine, the so-called Dryas flora of hardy shrubs was increasingly invaded by spreads first of birch and willow, and then, especially during the warmer Allerød phase of about 10,000-8500 B.C., of pine, and these trees survived the renewed cold of the time of the Yoldia Sea and the first thousand years of the Ancylus Lake.   These were the centuries of the Ahrensburg-

Lyngby group of cultures. From the end of the Finiglacial retreat, about 6800 B.C., the warm and dry climate known as Boreal supervened, when birch and pine were joined by hazel, and alder, oak, and other trees appeared. Finally, from 5000 B.C. the Litorina marine transgression was accompanied by a change of conditions to the no less warm but damp and rainy 'Atlantic' climate, in which alder and 'oak-mixed-forest', with hazel, became generally dominant. Since the technique of analysing the tree-pollen in stratified peat-beds has made it possible to assign any content of animal and human relics to its precise period in this climatic sequence, the Mesolithic record in the north, with its natural background geologically mapped and geochronologically dated, is now becoming one of the clearest chapters in early prehistory. We have seen that its inception was due to peoples of the tanged-point cultures, derived, it would seem, from East-Central Europe, and to these we must now return.

What we have seen of them so far has been all of pre-Boreal age; by Boreal times their tradition was in its older homelands obsolete, but it enjoyed a longer life among remoter colonies established on the West Norwegian coast, where in the Fosna province and elsewhere primitive flint-using communities of hunters and fishers maintained a Mesolithic existence until much later times. Indeed, among the later hunters and fisherfolk, who in Sweden as well as Norway were the descendants of Mesolithic colonists, the tanged-point and other ancient traditions lived on to make contact with the arrival of Neolithic civilization. Though on the shores of Oslo Fjord and the Kattegat there are groups of more primitive flints of still doubtful affinities, Mesolithic settlement in Scandinavia thus stands in positive archaeological connexion with the main North European story. The chief evidence for early prehistoric dating along the ocean coasts of Norway depends on the relation of sites to the old shore-lines now raised above sea-level, for here there was no shore-line oscillation as in the Baltic, but the land rose steadily out of the sea throughout post-glacial times, and the ancient levels may be geologically dated. Thus it is that the unique Stone Age culture of Finmark, along the narrow ice-free margin of the

Arctic Ocean, has been taken as far back as about 8000 B.C., nearly contemporary with the Fenno-Scandian moraines further south. Here, too, there are tanged points among the people's stone tools, but with these and some microlithic forms are many more direct reminiscences of the Palaeolithic, and the 'Finmarkian' is best ascribed to independent colonization by way of Karelia from Palaeolithic origins on the Russian plains. Its subsequent extinction finds a limiting date in its absence from the shore-horizons of around 4500 B.C. and after. Meanwhile, at the other end of Scandinavia, the Forest Cultures had come into existence with the invention of the axe.

In their earliest dwelling-site yet discovered, Klosterlund in Central Jutland, rough pick-like axe-heads flaked from flint cores are already a regular and quite plentiful type (Fig. 4, *o*), and there are a few flake-axes or *tranchets*, the cutting-edge always formed by striking off a single flake transversely across the implement's end, to leave a sharp raw edge ready for use.[1] Side by side with these, scrapers of varied forms and a series of gravers still strongly recall the Palaeolithic tradition, and some of the flake-knives have enough of a hafting-tang to suggest something of the old tanged-point tradition. There are also microliths in some quantity, for the most part simple forms without angular ('geometric') development. The age of the Klosterlund site, as determined by pollen-analysis, is near the end of pre-Boreal times or about 7000 B.C., and with the onset of the Boreal climate the whole land-mass barring the Ancylus Lake from South Sweden to North Germany became the centre of a further development of culture on the same lines. It is known as the Maglemose culture, from the great peat-moss at Mullerup in Zealand, which with Svaerdborg and Holmegaard near by ranks among its most famous sites. The type-site for the culture's earliest standard form is Duvensee near Lübeck, which, like all the settlements explored, is apparently the summer hunting-camp of a people living by hunting, collecting, and fresh-water fishing. Core-axes in the Klosterlund tradition are the rule, with flake-axes in a minority (Fig. 4, *u-v*), and the rest of the flint industry (*p-t*) includes tanged-point survivals, blades,

[1] Cf. Fig. 4, *u*.

scrapers, gravers, and a range of microliths in which 'geometric' forms and the micro-burin technique (p. 47) are considerably more in evidence, apparently owing to contact with the Tardenoisian peoples of the more open country to the south and west. There are also some stone 'pebble-axes' (Fig. 4, *w*), of which more hereafter. The famous sites in Zealand, though they show some growth of regional character, furnish the best all-round picture of the developed culture. Man appears here for the first time in human history accompanied by the domestic dog. His material equipment shows, side by side with the flint industry, a remarkable extension in bone and red-deer antler. Not only were axes and adze-heads made in antler, normally with a perforation for the haft, but flint axes were mounted in antler 'sleeves' (Fig. 4, *v*) similarly perforated, and among numerous tool-types in bone there are fish-hooks and an astonishing variety of bone points for use in fishing, fowling, and hunting. The barbed points, of which Fig. 4, *x* illustrates but one of many forms, are often called harpoons, but must in fact be spear-points, in many cases evidently of fish-spears, either single or composite. There are also 'leister'-prongs, and bone points slotted to mount flint flakes as side-blades or barbs, in the manner already conjectured (p. 46 : Fig. 4, *a*) for the mounting of microliths. The detailed study of these bone types and their distribution has clearly shown that, despite various purely regional features, the Maglemose culture was essentially a single entity throughout the area of its dispersion.

And that area was enormous. Not only west and south, but also east of the Ancylus Lake are its remains forthcoming: some of the best bone-work comes from Pernau and Kunda in Esthonia, and westward finds are scattered as far as Northern France, while South-Eastern Britain has produced not only characteristic implements like Fig. 4, *x* from Hornsea in Holderness, but settlement-sites with typical flint-work such as Broxbourne in Hertfordshire. Here, as wherever else dating by pollen-analysis has been carried out, there is proof of the same Boreal age, and from the tracts now beneath the North Sea dredging has brought up evidence for the same distinctive flora, associated in one case with a typical barbed bone point.

The evident mobility of Maglemose man was not limited to dry land: among the numerous wooden objects found on sites favourable to their preservation, both Duvensee and Holmegaard have yielded paddle-rudders implying quite sizeable boats, probably dug-out canoes, and were the Ancylus coast-line not now largely sunk beneath the sea, there would doubtless be more to show for navigation, as also probably for winter habitations—for sledges and skates there is evidence already. On the other hand, an inland variant may be noted in Central Jutland, where the so-called Gudenaa culture, recently explored, shows a predominance of flint-work, much in the Klosterlund tradition, but with its microlithic element influenced in especial strength by Tardenoisian contacts.

It remains to say a word on Maglemose art, which is mainly displayed on bone and antler objects of use, more rarely of adornment. It consists largely of simple geometric designs, but includes stylized net and chequer forms carried out in fine engraving, and also in pointillé, and arrangements of regularly bored holes, made probably with a bow-drill. Any sort of naturalism is extremely rare, though conventionalized animal and human figures are at times discernible, and while the art may reliably be credited with belated elements of Palaeolithic descent, its interest extended to little more than mere pattern.

The climatic change from Boreal to Atlantic about 5000 B.C., with the accompanying transgression of the Litorina Sea, made a great difference to life in Northern Europe. The submergence of so much land, and the wider and denser growth of deciduous forest in the far damper climate, had important consequences both for man and beast. Hunting facilities worsened, and the traditions of the Forest Cultures became largely concentrated, in an altered form, along the new and indented sea-coasts, where communities now found it better to live all the year round. For the easiest food-supply came from the edible shell-fish—periwinkle, cockle, oyster, and the rest, which abounded in the warm sea. Thus grew up the renowned 'kitchen-middens' or shell-mounds of Denmark, the accumulated food-refuse of these beach-dwelling communities, amongst which they persisted in living, cooking their meals on little stone hearths in the ceaselessly growing débris. Forest animals and birds were indeed still pursued, but the old fine equipment in bone and antler gave place largely to the bow and arrow, the latter tipped with a characteristic transverse-bladed flint (Fig. 5, *k*) which is really a form of geometric microlith, unknown in Maglemose times, but referable to the series of 'trapeze'-shaped angular microliths developed at this period in the not far distant Tardenoisian. The inland Gudenaa culture of Central Jutland was less affected by the climate-change, and continued much as before, but even more strongly influenced by the Tardenoisian, whence geometric microliths were evidently borrowed. Its combination of microliths, larger blade-tools, and flint axes is repeated with well-marked differences in the earliest kitchen-middens, and the culture embodied in the latter is best distinguished, by the name of a typical midden, as the Ertebølle culture.

Flake- rather than core-tools were now the rule (Fig. 5, *e, f, j*), and a new type of antler axe (*g*) appeared with the haft-hole socketed in a projecting tine-stump; but more remarkable is the production of a round-bodied axe in stone, pecked into shape and with a ground cutting-edge (Fig. 5, *h*), and the 'Limhamn' axe, flaked, but finished by partial polishing. Round and pick-ended stone 'maceheads', perforated for hafting,[1] had been devised already in Maglemose times, as had the simple pebble-axes above noticed,[2] and with these new axe forms, ground and polished like their inventors' traditional bone-work, stone attained a more important place in the Mesolithic equipment. Finally, we are for the first time confronted by vessels of pottery—big bag-like affairs of coarse-gritted clay, built up by hand in coils from a stump-pointed base to an out-curved rim, sometimes ornamented with finger-nail or stab markings. The problem presented by this momentous invention will be discussed presently (p. 201 : Fig. 19, 1). At this early date, it remained unknown in the outlying districts to the north, which now received the version of the same culture called after Lihult in Sweden and Nøstvet in Norway; this is distinguished by core-axes made in the volcanic rock of the

---

[1] Fig. 5, *l*.　　　[2] Fig. 4, *w*.

country instead of in flint.[1]   Such tools, made in trap rock, appear in settlement-sites right up to Northern Scandinavia, and it was without doubt in this Atlantic age that the hunting and fishing folk of all these 'Arctic' dwelling-places acquired the main foundations of their long-lived culture.   The conditions of these northern hunters' lives must have been not unlike those of the Upper Palaeolithic in Western Europe, and it is scarcely surprising that the animal art of the hunting-magic which had died with that age in the west should here have been born again into a new and rather different existence. Animal rock-engravings are in fact found in great numbers in Scandinavia, [2] and the oldest group, which has a northerly distribution and consists of drawings, most typically in ground-in outline, of reindeer, elk, bears, and sea-creatures, may by its relation to ancient shore-lines be dated from even before the beginning of this period.   We shall return to the Arctic Stone Age and its art in a later chapter (p. 205, with Pl. VI).

Not only northward, but also eastward, were axe-using Mesolithic cultures now distributed.   In the forest tracts of Poland, Russia, and the Baltic countries their vestiges are as yet not certainly datable, but in Finland and Esthonia settlements with distinctive material have been proved contemporary with the Litorina coast-line—those of the Suomusjärvi culture, with its short, broad axes in ground volcanic rock.   Here we are in a distinct eastern province of Forest Culture, now in no contact with Scandinavia, and foreshadowing a long-continued history on separate lines of its own: we shall shortly find the dwelling-places of people still rooted in Mesolithic life, but distinguished by a peculiar comb-ornamented pottery, spread across the whole vast forest region of Eastern Europe.   North-Eastern Germany, on the other hand, yields flint types substantially similar to those of Ertebølle, and the heavier Mesolithic flint-work of Silesia has lately been compared to that already earlier represented at Sandarna in Sweden.   Ertebølle was in fact the central culture for the hither side of the Litorina Sea, and though it has been thought to betoken the arrival here of a new people,

---

[1] Fig. 5, *i*.   [2] Pl. VI, 2.

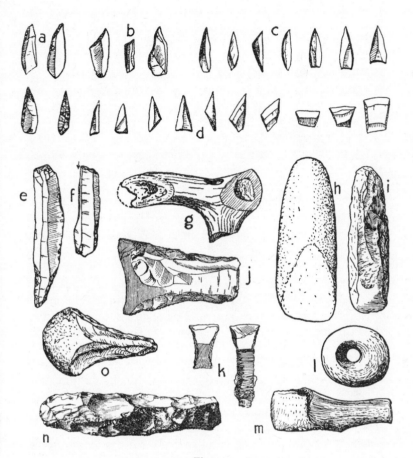

Fig. 5

MESOLITHIC IMPLEMENTS, II

a, Microliths, Mother Grundy's Parlour, Creswell Crags (pp. 34, 50);
b, Lower, *c*, Middle, *d*, Upper Tardenoisian microliths, Belgium (pp. 50, 66); *e, f, g, h*, Ertebølle scraper on tanged blade, angle-graver, antler-axe, stone-axe, Denmark (pp. 60-62); *i*, Nøstvet stone-axe, Norway (p. 61); *j, k*, Ertebølle flake-axe and transverse arrowheads, Denmark (p. 61); *l*, Ertebølle type of stone mace-head (p. 61); *m*, pebble-axe in antler sleeve, Falkenstein cave, Hohenzollern (p. 65); *n*, Halstow core-axe or 'pick', Thames (p. 67); *o*, Asturian stone pick, N. Spain (p. 68).

Scales : *a-f, k*, $\frac{1}{2}$; *g, i, l, n*, $\frac{1}{6}$; *h*, $\frac{2}{6}$; *j*, just over $\frac{1}{3}$; *m*, about $\frac{1}{8}$.

the differences between it and its Maglemose predecessor really require no such explanation. The evidence for continuity from 'transitional' Danish sites like Klampenborg and Bloksbjerg would doubtless be more striking if most of the Maglemose coastal areas had not been swallowed by the sea, but even as things are, the case stands reasonably firm. The peoples of Northern Europe have every right to their claim of unbroken aboriginal descent.

If the later Mesolithic saw any fresh arrivals in their neighbourhood, these might more plausibly be sought within the Tardenoisian. The change to Atlantic climate brought on really dense growths of forest on the heavier soils almost all over Europe, sharpening the contrast between these thick mixed woodlands and the thin-soiled open tracts which mainly supported Tardenoisian man, and with its onset his microlithic cultures are found in uniform development from south-east to west, right across the North European plain. In the caves of the Crimea the eastern counterpart of the Azilian gives place to a true Tardenoisian with advanced forms of geometric microlith (p. 59), and similar cultures are distributed over the Ukraine, Volhynia, Poland, and East and North-Central Germany. It was in this stage that the Tardenoisian influenced the Gudenaa and Ertebølle cultures of the north, and though all evidence for its bearers has perished save their flints, it is probable that their distribution is of underlying importance for the ensuing problem of the relations between North-Central Germany and the South Russian steppe. This whole range of Mesolithic development had a common Palaeolithic basis in the East-Gravettian type of culture (pp. 30-35) from which East-Central and Northern Europe had been successively brought into connexion with the steppe-land corridor out of Asia, and in the developed Tardenoisian, so remarkably uniform from South Russia to Germany, may lie hidden the final ethnic contributions to the folk for whom not only Nordic race, but Aryan language, will be claimed in a later chapter.

In Central Europe, on the other hand, the Tardenoisian retained much more of the ancestral, Azilian-like character inherited from the Magdalenian, and both in South Germany and Switzerland an essential continuity of population is claimed throughout the Mesolithic. While, for example, in Poland and Silesia the Tardenoisian makes a break with the old tanged-point tradition of the Swiderian, and its advanced geometric forms are well in evidence in the north of Bavaria, there is a good deal less to show for them nearer the Alps. In the stratified South Bavarian cave of Ensdorf, the proportion of geometric microliths is not overwhelming even in the latest layer, and the results were not dissimilar at Tannstock in Württemberg, where beside the Federsee a group of thirty-eight pit-dwellings has furnished precious evidence of the nature of Mesolithic habitation on an open lakeside. At the Falkenstein Cave in Hohenzollern (p. 48) the Azilian tradition, augmented here by the survival of typical harpoons and a whole industry in bone, remained dominant to a late stage, attested by the appearance of a big deer-horn hafting-mount or 'sleeve' containing a ground pebble implement recalling the round-bodied axes of the north (Fig. 5, *m*). The Atlantic forest growth engendered a contrast between the pursuit of a waterside existence, as in the basins of the Upper Danube and Rhine, and the ranging life which poorer groups continued to lead on the open uplands of the South German Jura, as at the Rappenfels site on the Swabian Alb; there such simple hunting-folk survived into Neolithic times unchanged, whereas we shall find it probable that the waterside dwellers entered directly into the Neolithic civilization of the Alpine lakes.

Further east, in Austria, Bohemia and Moravia, finds of microliths are sparser and scantier: in Hungary, away from the Polish border, micro-burin technique seems unknown, and a rarely found Mesolithic of archaic and simple type seems to have had a long survival on the northern fringes of the Hungarian plain; added to this, a heavy flint industry has been recognized in the Miskolcz district, where the so-called Avas culture vaguely recalls the ill-attested East European forest Mesolithic noticed above. There have been similar finds in South-West Rumania and Bessarabia. On the other hand, the sub-Alpine Mesolithic of Central Europe in the main rather corresponds to the Middle Tardenoisian of Belgium and the Sauveterrian of France (pp. 50-1), and the contrasts we have noticed with both north and east suggest that in its latest developments, as in its earlier Azilian origins, its main affinity was with the west. For it is in this Atlantic age that the Mesolithic of Western Europe reached its climax in the advanced geometric microlith-production of the Late or fully developed Tardenoisian. The French, as we have said, suggest restricting the name Tardenoisian altogether to this stage, though it is doubtful if the looser usage already familiar to us can be checked. If a French type-name is wanted to make a third to Azilian and Sauveterrian, one might well take it from the farm of Montbani, in the actual Tardenois district of the sandy Aisne country, where a rich flint-working settlement has furnished a typical microlithic series.

The culture's Late Mesolithic age is happily shown at the Sauveterre site in the Périgord, where the excavations at Le Martinet, noticed above (p. 50), have revealed it in a series of hut-floors stratified above the Sauveterrian layer, and distinguished therefrom by their regularly struck cores and sharply formed triangular and trapeze microliths. The industry in the first hut corresponds to that of Montbani, that in the second to the more evolved form found in another stratified site, Le Cuzoul at Gramat (Dépt. Lot), where the trapeze microliths include regular transverse arrowheads (p. 61) showing the secondary surface-trimming also seen on the Late Tardenoisian points of Belgium (Fig. 5, *d*) and of Holland.

This type of microlithic culture is unknown in Britain, where microlithic technique was never carried beyond the Middle Tardenoisian or Sauveterrian stage. We have already seen (p. 56) that our island's separation from the Continent may now be dated as far back as the middle of the Boreal period. At this stage the Straits can hardly yet have been wide, and the Narrow Seas between South-East England and the Low Countries were most probably still shallow and broken, but the separation was sufficient for Tardenoisian man, who was unconcerned with navigation. On the other hand, in the Atlantic age our south-eastern Mesolithic contains together with its microliths and other flint types a pronounced 'axe' element which is directly parallel to that of Ertebølle:

a type-site for this has been duly dated at Lower Halstow in Kent, and its core- and flake-axes remind us that in Boreal times South-East Britain had belonged to the Maglemose complex, which formed a common foundation for the Lower Halstow culture and its analogues across the now intervening waters.   Its core-axes, commonly known as 'Thames picks',[1] were a long-lived type, and closely resemble the corresponding tools which in France and Belgium have been called 'Campignian', after Le Campigny near the mouth of the Seine, a site which actually belongs only to the time of their later survival.   The flint-axe culture which they typify indeed lasted into Neolithic times from Northern to South-West Central France, as also in the Low Countries, where, however, excavation (e.g. at Rijckholt Ste.-Gertrude near Liège) has so far failed to prove the late Mesolithic date demanded by its character as an extension of the northern 'Forest Culture' parallel to Halstow.   The axe element seen in the latter became incorporated into the microlithic culture of the South-East British Greensand country, which has its most typical sites round Horsham in Sussex.   Among other features of this province of the Tardenoisian is a hollow-based form of microlithic point, and by excavating a group of these people's pit-dwellings recently at Farnham, Dr. Grahame Clark has begun to reveal a great deal concerning their industry and general manner of life which lack of such work has previously left obscure.

Outside the south-east, the British Mesolithic continued as has already been described (pp. 50, 66), and its microlithic tradition had a very long survival, especially in the west and north of England and in Scotland.   The same is true of Northern Ireland; but here geological horizons of Atlantic age have yielded larger-scale flake-cultures, tracing descent from the western fringe of the Upper Palaeolithic (p. 34) with perhaps a late Azilian extension, and also elements of North European affinity, perhaps related to the tanged-point tradition we have above discussed (p. 52).   There are, furthermore, signs of heavier industry of 'Forest' type as well, and in that too connexions are claimed not only with

[1] Fig. 5, *n*.

Northern but with Western Europe. We shall come to the suggested North French element in these when we consider the Irish Stone Age again in a later context; but another has been adduced with the Atlantic coasts further south, where the shore-line existence of the Ertebølle shell-fishers is paralleled in a peculiar form. On the Asturias and Biscayan shores of Northern Spain are the remains of great shell-middens, under overhanging cliffs and in cave-mouths, where they at times overlie earlier remains of Azilian occupation. The shells imply a warm sea, too warm for the *litorina* periwinkle which infests it to-day and was there also in Azilian times, and oysters, cockles, and above all limpets (mussels come only from the later levels) formed the diet of the shore-dwelling population, who could make rough pebble axes and scrapers of quartzite, but whose commonest tool was a simple pebble pick (Fig. 5, *o*) for detaching their shell-fish from the rocks. Beyond some rare bone implements nothing else is known of this wretched Asturian culture, though its association with the warm wet Atlantic climate-period seems certain, but elsewhere on the ocean coasts there are middens more closely related to European prehistory at large.

The shores of Brittany, like those of our Narrow Seas, were in Atlantic and later times gradually sinking in the course of the Flandrian sea-transgression, which reduced many of their peninsulas to islands. On one of these, now the Île Téviec near Quiberon, a midden has been excavated whose makers lived and cooked among the shell-fish débris and left an abundant flint industry of Late Tardenoisian type, with geometric microliths, micro-burins, and transverse arrowheads, some bone and antler equipment, and numerous plain pebble tools both small and large; moreover, they buried their dead crouched in the midden, accompanied by implements and a rich adornment of pierced shell necklaces and pendants in cairn-covered graves which we shall find significant in a later context (p. 147). The Late Tardenoisian, thus apparent in North-West France as well as from Belgium to the Périgord, appears also nearer the Mediterranean, where it succeeds to the Azilian in the stratified caves of the Narbonne region. And its geometric microliths, though less manifest in the Italian and Sicilian Mesolithic with its Grimaldian tradition (p. 34), are of course prominent in the old home of micro-burin technique in Spain. In the Peninsula, too, the Atlantic coasts attracted a population to shell-fishing, and the great middens on the Tagus estuary at Mugem, first explored seventy-five years ago, have yielded important evidence in more recent excavations. Here, in contrast to Brittany, the sea-level has sunk, and the Amoreira midden, facing a higher shore-line, is older than that of Arruda: its shell-fish indicate a warmer sea, and its microliths display a Sauveterrian stage of development, whereas at Arruda, where there were mussels as in the later Asturian, the industry has advanced to a full range of geometric and trapeze forms. Many dead, including broad-heads as well as the long-headed type christened *Homo taganus*, were buried in the middens, amid the squalor wherein the living dwelt and cooked their shell-fish, which they stored in small pits in the ground. Mugem, like Téviec, shows simply a rather specialized coastal form of the later Mesolithic of Western Europe generally. An industry of exactly similar microliths, similar bone-work, similar shell ornaments, similar cooking-hearths, and even similar storage-pits, was discovered when the Belgian archaeologist Siret explored the settlement of El Garcel, near the Mediterranean shore of South-East Spain. But there, beside all these native elements of Mesolithic tradition, he found great quantities of pottery, and with it highly polished fine stone axes of a kind absolutely new to Europe.

We have now followed, to something like two thousand years from the incoming of Atlantic climate about 5000 B.C., the fortunes of Mesolithic man in nearly every quarter of our continent. Obscure peoples inhabit the eastern forests, and other still more obscure are thinly scattered from North Hungary towards the Eastern Alps. Between, Tardenoisian hunters range the available open spaces from South Russia to the North European plain, while beyond them—and not unrelated—a great tradition of hunting and fishing life is firmly rooted in the shore-lands and forests of the north. In Central Europe along the Alpine fringe a rather simpler tradition has been long established: Italy, like large parts of the British Isles, maintains an even simpler seclusion. And from the Spanish Peninsula right across France, touching Alpine Europe and running out towards the northern plains to meet and mix with the life of the forests, stretches the open-country and coastal Tardenoisian culture of the west. With this picture in our minds we must now turn our eyes elsewhere.

3. THE DAWN OF CIVILIZATION

The Mesolithic Age has shown us how man in Europe adapted himself to the gradual but tremendous change from glacial to temperate and forest conditions. But though in its later phases he had done a good deal for the bettering of his material equipment, one can see no really radical change in his attitude to Nature as the provider of his livelihood. 'He had remained content to take what he could get'—in other words he was still, like his Palaeolithic forbears, a hunter, a fisher, and a food-gatherer only. The latent possibility of civilization remained unrealized. What was lacking was the revolution in human economy whereby food is not merely collected, but produced by man himself. Civilization is founded directly upon the cultivation of plants and the domestication of animals: from the steady practice of primary food-production comes the growth of both physical and mental fertility. Increasing in numbers with its assured resources, a food-producing community enlarges the range of orderly social life: extending its old day-to-day forethought to the span of the farmer's year, it learns not only to live in the conscious planning of measured time, but to employ its relief from hand-to-mouth anxieties in the issues, both material and spiritual, of slowly liberated thought. Hence come discoveries, inventions, and the specialization of crafts, the seeds of a trading economy; hence also the manifold adventures of the mind—the whole made fruitful in a quickening mastery of language. This revolution—actually a long and varied process of which archaeology can as yet only point to the results—took place in the Middle East. Before those results were effectively passed on to Europe, it was being succeeded in the river-lands of the Nile, the Euphrates, and the Indus by the momentous steps which led to the maturity of the commercial city and the integrated state. How then is its genesis related to the Palaeolithic and Mesolithic Ages of our European survey?

In recent years the account most usually given of the genesis of Near-Eastern civilization has been, broadly speaking, on these lines. With the retreat of the last European ice-sheets, the northward withdrawal of the Atlantic storm-track from the Saharo-Arabian belt left its huge tracts of grass and park-land a prey to desiccation. This process, already described (p. 46), thinned out both human and animal populations, and as their roaming-grounds fell away to desert, the survivors would be driven to the remaining oases and rivers for sub-sistence. Here, where man and beast were drawn together by necessity, the hunter's old relation with his game could easily become one of control, leading in time to regular domestication. Here, too, familiarity with wild grain-bearing grasses, ancestral to wheat and barley, would suggest to man the idea of their deliberate cultivation, sowing and reaping with the season. In particular, the cycle of seed-time and harvest would be provided in unique regularity on the banks of the Nile, where, in the rich soil deposited by the unfailing annual flood, grain would grow 'without human intervention'.

Such an account is of course a highly simplified version of the probable facts. To begin with, the period of desiccation cannot have set in long after about 12,000 B.C., with the waning of the last Würm phase of glaciation in Europe, and it is six or seven thousand years more before traces of the early farmer's life first appear in Egypt, or indeed anywhere in the Near East. Further, their appearance is preceded by a return from extreme desert conditions to some degree of humidity, for the rising temperatures which began to be marked in Europe from about 8000 B.C., to culminate in Boreal and early Atlantic times (p. 57), brought about sufficient renewal of rainfall to make subsistence in the Sahara and Arabian deserts feasible again, at any rate after the seventh millennium. All we know of the Middle East in the long dry interval is that Mesolithic cultures were persisting where they could—the Oranian and Upper Capsian in coastal North Africa, in Egypt a rather different tradition known as the Sebilian, and in Palestine another, named the Natufian, born somewhere in the south-west Asiatic highlands. Clearly these populations were restricted by drought to the neighbourhood of water. But there is nothing to suggest that this restriction led at all immediately to cultivation or stock-keeping. It is only in the ensuing phase of relative humidity—though the rainfall can never have been more than scanty—that food-production begins to be attested. The preceding dry period has rather a preparatory importance. It is possible that the earlier stage of the Natufian may belong to it, and therein were made composite tools (p. 46) with serrated blade-flints in a bone haft which resemble sickles and were used as such, for the straw or grass they cut has left its characteristic gloss on the flints. And grinding-stones were in use in the North African cultures. Grain-bearing grasses were then being sought out and gathered for food, though how early remains uncertain. At all events, the wild wheats emmer and dinkel are apparently native to South-West Asia, and so—with a secondary extension to North-East Africa—is wild barley. As for domestic animals, the sheep is certainly of Asiatic origin, but may already have extended to North Africa; small as well as large cattle were living in both regions. Here then are the pre-conditions for domestication and for grain-growing, and any increase in rainfall would by its promotion of fertility act as a stimulus towards their regular adoption. By 6000 B.C. our expectations may reasonably be heightened, and within the next thousand years at least we may believe that small communities of early farmers were scattered over some of the most favoured regions of the Near East.

But their ancestry and affinities are still everywhere doubtful. In Egypt the oldest known settlers, though they may have had Natufian connexions, seem to have had nothing to do with the North African Mesolithic as we know it: wherever they came from, it was apparently not the Sahara. Perhaps they came down the Nile from a Nubian focus of immigration into Africa from the east. In Palestine the analogous settlements seem later, and cannot adequately be explained by reference to the Natufian alone: here again, then, there is a tendency to look eastward. From Palestine to Syria, and thence round the rising fringe of the great Euphrates-Tigris basin as far as Elam on the Persian Gulf, stretch the lands, intermediate between mountain and plain, which Professor Breasted has strung together under the name of the 'Fertile Crescent'. In North Syria and Assyria a very early civilization has come to light, most notably at Tell Halaf (after which the culture is sometimes called) and at Arpachiyah near Nineveh; here, by a date which seems scarcely later than the fifth millennium, human material progress had reached a point which implies a civilized tradition already of some standing. The recent discoveries at Mersin in Cilicia have begun to throw light on a still remoter antiquity: the still incompletely known Samarra culture is yet earlier than that of Tell Halaf, and in Elam the first civilization of Susa is perhaps as early; while in the alluvial land of Sumer, through which the great rivers themselves flow into the Persian Gulf, we then have the related culture of the earliest settlers on such sites as Al 'Ubaid and Ur. But, though microliths have been reported from the virgin surface beneath Sumerian Kish, there is in these regions no ancestral Mesolithic either. The settlers arrived bringing their civilization from elsewhere, and their blade-tools of flint and the volcanic glass, obsidian, are actually rather Palaeolithic in appearance. If they came from the highlands to the north-east and east, their forbears may have taken the path of civilization directly from a very late Palaeolithic stage of culture. The region of the Iranian plateau should have witnessed an adoption of food-producing earlier, and in more immediate accord with theory, than the alluvial river-lands can show us.

At all events, by the time the founders of the Hither-Asiatic cultures had settled on the sites we know, they were already masters of small-scale cereal, dairy, and stock farming; they were also builders, and their equipment included not only blade-tools and hoes of flint, but axes and adzes of polished stone: furthermore, axes perforated with a shaft-hole were probably already being made of the earliest utilized metal, copper, of which small implements and ornaments—best known perhaps from Susa—were certainly being made. There will be more to say of metallurgy and its enormous importance presently (pp. 91, 285): a chemistry simpler than the coppersmith's must first confront us, and that is the craft of the potter.

Our Near-Eastern villagers must already have been weaving garments, originally perhaps of hair, thereafter of wool, as sheep began to be bred for their fleeces, and (in Egypt anyhow) of flax. Archaeology has recovered the spindle-whorls which enabled them to spin. And weaving spun thread on a frame or primitive loom is a complicated business compared with the weaving of basketry. Basketry, no less than netting, seems to have inspired some of the criss-cross motives of Maglemose art (p. 60), and the craft must be at least as old as the Mesolithic. But for a basket to hold liquid easily it must be lined with clay, and if such a vessel chance to be burnt, the clay lining is seen transformed by the fire to a semblance of stone. It was only a matter of time before human adaptiveness was devising vessels made of baked clay alone, in which liquids could be held and food cooked on the fire, and such novelties were naturally first made in the outward likeness of the already familiar basket, gourd, or leather bag. Thus the earliest pottery, both in form and ornament, embodies the memory of its makers' existing equipment of vessels made in perishable materials. Basketry forms may be either round- or flat-based, but will indicate their prototypes most clearly in the ornamental patterns wherewith the natural conservatism of simple minds liked to give them the familiar woven look. The hemispherical gourd form will be embellished with lines giving the zigzag appearance of a carrying-sling, and leather bags or bottles will have their forms faithfully reproduced in smooth-faced plain pottery, occasionally with the incised semblance of a girth-band, or perhaps rows of impressions to represent stitches.

Different clays, and different fuels for firing, produce pottery of various colours. The fiercely burning woods of hot, dry regions will fire many clays pinkish, or buff, while the smoky fire got from damper growths burns black or greyish, unless the pot can stand free of the charcoal for its iron content to oxidize red. By experiment the potter can learn to control these seeming mysteries and produce colour effects at will. A clay rich in iron oxides can be applied as a 'slip' coating to give a rich red surface, with which a black top will make an effective contrast if the mouth of the vessels is buried in charcoal while firing—or black can be obtained by applying matter which will char of itself. A refinement of the idea of a slip is the painting on the unfired pot of a pattern which will burn red or black, while the background fires pale pink or buff. Such a light ground can be reliably produced only in the intense but smoke-free heat of a built oven or kiln, and the potter's art in Hither-Asia had already encompassed this invention in the earliest ages yet known to archaeology. Obviously its development was a communal growth: the women in simple societies are all potters together, and their inventions became embodied in a steady tradition of workmanship. Thus style in the shaping and ornamentation of pottery is the archaeologist's most reliable index to the identity and contacts of an ancient culture. The early cultures of the Near East form, in fact, two broadly contrasted groups in this regard. One group had in centuries unknown to us already developed painted pottery: the painted designs on their pale background are most essentially the weave-patterns of basket prototypes, though the artist's freedom now leads to the inclusion of freshly conceived animal, plant, or abstract motives. In the other, plain surfaces are the rule, from black and grey and brownish to rich red; here leather and gourd prototypes are especially marked among the forms, and when sling or binding is occasionally commemorated, or when the model is in fact a basket one, decoration is most often incised, and may be emphasized by a white filling.

This conception of Painted-ware and Plain-ware cultures has played a great part in schemes of interpretation in Near-Eastern prehistory, and though their analysis is not here our concern, it is at least clear that the Tell Halaf culture in North Syria and Assyria, and the more southerly Susa-Al 'Ubaid cultures in Elam and Sumer, are rooted in a painted-ware tradition, while in Egypt the earliest communities known are plain-ware people, and the same is independently true of Anatolia, which has been suspected to be the true home of plain-ware elements which appear in more than one early context within the painted-ware province. More probably Anatolian and, by a more roundabout route, Egyptian plain wares represent early offshoots of the craft from the original centre of its creation somewhere in South-West Asia, say in the sixth millennium, while its original creators had already advanced from plain to painted ware when we first encounter their traces in the north and east of the Tigris-Euphrates basin. For the beautiful pottery of Tell Halaf or Susa must have a long history behind it, and knowledge of the plain essentials of potting can have spread by diffusion at an earlier stage than any we yet know, and travelled both south and west. It is even conceivable that it may, in some way yet utterly obscure, have filtered across the forests of Eastern Europe to reach the Ertebølle people of the northern sea-coasts, whose primitive earthenware we have already (p. 61) seen to be at 5000 or so B.C. the earliest well-attested pottery in Europe. That is conjecture: what is certain is that a thousand years later those beginnings had in their homelands long been left behind; self-reliant, productive culture, of which pottery was but one of many symptoms, had itself spread well beyond its cradle, and while from Assyria to Elam, and in the Indus valley beyond, the foundations of further progress were forming, men had come to settle and do likewise in the fertile hinterlands of the Eastern Mediterranean. From among these communities diffused the true Dawn of European Civilization.

Within the broad promontory of Anatolia, populations whose precise antiquity is as yet unknown become visible in the course of the fourth millennium, when their combination of stone industry with some knowledge of copper earns their culture the name of Chalcolithic. The east-central group on the highland plateau appears distinct from the western, which bordered the Aegean and the Straits and is best known towards 3000 from the first settlement at Hissarlik, the site of Troy, and the earlier occupations at Thermi in Lesbos—though at Kum Tepe in the same region a still older stage is suspected. Anatolian pottery, based most clearly on leather prototypes, is typically black or brownish, and the red-ware technique which predominated in the subsequent Copper

Age is thought to have reached the plateau from the east, or from Cilicia in the south-east, which Mersin has recently revealed as already the home of settled civilization so long before. The most important extension of the Anatolian province as a whole is the earliest culture of Crete, where plain dark-faced ware of simple bag and bowl shapes seems probably as old as 4000 B.C., and became improved to a black burnished fabric often bearing incised and white-filled ornament, which may perhaps reflect an element of African derivation. The polished stone axe or adze is typical of all these cultures (Fig. 7, 1-2), and as well as bone tools there is a universal blade-industry in flint and obsidian, which in East Anatolia is native but in Crete was imported from the Aegean island of Melos. Thus early in seafaring activity attested in the Aegean, which in the sequel became the home of an essentially maritime civilization. Crete has in this regard a uniquely favoured position: it is in fact the inevitable centre of East Mediterranean sea-routes, on the edge of the Aegean, and in the path westward from the Asiatic shores and north-westward from Egypt.

In the Egyptian delta, whence Cretan culture was to receive the most vital of its seaborne influences, the village civilization we have been discussing was by now well established. At Merimde near the Delta's western margin, a settlement has recently been explored where the villagers kept cattle, pigs, and sheep, or goats, and cultivated emmer wheat beside the Rosetta branch of the Nile, threshing their grain on hollow clay floors and storing it in basket-bottomed pits. The pottery is a simple dark plain ware based on leather and open basket forms, often with lugs for hand or string-hold, and includes distinctive spoons or ladles.[1] To a flint blade-industry, including serrated sickle-blades, are added flint as well as polished stone axes; fine hollow-based arrowheads attest continued hunting, and the bone-work comprises harpoons. The related culture not long revealed beside the Fayûm lake has points of resemblance and some of individuality: grain-pits lined with straw matting are distinctive, the hollow-based arrowheads are especially fine, and the pottery, generally similar, is of simple

---

[1] Fig. 6, A 2.

bag forms normally devoid of lugs.¹ Finally, at Deir Tasa
up the Nile in Middle Egypt, the rather less developed Tasian
culture, in which agriculture is scarcely in evidence and life
in general less settled and organized, has similar stone axes,
and leather-bag pottery, including peculiar trumpet-mouthed
beakers, with incised ornament suggestive of a derivation from
basketry bindings. The semi-nomad life of the Tasians was
far outstripped by the Badarian culture which followed:
emmer cultivation was regular, cattle and sheep were
domesticated, cloth was woven, hollow-based and leaf-shaped
arrowheads and beautiful laurel-leaf blades appear in the
flint industry, while the pottery, with its fine red surfaces
black-topped by the firing-process described above (p. 75)
and its marvellous rippled finish, is of the highest excellence,
though cruder brown fabric was also made.² Leather-bag
shapes still predominate, but flat bases are commoner and
the bowls may have a carinated outline, recalling perhaps
a withy hoop employed to stretch the leather models to a
similar profile. Spoons were now finely carved from ivory,
and finally an industry in hammered copper had made an
appearance. From the Badarian civilization the First Predynastic or Amratian culture of Upper Egypt seems directly
descended, with the incorporation of new elements from the
semi-desert margins, and dates for these early cultures can
be estimated by reckoning backwards from the known
beginnings of Dynastic Egypt about 3000 B.C. A thousand
years is an agreed minimum for the Predynastic sequence,
and it is safe to place the Badarian before 4000. As it was
confined to Upper Egypt, the Merimdian of the Delta may
well be contemporary, while the Fayûm settlements may on
the whole be somewhat later: their lower dating-limit is
provided by the new civilization which entered Egypt in the
fourth millennium with strong Asiatic affinities, known as the
Second Predynastic or Gerzean.

We have no need to describe it in detail, but among its
introductions was not only a more advanced metallurgy in
copper, but painted pottery with designs in red on a pale
ground, of forms modelled on contemporary vessels of ground

¹ Fig. 6, A 1.   ² Fig. 6, A 3.

stone of which a tubular lug handle is but one of many distinctions. The final union of Egypt was effected by a fusion of these new people with the old, and though the precise eastern origin of the Gerzeans is unknown, it is notable that

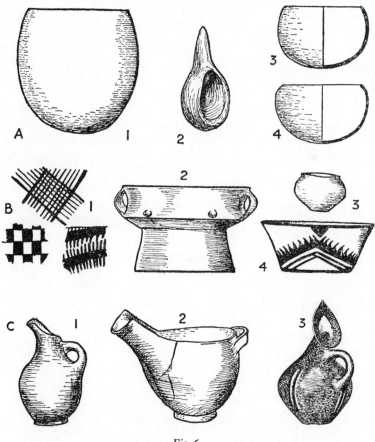

Fig. 6

A, EARLY POTTERY FROM EGYPT (1, Fayûm; 2, Merimde; 3, Badari: pp. 77-8) AND SPAIN (4, Gibraltar: pp. 83, 129-30).

B, FIRST-THESSALIAN POTTERY AND PAINTED DESIGNS (1, Chaeronea and Sesklo; 2-4, Tsangli: pp. 80, 90 ff.).

C, EARLY MINOAN (1, Palaikastro), EARLY CYCLADIC (3, Melos), AND EARLY HELLADIC (2, Chalandriani) POTTERY (pp. 87-9).

Scales: A 1, 3-4, $\frac{1}{7}$; 2, about $\frac{1}{4}$. B 2-4, $\frac{1}{7}$. C 1-3, $\frac{1}{6}$.

the centuries before about 3500 B.C. are marked by other westward extensions of Painted-ware culture. Painted pottery began to be adopted in Palestine and Syria, where in the north influence from the Tell Halaf tradition is unmistakable: the same thing appears by the side of the above-mentioned red ware also in Cilicia, and the two together distinguish the earliest settlements in Cyprus. Further extensions remain to be traced along the coast and hinterland of South-West Asia Minor, but this is most probably the quarter whence the first known settlers arrived on the mainland of Greece.

For there, in Central Greece and parts of the Peloponnese, and above all in Thessaly, the earliest recognized communities appear with pottery traditions quite unlike those of Crete, issuing in burnished red ware and a distinct painted series with basketry designs generally in red on a pale slip ground.[1] It is from Sesklo and other sites in Thessaly that this culture has been longest known; the people lived a farming life in regular villages of square or round huts, and among their polished stone axes bevelled adze forms [2] appear which suggest specialization as hoe-blades, a specifically European development of which we shall have more to say in the next chapter. Here, then, perhaps from about 3500 B.C., the periphery of Near-Eastern civilization is found at last on European soil. And the Thessalian form of the culture reached Servia in W. Macedonia, whence the mountain passes lead northward to the valley of the Danube leading out of Central Europe. Presently, in and beyond that valley, the essentials of the same pattern of life reappear. Villages of peasants, raising grain and domestic stock and making good pottery and polished stone hoes, here look in the main and south-eastward for the origins of their culture. But the origins are unmistakable in general while remaining dim in detail. These earliest known civilizations in South-East Europe will meet us at closer quarters in the next chapter, and we shall not find any Anatolian (or Aegean) cultural ensemble reproduced among them with exclusive fidelity. On European soil, in fact, features of Oriental derivation become blurred, partly by their blending with new elements of local contribution, and partly by the

[1] Fig. 6, B 1-4.   [2] Fig. 7, 4.

PLATE I

Photo : T. D. Kendrick

STONEHENGE : A VIEW SOUTH-EASTWARD FROM THE CENTRE

The two standing trilithons of the sarsen horseshoe, part of the " blue-stone " horseshoe
in front of them, and glimpses of the outer circles behind. The recumbent stone on
the right is the " altar stone." See pp. 316-7

PLATE II

THE " VENUS OF WILLENDORF," AND TWO SMALLER FEMALE
FIGURES FROM THE GRIMALDI CAVES

From casts in the British Museum

Scale 5 : 6

See pp. 38-9

filtering and impoverishment that they must have undergone
in the varied lands beyond and bordering the Aegean.   The
impoverishment must in any case be a cardinal fact: the
filtering, like the blending with native elements, is a process
still far from clear; but it was evidently along these lines that
the Near-Eastern cultural tradition, itself already old in its

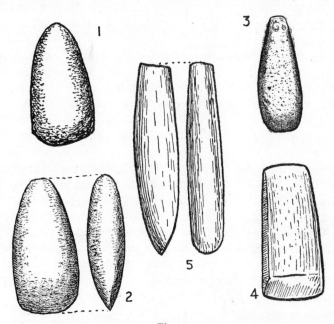

Fig. 7

STONE AXES (pp. 73, 77 ff.) FROM THE NEAR EAST (1, Asia
Minor;   2, Cyprus), SPAIN (3, Alhama de Granada), AND
THESSALY (4);   DANUBIAN 'SHOE-LAST CELT' OR
HOE (5, Worms: pp. 94 ff., 123).

Scales: 1-4, ¼; 5, ⅓.

homelands, became in the fourth millennium B.C. established
in South-Eastern Europe, in the hands of related but distinguishable groups of peasant settlers.   Thence, at least by
3000 B.C., simple peasant civilization began to spread into the
interior, particularly on the broad stretches of loess and
'black-earth' soils, which attracted settlers by a fertility beyond
the dreams of the Mesolithic hunter.   Its diffusion thus began

by colonization, but soon native European peoples were drawn into its orbit, and within the next millennium prehistory has to record the shaping of province after province of distinctively European culture.

In North Africa things were rather different. There the immense tracts of half-desert country carried a population of strong Mesolithic tradition, whose essentially hunting life can have been but little modified by such acquaintance with grain-growing as they had gained; small-scale garden-culture, no less than herding, is easily grafted on to nomad habits, and in absorbing traits of civilization from the progressive peoples of Egypt they did little to mitigate their barbarism. Incomings from the desert mark decay in the culture of the Fayûm, and though others were successfully absorbed into Predynastic civilization, that civilization remained of necessity dependent on the Nile. Thus while the making of stone axes, pointed flint arrowheads, and pottery became gradually disseminated among the nomad peoples as far west as the coasts of Morocco, these simple crafts no more imply civilized progress here than among the Arctic Stone Age peoples of Northern Europe (p. 62). And as there, too, animal rock-engravings vividly display the continued dominance of hunting and the hunter's mentality. For the rock-engravings and paintings of North Africa have been shown to belong in the main to this long-continued stage of Mesolithic tradition, and the series is unbroken down to the appearance among them of the horses and chariots which take the story of barbarian borrowings from Egypt on past the middle of the second millennium B.C. The stone axes show that it began early, for Egypt had abandoned them already in Predynastic times, but the pottery reflects not only the early plain wares of the Nile, but also certain Predynastic features such as blunt-pointed bases, tubular lugs, and various elements in the incised decoration, in the main referable to basketry models, which it frequently bears. In this way faint echoes of a thousand years' development in Egypt may be vizualized slowly reaching the cave-dweller of the North African Atlas, and at last they were actually carried across the Straits to issue in the 'cave culture' of South-Central Spain.

In addition, however, to these barbaric echoes of eastern culture among the southern sierras, stands the fresh current of civilization with which our last section ended on the south-east Spanish coast. The settlement at El Garcel, with its grain-pits, its sickle-flints, finely polished stone axes, and big-bellied jars of plain pottery, recalls Egypt more closely—though we have seen (p. 69) that geometric microliths attest also a native Mesolithic element. It seems that the coastal province of Almeria was actually colonized by a new people, whose skulls proclaim them to be of 'Mediterranean race', the ancestors of the historic Iberians, and whose culture was in some distinct sense derived from Egypt. The round-bottomed bowls from Tres Cabezos, another early Almerian site, point in the same direction, and examples of the simpler bowl type of Fig. 6, A 4, are indistinguishable from early Egyptian work (A 1, 3). This distinctive 'Western Culture' must await fuller description later (p. 125): it is evidently the child of the plain-ware province of the Eastern Mediterranean, with a prominence of certain Egyptian characters, and its recognition requires us to believe that, as well as a gradual seeping of ideas from Egypt among the North African barbarians, some definite outgrowth of early Nilotic civilization itself managed to pass westward to the coast of Spain, and, as we shall find, far wider tracts of Western Europe too. It still remains for archaeology to find traces of its passage. Professor Bosch Gimpera would look to the Western Sahara, and others have spoken of a coastwise migration, but in any case its arrival in Europe seems to fall after 3000, though well before 2500 B.C. (pp. 128-9).

The Mid-Mediterranean regions past which it would have travelled seem to have been left untouched; they were apparently settled already by a movement rather similar to that which brought the cave-people to the South Spanish hinterland. The earliest traces of such settlement in Sardinia and West Sicily are still obscure, but the basis of later developments there seems to have been a lowly culture somehow allied to the Spanish (p. 126), while in East Sicily the first settlers (seemingly unconnected with their Late Palaeolithic or Mesolithic forerunners) display a more advanced version of the same kind of thing. Though apparently not agriculturalists like the western colonists of Almeria, they lived in regular villages, not merely in caves; the sites of these at Stentinello and Matrensa reveal them as established pastoralists, and though instead of polished stone axes they were usually content with picks of chipped stone or basalt, their pottery, with its basket-like designs incised or formed by stamped impressions, is almost as much like the Cretan as anything yet known in Africa. This culture may be compared with the later stages of the basic civilization of Crete, and there may be an East-Mediterranean element here reflecting that which we shall encounter (p. 153) in Malta, but its affinities further west, in Sardinia, and in South Spain, leave us able to do little more than emphasize its archaic Africo-Mediterranean aspect in general. From Sicily it spread to South Italy, but further developments in these regions belong to a later chapter, when we shall find the whole nexus of Mediterranean culture roused to more positive activity through the channels of maritime trade.

Trade among the simple peasant communities we have hitherto been discussing is indeed perceptible, but for self-sufficing villages it had as yet little primary significance. And it would be a mistake to ascribe its beginnings to purely economic motives. The ancient belief in magic forces, which we have seen animating the hunting-peoples of the Old Stone Age, was naturally stimulated to new forms by the changed preoccupations of a peasant life. The primitive urge for human fertility, which had inspired the 'Venuses' of Palaeolithic times, became now entwined with the desire for the fertility of Mother Earth, and in the generically similar female statuettes, usually of clay, which occur so commonly on all these early sites in the Near East, and in South-Eastern Europe, and even once at El Garcel in the West also, we may see a fertility-cult extended to the conception of Earth as a 'Mother-Goddess', responding to the paternal moisture of sky or river. The marriage of earth and sky, and the embodiment of their fertility in human shape, are concepts of great antiquity in the religious history of civilization. But the magic of charms and talismans could extend much more widely. The cowrie-shell, from its resemblance to the vulva,

has a long history as a fertility-charm, and the virtue of
ornaments, at once decorative and mystical (cf. pp. 94, 111),
accounts for the constant presence of sea-shells in these
settlements, however far from the sea. And traffic in magic
shells and precious pebbles not only found an economic
counterpart in trading of the craftsman's obsidian and stone,
but itself, no doubt, led to the discovery of the enduring yet
workable treasure gold, and of substances—the oxidized ores
seemingly preceded by the purer material malachite, first
known in Egypt as an eye-paint—transformable into copper.
Though the Badarians indeed could only work it cold, the
fusibility of copper, and the technique of casting it molten
in a clay mould into any suitable shape that might be desired,
were discovered in the Near East at a very early date, and
with the first mastery of metallurgy trade and industry finally
interlocked to open a new era of human achievement.

It is impossible here to detail the momentous course of
discovery, invention, and organization which led the Near
East through the centuries preceding 3000 B.C. to the primacy
of higher civilization. Coppersmiths were only one class of
the specialized workers who could be maintained on its
mounting surplus of primary production. The carpenter
became master of the wheel, the boat-builder became the
ship-builder, and transport could thus equip itself to the
greater service of the long-distance trade on which industry
must more and more rely. Wealth demanded organization
for its disposal: the primitive amulet became the graven seal,
and from signs for ownership and for number, systematized
along with pictographic symbols as reckoning advanced to
the complication of accounts, emerged the vital invention of
writing. The specialists in the ever-compelling magic, inevitably at the centre of the community's life, commanded and
propelled the furtherance of progress both intellectual and
economic, and side by side with the priestly corporation of the
temple, the dynamics of civilization created the king, in whom
supernatural sanction vested the powers of law and order,
and of leadership in the warfare which defence against un-
civilized and rivalry with civilized neighbours would alike
necessitate. In short, there came into being the State.

Dynastic supremacy over the Sumerian cities began about 3000 B.C., and at about the same date the powers of Upper and Lower Egypt were united under the first of the Pharaonic Dynasties.

But in Europe it was only these same centuries that saw the first humble stages of the process—the implanting of simple peasantries, linked by no more than petty trade. And the stimulus to further progress came not so much from Egypt and Mesopotamia direct, as from the less advanced cultures of Anatolia, Crete, and the Aegean, which developed on their own lines in contact with the great Eastern centres on the one hand, and with the primitive Europeans on the other. It was thus the Aegean world which first passed the dawn of Western civilization, just as it was later destined to win for Europe its primacy from a stagnating Orient. But the same dawn broke gradually over all the Continent, and it was in mingled dependence and reaction that the peoples of Prehistoric Europe grew up to transfuse its light with their native potencies, till they too came into history to make the primacy at last their own. Of that growth the chapters that follow imperfectly essay a record.

Chapter Four

THE SOUTH-EAST AND THE DANUBIAN
EXPANSION

I. AEGEAN CULTURES AND THE NEOLITHIC HINTERLAND

(Map III and Table III: at end)

THE island of Crete, as we have already seen, lies in the
forefront of the Aegean world over against Egypt and the East,
and if its humble earliest culture came to it from Anatolia, its
development was more vitally affected by Egyptian contacts.
The union of Upper and Lower Egypt under the First historic
Dynasty, to be dated, as was said above, about 3000 B.C., may
possibly have led to an actual migration to Crete of refugees
from the Western Delta, fleeing before the new royal power.
The archaeological links with Egypt are indeed not so firmly
datable as one would like, but they can yet justify the belief
that if not quite as early as 3000, at any rate within two centuries
or so thereafter, one may in part date and explain the beginnings
of the civilization which its discoverer, Sir Arthur Evans, has
made known to all the world as the Minoan. But it arose
directly from the island's ancestral culture already described
(p. 77), with any discernible foreign elements as a fertilizing
admixture. Stone and obsidian begin gradually to be joined
by metal: the earliest metal objects seem to be Egyptian copper
imports, and are very rare, but before the end of Evans's
Early Minoan I period, which may be a century or there-
abouts on either side of 2700 B.C., native metallurgy has
become perceptible. We can believe that the people kept
domestic animals and practised some primitive agriculture,
while their stone dwellings, at first square one-roomed
structures, reached in Early Minoan II (to about 2400) considerable size, with a number of rooms and even of storeys.
Early Minoan pottery is varied both in form and decoration.
The old island tradition is strong at first, but its black ware

became refined into what may be called 'bucchero', which was decorated with incised or impressed patterns, and also used for stemmed goblets suggesting a wooden model. There are also fine light brown wares, and Anatolian-like jugs (Fig. 6, C 1), first decorated in red varnish, lead on to the so-called 'Vasilikì ware' of Early Minoan II, in which the varnish is fired to red and black in varying pattern. Forms, especially under the influence of Egyptian types in metal and stone, multiply, and in Early Minoan III (roughly to 2100) some standardization sets in; while Vasilikì ware degenerates, a new ornamental technique appears of patterns in white on a black varnish ground. It was Eastern Crete that led the way in Early Minoan culture, not least probably by reason of its veins of native copper. Flat copper axes appear beside the old plump stone type, and triangular knives and daggers soon become common and achieve in time quite an effective length. Early Minoan goldsmiths had also made a brilliant appearance, and the progress of the crafts is accompanied by mounting evidence for trade and intercourse in which the Aegean world joined hands with the whole Eastern Mediterranean. Of the opening of sea-ways further west we shall speak later on; next to be noticed come the Cycladic islands of the Aegean itself.

Despite their close relations in seaborne trade, Early Cycladic culture shows decided differences from Early Minoan. It was apparently first established by independent colonists from Western Asia Minor, and their pottery belongs generically to the Anatolian plain-ware family. It may be unburnished or, as most notably in Melos, burnished black or red: a leading shape is a big jar with a conical neck, and on these and other forms incised ornament became popular, while leather-derived jugs rather like the Anatolian were elegantly formed with stylized projecting spouts (Fig. 6, C 3). Most of this pottery comes from the tombs which will be noticed below, and of habitations there is on the whole less to record, but mode of life must have been similar to the Cretan in general. Our picture will become clearer when evidence from the important town-site of Phylakopi in Melos begins in the Early Cycladic period III, from round about 2400 B.C. But the culture's traditions were by then already fairly mature, and we can see that out of Anatolian origins and Cretan and more distant contacts something quite distinctive had been created. Copper-smiths had become established, using, no doubt, the native ores of Paros and Siphnos; flat axes and daggers are known, and the tombs show quite a wealth of copper and also silver personal ornaments, mostly of types found also in Crete. We shall soon find some of these travelling far afield, but more widespread still are the affinities of the most famous of all Early Cycladic creations, the marble idols (Pl. III, A). We have already spoken of the 'Mother-Goddess' figurines of the Near East and their significance (p. 84): such were made abundantly in pre-Minoan Crete, the arms clasped round the breasts and the exaggerated lower limbs either squatting or in a seated posture. It is with the latter form that the simple type of Cycladic idol seems most closely connected, though it must have been from Asia Minor [1] that the peoples of all the islands brought the whole conception originally, and the more elegant extended type here illustrated has probably direct Asiatic connexions. They are often found buried with the dead, and though their exact significance may be disputed, the religious idea which they embody is distinctive of all these Eastern-derived cultures and their more distant outliers which we shall meet on European soil. Though figures like that of our Plate may show the female form in a stylized rendering of great beauty, the simpler type may be conventionalized into mere schematic fiddle or half-fiddle shapes, such as occur also in Crete and in the Anatolian civilizations (Pl. III, B 2).

Early Cycladic culture has an especially close counterpart in the Early Helladic of mainland Greece, which is indeed regarded as introduced by colonists from the islands. The dating of its pottery has evoked more than one interpretation, but there seems little doubt that the dark burnished ware which was the earliest found at the stratified settlement-site of Korakou near Corinth is, in fact, the culture's original fabric, and this, with its incised or impressed ornament and its 'leathery'-bodied and spouted forms,[2] is of just the same kind as the Early Cycladic. However, the next and generally most abundant fabric introduces a different tradition, and is best

---

[1] Cf. Pl. III, B 1.　　　　　　　　[2] Fig. 6, B 2.

ascribed to influence from Early Minoan Crete: the forms
continue Helladic conventions, but the surface was covered
with a thin lustrous slip-paint or varnish, red to black in colour,
and clearly recalling the Cretan technique that culminated in
Vasilikì ware. This spread also to the Cyclades, and the white
pattern ornament of Early Minoan III came to be emulated
with indifferent success both there and on the mainland. In
the Early Helladic period III thus distinguished, the culture
had been carried as far as Central Greece, where it abruptly
replaced the old painted-ware civilization described in our
last chapter and best represented in Thessaly. But it penetrated no further, and we are thus brought face to face with the
fact that the metal-using cultures of the Aegean never themselves advanced northward into Continental Europe; their
civilization remained essentially maritime, and it was not the
Early Helladic but the preceding peoples who had brought
red and painted pottery into Greece from the East before them,
who connected the Aegean on this side with the peasant
colonization of the Danube basin and the lands beyond.

Of the First Thessalian culture, as found at Sesklo and
elsewhere, we have already spoken, and one closely similar
had been settled beyond in W. Macedonia (p. 80). Here we
have one set of connexions for the settlers of the European
hinterland. For the rest, we can only look to Anatolia. But
for connexions truly primary we must look beyond the West
Anatolian civilization of Troy and Thermi, which we saw
above to have been established by 3000 B.C. in the region of
the Straits. That civilization was then already differentiated
(p. 76) from the Chalcolithic culture of the Central Anatolian
plateau. And it is with Central, not Western Anatolia, that
South-East Europe beyond the Aegean shores has in its initial
period of settlement most in common. Round the lower
Danube, Troadic parallels are no more than elements of a
partial family likeness between collaterals already divergent.
For the West Anatolian culture from the first inevitably
responded to its unique position in geography, at the junction
of two continents and two seas, and became specialized as a
focus of trade and its corollary power: Troy I was no peasant
village (as used to be thought) but a stoutly fortified acropolis,

foreshadowing already its successors' greatness. On the other hand, the settlers in Europe were fated, by their relative isolation and continued dependence on subsistence agriculture, to maintain the essentials of the old Anatolian Chalcolithic whence we must believe they had sprung, kept beyond the reach of its Copper Age successor by the developing barrier of Troy and its like, and modified only by contact with still unknown Mesolithic natives and the Macedonian-Thessalian connexions of their southern flank. It may be guessed, then, that their original immigration from the East goes back behind the inception of Troy and Thermi, just as that of the First Thessalians goes behind the Early Helladic, into the mists of the fourth millennium. Out of those mists they established for themselves a culture distinctively European. Yet they did so by naturalizing in Europe what the East had been the first to learn, and they did not pass beyond the reach of further lessons.

The civilization thus planted in Europe is conventionally known as Neolithic. It is thereby labelled as a 'New Stone' culture: new in its peasant communities and their livelihood, but equipped with nothing nearer to metal than polished stone. The term was originally coined when it was thought that this 'New Stone Age', following on the 'Old Stone' or Palaeolithic Age (with the Mesolithic later added as a Middle term between), had universally preceded the Ages of Metal. It has not yet been used here, because this orderly sequence of events cannot be applied to the whole Old World indiscriminately, and we have instead seen that food-producing civilization began independently in the East while the European Mesolithic was still running its course. Furthermore, the discovery of metal was there, broadly speaking, part and parcel of that same 'revolution'—or so it seems at present. But among the elements of primitive civilization metallurgy is peculiarly difficult to spread. Not only does it require special skill, but its requisite supplies of raw material need, if present naturally in a new country, to be sought and found, and if absent must be imported from elsewhere. There will be more to say about this later, but since long-distance transport or trade and long-distance prospecting for ores can obviously neither of them be very primitive developments, civilization will spread at first, where it spreads at all, without its metallurgy. Agriculture, pastoral pursuits, and the peasant homestead will take the polished stone axe with them when, through emigration or contact between cultures, they travel to new homes, but the art of making a copper axe cannot so easily be diffused. Its diffusion can, in fact, hardly be brought about effectively until the maturity of civilization in the metal-using centres has given them fresh power for the distribution of their knowledge. But peasant culture began to propagate itself in Europe before that power overtook it. The mysteries of copper and gold trickled into the Aegean world only after it had been established there already, and it is from that prior establishment that it began its spread inland. Similarly it passed ahead to the islands and coasts of the West. It is this stage of food-producing culture diffused beyond the range of its metallurgy which is the true Neolithic, and in that sense we shall use the word in these chapters.

2. THE SOUTH-EASTERN PEASANTRIES

(Map III and Table III: at end)

The most famous Neolithic site in the whole East Danubian region is Vinča, on the river's right bank below Belgrade. It lies on a ridge of firm open loess, in which the first settlers dug pits beneath their dwellings, to be buried in course of time under an accumulation of successive occupation-floors and débris, till the deposit reached a height of over ten metres. The material history of this long-lived settlement cannot be divided up into distinct stages at present, and we shall not here seek to isolate a 'Vinča I' or a 'Vinča II', but the excavations there are soon to be definitely published in English, and meanwhile it is already clear that the evidence, taken in its broad lines, shows the uninterrupted progression of a single culture, ever open to influence from without but essentially self-contained from the start. The start is illuminated by the contents of the pits in the virgin loess at the bottom, and here the pottery comprises rough brownish ware with a hummocky 'barbotine' coating of unevenly applied clay, and finer smooth red or black ware [1] with angular or curving ribbons [2] of incised design, punctuated with stab marks. The barbotine ware seems a fresh embodiment of a coarse-potting tradition originally common to Central Anatolia, where it appears with finger-nail ornament, and the Troadic region; incised design was already diversifying Anatolian plain ware in the Chalcolithic, and the supervening Copper Age in Central and distinctive evolution in Western Anatolia left the old convention here to independent development. Plain ware itself, finely burnished,[3] appears early at Vinča also, and there is a further class with a fine shallow-tooled surface fluting or ribbing, not unlike the rippled ware of Thermi or even of pre-Minoan Crete, and also another with a lustrous red slip. This seems Anatolian too, but reminds one also of the red-ware technique of the First Thessalian culture,[4] whence we shall presently find cause to suggest the technique of painted ware spread northwards also. This red ware is most commonly used for pedestal bowls, a form palpably derived from the Anatolian Chalcolithic to take on here a distinctive embodiment, and the rimmed bowl-forms [5] which characterize the site's better-class pottery in general fit, broadly speaking, into the same picture. In short, the early Vinča pottery shows Anatolian tradition Europeanized, with a partial instalment of influence from Thessaly and Macedonia, and some also from the Thermi-Troadic development, where, however, its curious hollow pot-lids, moulded and incised in the likeness of a horned and owl-like human face,[6] are only answered in the age of the Second city at Troy, contemporary with a later stage of the Vinča occupation. It has, in consequence, a character very much of its own.

This originality was born, no doubt, partly of mere isolation, but it may also be ascribed to some aboriginal Mesolithic element assimilated by the immigrant settlers. Among the bone and antler tools, barbed harpoons suggest this strongly,[7] though while the Balkan caves remain unexplored nothing more positive can be said. Blade-tools are common in local flint,[8]

---

[1] Pl. IV, A 6-8.   [2] Pl. IV, A 6.   [3] Pl. IV, A 7-8.
[4] Cf. Fig. 6, B 2-3.   [5] Pl. IV, A 8.   [6] Pl. IV, A 2.
[7] Pl. IV, A 5.   [8] Pl. IV, A 3, 4.

but the flint industry is seen extended to the service of the immigrant art of farming in the serrated sickle-teeth [1] above noticed (p. 72) in the Near East. The ground was tilled with the plano-convex stone hoes,[2] already mentioned with the bevelled adzes of Thessaly (p. 80), commonly known as 'shoe-last celts' and characteristic of this whole European peasant culture.[3] Above the irregular pits of the lowest level, Vinča has yielded the remains of rectangular timber-framed huts with wattle-and-daub walls, and the whole material culture bespeaks a sedentary farming-life. Female figurines of the form which we have already encountered in the Near East and the Aegean (pp. 84, 89) are plentiful (Pl. III, B 3): they belong to the culture's Anatolian inheritance, and thus also recall, more or less crudely and in baked clay, the Asiatic type of the Cycladic idols, which has rather different representatives in Thessaly, or else display squatting or seated postures. There are male figures too, and in all the head may be perforated behind to hold some sort of head-dress. Animal statuettes are also found, and thus the simple religion of fertility appears embracing all aspects of the community's living. Personal ornaments were plentiful, and some are made from shells which can only have been imported from the sea-coast: marble and other foreign substances were also in demand, and we can thus see that some sort of trade was plied between the villagers and Aegean regions. The site has even yielded little beads and scraps of copper, and the cinnabar obtainable near by at Šuplja Stena is the best-attested among exchange productions, which may have included even the gold of Transylvania beyond the river.

Some twenty other settlements of the Vinča culture have been identified along the Serbian bank of the Danube, and also southward up the Morava valley, which can be easily reached, by way of the Vardar, from the north Aegean coast. But if immigration came this way, its course is as yet unrecorded by any showing of a south-to-north chronological sequence, and at present Vinča itself seems the inland centre of the culture's diffusion. It has been suggested that it came thither up the Danube from the east, but the famous gorge and rapids

---

[1] Pl. IV, A 3.   [2] Pl. IV, A 1.   [3] Fig. 7, 5.

of the Iron Gates, with their forbidding mountain flanks, make a fatal obstacle compared with the easy route by the Vardar and Morava.

Our account hitherto has been as far as possible confined to the lower levels at Vinča, but, as already mentioned, it is not easy to divide the material into successive stages owing to what are at present uncertainties of stratification, and one naturally turns for complementary evidence to analogous sites elsewhere. This quest takes us across the Danube into the Banat and Western Rumania, whither a branch of the same culture seems to have penetrated up the tributary rivers which flow down west and south. The best-known Rumanian site is Tordos (Turdaş) on the Maros, where excavation has revealed three successive strata of occupation. The basic material is in general similar to that in the lower levels of Vinča, and the sequence above shows mainly an improvement of the same pottery tradition, with burnished and red-slip ware and incised ornament; clay figurines are abundant, and the chief stone tool is, as before, the 'shoe-last celt'. Similar material is quite widely distributed in the West Rumanian valleys and the plain of the Banat between the Danube and the borders of Hungary; the accompanying coarse ware answers to the barbotine pottery of Vinča, with lumpy and finger-marked rough surface, and the finds as a whole bespeak the same peasant culture in a rather elementary version. From South Hungary its territory runs eastward also up the Körös River, which flows parallel to the Maros on the north, and the sites in this area have given it the name of the 'Körös group'. Like the Vinča group south of the Danube, it is the first and basic peasant culture of its region. The incised pottery-ornament comes to include not only angular but curvilinear 'spiral-maeander' patterns, which make a parallel appearance at Vinča too, and we shall in the next section return to this very distinctive convention when the spread of civilization has to be traced north-westward into the heart of Europe. Meanwhile the sequence of levels at Tordos introduces us to a fresh element in the picture, for the uppermost stratum there has also yielded a distinct class of pottery, namely painted ware. Its makers were evidently familiar with the same tradition as we have seen dominant in Thessaly, of designs in red on a white slip ground, and some of their work preserves this scheme, but the white slip was apparently difficult, and the painting is often done in red or brown on a natural buff-fired surface. The same sort of thing occurs on a number of other sites in and near Western Rumania, and as the general tendency is for the pot-clays to fire brown or red rather than buff, the painted patterns naturally take to darker browns and black. Such black-on-red painted ware actually appears sporadically at Vinča itself, and sepia-on-red at one of the Morava sites (Prokuplje), but it is far more plentiful on the opposite side of the Danube at the interesting site of Starčevo, where it seems to exclude incised ornament, supervening on a repertory of plain burnished and rough barbotine pottery only, with a somewhat altered range of forms, among which the painting is virtually confined to pedestalled bowls. The patterns [1] are most often angular and criss-cross, with a strong look of basketry, but there is also a variety of curvilinear spirals, and the colours run from black and red to brown and buff, with a partial use even of white.

This West Rumanian painted pottery is clearly not an original element of the peasant culture of these regions, as Starčevo and also the stratification at Tordos show: it is not an integral part of the Körös-group tradition, though it arises within its general ambit. It is most natural to look for its immediate inspiration to Thessaly, though the First Thessalian culture is in Macedonia as yet known only from Servia. The tall pedestalled vessel-forms which tend to accompany it are simply extensions of the red-ware pedestal type, and they have Thessalian analogues, though they continue to recall the Anatolian prototypes which point back behind them to the Asiatic painted-ware civilizations which ultimately lie at the root of the whole matter. It was indeed formerly suggested that the painted wares of Continental Europe have some kind of direct derivation from Mesopotamia or its periphery, perhaps by the southern Black Sea coast, perhaps by the Caucasus and South Russia. But since we have here proposed to derive the Thessalian painted ware from the Tell

[1] Fig. 8, *a*.

Halaf culture by way of Southern Asia Minor, the Asiatic connexion is far better thus supplied through a Thessalian medium, and any further contacts with the Orient by trade need only be reckoned as secondary factors. In any case, when the ancient tradition of painted pottery found a new home in and beyond the Danube basin, its most striking feature is not derivative but original: namely, its wonderful development of curvilinear and spiral design.

To see this essentially European development in its proper place, one has first to recognize that peasantries without painted pottery at all, like the first settlers at Starčevo and elsewhere in the Vinča region, were established previously in the regions where it arose. We have already seen this in the West Rumanian neighbourhood: when the earliest settlers wanted to decorate pottery, they did it by incision. And the same is true of the other regions which we shall now consider.

The Iron Gates have already been defined as marking a natural barrier between the Lower Danube and the territories that encircle Vinča. It is not surprising, then, to find a different form of Neolithic culture in the lands downstream. This, a rather recent discovery, is called the Boian A culture after the island in the Danube where it was first recognized. It seems to be an affair of peasant communities as already described, but oddly enough the usual female figurines have not been found on any of its sites, and its pottery is of distinctive type. It consists mainly of various forms of bowl, not unlike the burnished shapes at Vinča, but ornamented with close-set rows of incised linear patterns, zigzags, chevrons, or simple horizontal rilling, the lines neatly filled with white inlay so as to stand out against the red-brown or dark ground. These may be set off by rows of angular 'chip-cutting' with the same finish, and the patterns also run to forms of spiral. The best-known sites are in the Wallachian plain (e.g. Glina and Vidra near Bucharest), but there are others across the Danube in Bulgaria, and settlers seem also to have passed northward up the Alt valley into Transylvania, so bordering on the Tordos region. The culture is probably best regarded as an offshoot of the same root as the Vinča-Körös group which took on a specialized form in isolation on the Lower Danube. But more than this can scarcely be hazarded, for we cannot be sure how far back in its history our present evidence of it takes us. The stratification of Glina and Vidra shows it antedating the rise of painted pottery in this region, but that, though presumably valid for Transylvania also, will not be found, when we come to consider absolute dates, to take it further back than the middle centuries of the third millennium. Further, its characteristic type of peg-footed pot has been found represented on a Hungarian site (Kökenydomb) of the Theiss culture, which the next section will reveal to be not the contemporary but the successor of the Körös group. Thus, though some little time should be allowed for the Boian A culture's specialization, its antiquity must at present be left several centuries short of what we have claimed for Vinča.

Beyond the Carpathian mountain angle the Wallachian plain is met by the Moldavian, through which it opens northeastward to the Dniester and the whole fertile expanse of the Ukraine and South Russia. The rich 'black-earth' soil of this excellent country makes it ideal farmer's land, and inevitably it attracted further groups of Neolithic peasant settlers. The earliest stage of their occupation has until recently remained undiscovered, but in 1936 its remains were at last brought to light at Izvoare on the Bistritza River in Central Moldavia. The excavations revealed two habitation-strata, one directly above the other. The upper belonged to a settlement with painted pottery to which we shall shortly come: the lower, Izvoare I, preceded this with monochrome pottery bearing a distinctive range of incised designs. There are straight or curving bands of rilling, sometimes separated by punctuations, broken lines stamped with a tooth-comb, cross-hatched 'ribbon' lines with white inlay, and simpler linear patterns including spiral forms. The style has thus points of resemblance to those of Vinča, Körös, and even Boian A, with yet a clear individuality of its own. With the pottery are female clay figurines, a few polished stone implements and flints, and two or three little objects of hammered copper, including a pin and a needle. Further north-east across the Dniester, incised monochrome pottery closely similar to this forms one of the basic features of the great peasant civilization which became established in South Russia, or more precisely in the Ukraine and the neighbouring western borders of the 'black-earth' and loess plains. In general character this civilization is thoroughly allied to its counterparts in the Danubian lands, and thus there can now be little doubt that it originated in the same quarter, and was not brought in directly westwards out of Asia. It is known, after the first site of its discovery, as the Tripolye culture, and while its later or Tripolye B phase will lie outside our scope here for the present, the earlier or Tripolye A culture now demands our attention.

It is in the country round Kiev on the middle Dnieper that the Tripolye A settlements are best known. They consist of circular groupings of huts, placed close to running water. The inhabitants grew grain, and among their stone implements the 'shoe-last celt' hoe is prominent. They kept pigs, sheep, and cattle, and horses' bones are also found. Clay figurines, both female and male, occur, though not too commonly. At first, the pottery [1] is mostly monochrome ware decorated with incised linear and punctuate ornament and bands of parallel rilling; the patterns include a straight-line element, but there is also plenty of simple broad spiral design, especially on the wide-shouldered pots and beakers or bowls. In addition, there is painted ware, but it is much rarer on the Dnieper than further west, where on the Dniester and on the Galician loess there are other groups of settlements; their pottery is reddish, painted with pale spiral bands with black edging, or with black and red ones on a pale ground. It has been suggested that the former, typified at Niezwiska, mark an earlier stage in Galicia than the latter, represented at Zališčyky; pottery-painting certainly took root first in these western areas of the culture. The Bukovina, between the Upper Dniester and the Carpathians, shares with Galicia a third style, the contemporary rather of Zališčyky, with black and white painting on red, or red on white, best known from the first settlement at the site of Schipenitz. Throughout the culture also, however, is found coarse ill-fired pottery, with nothing but barbaric comb ornament. This never occurs in the Danube lands, where the coarse ware, e.g. the barbotine of Vinča and Starčevo, is of a

[1] Fig. 8, *f*.

different order: it evidently shows some absorption by the Tripolye people of a more primitive native population with simpler ways of doing things. In the dune country of the northern Ukraine, and along the Bug River in neighbouring Volhynia, we shall indeed meet these native folk in the next chapter, and shall find them to be southerly members of that widespread East European population, still rooted in Mesolithic ways of life, whose formation we have already touched upon above (p. 62). Such absorptions are of the essence of cultural diffusion.

By the time that settlements like Zališčyky or Schipenitz had reached their prime, like traditions of painted pottery and much else had become established in Moldavia. At Izvoare, the earlier settlement already noticed (p. 98) was succeeded by that of Izvoare II, which is indeed linked by certain traits to its predecessor, but shows a culture transformed into admirable maturity. This will be best described from the famous type-site of Cucuteni, rather further north in the region of Jassy, where, beneath the later occupation which we shall encounter in due course as Cucuteni B, that of Cucuteni A represents this earlier painted-pottery culture in full vitality. Here, too, there is self-coloured ware with incised and punctuated ornament, both angular and curvilinear, and also monochrome red ware, but both are rare, and the painted fabric was the potters' dominant interest and pride.[1] The designs are executed in red or warm yellow-browns, outlined in black, on a white slip ground, or still more often in red or brownish, black, and white directly on the fine reddish clay. The leading motive is a long S-spiral, standing out in white against a polychrome and often banded field; analysis can show how the free spontaneity of this swinging, graceful style was transcended by ideas of balanced composition, and though our illustration can do little to represent the wealth of the designers' repertory, it is clear that the old basketry or 'textile' inspiration is here far out of mind, and a genius for abstract art is finding wholly original expression. The shapes comprise open and shouldered bowls, cups, and covers; the range is wide, and pedestal feet are a notable feature, with an extreme

[1] Fig. 8, *c.*

form in tall 'fruit-stands' and separate hollow 'supports'. Clay figurines may have their surface decorated with tooled design in the same spirit as the pottery; stone, flint, bone, and horn implements cannot here be described in detail, but as a whole the culture strikes one as an outstanding achievement

Fig. 8

EARLY PAINTED POTTERY AND DESIGNS FROM
SOUTH-EAST EUROPE

a, Starčevo designs (p. 96); *b*, Erösd (p. 102); *c*, Cucuteni A type (p. 100); *d*, Dimini designs, Dimini and Sesklo (p. 105); *e, f*, Tripolye A types (p. 99 : *e*, 'binocular', p. 236).

of our peasant civilization. Moldavia and Bessarabia have produced a number of similar sites, of which the best explored is Fedeleşeni rather nearer the Carpathians, and westward across those mountains in the valley of the Upper Alt a group of over a score forms a distinct but closely related province of painted-ware culture.

The chief of these is the famous settlement of Erösd or Ariuşd, after which this Transylvanian province is sometimes named. The excavator found there three strata: the dwellings in the earliest and smallest were recognizable only as pits in the ground, while thereafter they come to include an oblong timber house with a porch at one end, familiar in archaeological literature as the proclaimed prototype of the Homeric *megaron*. A notable feature, which Erösd shares with Cucuteni A, is fortification: Cucuteni was surrounded by a rampart and ditch, and Erösd stands on a steep hill-spur with its neck similarly defended. Tool-equipment and evidences of peasant farming meet us here as before, as do the clay figurines, and the painted pottery, with its bowls and cups, pedestal feet, and tall hollow supports, is of the same order ;[1] the designs, in polychrome of red, black, and white, are angular or curvilinear, with graceful long S-spirals and maeanders as leading motives. Regularity of composition was sometimes obtained by stencilling; the ware is uniformly good, and part of one of the potters' kilns has been excavated, very like the oven discovered at the Macedonian painted-pottery site of Olynthus. Though the dwellings of at least the first two strata had been destroyed by fire, the same civilization seems to run throughout; it may be argued to be on balance rather later than Cucuteni A, but the two are so closely alike that they must be largely contemporary. Erösd may be allowed to be later than the Boian A penetration of Transylvania indicated above, but the point of crucial importance is its relationship to the West Rumanian painted-ware group (p. 96). This is really only one aspect of the whole question of the genesis of the European painted-ware cultures in general, for within the broad outline we have given of it, precision has only partly emerged from doubt.

We must first observe that the Erösd and Cucuteni cultures

[1] Fig. 8, *b*.

stop short southwards at the Lower Danubian plain. There, in Wallachia and Bulgaria, the sequel to Boian A is something different: in the Little Wallachian region west of the Alt appears the unique development revealed at Vodastra, where the pottery bears white-inlaid incised and chip-cut patterns incorporating spiral and fret motives in a manner peculiarly its own, while on both banks of the river lower down emerges the hardly less distinctive culture now named after the type-site of Gumelnitza. The Boian A pottery style did not die out without some slight adoption of painting, in which the use of graphite is recognizable, and when the Gumelnitza culture followed this was more regularly adopted, while incised mono-chrome pottery appears in new forms. These and its other leading features—clay figurines in abundance and also bone ones, spouted jugs, and 'face-urn' vases in human shape on the one hand, and, for instance, barbed harpoons of antler on the other—show that, while taking over pot-painting in a specialized form of their own, these people were drawing deeply on Aegean and Anatolian contacts, while also retaining elements of Mesolithic tradition. Stratified excavation indicates three phases in their development, of which only A is contemporary with Erösd and B and C will require notice below, but meanwhile it is plain that Erösd, Cucuteni, and their like find no primary elucidation in this quarter. Indeed, it is just the Anatolian and Near-Eastern features which their pottery carries, in form most notably its tall 'fruit-stand' pedestals and hollow supports, and in ornament of course the whole fact of its painting, that, as representing old Chalcolithic derivations matured together on European soil, contrast most sharply with Gumelnitza's reflexions in jugs and face-urns of Aegean and Troadic-Anatolian fashions contemporary with itself. Those reflexions are obviously the result of the culture's geographical position so near to the Aegean and the Troad; its basic composition, however, is no more Troadic than that of its more distant neighbours, and is best ascribed to the action upon Boian A of a movement from the eastern hinterland of Macedonia, where Dikilitash in the Struma valley points to an outcome of a Macedonian version of the painted-pottery tradition with a long survival.

Before suggesting the connexion of this with what befell the Macedonian coast lands just after the middle of the third millennium, we must go behind the specialities of Gumelnitza to an aspect of South-East Europe's relations with the Aegean and Anatolia which pervades the whole nexus of its territories —that of trade. Throughout the complex of Tripolye A, Cucuteni A, and Erösd, the knowledge and use of copper was quite appreciably diffused. Tripolye A has yielded flat copper axes and even moulds for casting them: another belongs probably to Cucuteni A; while the Alt valley folk had copper pins, awls, and fish-hooks, and even bracelets and tube and spiral-ring beads among their simpler finery of shells, teeth, and stone. But little copper beads and pins had appeared already at Vinča (p. 94), and at Izvoare I, and this small-scale use of the metal is carried no further at Erösd than one would expect from a district open to the rudiments of trade with the metal-using civilizations. To such traffic, however fitful at first, the discovery of Transylvania's natural copper wealth must have been due, and its abundant gold must likewise have early attracted attention: e.g. two gold trinkets occurred in the earliest of the Erösd strata. The copper axes of Tripolye indeed look directly eastward to the Asiatic bridgehead of the Caucasus, and another Tripolye A find recalls the axe-adzes to be noticed in that region presently, but in the main these commercial and economic links between South-East Europe and the higher civilizations seem to have been with the Anatolian-Aegean borderlands. But their existence must not be allowed to confuse the matter of the origin of the European painted-pottery cultures themselves. The old theory of the possibility of their direct derivation from the Near East round the Black Sea is not made any more probable by the infant trade connexions which we have sketched.

In any case, the vital originality of the European pot-painters' style must demand an explanation of its own. If, as we have been suggesting, the knowledge of pottery-painting first came to Europe with the First Thessalian-Macedonian culture, and thence subsequently spread across the Danube above the Iron Gates by way of Starčevo and Western Rumania, diffusing thereupon to the peoples of the Erösd, Cucuteni, and Tripolye cultures (Gumelnitza receiving it from an East Macedonian source of its own), the fact yet remains that its recipients used it to create a spontaneous art of pure line and spiral. The actual process of that creation is still indeed obscure in detail; but the Starčevo and West Rumanian painted ware has surely brought the solution of the problem to close quarters, and we can at least define its terms as immigrant influence and a transformation wrought by native originality. But what lay behind the originality we can only guess. Curvilinear essays appear early in the incised work with which all this pottery-ornament begins, and the belief that Neolithic newcomers incorporated Mesolithic natives may incline us to take the 'spiral-maeander' style with them back to Palaeolithic roots. Is it mere coincidence that precisely in the Tripolye country the East-Gravettian (pp. 30-1) site of Mézine should have produced a perfect maeander pattern engraved in mammoth ivory? We have already adduced the comb pottery of Tripolye as a link with the aborigines of Eastern Europe, and it is also worth noting that both in Cucuteni A and Erösd, and Gumel-nitza A also, animal-head stone carvings have been found, which recall those of the East Baltic comb-pottery people to be described below. However much in its formation remains mysterious, our culture emerges with no lack of distinctively European character.

And the next event to be recorded is its overflow back into Macedonia and Thessaly. The new culture which superseded the First Thessalian at Sesklo, and is best known from the fortified settlement its bearers founded near by at Dimini, is unmistakably similar to that of the painted-pottery peoples beyond the Danube. The multiple ring-walling of Dimini is an advance on Erösd or Cucuteni, but fortification had previously been unknown in all Greece; the rectangular *megaron* type of house, with its central hearth, is likewise absent in the earlier culture, while familiar at Erösd; and the Dimini painted pottery, decorated in polychrome spirals and maeanders, is virtually that of Erösd over again.[1] A break with the older culture is also seen in types of stone axe and of clay figurines, and amongst other novelties metal (e.g. flat copper axes and

[1] Fig. 8, *d*.

gold for ornaments) is now first encountered. The Dimini culture stopped short at the wooded country of West Thessaly, where the older 'First Thessalian' traditions continued but slightly modified, but its abrupt appearance in the more accessible eastern region was formerly explained as an invasion from Erösd or some other trans-Danubian district. Yet the fact of the matter seems not so simple. In Macedonia, the old First culture was similarly broken into by a new one, the 'B' culture, with northward affinities. But its pottery is not just a half-way house between Erösd and Dimini: on the contrary, the commonest fabric is plain burnished and ribbed ware like that of Vinča, and colour-painting is rarer and less often polychrome than black on buff or red as at Starčevo or Tordos. The culture is in fact simply a southward extension of the Vinča-Körös growth, which was now carrying the practice of pottery-painting in the pre-Erösd stage which Starčevo and Tordos have revealed. Thus the ensuing polychrome styles of Erösd and Dimini are not parent and daughter but half-sisters. The extension must have travelled by the Morava and Vardar valleys, and may be conveniently called by those rivers' names. In support of this explanation, we may notice that the newcomers in Macedonia were not past other experiments in pot-painting: much of their work is in dark grey on grey, a style also found in Thessaly (where it used to be thought later than this), and they also practised a clumsy sort of 'crust' painting done after the firing of the pot instead of before. Now this badly imitative 'crusted ware' occurs also at Vinča and elsewhere on the Middle Danube, and the same is true of distinctive incised pottery, which is found with it in Macedonia and scattered also in Thessaly and even further south. On the Danube this marks an advance on that of the early Vinča-Körös group, and is in fact characteristic, with the 'crusted ware', of its successor, which we shall meet in the next section centred in Hungary and named the Theiss culture. The Morava-Vardar extension then carried south elements drawn from well up and beyond the Danube, and in a moment we shall have to notice its inclusion of something corresponding to yet another pottery style, which will take us into the heart of Central Europe.

What was the date of this extension? It is clearly a key point in all these territories' chronology. The Dimini culture has usually been dated in Aegean terms from about the middle of Early Minoan II, or 2600 B.C. It has further been argued that this was the source whence the spiral motive, prominent on Dimini as on Erösd, Cucuteni, and Tripolye pottery, became gradually adopted into Aegean art, where it reached full flower with the beginning of Early Minoan III at 2400. But it was familiar a good deal earlier in Minoan metal-work, and our Morava-Vardar chronology can be more reliably checked by turning to the parallel civilization of Troy. We have seen (p. 76) that the first establishment at Troy and the first two near by at Thermi cover a period going back at least to 3000; there is then a phase best represented by Thermi III, and thereafter was founded the famous fortified citadel of Troy II. This Second City was formerly thought to have had a life of five or six centuries, from about 2500 until 2000 or 1900 B.C., but it is now known, from the recent American excavations, that the settlements which followed its destruction, Troy III and IV, were still importing Early Helladic pottery, and so cannot be later than the end of Early Minoan times at 2100. The end of Troy II must therefore be earlier, and since, furthermore, the two-handled goblets then characteristic of its pottery were being imported or imitated in the Copper Age culture of Central Anatolia at Alishar, which came to a violent stop there between 2400 and 2300, its destruction must be dated about 2300 and not after. On the other hand, while its life was long enough to consist of three distinguishable phases, and estimates for its foundation-date have lately been put as far back as 2700 or 2800 B.C., it is now the opinion that its lifetime has up to now been over-estimated, and that the traditional foundation-date of 2500 is substantially correct. And this bears directly upon Macedonia, for only a short while after the Morava-Vardar extension thither from the north, an offshoot of the civilization of Troy was carried in from the east. The invaders who brought it took possession of the coast-lands, and confining the painted-pottery tradition to the hinterland, moved westward, founding the culture known as Early Macedonian. And their pottery corresponds initially to that of the first phase of Troy II—as can be closely checked from the sequence established at Thermi. The date of their intrusion from the Troad will then be scarcely later than 2500. But the site-stratification even in West Macedonia shows that their Morava-Vardar predecessors cannot have been established more than about a century by the time of their arrival. The Morava-Vardar extension and its 'B' culture may therefore be dated from soon after 2600, and the answering Dimini culture be reckoned established in Thessaly by 2500, shortly before the Early Macedonian wedge from the Troad severed it from its northern relatives.

With this outlined, we can turn back to those northern relatives again. First of all, it may be recognized that the Early Macedonian intrusion, by confining what remained of Macedonia's painted-pottery tradition to the mountain valleys of the hinterland, provides just the initial impulse needed to start its carriers moving northwards from East Macedonia to found the Gumelnitza culture of Bulgaria and the fertile plain of the Lower Danube, as already suggested (p. 103). And thus a date about 2400 becomes acceptable there for its entry, leaving Vodastra on one side, upon the inheritance of its predecessor, Boian A. Next, we have seen that the Morava-Vardar, Starčevo-Tordos stage of the evolution of painted pottery higher up the Danube and in West Rumania was in being at 2600, so that its outcome, the Erösd civilization of the Alt valley, can only have formed after that. Time must be allowed for this formation, and the spread of pottery-painting eastward to the wide territories of Cucuteni and Tripolye; further, not only may an imported Cucuteni-type vase at Vidra serve to equate Cucuteni A with the Gumelnitza horizon there of after 2400, but in Hungary painted pottery of Erösd style has been found as late as the stage which followed after the Theiss culture, itself already (p. 106) equated, by incised and 'crusted' pottery, with the Morava-Vardar horizon in Macedonia. Erösd and Cucuteni A were, then, flourishing not merely after 2400, but still later, for this successor of the Theiss culture in Hungary is the Bodrogkeresztur culture of the Hungarian Copper Age, to be dated in a later chapter (p. 242) from about 2200. 2400 B.C. may then be reckoned no more than an upper limit for the emergence of these painted-pottery cultures, stretching with Tripolye A far eastwards into the Ukraine, from the earlier stages of peasant settlement during which the art of pottery-painting came in from the south by way of West Rumania, gradually to captivate the makers of the monochrome linear-ornamented ware of Izvoare and their still obscure counterparts who first tilled the Ukrainian Black-Earth. Finally, this chronology can be made to extend in the other direction up the Danube into Central Europe. For among the Morava-Vardar pottery of Macedonia occurs a peculiar ware which we have as yet only just mentioned (p. 106), a development from the linear-ornament tradition which is incised in lines not continuous, but formed by rows of discontinuous strokes made with a sharp tool. And such 'stroke-ornamented ware' is well known: it was developed up the Danube in the Central European province whither we must now penetrate, and the occurrence of outliers of it at the Morava-Vardar horizon in Macedonia shows that it was already in existence in the century before 2500 B.C.

3. THE SPREAD OF DANUBIAN CIVILIZATION

(Map III and Table III: at end)

Until lately it was difficult to see any actual continuity of connexion north and north-westward between the earliest Neolithic of the Vinča-Körös area and the region beyond the Danube elbow north of Budapest. The swampy margins of the great river itself will have kept settlers away, and it has only been recent work in the undulating country flanking them in West Hungary that has added continuity on the map to the long-assumed cultural relationship between the initial Neolithic of South-Eastern and of Central Europe. West Hungary is in fact the southern province of a great territory of peasant culture, with its centre of gravity in Moravia, where south-eastern impulse brought to birth the essentially Mid-European civilization known as the Danubian. Its mode of life was an outgrowth from the south-east, but it was no mere extension of south-eastern culture. Its coarser pottery is indeed a finger- or wart-ornamented fabric analogous to the barbotine ware of

Vinča, but the burnished and red-slip Vinča wares have
vanished, and their accompanying incised ware appears translated into a new form, with linear ornament in spiral and
maeander 'ribbons' running freely over a hard-baked, dark-
faced pot-surface.[1] The usual shape is a hemispherical bowl
recalling a gourd vessel, and it is significant that this only
appears here, where one passes out of the gourd-growing
country of the south-east: it is in fact a gourd substitute.
Thus, just as on the other flank of South-Eastern Europe the
further marches of peasant civilization were first peopled by
makers of monochrome linear pottery, who only later took to
painted ware, so here the Danubians are characterized from
the first by a linear pottery essentially their own, on which
further south-eastern developments only later supervened.

The independence thus made manifest suggests that here,
just as there, Neolithic culture was the creation of immigrant
settlers from the south only in combination with native
Europeans of still obscure Mesolithic descent. At any rate, in
comparison with what we have seen in the south-east, the
Danubians display both originality and impoverishment: clay
figurines are very rare, and there is not the smallest hint of
metal. Their simple hoe-tillage kept them to the rich loess
soil, which we have already commented on (pp. 8, 81) and
seen selected from the start at Vinča (p. 92); indeed, its
distribution, like that of the related soils of the 'black-earth'
country beyond the Carpathians, is the key to the whole
pattern of Neolithic settlement. The loess-lands of Moravia,
with parts of Slovakia adjoining, were the core of the Danubian
territory. But even so, without manuring or rotation their
corn-plots would soon be exhausted, and the expansion across
Central Europe which they came to achieve can thus be seen
to be due to a sort of slow-motion nomadism in the easy
pursuit of fresh fields to till. Everywhere they took the same
culture: villages of huts with pit-scooped floors, cultivation
mainly of wheat, including emmer and spelt, with the 'shoe-
last' hoe,[2] domestic cattle, sheep, goats, and swine—simple
peasant economy and very little else. They could perforate
stone disc-tools, and sometimes their 'shoe-last' hoes or adzes:

[1] Fig. 9, *a*.   [2] Fig. 7, 5.

they had a few bone and flint tools; trade appears only in a little imported obsidian from Hungary, and *Spondylus*-mussel shells from the distant Mediterranean for beads and bracelets. From Moravia they spread into Bohemia, and beyond into Central Germany, Silesia, and east at last to Galicia, where scraps of their typical pottery ultimately turn up even in the painted-ware settlement of Niezwiska. Pottery-ornament indeed shows some development: punctuation became more popular along with the 'ribbon' lines, and a music-stave effect with 'note-head' dimples appears in Moravia and in Austria, beyond which the culture also spread on to the loess-lands of Bavaria. The spread was slow: we need to allow for retardation in applying Middle Danubian chronology to regions of colonization further afield; but their culture may be reckoned forming and on the move in a century or so from 3000 B.C., as that chronology may reasonably allow. Of particular importance is the 'stroke-ornamented ware', which we have already seen attested for the century 2600-2500 B.C. by its Morava-Vardar outliers in Macedonia (p. 109), for this new departure marks a second stage in the Danubian development.

It is in Moravia that excavation has done most to demonstrate the succession: essentially, the culture remained as before, but the appearance of the new decorative style on the pottery is thought to point to the inclusion in it of a new element of European-Mesolithic descent. Its patterns, with their bands of tool-point strokes,[1] sometimes recall the form of the string carrying-sling probably responsible for inspiring it: in any case, they contrast with the old spiral-maeander work in showing a regularly planned design, adapted to the form of the pot, instead of a mere rambling free-style. As time went on, decoration and also pot-forms became more varied, and varieties of the style appear not only in Moravia but Bohemia and the regions north and east of it, and Bavaria also (the so-called Münzingen ware). In Austria it seems rare: the stave or 'note-head' style died harder in the 'Zseliz' pottery that had now developed there, and in West Hungary, where this is also found, the old tradition of linear ornament still flourished, though in appreciably altered forms. How long the latter

[1] Fig. 9, *d*.

lasted may be seen by reference to the quite different course of events in North and East Hungary across the Danube.

Here, from very early roots in the initial stage of the linear-pottery culture, a specialized form of it was engendered among the people who came to dwell in the caves of the North

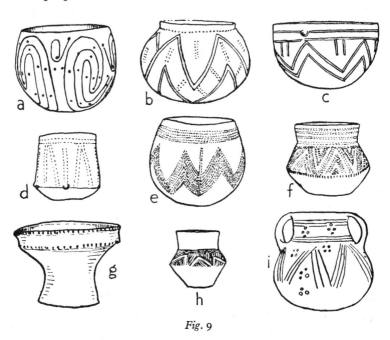

Fig. 9

DANUBIAN POTTERY FROM GERMANY

a, b, c, Linear (spiral and maeander), Rhineland : *a*, Early ; *b, c*, (Köln-Lindenthal) Later (pp. 110-118); *d, f*, Stroke-ornamented, Early and Later, Central Germany and Silesia (pp. 111-122); *e*, Hinkelstein type, from near Worms (p. 121); *g, h, i*, from groups related to Theiss Culture: *g*, Münch-shöfen (p. 116); *h*, Aichbühl (p. 119); *i*, Jordansmühl type (pp. 116, 118), Silesia.

Scale : $\frac{2}{11}$.

Hungarian Bükk mountains, and in village settlements elsewhere in Hungary east of the Danube with some extension northward into Eastern Slovakia. Despite their partial addiction to cave-dwelling, the authors of this Bükk culture were peasant farmers no less than their Danubian neighbours: they cultivated the same grains and kept the same domestic

PLATE III

A. CYCLADIC MARBLE IDOL (height 8.1 in.)
British Museum

See p. 89

B. FEMALE FIGURINES FROM ASIA MINOR AND S.E. EUROPE
Clay : 1, Adalia (S.W. Asia Minor) ; 3, Vinca ; 4, (from a cast),
Schipenitz   Marble : 2, Troy   Scale, 1 : 2
British Museum

See pp. 89, 94, 99-101 & 236

PLATE IV

A

B 1 above ; 2 below   C

A. POTTERY AND IMPLEMENTS FROM VINČA :
    1, Stone " shoe-last " hoe ; 2, Owl-face pot-lid ; 3, 4, Flint sickle-blade and end-scraper ;
    5, Bone harpoon ; 6, Decorated and 7-8, Plain burnished pottery
    Scale in inches   See pp. 92-5

B. 1, BÜKK, AND 2, THEISS POTTERY FROM HUNGARY
    Scale 1 : 4 (nearly)   See pp. 112-6

C. BOWL OF RÖSSEN POTTERY FROM NEAR MAINZ
    Diameter 4.8 in.   See pp. 118-9

animals, they used the same 'shoe-last' stone tools, and had
a bone and flint industry of much the same order, though
naturally more strongly supplemented by their country's
native obsidian.   But remembering that North Hungary has
not failed to yield traces of an older Mesolithic population
(p. 65), we may suspect that here, too, the incorporation of
such aborigines by peasant settlers had much to do with the
culture's individuality.   This is most manifest in its pottery:
typically Danubian forms of hemispherical and bulging bowl
were made both in simple coarse ware and in finer fabric, but
the latter is distinctive both in its thin, elegant quality and in
its beautiful ornament.[1]   Bands of finely cut lines, often with
white or even red inlay, are disposed in intricate maeander,
volute, arcade, or zigzag patterns of almost infinite variety,
with occasional dotting and shading; Dr. Tompa's studies
have distinguished three stages of the style's development—
the first dominated by maeandering multilinear ribbons, the
second by volute and various angular designs, and the third
by further diversities of complication.   With these, rarely in
the first stage, and increasingly in the second and third, bands
of dark-reddish or whitish painting appear: though always
subordinate to the linear patterns, these at least show that the
painting idea from the south spread to some extent here as
well as eastwards, and whether or no the Bükk pot-painters
contributed to the eastward spread too, and influenced the
polychrome styles of Erösd and Cucuteni, they certainly
exerted influence westwards, for imitative work, the paint only
applied after the pot's firing, may be seen in the Šarka ware
or later spiral-maeander pottery of Bohemia, and other painted
ware will soon meet us in a rather different context in Moravia.
   Meanwhile the Bükk people formed an important element
in ensuing developments in Hungary itself.   A Bükk II bowl
has been found at Nagyteteny near Budapest together with an
imported piece of 'note-head' Zseliz linear ware from the
west, and in their later stages these two cultures appear somewhat assimilated; but the stroke ornament which meanwhile
arose in Moravia was excluded from this inheritance in Hungary,
and instead it was the old Körös-group tradition from further

[1] Pl. IV, B 1.

south (p. 95) which now issued, in the next main stage of Hungarian civilization, competing with and finally incorporating both the Bükk and linear traditions. The result came at last to embrace the whole region of the Middle Danube, and finally spread out to supersede the tradition of stroke ornament in Moravia, Bohemia, and Silesia, flooding Austria too as well as West Hungary, and also penetrating south and south-east into Jugoslavian territory. This new culture is called after the Hungarian river Theiss or Tisza, in whose basin sites like Polgar and Kenezlö well attest its formation. Its general uniformity carries a certain regional variation: in the south, where we have already encountered its pottery among the material of the Morava-Vardar complex and its extension into Macedonia, this is particularly marked, and it is through its southern province that the Macedonian chronology already reviewed (p. 107) supplies an initial date for its formation about 2600 B.C. The designs of its incised pottery,[1] and the 'crust'-painted ware that accompanies it, are characteristic (representing at Vinča the stage that has sometimes been called 'Vinča II'); the sequence at Tordos (p. 95) leads to a corresponding stage, and while the rise of the Erösd painted-ware culture came to limit its eastward extension, the same version of it is found spreading into Jugoslavia westwards up the Drave and the Save, and south-west to the well-known settlement of Butmir in Bosnia. At Butmir indeed it appears in a further specialized form, typified in incised, hatched, and pointillé pottery-ornament in angular ribbons, chequers, and abundant running spirals—perhaps yet another native Meso-lithic contribution—and there are southern connexions here which will be best discussed in a later context (p. 151), but the general impression given by all this southern region is the same—a culture in which earlier elements have been overlaid and transformed by currents coming from Hungary. The connexion of those currents with the Morava-Vardar extension into Macedonia and Thessaly is not only evident in material parallels with those countries, but will account also for the reflex movement of Aegean influences back into the homeland of the Theiss culture itself.

[1] Pl. IV, B2.

For in its absorption of Aegean and Anatolian elements into a characteristically European mould, the Theiss culture is the analogue of its eastward neighbours and contemporaries, the painted-pottery cultures. At Hungarian sites like Polgar and their numerous counterparts in Moravia, what does duty for painted ware is the 'crusted' pottery which we have already encountered further south: the well-made black-polished bowls and beakers were decorated after firing with a wide range of patterns in red, yellowish, and white 'crust', from simple stripes to all sorts of angular and maeander forms and some spirals, and there is a certain amount of linear-incised ornament as well. Red ware and various red and white designs occur also at Polgar, and in Moravia they characterize a distinct group of 'Moravian painted pottery', the neighbour of the later Bükk and Šarka phases (p. 113), and answering in the main to the Theiss culture's middle period. On the other hand, the potters might also keep their black-polished ware un-crusted: much of the Central Hungarian ware is of this kind, and it is typical west of the Danube at Lengyel, an important settlement and cemetery-site which has led many to use the term 'Lengyel culture' as one of general application.

Lengyel pottery types, as well as including bowl, bottle, and beaker forms evolved from the old Danubian repertory, run to handled and polypod vessels pervaded by a strong feeling of Aegean-Anatolian inspiration, and the pedestalled forms emerge from the Vinča-Körös tradition impressively enlarged and recalling their Anatolian prototypes no less than their half-contemporaries of Erösd or Cucuteni. Some handled types may imitate metal prototypes current at Troy, and small cube-block pots copying Cretan originals of stone join in supporting the culture's chronological equation with the latter part of Early Minoan times. Similarly, while copper trinkets found both at Lengyel and Polgar serve in general to show the use of metal gradually on the increase, chronology is again assisted by the appearance before the culture's end of little double-spiral ornaments of copper wire, which are copied directly from a type well known in Troy II. Female clay figurines become much more prevalent, and their forms more sophisticated and Eastern, while traders brought in various

Mediterranean shells for personal ornaments. Finally, the clay stamps or so-called *pintaderas* characteristic of the culture —and likewise of that of Erösd and other more or less contemporary sites—are manifest imitations of the widespread Near-Eastern stamp-seal, which, though known to the First Thessalians and in Chalcolithic Anatolia, was general in the Anatolian Copper Age and at contemporary Troy. But the European elements of the culture are always fundamental. Angular-incised pottery-ornament looks back to the old linear Körös-group and Bükk traditions; the old shoe-last stone hoes and adzes continue; Hungarian obsidian was widely used for blade-tools, and implements of bone, horn, and antler carry on without much change from earlier times. The Lengyel type of culture became extended to Southern Moravia and Lower Austria, where it went on to develop as the so-called Wolfsbach culture, and further up the Danube to Upper Austria and as far as the loess-lands of Bavaria, where its incised and pedestalled pottery and other traits took the regional form known as the Münchshöfen culture.[1] Another branch went into a part of Central Germany, and nearer home in Bohemia, in Moravia, and in Southern Silesia, where its history opens with the formation of the so-called Ottitz group, there presently arose another and greater regional grouping familiar under the name of the great Silesian site of Jordansmühl. We shall return to the later developments in these various regions below. Meanwhile this tale of Danubian diffusion has brought us as far as the time of the end of Troy II, about 2300 B.C., or a little further—anyhow, well into the Early Minoan period III, and we must now turn to see what progress had by then been made still further afield by the bearers of the earlier Danubian traditions associated with linear- and stroke-ornamented pottery.

Of the two we have seen the linear to be the original one, and with this fact accords not only its simplicity but its universality. It is an affair of elementary self-expression by folk living close enough to bare essentials to have at first little margin for innovation; that came later, when with a background of some centuries of security the stroke-ornamented style was

[1] Fig. 9, 8.

devised on the Middle Danube, and the various groups of settlers now scattered over all the surrounding loess countries attained their different regional conventions. These in due time were unified by the fresh currents which issued from Hungary with the Theiss culture; but away in the middle of Europe men rooted in the older ways had a long start, and our peasant diffusion had nearly reached its maximum before their basic pot style became exhausted. This linear 'ribbon' mode of ornament, which gives Danubian pottery its German name of *Bandkeramik*, was in fact transplanted out of Central Europe north-west into the heart of Germany, and west into the basin of the Rhine. The slow but ceaseless quest of new tillage carried the Danubians across the upland divides which the Atlantic climate (p. 57) had wooded so thickly; it was thus that from Bohemia they reached the Central German loess-lands watered by the Elbe, the Saale, and the Upper and Middle Weser, and from the Upper Danube those of the Main and Neckar, and the Rhine from Alsace to Cologne and beyond—while a handful from Silesia even reached Pomerania along the Lower Oder. Everywhere the simple linear style of ornament is found. But the occurrence in the same regions, and sometimes in the same deposits, of various forms of stroke ornament has often led to the belief that this whole west and north-westward movement was retarded till after the spread of the latter from its Middle Danubian home. The truth has recently been revealed by one of the finest achievements of modern archaeology—the total excavation of the great settlement of Lindenthal near Cologne, in which the whole history of the *Bandkeramik* culture in this far north-western region has been exposed in detail.

The excavators' superb technique disentangled the complex agglomeration of traces left by dwellings, pits, sheds, and barns in the virgin loess into an orderly series disclosing four periods of occupation, distinguished each by its own range of pottery types, and fixed in chronological sequence by inter-locking stratification. The priority of the pure linear style has thereby been proved, and this proof so far from the Danubian homeland necessarily covers the connecting regions in between, among which the Middle Rhine has furnished a type-site for this first period at Flomborn near Mainz, while the same priority has been worked out independently on the Elbe and Saale. The Danubian colonization in Germany may thus be dated well back in the first half of the third millennium, and by about 2700 B.C. the countryside round Lindenthal may be pictured dotted with little hamlets, whose inhabitants stored their crops in the large oblong barns, built on stilt-posts, of which over a dozen stood together with a few dwellings on the central site. In time this granary-village grew in size, and the second period brought new barns and sheds and more numerous dwellings, enclosed in two contiguous ring-ditches, the larger affording open space for flocks and herds. The potters now combined the old linear style with the growing influence [1] of stroke ornament, for these were the years, rather after 2600 B.C., of its gradual extension north-westward to rival its predecessor. Finally, perhaps about 2500, there came a break: the old inhabitants deserted their homes, and when new settlers arrived, stroke ornament had become the dominant style. Though this third phase was relatively short and terminated by fire, it was followed directly by the establishment of a much larger colony of the same culture still further developed, which made the fourth period, lasting perhaps till rather after 2300 B.C., the richest and most populous of all.[2]

The stroke-ornament people had, in fact, been now for some time in evidence in Central Germany, and in the south as far as the Middle Rhine. In both districts their culture lived long: pottery-ornament developed,[3] and in Saxony and Thuringia, as in Silesia and Bohemia, the tradition lasted to receive the influence of the Theiss culture, manifest in pedestalled pot-forms evidently derived from the type of Jordansmühl (p. 116). In Bavaria similar contacts ensued with the Münchshöfen settlers, but from the first the stroke-ornament people showed a civilizing force of their own, which was exerted on the Mesolithic natives, probably very largely (p. 111) their own kin, whom they found in Germany. Such a further fusion of Danubian and native is what best explains the rise in Central and South Germany of the so-called Rössen culture. Rössen is near Merseburg in Saxony, but the culture spread over

---

[1] Fig. 9, *b, c.*   [2] Fig. 10, *b.*   [3] Fig. 9, *f.*

much of South and West as well as of Central Germany, and in North-West Bohemia too, and its Danubian relationship is thus borne out by its geography as well as by its material, in which the stone implements are all Danubian and the pottery is simply a specialized form of stroke-ornamented ware, with stab and jabbed-line decoration, filled with white inlay, on hollow-necked bowls and deep dishes, both usually ring-footed (Pl. IV, B 3). But an abundance of triangular flint arrow-heads, and the stags' teeth used for necklaces, show an addiction to hunting quite foreign to the Danubian peasants, and the Rössen distribution covers much of the Thuringian-Swabian upland country which (p. 65) had supported the old Meso-lithic hunting-population. The best-explored Rössen site in South Germany, for instance, the Goldberg near Nördlingen, is on a commanding hill-top, and in their combination of hunting with husbandry the Rössen folk represent the blending of new and old typical of highland zones. The Goldberg excava-tions have shown their houses to have been rectangular pitch-roofed structures, walled with timber uprights and partitioned within, with the door under the roof-gable in the short end. Though in a sense analogous to the *megaron* houses of South-East Europe (p. 102), the type's development is as yet obscure; it has been widely claimed as 'Nordic', but woodland environ-ment was doubtless the determining factor. Similar houses,[1] sometimes porched in the *megaron* manner, have been excavated in the lakeside settlement of Aichbühl on the Federsee, again in a context of probable fusion between Danubians and natives of local Mesolithic descent (p. 65): Aichbühl pottery[2] is another variant on the stroke-ornament theme, and its occurrence also at the Goldberg marks the overlap between the Rössen culture and this analogous development on the Alpine fringes, about or soon after 2300 B.C., and contemporary with the Münchshöfen culture near by in Bavaria.

Before this the Rössen people had passed over into the Rhineland, where among the earlier-established Danubian inhabitants distinct varieties of culture had now grown up, each with its distinguishable pottery style. In addition to that of Alsace, there was one in the Wetterau country on and

[1] Fig. 10, *a*.   [2] Fig. 9, *h*.

beyond the Lower Main, another in the Worms district, and
a third further down the Rhine round Plaidt in the vale of

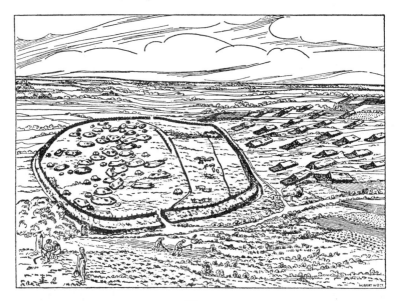

Fig. 10

RECONSTRUCTIONS OF THE NEOLITHIC SETTLEMENTS AT
AICHBÜHL (*a*, above) AND KÖLN-LINDENTHAL (*b*, below)

Neuwied, while the fourth occupation at Köln-Lindenthal
typifies yet another. The Rössen immigrants cut right across
the first two of these, and the position about 2400 B.C. then

becomes further complicated by the reinforcing of the influence of the stroke-ornament people, who were now appearing, side by side with Rössen settlers, in the region of the Neckar, whence some came down into the Rhineland. The result was the formation of the distinct Middle Rhineland culture known by the type-site name of Hinkelstein: its pottery is distinguished by stroke-and-ribbon decoration of a peculiar kind,[1] and in general it seems stronger than the Rössen culture in true Danubian elements, though here too flint arrowheads, of the transverse type (p. 61) attest a Mesolithic-derived hunting strain. Side by side with it the Rössen people continued on the Rhineland margins, sporadically further north and more intensively further east and in the Neckar region, where in contact with the stroke-ornament folk beyond again, and later with their Münchshöfen and Aichbühl successors, there flourished a plethora of local groupings with names that need not here be recited.

Throughout this whole complex of populations, regional isolation was always offset by mutual intercourse. Comings and goings are constantly being proved by the discovery of objects traded from one group to another. *Spondylus*-shell for bracelets, imported from the distant Mediterranean, must have been circulated in this fashion, and the trading about of pottery itself has been strikingly demonstrated by the mineral-analysis of 'foreign' pieces found in the Lindenthal settlement. Among these the fourth occupation-period produced a typical Hinkelstein piece made in the neighbourhood of Mainz, and others from Plaidt or Neuwied occurred both in that period and the preceding one. And Plaidt pottery was exported even further afield, for a specimen has now been identified by the same method in a still more westerly region of Danubian expansion, that of the 'Omalian' group in the Liège province of Belgium, whither the culture's unmistakable traditions had also been brought, by colonists who made pottery with forms both of linear and stroke design, and apparently traded some of it in turn back to Lindenthal. Others had settled likewise on the loess of the southern extremity of Holland, round Maastricht: at Caberg there is a big site, enclosed by ditches

[1] Fig. 9, *e*.

like Lindenthal, where the pottery resembles the Omalian, and one of its neighbours at Geleen is perhaps one of the latest of all westerly Danubian sites. But this province was not able to emulate the long survival achieved by the stroke-ornament people of the far north-east (p. 118), side by side with the later comers of Jordansmühl. The defences of Caberg and Lindenthal suggest that their wealth became coveted by enemy neighbours, and in the first instance these were probably predatory bands of Rössen hunters, since such are known to have been active on the margins of the Rhineland at the time. But at this point the further west of Europe, which, despite their occasional traces as far into France as the suburbs of Paris, the Danubians could never properly colonize, has to be brought into the picture. For it had become the home of another Neolithic culture altogether, which from the spearpoint of its territory in the Jura and Western Switzerland was already by 2300 B.C. being carried down and across the Rhine, to the undoing of this whole province, weakened as it may often have been by Rössen borderers, of the Danubian civilization. But the culminating phase of that civilization, before it broke up and gave place to this incoming Western Neolithic, is so well epitomized at Lindenthal [1] that it is worth taking a vantage-point here to review and sum up the Danubian achievement as a whole.

From first to last, Danubian civilization retained its adaptation to farming-life on open loess-land. Thus the form of the dwellings, in the final Lindenthal period no less than earlier, remained the irregularly rounded hut with its interior scooped out into pits and hollows in the ground: never the woodlander's log cabin. But for his barns, the paramount need of dry grain-storage made the Danubian practise solid timber building, and these formidable structures, with their drying-platforms in front, give us in their stilt-post construction a striking anticipation of the Roman granaries of long afterwards. The root of the tradition was the farmer's need: the traces of similar barns have been found in South Germany, most notably at Herkheim near Nördlingen, and as far away as Silesia and Bohemia, and the general uniformity of the culture's building-

[1] Fig. 10, *b*.

customs was probably no less widespread than its uniformity of tool-equipment. The 'shoe-last celt' or adze is already familiar (Fig. 7, 5) as the Danubian's hoe, and among its forms some of those perforated for attachment are so massive that they can only be explained as ploughshares; that is, the stone-bladed hoe was becoming liable to transformation into the traction-plough, though it may well have been human and not animal power that first dragged it. Of the flint sickle-blades with which the crops were reaped we have already spoken (p. 94): the grain was ground on simple 'saddle'-querns, and numerous finds reveal that the chief crop was 'little' wheat (*Triticum monococcum*), though forms of true bread-wheat (*T. vulgare*) were already current. Our earlier sections have made clear the origin of grain-growing in the Near East, as also of animal domestication, and the European naturalization of farming remains the Danubians' prime and characteristic achievement. Their social organization was of peasant simplicity, and the typical family dwellings are normally of equal size: at Lindenthal in the last period there were 30-35 of them, giving a population of some 250-350 (the second period total was about 100 less, the first and third still smaller). The whole life of the settlement is reckoned at close on 500 years. Of this roughly half is accounted for by the two last periods, in which, as we have seen, stroke-ornament people from the south-east reached the site from further up the Rhine, and made here in the Cologne district a regional grouping of the culture, answering to the others we have already named. Though a linear element still persisted in their pot designs, stroke ornament dominated, and in particular the developed form of it executed by impressing a comb-like stamp on the clay instead of making each stroke separately. The same technique was employed, but in a different way, by the contemporary group in Alsace, and its offshoots westward into France, best attested at the village-site of Ante in the Marne. Despite such local divergences, the culture as a whole remained essentially homogeneous, for its character was maintained by a unitary manner of life, and supported by the trading-intercourse of which we have spoken.

It remains to ask whether the Danubians were racially one

people, or in any case what their racial complexion was. We must then consider briefly one more subject, the graves which have yielded their physical remains. In South, West and Central Germany, and in some cases on the Middle Danube also, the dead were cremated, especially in the late or stroke-ornament period, and often under their hut-floors. But over most of the Danubian territory inhumed burials have been found, usually in a gently flexed position (though the Rössen corpses were fully contracted, and at Hinkelstein they lay stretched on their backs), and the more easterly Theiss culture is best known from its great cemeteries, such as Lengyel and Jordansmühl. On the whole, the skulls show a good deal of variety, from long to medium forms, and 'Mediterranean', 'Nordic', and 'Crô-Magnon' elements have all been discerned by one writer or another. There will be more to say on this matter later, but meanwhile it is plain that there was here no 'pure' race, and in particular no dominating strain of Near-Eastern immigrants: the Danubians form a typically European blend, and their racial composition must have been matured on European soil. Indeed, it may be reckoned the honour of their civilization to have knit and multiplied together a diversity of human stocks in a great cultural unit, which from East to West laid the first foundations of ordered and self-reliant livelihood across the whole centre of Europe.

Chapter Five

THE WEST, THE SEA-WAYS, AND THE NORTH

I. THE WESTERN NEOLITHIC

(Map IV and Table IV: at end)

IN our third chapter (pp. 82-84) we saw how second-hand elements of early Egyptian culture were seemingly disseminated among the peoples of North Africa, until such things as stone axes, flint arrowheads, and decorated pottery became adopted by the cave-dwellers of the Atlas as far west as Morocco and the Straits of Gibraltar. We also referred in the same context to the colonization of those three most accessible outposts of the European continent, Sicily, Sardinia, and Southern Spain.

It is from this point that the story of Neolithic development in the West must now be taken up. The East Sicilian settlements in the neighbourhood of Syracuse, Stentinello, Matrensa, and their like, reveal a mainly pastoral people whose pottery has affinities at once African and Cretan. Its incised and stamp-impressed designs, usually with white filling, suggest the basketry models already remarked on (pp. 75, 77-8, 82) in various North African connexions, and also the white-filled ornament of some of the pre-Minoan pottery of Crete (p. 77). If the East Sicilian colonists had, as seems most probable, a North African origin, their lack of true agriculture, the primitiveness of their tool-equipment, and their resort to cave-dwellings as well as villages, suits a derivation from outside, and presumably west of, the focus of higher civilization in Egypt; but they were obviously not so far beyond it as the more westerly migrants to Sardinia and Spain, their relation to whom has been already touched upon (pp. 83-4).

And as their culture spread over Eastern Sicily to the Italian mainland and up the Apulian coast, it lay open to currents of civilization from an eastward direction, transmitted by the Otranto Straits from the Balkan Peninsula. The

Apulian sites, both villages like Molfetta, Matera, and Settiponti, and caves as at Ostuni, yield not only incised pottery like the East Sicilian, but fine painted ware, decorated mostly in black on buff with angular patterns and also rudimentary spirals, which at once recall, though with a certain vagueness, the Dimini ware of Thessaly (p. 105). The exact dating of this surely Balkan introduction, by which painted pottery was naturalized in Italy in a quite distinctive form, is not yet firmly fixed: the Thessalian analogy points to the middle centuries of the third millennium, and the ensuing innovations in Sicily to be noted in the next section suggest an initial date scarcely after 2500 B.C. The Mediterranean, apparently African-derived, matrix of the culture, seen at its purest in the East Sicilian sites like Stentinello, should have begun its career a good deal nearer to 3000. But the growth of this civilization will be best discussed below, when we can extend our survey to include subsequent developments. Meanwhile it remains to notice that the villagers lived in square or round huts, sometimes sunk into the ground, and often protected their settlements with simple earthworks, while their graves were single pits or trenches, in places walled with stones, in which lie huddled the long-skulled skeletons attesting the 'Mediterranean race'.

To pass next further west, the earliest settlers in West Sicily and Sardinia are far less well known. Their traces are confined to caves: in West Sicily one cannot yet date their beginnings, though the Villafrati Cave (p. 252) will presently attest them in the late third millennium, but in the distinctly similar Sardinian culture the San Bartolomeo Cave near Cagliari has an upper stratum of that period (p. 252) with below it an earlier deposit, which suggests that both cultures may go back to the times we are now discussing. It contained remains of burials, tools of bone and local obsidian, and pottery, partly plain, partly ornamented with incised 'ladder' designs, which recall not only the West Sicilian, but also the South Spanish cave-culture; and with this we have in the third place now to deal. The probabilities of a close affinity going back to Mesolithic times between the peoples on either side of the Straits of Gibraltar have been discussed above

(p. 47); thus, though there is no demonstrable warrant for making those on the Spanish side actual Capsians and so carrying back the affinity into the Palaeolithic (p. 44), yet their African connexions at the time now under consideration may be taken as close enough to make a Spanish extension of the Atlas cave-culture in no way a surprise. Further, the distribution of this South Spanish cave-culture on the map is clearly based upon the Straits themselves, and one may recognize in it a diffusion of the elements introduced by migrating African cave-dwellers among their Peninsular kinsmen.

What those elements were we in part already know: simple ground forms of round-bodied stone axes now mingle with various bone implements and the old flint-flaking tradition of the Mesolithic, in which true microliths are not yet extinct, though the commonest tools are plain flake-knives. There are a few simple grinding-stones, but nothing to attest true agriculture, though the bones of cattle besides deer show that herding had come to supplement the chase, whose ancient magic was still kept alive in the schematic rock-paintings noticed in an earlier chapter (p. 43). The pottery, coarse and black to reddish, is ornamented with various forms of incision: a scatter or rows of stab or nail marks, plain and dotted lines, zigzags, herring-bone, and hatched bands of 'ladder-pattern'. In so far as these bear any positive explanation, they may stand as degraded versions of basketry or 'sling' motives (p. 74), as in North Africa, while some of the dotting and hatching, and the curious concentric semicircles which, with 'ladders', occur also in Sardinia, and seem of some magical significance (pp. 172-3), look like remote renderings of the painted vase-patterns of Gerzean Egypt (p. 78). Broad lug handles likewise recall Egyptian tubular lugs, and the whole harmonizes well with the account of the parent North African pottery already given on these lines.

The numerous caves at Gibraltar, those of los Murciélagos and la Mujer in Granada, and of Hoyo de la Mina and la Pileta in Malaga, have yielded the best part of the South Spanish material; the Malaga caves are interesting not only for schematic rock-paintings (la Pileta), but for the appearance of yet one more technique of pottery-ornament, the 'stab-and-drag' line, important in view of the sequel to this culture in South Spain, and becoming more strongly typical as it spread inland to the mountains flanking the basin of the Tagus. There, among the caves of Extremadura and Segovia, is the well-known site of Boquique, which has given its name to this distinctive technique, and we shall shortly find similar pottery both further west in Portugal and north-eastwards in Soria and Burgos and beyond again in Catalonia. But here in North Spain it is not only later but relatively rarer, for the southern culture's arrival brought a distinct North Spanish cave-culture into being, which is marked by pottery with plastic ridges and bands decorated with finger-printing, inspired no doubt by stitched or plaited girth- and collar-bands on leather vessels of aboriginal tradition. In time this 'finger-tip ware' became characteristic of the cave-dwelling population of the whole mountain zone from North-Central Spain by the Pyrenees and the south of Mid-France to the Alps and North Italy; but that belongs to a later stage of our narrative (p. 156). An initial date for the South Spanish cave-culture is not easy to fix; but the parent diffusion across North Africa need not have been at all rapid, and the figure should probably be lower than that for Stentinello in Sicily, in fact appreciably later than 3000, for, as we shall see, the culture's arrival cannot long have preceded the higher and quite different civilization, to which we must now turn, in Almeria on the south-east Spanish coast.

The primary Almerian site of El Garcel has already been signalized (pp. 69, 83) as marking the first West European appearance of true Neolithic culture, in the sense above defined (p. 91). In actual fact it has yielded copper slag, which shows that the settlers knew metal and were from the first on the look-out for its ores in their new home. It does not need stating that in Spain they had found one of the richest mineral countries in the ancient world, and very soon this mineral wealth becomes the most powerful single factor in Spanish prehistory. But there is as yet little to show for it in these earliest years of Almerian colonization, and at El Garcel and Tres Cabezos we have what is virtually a pure

Neolithic economy, in which the Egyptian-looking plain dark pottery, polished stone axes, and agricultural equipment of the colonists mingle with the microliths and scrapers of the native Mesolithic. Almeria is the first easy landfall in Spain for westward voyagers keeping touch with the North African shore, and the difficulty already alluded to (p. 83) of detecting the route of these first Iberian settlers may be largely due to their having come a long way by sea. Even if Professor Bosch Gimpera is right in looking for their immediate origin to the Saharan fringe behind Oran, it is clear that they differ from the cave-culture people in coming from inside, not outside, the orbit of Egyptian-centred civilization. Theoretically, their cultural affinities to the Neolithic Egyptians of Merimde or the Fayûm (p. 77) can suggest for their coming a date many centuries earlier, but even by the Nile itself primitive pot-forms had a long life alongside their typological successors, and a whole culture of this type may easily have survived into Dynastic times in a yet undiscovered marginal region. But with no specific reflexion of the commercial activity of the Old Kingdom or the maturer years of Early Minoan Crete, no date under a century or two before 2500 B.C. can pass as plausible, and, indeed, in Spain as in Sicily (pp. 151-2) we shall find that limit followed by new developments which the culture's first beginnings must precede by a definite margin. The dating of its sequels further away in Western Europe points in the same direction, while on two Almerian sites (La Gerundia and los Tollos) incised pottery shows an overlap with the neighbouring cave-culture. On present evidence, then, 2700 B.C. is not too early for El Garcel, and by 2600 the Almerian may be reckoned an established civilization.

For what must have been an Eastern metal trade soon began to foster its development. The copper implements found in the hill-top village of Parazuelos indeed show the same types as the ensuing period, to which, like its fellow at Campos, it may in part belong, but its surrounding rampart is no argument against early date, for we shall find earthworks typical of the same culture's more distant extensions. Perhaps partly for barter with the natives with whom they were mingling, the settlers introduced pointed flint arrowheads finely flaked in the Egyptian manner; these are tanged and barbed or more simply lozenge- or leaf-shaped, while the triangular or hollow-based type, extinct in Egypt since Early Predynastic times, show signs of re-creation from the native angular microlith, in such 'transitional' forms as from the grave of Puerto Blanco. This was a stone-walled sepulchre for the collective burial of eight or ten bodies: smaller interments were, however, more usual, the slab-cist of La Pernera containing a flat stone idol of the Eastern-derived type already (p. 84) noticed at El Garcel, while the still simpler trench-burials of Palaces recall the graves of South Italy (p. 126), and at Velez Blanco there were stone grave-cists each under a round cairn. We are reminded that the simple North African pit-grave, in Egypt the starting-point of a development of funerary grandeur which needs no recalling, took on the Saharan margins very similar stone-cairn forms, while in Crete, side by side with natural rock-tombs, not only were small rock-cut grave-cists appearing in just this period (Early Minoan II), but the distinctive rite of collective burial was already also established, in 'family vaults' which will soon emerge (p. 148) as of vital importance for the archaeology of the West, and seem already reflected here, e.g. at Puerto Blanco. So buried, with their belongings and finery of stone and shell beads and bracelets, the early Almerians reveal the long-headed 'Mediterranean' skeletal type in a form which marks them out as the ancestors of the historic Iberians, and their ensuing spread covered the whole of the coast and hinterland of Eastern Spain.

Though the primitive Almerian bowls (Fig. 6, A 4) from the Gibraltar caves attest some westward movement on to the cave-people's coasts, the latter's absence from the seaboard to east and north favoured Almerian expansion towards Catalonia and the south of France. Coasting voyages naturally preceded permanent penetration of the rugged interior, and in the hinterland of Murcia and Alicante an early site like Mola Alta de Serelles leaves the majority answering rather to Parazuelos or Campos than, say, to Tres Cabezos. But both here and beyond in Valencia such inland settlement implies an earlier foothold on the coast, just as the parallel advance

up the Ebro carried with it unchanged the culture's most
primitive pot-forms, the round-bottomed bowls of Fig. 6, A 4,
as found in the rock-tomb of Canyaret near Calaceite. Thus it
is not surprising that an abundance of graves of the Almerian
types of Palaces, La Pernera, and Velez Blanco should mark
a colonization of South and East Catalonia beginning equally
early along the coast past Tarragona and Barcelona; in fact,
the *Pectunculus*-shell bracelets, whose coastwise distribution
well reflects the whole movement, are in Almeria confined to
the initial phase of Palaces and El Garcel. Finally, beyond
the bastion of the Pyrenees, the Aude valley opens into an
ideal settling-ground in the fertile coastal plain of Narbonne,
and the early arrival of Western colonists there has been
attested by M. Héléna's discovery of typically primitive plain
pottery (and the leaf-shaped flint arrowhead) in the cave of
Bize, stratified over a Mesolithic layer and under one with
decorated ware to be dated below towards 2300 B.C. (p. 159).
So the Western culture reached France, and the fidelity with
which we shall there and beyond find features native to its
North African home preserved, confirms the early date of its
arrival no less than the divergence, which thereafter becomes
more and more marked, between this and the Almerian branch
of the common stem. The cave of Bize must have been
occupied by these people about 2600 B.C.

Thus while the future of the Almerians became bound up
with the trade in Spanish metals, their relations brought to
South France, where ores were not discoverable, a pure
Neolithic economy. Plain round-bottomed pots, bag-shaped
and often with lugs which may be perforated for suspension,
round-bodied polished stone axes, leaf-shaped and sometimes
barbed and tanged flint arrowheads, simple tools of flint and
bone, and ornaments of shell, bone, or stone, remained long
the basic elements of material culture along the foothills
between the Pyrenees and the Lower Rhône. And though
we know as yet little of the initial phase there, further expansion
may be followed in two directions. Eastward beyond the
Rhône there are caves in the Ligurian Alps which have yielded
much evidence of Neolithic and later habitation, and though
Italian excavators have not been able to distinguish them by

stratigraphy, it seems certain that several stages succeeded one another, beginning with a Neolithic recognizable in just such pottery, axes, arrowheads, and ornaments. Not only are the round-bottomed bowls distinctively Western, but they are accompanied by clay ladles or spoons, which are typical of this culture in its North African home as far back as the days of Merimde (p. 77: Fig. 6, A 2). A vaguer element of the same sort appears beyond again in the caves of Tuscany; across the mountains in the plains of the Po and along the Adriatic coast, however, such signs die out in a derivative Neolithic drawing also upon other influences (p. 157). Northward, the Western people mounted the Rhône valley into Central France. At the famous fortified site of the Camp de Chassey in the Saône-et-Loire, stratified evidence is once more to seek, but the plain early round-bottomed pottery [1] stands out both in form and fabric from the decorated ware to be noticed in its later context below (p. 158), and the distinction is confirmed at the cave of Nermont, further north near St. Moré in the Yonne: there the pottery consists solely of such bowls, associated with clay spoons of the type just mentioned, which indeed occur at Chassey also. Finally, though it is still impossible to detect their presence at this early date in the north of France, our Neolithic colonists must have passed on thither, for, in a form which preserves its original features in unmodified simplicity, their culture next appears in Southern Britain, where we know it as Neolithic A, the initial culture of the renowned Wiltshire type-site of Windmill Hill.

But before reviewing this first Neolithic civilization of our island there is a good deal more on the Continent that requires our notice. The north of France, which the Windmill Hill people must have traversed on their way to Britain, was the home of a considerable Mesolithic population. There were the Late Tardenoisians of such sandy country as the Aisne district (p. 66), and more evenly spread from the confines of the Omalian in Belgium (p. 121) right across to the Loire and beyond was the straggling Western equivalent of the North European 'Forest Culture' of the Atlantic phase

[1] Fig. 11, 1.

corresponding to Ertebølle in Denmark and Halstow in South-East Britain. We remarked above (p. 67) that these people, vaguely though plentifully attested by their flint core-axes or 'picks', have been called Campignian, and it is now that the name-site of Le Campigny near the mouth of the Seine claims explanation, for there, in the débris on hut-floors scooped out of the natural gravel, a flint industry almost wholly of this Mesolithic type, with 'picks', flake-axes or *tranchets*, scrapers, points, and gravers, was found associated not only with grain-grinding stones but with our Western Neolithic pottery. And although this included a little of the decorated ware of the culture's second phase to be noticed below (p. 158), the site is of immediate interest to us here as demonstrating a fusion between the Neolithic colonists and the Mesolithic natives which must have been widespread throughout this North French region. The innumerable surface sites so beloved of the French flint-collector habitually yield just this mixture of Mesolithic and Neolithic industry, and it was clearly thus that the colonists were introduced to the greatly extended use of flint typified in the translation of their traditional polished stone axes into chipped or chipped and polished flint. Contact with the Tardenoisians, whose sandy hunting-grounds were no attraction to the Neolithic cultivator, is at this stage relatively insignificant.

In the Central French uplands there was analogous fusion: the Azilian tradition of utilizing deer-horn seems responsible for the antler's 'sleeves' in which the Chassey people took to mounting their axes in the wooden haft, and this device becomes absolutely typical (Fig. 11, 5), when we follow our Neolithic culture into the sub-Alpine region, where such a sleeve has already been remarked among the Mesolithic folk (p. 65 : Fig. 5, *m*) who when faced with the Atlantic forest-growth had taken to a largely waterside existence. It was the impact of the Western Neolithic on these folk that seems to have been responsible for the earliest of the famous pile-dwelling cultures of the West Alpine lakes. Finds near Chambéry in Savoie, and a pile-settlement on Lake Chalain in the French Jura yielding typical Western bowls,[1] axes, and antler sleeves, point

[1] Fig. 11, 2.

the way from the Chassey district into Switzerland, and there the excavations of M. Vouga on the Lake of Neuchâtel have revealed what is called, from one of his sites, the Cortaillod culture. The Cortaillod sites, Chalain, and Chassey are so closely linked by their plain pottery, implements, and such details as amulet-pendants recalling Predynastic Egyptian types, that they should be virtually contemporary, and collation of the lake-flood deposits of Neuchâtel with those of the Eastern Alps shows Cortaillod to be no later, and more probably earlier, than the Danube-derived site of Aichbühl, already dated about 2300 (p. 119). Thus a date about 2500 for the start of these Western culture-groups will fit the Alpine as well as the Mediterranean evidence.

The Cortaillod culture extends no further towards the Danubian provice than Zürich on the east and the Black Forest on the north; among a number of sites within these limits, Vouga's at Port-Conty is the most fully known, though nowhere are the habitations represented by more than the stumps of their supporting piles in the shallows of the old lake margin. But the relics of the occupation, found stratified with them in the mud beneath the flood-deposit which marks and explains its eventual end, are abundant and well preserved. The stone axes are either round-bodied or have squared sides, and their antler sleeves are undivided into body and tang:[1] picks and other objects of antler and bone are numerous, and in flint (mainly a dark brown imported variety) there are blades, points, and scrapers, rare triangular arrowheads, and quite a number of microliths representing the culture's Mesolithic element. Ornaments, besides the pendants already noticed, include pierced boar-tusks and bone and stone beads. The smooth dark pottery bowls,[2] open, bag-shaped, carinated, or bottle-shaped, usually have lugs, often with single or multiple [3] perforations for suspension, while the ladle reappears in wood.. Baskets and fishing-nets were made, and a bone comb and clay loom-weights attest cloth-making, probably of flax as well as the wool of the sheep, which with goats, pigs, cattle, and dogs represent the domestic animals. Only deer were regularly hunted. Lake-shore agriculture is attested

[1] Fig. 11, 5.   [2] Fig. 11, 3.   [3] Fig. 11, 4a.

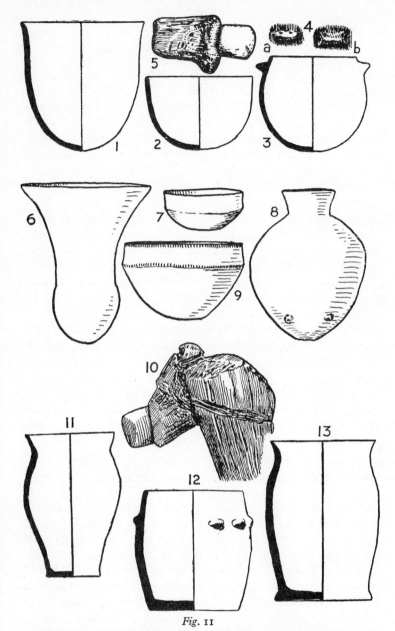

Fig. 11

WESTERN NEOLITHIC POTTERY AND AXES

1, Chassey; 2, Chalain; 3, 5, Lake Neuchâtel, Cortaillod culture (pp. 132-6); 4, Lugs; *a*, multiperforated; *b*, trumpet (pp. 134, 146). Michelsberg culture (p. 136); 6, Lake Constance; 7-9, Baden (8, 9, Michelsberg). Seine-Oise-Marne culture (pp. 198, 260, 283): 11, Long cist of Les Mureaux; Horgen culture (pp. 198, 244): 10, 12, Lake Neuchâtel; 13, Lake of Zürich.

Scales: 1-5, $\frac{1}{4}$; 2-9, $\frac{2}{11}$; 11-13, $\frac{1}{8}$.

not only by antler and axe-like stone hoe-heads and even ploughshares, probable sickle-flints, and abundant grain-grinding stones, but by finds of carbonized wheat-grains. In other words, though the people had not the highly developed agriculture of the Danubians, they had all round a very adequate Neolithic economy of their own. The few skulls found are long and of Mediterranean affinities.

After the ruin of their settlements by flood, the Cortaillod people disappear from Switzerland, and a new people coming south-east from France eventually took their place (p. 198), but since from Lake Thun their culture reappears beyond the Alpine passes on Lake Varese, some of them must have retired southward and continued their existence in the North Italian lakeland. But the way northward was easier, and here the lake-dwelling civilization had perhaps already, as at the Altenburg in the Black Forest, been taking on a new form, in which Western elements mingle with some fresh ones, and others due to contact with outliers of the Danubian province. The result is known in some pile-dwellings on Lake Constance, and in log-raft villages (recalling Aichbühl) on lakeside peat, as at Weiher (Thayngen) near Schaffhausen, but better from settlements on dry land, of which the most famous are fortified, including that of Michelsberg in Baden which has given this culture its name. The smooth baggy pottery[1] is developed into big oval bottles with upstanding necks, carinated bowls, handled jugs, and 'tulip'-shaped beakers suggesting a traditional form of leather bag, made from an animal's scrotum, that had not been thus translated into clay since Tasian times in Egypt. In addition, there is rough-faced coarse ware, used for tall slightly shouldered pots ornamented with plastic strips and finger-printing, and round flat baking-plates. Danubian perforated axes occur with the plain Western ones, whose antler sleeves tend to a 'heeled' body with a distinct tang. Domestic crafts, stock-farming, and agriculture are attested as before, but arrowheads and bows show hunting intensified, and in general the new contacts show up well in the broader basis of the culture: in fact, before long, Danubian connexions were bringing in occasional tools and ornaments

[1] Fig. 11, 6-9.

of copper. Beyond Lake Constance and on the Upper Neckar
the Danubian element was strong enough to form a distinct
offshoot, in which, as at Schussenried and a second settlement
at Aichbühl, incised pottery-ornament and the handled jug-
forms are clearly related to Central European groups like
Jordansmühl (p. 116). But the course of pure Michelsberg
expansion was down the Rhine. Here the last Danubians,
Hinkelstein and Rössen people, were ousted from the loess
of Alsace, Worms, and Mainz, and thence the invaders
overflowed the Wetterau north-east into Central Germany,
just as from the Neckar they usurped the Rössen settlement
on the Goldberg (p. 119); at last, from the Saale and Elbe,
they gained a substantial foothold in Northern Bohemia.
Thus, by a sharp reversal of the current, this whole great
segment of the Danubian heritage became Westernized by
the Michelsbergers' immigration. It must have been spread
over a good few generations: if the culture was starting to
form about 2400, we need not date its fullest expansion before
2300 or 2200. But its Western (and partly Alpine-Mesolithic)
contribution to the mixing-bowl of Central Europe is none
the less a matter of importance, as the sequel will show.

However, the first movement northward went further than
we have yet followed it: there are traces of the Michelsbergers,
superseding the Danubians, from Eastern France beyond
Alsace, and from the Rhine as far below Mainz as near Köln;
so they would seem to have supplemented the Rössen peril
(p. 122) which prompted the fortifications of the fourth period
at Lindenthal, and probably brought about its final dereliction.
Lastly, joining hands perhaps with their earlier-arrived
Western cousins of North France, they settled in Belgium,
whence the Omalians disappear. Boitsfort in Brabant is, like
Michelsberg, itself a fortified hill-spur, though of such fortified
sites the most distinctive are those of Mayen and Urmitz
near Koblenz on the Rhine, which answer closely to the
'causewayed camps'[1] of the British culture of Windmill Hill.
For the ditches are divided into stretches, longer at Mayen,
shorter in the double line round Urmitz, by solid causeways,
defended at the latter site by stockade-works protecting gates

[1] Fig. 12, *b*.

in the palisade behind. Within all the settlements the dwellings, though often half scooped in the ground, might also (as at Mayen and the Goldberg) be surface-floored rectangular structures of timber, which in raft-villages like Weiher and Aichbühl II were divided into two rooms. The dead were usually buried, in a contracted position and some-times under their own huts, which were therewith destroyed, but the Belgian group burnt the dead in mound-crematorium cemeteries, as at Boitsfort in Brabant—a practice at present unexplained. This was not its only peculiarity: in common with North France, there was a strong Mesolithic substratum here, to supply the new culture with a 'Campignian' element, which appears most plainly in the 'picks' and other tools of an abundant and conservative flint industry. The natives must long have known that the best flint was to be dug from the chalk, and the Neolithic settlers soon turned their more organized resources to exploiting this by sinking regular mines for its extraction. In the Hesbaye towards Liège, and near Mons at sites like Obourg, and above all Spiennes, flint-mining became an established industry, whose products were traded all round the country. The same industry occurs wherever else Western Neolithic culture came in contact with a Mesolithic flint-tradition of this type—in North and West France, and no less prominently in Southern Britain. Where the chalk with its seams of flint was easily reached, open or at most bell-bottomed pits could be dug: where, however, thick overlying gravels or sands had to be penetrated, a narrow shaft was sunk with level galleries radiating from it at the bottom (Fig. 12,*a*). The latter might be dangerous if the chalk was not solid, as is grimly shown in one at Obourg where a miner's skeleton was found buried by a roof-fall, and the various forms of workings are thus to be explained by varying natural conditions. Pre-Neolithic attempts at mining are unrecorded, and the industry as we know it is the creation of the Western Neolithic peoples established where the use of flint was natural and traditional. In Britain a long line of flint-mines has been explored along the Sussex Downs, from near Eastbourne by Cissbury and Harrow Hill to Stoke Down above Chichester, and again on the Wiltshire border at Easton

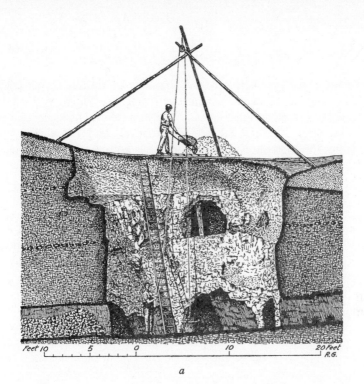

a

b

Fig. 12

a, SECTION OF A FLINT-MINE AT HARROW HILL,
SUSSEX.

b, PLAN OF THE NEOLITHIC CAMP AT COOMBE HILL,
JEVINGTON, SUSSEX.

Down; though their use, most notably at Easton Down and in Sussex at Blackpatch, continued well into the Bronze Age, the earliest pottery is typically Neolithic A. The deer-antler pick (Fig. 13, 5), the blade-bone shovel, and the chalk-cup lamp are characteristic of the miners' equipment; the mined flint was in demand mainly for axes (Fig. 13, 9), which were manufactured on the spot, and whole floors of waste flakes, with discarded 'rough-outs' and half-finished as well as perfect axes, are typical of all the sites.

The most famous British flint-mines are Grime's Graves in West Norfolk, where workings of every type crowd an area of some twenty acres. The industrial remains are very much the same, but whereas in Sussex the Western A culture is the only Neolithic represented, the Neolithic pottery here is of two kinds. Besides the plain baggy A bowl there are pieces of quite different vessels, with peculiar everted rims and close-set ornament impressed with twisted cord and small bird-bones. Here in the east of Britain, in fact, Neolithic A overlaps with another, quite distinct culture known as Neolithic B, of which this pottery, sometimes called Peterborough ware after the place where it was first found, is characteristic.[1] Now we have seen above (pp. 66, 133) that in Mesolithic times the east of Britain was part of a great cultural unit centred on the West Baltic region, of which the 'pick' traditions of Halstow and Campigny are peripheral offshoots. It is not surprising, then, to find that while the Western Neolithic was entering Southern Britain from France, a Baltic type of culture makes its appearance on our eastern shores. For, as will soon be seen, this pottery with its peculiar decoration is definitely of Baltic affinities. How early it was introduced is yet unknown, but we shall presently (p. 202) find it must have been well before 2300, and the two cultures, A and B, may here be treated as roughly coeval. In this section we need only note that just as the carinated bowls of A may perhaps have prompted the B potters to adopt distinctive shouldered bowl-forms, so the rich ornament of the B tradition became reflected in the shallow tooled decoration which in course of time invades that of A. But, broadly

[1] Fig. 13, 7.

speaking, the two cultures remained for a good while apart, not only as based upon different coast-lines, but since the B people, like their Mesolithic forefathers, kept to low riverlands and the watersides, while the A people, who wanted open country for their pasture and tillage, preferred upland like the chalk Downs. And to make a third with the pair of them, the Mesolithic hunting-folk of Tardenoisian tradition still dwelt on the Greensand ridges of the Weald and other such barren country, just as they still ranged undisturbed over the hills and moorlands further north and west.

In the middle of the third millennium B.C. the earlier Atlantic subsidence had left South-East Britain still much easier of access than at present from the Continental coast-line stretching from Denmark to the mouths of the Rhine. The links between our Neolithic B people and their Baltic relatives must now be largely submerged, and on the Essex coast at Dovercourt, Walton, and above all Clacton, Neolithic occupation, both A and B, has been found on a land-surface now sunk below high-tide mark, and revealed only by the modern erosion of anything up to a foot of peat and ten feet of clay covering them. With the Neolithic remains are those of later comers who made grooved and beaker pottery; these await our attention below (p. 269), but they serve meanwhile to show that the submergence of this 'Lyonesse' surface was delayed for a good few centuries after the first Neolithic arrivals. The Fenland Research Committee's excavations in East Cambridgeshire have shown likewise how the encroachment of peat-fen on the district's original sand-hills proceeded gradually from Boreal through Atlantic times, to be abruptly succeeded by a submergence which brought in six to seven feet of clay and silt from the sea, and made the sand-hills islands amid half-brackish water. The sections at Peacock's Farm have disclosed the place of the local Neolithic A in this series as over two feet below the clay, with a Mesolithic (Late Tardenoisian) horizon below again at four feet, and the vegetation and pollen-analysis of the 'lower peat' in which both are thus stratified established their age in terms of the climate and forest history of the region. While the Mesolithic horizon comes close to the Boreal-Atlantic transition, the

Neolithic A occupation lies in the later Atlantic period of relative stability between sand-hill and alder-fen, and it was followed by an appreciable interval of first drier and then wetter conditions before the great submergence took place. The story of our southern coasts is still comparatively undefined, but while actual separation from the Continent had occurred long before, at the start of Atlantic times (p. 56), the crossing from North France in the middle of the third millennium could undoubtedly be much easier than it later became. We do not indeed know precisely how or where the first Western colonists passed across, with all the stock of their pastoral and agricultural livelihood, to found our Neolithic A culture. But that culture's initial freedom from Continental developments of the age of Michelsberg bears out the Fen and Clacton evidence for the relatively early date of their arrival, and Continental and British evidence will alike be met if we put this not very much later than 2500 B.C.

As we have already seen from the flint-mines, it was on the open chalk of Wessex and Sussex that the immigrants settled most thickly. On the Trundle hill above Goodwood their culture is well shown (though probably not at its earliest) in a 'causewayed camp' with an inner ring of 3 acres, probably for cattle, and part of an outer one 100 yards or so outside it, with a string of short dwelling-ditches or pits straggling in a sort of spiral line between them. Near Jevington in East Sussex there is another causewayed camp on Coombe Hill (Fig. 12, *b*). Windmill Hill itself displays the causewayed plan in classic form, with three concentric ditches enclosing 23 acres in all, the outer 8, the middle 5, and the inner 3.4 feet in average depth. The bone-finds show that with dogs, sheep, goats, and pigs, cattle were kept in great numbers, of a small but long-horned breed; grain was grown, reaped with 'composite' flint sickles (p. 72), and ground in local sarsen-stone querns. Bone and antler implements were abundant, though sleeves were not used for mounting the polished flint axes (Fig. 13, 8) in which the polished-stone tradition of Mediterranean Europe was consciously kept up; among the smaller flaked flints serrated saw-blades are notable, and the arrowheads (Fig. 13, 4) are finely leaf-shaped, though some trans-

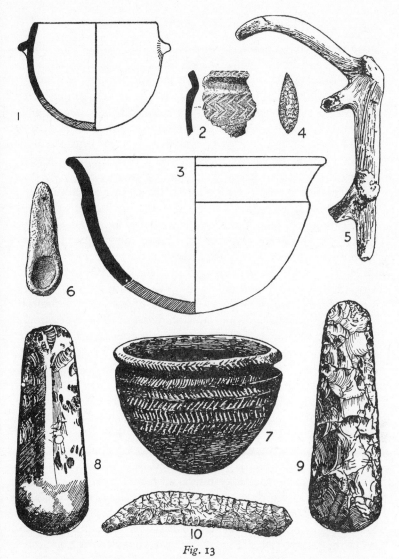

Fig. 13

NEOLITHIC POTTERY AND IMPLEMENTS FROM BRITAIN

Neolithic A pottery (pp. 132, 140-5): 1, Norton Bavant, Wilts; 2 (assimilated to B), Whitehawk, Sussex; 3 (carinated), Ehenside Tarn, Cumberland; 4, Leaf-shaped flint arrowhead (p. 142); 5, Flint-miner's antler pick, Grime's Graves (p. 140); 6, Pottery spoon, Sussex (p. 144); 7, Neolithic B bowl, Thames at Mortlake (p. 140); 8, Polished, and 9, Chipped flint axes (pp. 142, 140); 10, Curved flint sickle, Grovehurst, Kent (p. 213).

Scale : ¼.

verse forms suggest contact with a Mesolithic tradition. The archer's main quarry was roe and red deer, and here as elsewhere wood-flora and mollusc-shells indicate an 'Atlantic' climate damper than at present, with a higher spring-line. But Mr. Keiller's excavations have revealed more than this: the outer ditch has furnished a stratification, in which the lowest levels, representing the initial half of the settlement's life, are characterized by plain baggy bowls, shallow hemispherical, or deep, with simple lugs and rims (as Fig. 13, 1); these, therefore, typify the earliest phase of the culture in South Britain, answering, more closely than those of even the Trundle, to the simple Continental types already described (Fig. 11, 1-3). Pottery spoons, related to those noticed above in the same Continental context, are also known to occur in the British culture.[1] But the middle levels at Windmill Hill introduce carinated or shouldered bowls with more distinctive lugs and rims and a greater frequency of tooled and comb-stamped ornament on rims and shoulders. These features reappear at sites which, like that on the Upper Thames gravel at Abingdon, may be regarded as late in the Wessex history of the culture, and while further west they die out, they are more firmly marked as one passes eastward. And at White-hawk, on the racecourse above Brighton, the excavation of a fine causewayed camp, with four concentric ditches enclosing in all $11\frac{1}{2}$ acres, has revealed beyond doubt that the ornament owes its inspiration to the rich decorative repertory of the East British Neolithic B ware, referred to above (Fig. 13, 2). The best of such ornament, in fact, all comes from the easterly region of Neolithic B contact: Maiden Bower near Dunstable, or the Hayland House sand-hill in the Fens, provide good examples. But for the carinated bowl-forms, especially the splay-mouthed type of (Fig. 13, 3), this derivation will not do. They are, in fact, foreign to the ancestral tradition of Neolithic B (p. 202 below), and are perhaps best explained, like the antler combs sometimes found with them, as introduced by further drafts of Neolithic A people from the Michelsberg province of Belgium, where this sort of bowl (in place of the 'tulip-beaker' of South Germany) is at home unornamented. Before

[1] Fig. 13, 6.

the submergence around the Narrow Seas such incomings
would not be difficult, and it was probably only this addition
to the A people's strength in the east which led to the B
contact responsible for their adoption of pottery-ornament.
But it led more directly also to an expansion northward,
across what later became the Wash, for though what little
A pottery is known from Lincolnshire is relatively late, it
carries on precisely this tradition of shouldered form and
plain surface, while beyond the Humber on the Yorkshire
Wolds the same tradition is represented in its prime. Our
Michelsberg chronology will allow a date for the movement
between roughly 2300 and 2200 B.C., the results of the
incidental B contact spreading westward during the following
century.

No causewayed camps are known in Yorkshire, but long
ditch-like pit-dwellings, recalling those of the Trundle, have
in two cases been found, burnt out and buried full of bones
and charred matter under what are evidently sepulchral
mounds or barrows. Here, in fact, at Hanging Grimston and
Kemp Howe, we seem to have the Michelsberg rite of
destroying a dead man's hut to serve as his tomb (p. 138),
compounded with the Belgian habit of mound-cremation.
But under another such mound at Garton Slack (where the
burning had been done in a specially made crematorium-
trench instead of a real dwelling), there were also inhumed
burials, and the co-existence of the two rites well suits the
mixed Belgian and South British origin we have suggested
for the Yorkshire Neolithic settlers. For inhumed burials
have been several times found in the Neolithic A settlements
of South Britain, and the long-skulled skeletons in both
regions agree in recalling the 'Mediterranean' type already
associated with our culture abroad. And if such casual
settlement-burials—there are even hints of cannibalism—were
originally typical of the South British settlers, they had by
the time now under notice adopted, for their most honoured
dead, a form of ceremonial interment under barrows of which
the mounds of Yorkshire are simply a distant reflexion. For,
as is well known, the typical Neolithic tomb-form in Britain
is the Long Barrow.

Long barrows are mounds of earth or other material, elongated in plan, covering burials of a number of people together, and to understand how this distinctive kind of sepulchre and its associated complex of ritual practices first came to our island, we must make a fresh start abroad. For throughout the progress of the Western culture from South-West Europe to Britain there has hitherto been nothing of the kind, and the main distribution of the barrows, between our Mid-Channel coasts and the Lower Severn, points to their being a fresh introduction from the south by sea. Further, since the majority lie west of the longitude of Southampton Water, their immediate origin might be expected in Brittany rather than further up-Channel. And there is in the west of South Britain a distinct province of Neolithic A culture which is suspected of a Breton origin likewise. If, in the primary diffusion of the culture across France one branch went north-west to colonize the Breton peninsula, and thence the coasts of Cornwall, Devon, and Dorset, that province would be explained. For though assimilation to the Wessex and Sussex provinces is evident in its causewayed camps at Maiden Castle in Dorset and Hembury in Devon, yet a westerly focus is suggested both by settlements as far away as Carn Brea in West Cornwall and by a proved trade in Cornish stones for axes. Together with hut-plans, both round (Hembury and Carn Brea) and oblong-rectangular (Haldon near Exeter), the most distinctive feature is the pottery, all of very simple bowl-forms, never ornamented at all, and with lugs including a tubular type with 'trumpet'-expanded ends[1] which can be paralleled in Brittany. This sort of pottery characterizes at least one long barrow (Holdenhurst near Bournemouth), and though at Maiden Castle a long barrow has been found to be not the contemporary but the successor of the causewayed camp just mentioned, this need not upset the suggestion that these south-western Neolithic A people were perhaps the means of first introducing the long barrow, or more correctly the long mound, into Britain.

For while our long barrows come to incorporate types

[1] Fig. 11, 4*b*.

of chambered tomb-structure which will concern us only in the next section, in their most primitive form they are simply oblong mounds covering multiple (but simultaneously deposited) burials, such being distributed mainly in regions open to south-western immigration. And unmistakable parallels to our south-western pottery come from equally distinctive oblong mounds in Brittany, e.g. at Manio, revetted with stone walling just as the Holdenhurst mound, for instance, is with turf, and forming a collective covering for numerous burials in curious little cists, each under a pile of stones. The burials under British long mounds are covered (in the absence of suitable stone) by analogous piles of mould, and the presence in both groups of a larger dome-like structure on the central axis, covering a ritual deposit of some kind, and of a standing stone or post near one end, may be taken as further evidence of their kinship. Now, on the Mediterranean coast of Spain the Neolithic graves (p. 130) include forms of stone cist, and there are certain cist-burials in the west of France which may indicate the route taken by the colonists of Brittany, where there are more numerous cist-graves, of which some, whether or no beneath small round cairns, may well be as early as this same initial colonization; though such are not attested for the main spread of the culture further east, Breton stone lends itself readily to the usage. But the form taken by such cists when grouped under a long mound, and the phenomenon of the long mound itself, can best be explained in terms of the colonists' fusion in Brittany with Mesolithic natives. For the same piles of stones over graves, whether of one or several bodies, and the same dome-like structures covering ritual deposits of burnt funeral offerings, have been found in the Mesolithic cemetery of Téviec remarked on above (p. 68), grouped in a part of the communal midden, and it may be that the Breton long mound is just a walled-off artificial version of this ancient Mesolithic mode of sepulture, created by more civilized ideas about the disposal and segregation of the dead introduced by the Neolithic settlers—whose cultural fusion with natives is attested in these same mounds by the association of their pottery and axes with microliths. In the sequel we shall meet the long mound as a recurrent feature of Neolithic burial in this corner of Europe. But the Breton origin here suggested is far from explaining the whole long-barrow complex without remainder. Even in the simplest British mounds the burials are concentrated in one spot, and when to this significant change we have to add internal developments of tomb-structure quite foreign to the original long-mound idea, it is time to return to the Mediterranean starting-point of the whole Western Neolithic culture, and seek there a fresh and more far-reaching impulse in explanation. Up to this point the main story of the West European Neolithic has been that of a fairly homegeneous Southern people bringing a pastoral and small-scale agricultural civilization, of ultimately Egyptian affinities, northward from the Mediterranean coasts, and separating into various regional groups, in varying degrees of combination with Mesolithic natives. Only in East Spain did the Almerian group specialize from the first in the winning and trading of metals. It was along the channels of that trade that the new impulse came of which we have next to speak.

2. TRADE, RELIGION, AND CIVILIZATION FROM THE MEDITERRANEAN TO THE ATLANTIC

(Map IV and Table IV: at end)

Our brief sketch of Early Minoan and Cycladic culture (pp. 87-90) stopped short of describing its funeral customs, and by making good that omission here we shall obtain a fair perspective for the remarkable developments which now await attention in the West. The Early Minoan dead were buried either in natural caves or in rock-cut or stone-built tombs, but while both the latter might, as in East Crete, be small single-graves or cists, there appeared on the Central plain, at the beginning of Early Minoan II, a form of stone-built tomb distinctively adapted to the rite of collective or family burial. This was the so-called tholos or 'beehive', a circular building of dry-stone walling with the upper courses offset in succession inwards, and the roof either completing this in a corbelled vault (Fig. 16, *a*), or else, as it is often safer to suggest, in wood and thatch, and closed with a single capstone at the top. It was entered through a narrow portal with monolithic jambs and lintel, from a square yard or pit outside, above the height of whose walls (some 6 feet) the structure was free-standing: 20 feet might be an average height, the chamber's diameter varying from 40 feet to 20 or even less. While such corbelled vaulting is exemplified in brick in Egypt, it had perhaps long been understood in the Near East, for at Arpachiyah in Assyria (p. 73) similar beehives, often fronted by a rectangular approach, have been found and explained as temples. The device, in fact, enabled the primitive round-hut type of human dwelling to be reproduced in stone as would benefit a supernatural occupant, and its adaptation for the dwellings of the ghostly dead is a natural sequel. While in Egypt ideas concentrated on the tomb as a place of preservation for individual grandeur, social structure in the Aegean world favoured the collective burial of the family of equal clansfolk, the successive interments, accompanied by great purificatory fires, accumulating, regardless of confusion, to the number of many hundreds. But behind and together with the hand-built dwelling was the tradition of the cave, as the home of the dead as of the living; the mother-womb of Earth was the abode of the mysteries of birth and death alike, and it is not surprising to find the tholoi made to be entered as from an earth-sunk pit, and, answering equally to these and natural cave-sepulchres, rock-cut tombs in the Cyclades entered likewise by an artificial pit or adit, and roofed with the same beehive-corbelling, if not tunnelled entirely in the living limestone. These Early Cycladic tombs, whose pottery and marble idols were described above (pp. 88-9), include small slab-cists as well as such pit-and-chamber forms, and the more prevalent rite was not collective but individual burial in a contracted position, somewhat as in Eastern Crete. But the chamber-tombs reached as far as Euboea,[1] and on the Greek mainland the Early Helladic people whose island affinities have been already noted (p. 89) buried their dead collectively (though not in great numbers) in pit-caves or rock-cut chambers of the same sort. Thus by the middle of the third millennium the Aegean

[1] Fig. 16, *b*.

world from East Crete to Western Greece had, despite its diversities, a unity in religious ideas no less than in material culture.

In fact, it may be reckoned a sort of cultural confederacy, bound together in a growing intercourse by maritime trade. And to the north-east, the West-Anatolian civilization of Troy and Thermi had made answering strides. The strong walled city of Troy II, founded, as has been seen (p. 107), about 2500 B.C., was a centre of far-flung commerce, maritime as well as European and Asiatic, which brought its rulers riches vying with those of Eastern Crete, and their diadems and spiral ornaments and pin-heads of precious metal find relations both there and in the Cyclades, where gold, silver, and copper ornaments and toilet-instruments are widely found in the tombs; Trojan flat marble idols,[1] too, attest the same Mother-Goddess so honoured in the Aegean. The copper tools and weapons which were now gaining on Aegean obsidian and stone — plain flat axes, rivet-heeled Cretan daggers, and slot-fastened Cycladic spearheads, with the famous Minoan double-axe, most significant as a cult-symbol and rendering like the shaft-hole axe-adze a Sumerian model—are replaced at Troy by flat axes and rather different dagger and other types made in true bronze: that is, copper with a 10 per cent. alloy of tin. The source of this Trojan tin will be reverted to when we turn once more to Central Europe: it was a secret not passed on to the Aegean world in Early Minoan times, but much Aegean silver probably came through Troy, and the community of Trojan with Aegean trade is shown in the distribution of even quite humble objects such as bone tube-ornaments and strip-plaques, while Trojan pottery found especially in Euboea suggests regular trading-colonies. We have seen (pp. 107-8) that Troadic immigrants invaded Macedonia soon after 2500: rather later the same element reached Thessaly also, and this Anatolian dominance in the North Aegean, answering to the Minoan-Cycladic in the South, had sequels of vital importance, as will be seen below.

Meanwhile the Morava-Vardar extension from the Danube which preceded it in Macedonia, and had resulted in the

[1] Pl. III, B 2.

Dimini culture in East Thessaly (p. 105), had also affected the Aegean world on its Helladic side. While the Dimini people flourished near the Thessalian coast, Danubian elements that had come in with the same Morava-Vardar movement were not only fusing with the older Neolithic tradition inland, but reached further south and south-westward also. Inferior painted wares, black on buff and grey on grey, and crusted ware of Theiss-culture character (p. 115) belong to this context, as do the incised designs, some of them spirals, which occur more sporadically not only with them in Thessaly among the more normal pottery in monochrome, but also in the Early Helladic province further south; there too recur the 'hour-glass' vessels and beaked jugs which in the north seem due, along with two-handled cups and footed bowls, to oversea contacts with Troy and the Cyclades. And such types appear also in West Greece, and meet in Leukas outliers of the Early Helladic culture already mentioned. The parallel movement of Theiss-culture elements towards the same sea-coast further north has been noticed above in connexion with Butmir in Bosnia (p. 114), and since we have also already observed the appearance of Balkan- or Thessalian-like painted pottery on the opposite shores of the Ionian Sea in the heel of Italy and Sicily, it is not strange to find with it peculiar projecting bowl-handles exactly as developed in these centuries in Thessaly and Macedonia, and among the Siculan painted pottery 'hour-glass' vessels of unmistakably Early Helladic derivation. Helladic and Danubian, in fact, were not only crossed on the Greek mainland, but in extensions to the South Italian region likewise, and it was on the maritime fringes of this still rather obscure Balkan-Danubian-Italian province that the Aegean traders began the westward propagation of their material culture and modes of thought and custom.

For in Sicily the distinctive painted pottery to which the 'hour-glass' mugs belong comes, together with the island's first signs of the use of copper, from rock-cut tombs [1] almost exactly similar to those of South Greece and Euboea: oval or round chambers, entered by a pit or an adit running

[1] Fig. 16, *c*,

downwards or inwards from a rising cliff-face, through a narrow portal or window closed with a sealing-slab. And collective burial was the custom: up to a hundred dead have been found in one tomb, deposited successively, with fire and funeral feast, apparently after reservation elsewhere (or even deliberate stripping) had removed the corruptible flesh. The tombs were grouped in cemeteries, of which Castelluccio near Syracuse is a well-known example; Monte Racello, not far off, exemplifies also the natural cave-tombs which were in like use, and in two further cases tombs of analogous form built of big stone slabs, with a window-entry in one end. In South Italy the rock-cut and slab-built sepulchres are similar in form and burial-rite, and the Aegean inspiration of the whole complex is shown not only in these characters but by some of the grave-goods: as well as 'hour-glass' mugs, there are two-handled cups from Sicily, and the mainland too; some of the copper ornaments, e.g. of double-spiral form, look the same way, and contact with Troy II is attested by a knob-like type of weapon-pommel familiar there, by ornamented strip-plaques (rendered in copper), and by bone ornaments with the peculiar relief-decoration of a row of bosses sculptured amid an incised pattern, identically matching specimens believed to be from that city's middle phase, that is, towards 2400 B.C. These 'Chalcolithic' civilizations (so called, like their earlier counterpart in Anatolia (p. 76), from their use of copper with a strong survival of stone and flint—that of Sicily is further distinguished as 'Siculan I') had, it is true, a long life thereafter, but their inception well before the outgoing third millennium seems thus difficult to deny, despite the fact of their continuance as late as the middle of the second. We shall find that the Middle Minoan culture, to be reached in a later chapter, turned its back on the West, and before Late Minoan times and the equally late arrival of Bronze Age civilization down the Italian peninsula, there was nothing to modify or disturb the culture implanted by these early colonists.

A more extreme case of dependence on seaborne contacts, leading not merely to stagnation but cultural death once Aegean shipping had ceased to ply westward, is the wonderful early civilization of Malta. Its genesis is proverbially mysterious, but three facts stand out from which its place in our picture of Mediterranean origins may at least be guessed. The first and most famous is that, though Malta has its rock-cut tombs like Sicily, its chief monuments are not tombs but temples. The great stone-built structures of Hagiar Kim, Mnaidra, and Hal Tarxien, with the Gigantea in Gozo near by, betray both in their design (Fig. 16, *g*) and their contents the practice of a complicated cult, while the enormous rock-cut Hypogeum of Hal Saflieni, which reproduces similar features below-ground, was likewise a great shrine before becoming an ossuary for innumerable human remains. Yet their plan, essentially a sort of court approached through a portal and branching into lateral and terminal apses, is just that of a rock-cut tomb enlarged, as at times in Sicily and more strikingly (p. 155) in Sardinia, by multiple extensions of the chamber, and the corbelled vaulting of the apses answers precisely to that of a Cretan tholos-tomb. We are reminded that at Arpachiyah (p. 149) the tholoi were not tombs but rather temples, and the notion that in Malta we have a remote elaboration of the same Near-Eastern temple-form which in the Aegean was turned to sepulchral uses is supported by what these structures have yielded. Animal figures in bas-relief have a distinctly Near-Eastern look; stone phalli are Asiatic rather than Aegean; the corpulent female statues and statuettes of the Mother-Goddess (Pl. V, 1) are everywhere based on rotund forms untouched by Aegean convention, which look straight to the Asiatic mainland, and outside it have their closest parallels in the Thessalian Neolithic derived above (p. 80) ultimately from the Tell Halaf culture to which Arpachiyah belongs, the whole character of the cult, with its abundant animal sacrifices, peculiar votive offerings, ritual hearths, stone altars, and oracular chambers, carries a complexity foreign to Early Aegean practice. In the second place, the pottery, with its superb paste and polish, suggests, as the excavator of Arpachiyah has himself remarked, a Near-Eastern tradition, and though some of the forms, especially big conical-necked jars, recall Early Cycladic models, the 'bucchero' finish and finely incised ornament remind one of the Anatolian-derived style of pre-Minoan Crete, while the 'tunnel' handle (Pl. V, 2), suggesting derivation from a type devised for of a stone vessel, has relatives in Crete and the Cyclades and no less at Anatolian Troy and Thermi, and splayed and especially pedestalled bowl-forms recall the same Thessalian Neolithic as the statuettes. It looks as if an Asiatic migration, related to the Thessalian but crossed with an already Mediterranean element reflecting the implantation of tholos-architecture in Crete, had passed on westward to colonize Malta as a sort of Sacred Isle, at a date which its independence of parallel Aegean developments argues to be not later than 3000 B.C.

The third point which strongly confirms this high initial dating is the absence of all trace of metal from the culture: it inevitably suggests beginnings early enough to be here beyond reach of metal, and so requiring an exclusive reliance on stone tools which became protected by a ritual tabu. For the island's relations with Neolithic Sicily, attested in imported stones and Lipari obsidian and, recalling the suggestion (p. 84) of Eastern affinities there too, in some pottery-parallels with Stentinello, were succeeded by a much stronger influence from the Siculan-Italian-Balkan Chalcolithic, and metal finds would otherwise be inevitable when the growing maritime intercourse of around 2500 and after was bringing in not only Aegean pottery-forms and bossed bone ornaments like those of Troy and Castelluccio, but a Balkanic enlargement of the potters' decorative repertory in incised, hatched, and punched designs, coloured inlay to reproduce painting, and above all the spiral. The three temples of Hal Tarxien form a proved chronological series, and while the stones of the first are plain, apse-entrances in the second display spirals in relief (as do some tomb-slabs at Castelluccio), which in the third have been developed in a unique stalk-like branching design, reappearing not only on pottery but in the roof-painting of the Hal Saflieni Hypogeum. But all such reflexions of the outer world in the Maltese temple-culture cease after Early Minoan times; though some of the pottery from Borg-en-Nadur in the south of the island has a late look in its heavily incised ornament, the great temples were at last utterly abandoned, and when a Bronze Age cremation-cemetery of the second millennium was established over the ruins of Tarxien, their floors lay buried under three feet of sterile silt.   The Bronze Age pottery has reminiscences of Borg-en-Nadur, and Malta may never have been wholly deserted, but the cemetery-material as a whole really recalls rather the Bronze Age of Sardinia; and, indeed, before this gap of some five centuries which so plainly bespeaks the end of third-millennium seafaring to the Maltese sanctuaries, Sardinia was already closely connected with Malta, as with Sicily and Italy, in the intercourse which that seafaring spread throughout the Middle Mediterranean.

While Malta seems thus to have been an early outpost of Eastern religious culture which was caught up, in the centuries from about 2500, in the maritime activity spreading westward from its Aegean counterparts over all the Ionian and Sicilian seas, Sardinia had been first settled (pp. 126-7) by a primitive people of African origin, culturally akin both to the Neolithic Sicilians and to the cave-dwellers of Southern Spain.   To those little-known beginnings this activity brought a great increment of civilization.   No Oriental temple-tradition held the Sardinian field: the island doubtless gained prospecting voyagers' attention for its native copper and silver, and the culture thereupon established must have been Chalcolithic from the first.   And its known manifestations are at least as Aegean in character as those of Sicily and South Italy.   For the leading monuments here also are rock-cut collective tombs. Though widespread in the island and lasting even after the term of the Siculan Chalcolithic, this tomb-type can hardly have been introduced much later than the same initial date, about 2500 B.C.   The simplest tombs are identical with the Siculan or Cycladic, more or less hemispherical rock-cut chambers entered through a narrowing portal from an adit or stepped pit-entry; the complications best known from the great cemetery of Angelu Ruju[1] consist in interpolating an antechamber and opening subsidiary cells off a main chamber, often enlarged and angular, in which supporting rock-pillars were occasionally left; but the essential similarity of type is beyond doubt.   And when Early Aegean-like beaked jugs

[1] Fig. 16, *d*.

occur in the island, and the tombs themselves contain other vessels indubitably matched in contemporary Crete, amid a varied assortment of stone, bone, and shell ornaments, flint, stone, and obsidian implements, and occasional objects of copper and silver, the beginnings of the culture must definitely be classed as Chalcolithic and associated with the same sea-borne impulse from the Aegean—a conclusion clinched not merely by an ornamented strip-plaque but by marble statuettes copied from Early Cycladic models, and sculptured symbols on some tombs showing the sacred Minoan bull-head and the high-prowed boats in which these early navigators made their voyages. We may conclude that trading-enterprise was followed up before the end of Early Minoan times by actual colonization, and so add Sardinia to the chain of Aegean outposts established westward along the Mediterranean. The next early link in that chain is East Spain, which will shortly lead us to the Atlantic coast-lands, the British Isles, and even further away, but before following thither we have to emphasize that the Mid-Mediterranean region of Sicily, South Italy, Malta, and Sardinia served as more than a connexion between the Aegean and the Atlantic: it was the starting-point of offshoots branching away to the north. And an important part was played both by Sardinia on the west and by South Italy on the east in their transmission to the North Mediterranean mainland.

We have already (p. 128) anticipated the formation there of a cave-culture whose western province was North Spanish but which spread round the whole North Mediterranean mountain zone as far as Italy; in Spain, its indebtedness seems primarily to the African-derived South Spanish cave-culture, but in Catalonia and the south of France it was further influenced by the immigrant Western Neolithic described in the first section of this chapter (pp. 131 ff.), and this is likewise true of the Ligurian and Tuscan cave regions, where its typical plastic-ridged and finger-printed pottery is found side by side with the Western round-bottomed bowls. The natives of North and North-Central Italy are, in fact, found with that distinctive pottery (simply a crude clay rendering (p. 128) of leather vessels) even on the uttermost fringes of direct Western influence, and this derivative Neolithic culture occurs not only in caves, but in hut-villages in North Italy and as far east as the Vibrata valley. But there on the Adriatic coast it was within reach of the influence of South Italian civilization, to which primitive folk like those of the Monte Gargano were already reacting in local forms of Neo-lithic economy; indeed, the Vibrata hut-villages are paralleled by a string of others right up to the North Italian plain. And there the well-known discoveries of Reggio Emilia show yet a third influence, that of Danubian civilization inland to the north-east, transmitted from Austrian or Croatian territory across or round the head of the Adriatic by some contact like that of South Italy with Butmir and the Balkans. From these obscure beginnings civilization in North and Mid-Italy was thereafter stimulated by a more potent and direct current apparently of metal-prospectors and traders from Crete itself, and the Early Minoan II dagger-form encountered in this new province of Chalcolithic culture (Fig. 15, 3) may perhaps take its beginnings some way back towards the middle of the third millennium. We shall revert to this Remedello culture (so called from its famous type-site near Brescia) below; but it was the earlier inception of the North Italian Neolithic that provided the soil for its roots, and the Southern and Eastern influences manifest in that were meanwhile answered further west by those transmitted from Sardinia through the Tuscan and Ligurian cave-peoples, supplementing the effects of their primary Western inspiration.

The Ligurian caves have yielded square-mouthed bowls with Early Minoan prototypes, and a sort of hour-glass mug suggesting the Aegean forms of Siculan I, but with and beyond these, in North Italy and Tuscany too, appears decorated pottery derived from the native Sardinian tradition which had been taken over into the island Chalcolithic. As we have seen (pp. 83, 126), its repertory was one of incised design, related on the one hand to the Stentinello style of East Sicily and on the other to that of the South Spanish caves. The cross-hatched 'ladder-pattern' present from the first at San Bartolomeo (p. 126), and abundant at Angelu Ruju and other Chalcolithic tomb-sites, is found copied on the Italian mainland, and so also is the peculiar pattern of concentric semicircles which, as in Spain (p. 127), was probably likewise an original feature of the tradition. There are analogous concentric-curve designs at Stentinello, and the pattern passes over into the twin-eye motive which appeared early in the Aegean and embellished the eye-like openings of tunnel-lugs in Malta (Pl. V, 2). Tunnel-lugs identically treated in the cave of San Michele Ozieri confirm Sardinia's claim (p. 155) to Maltese connexions, and with or without this specialization the design reached not only North Italy, but the Western Neolithic population of Southern France. We shall shortly find it and its distinctive 'channelled' technique carried further west, with the Mediterranean rite of collective tomb-burial, in the opening-up of the Atlantic coast-lands, where the Sardinian contribution joined hands with its Spanish counterpart. But Sardinia's Mid-Mediterranean position is yet further reflected in her artistic repertory, for the incised pottery of the Chalcolithic tombs also displays handle-forms, hatched and fine-punched zigzag, chequer, and triangle designs, and even spirals like those of Malta, which, as there, seem to recall Butmir and the Balkanic element guessed above (p. 151) to have diffused throughout the Mid-Mediterranean region.

Cross-hatched designs suggesting this enrichment of Mediterranean style are likewise found in North Italy, and in great abundance in South France, where their sudden adoption into the hitherto purely plain-ware tradition of the Western Neolithic marks a fresh phase in that culture's history. To this belongs the stratum sealing the plain-ware layer previously noticed (p. 131) in the cave of Bize, and throughout the Aude, the Hérault, and the Gard the Western cave-dwellers are found enhancing their old plain potting not only with long multi-perforated lugs, but with triangle and zigzag patterns in fine hatched and pointillé work liberally inlaid with white and red colouring. Further, the style spread northwards up the Rhône valley, and finds its best-known expression in the similar decorated ware of the Camp de Chassey (p. 132). The same current touched the Michelsberg settlers in Alsace, and in North France, where there is a glimpse of it at Le Campigny (p. 133), it forms an integral part of the developed Western culture known from the important centres of Catenoy (Oise) and Fort-Harrouard on the Eure. We shall return to this culture and its subsequent extension to Brittany below; it marks the furthest limits of Mid-Mediterranean influence on the inland Western culture of Europe, and a date about 2300 B.C. is suggested not only by the Michelsberg synchronism in Alsace (cf. p. 137), but by the absence of its fine-incised pottery from the original Sardinian contribution to adventure in the Atlantic West. It was the 'channelled' concentric-semicircle design, accompanied by other cruder incised work only, that accompanied that (p. 173); and though the two conventions occur together in the South French caves, the way to the West must have been occupied by the carriers of those native Sardinian characters and the collective-tomb ritual brought them by the first Aegean voyagers, by the time that Italo-Balkan pot-styles, only then beginning their spread as far afield as Sardinia, became able to follow and find the way up the Rhône alone open to their bearers.

It is time now to return to the main stream of Aegean enterprise westward along the Mediterranean to Spain. Neither its direct northward offshoots like Remedello, nor the more indirect such as preceded Remedello up the Adriatic or spread from Sardinia so far northward into France, carried far with them the distinctive sepulchral practice of the rock-hewn or built collective tomb. Such tombs are not found in Italy north of Rome, and their spread from Sardinia up the Rhône can have been no more than a miniature affair (p. 167) till near the end of the third millennium; but it cannot be too strongly insisted that the potent religion which inspired this treatment of the dead was to the main current of westerly trade and adventure a thing as vital as in its own way the Catholic religion was to the Spanish adventurers in the Indies, Mexico, and Peru. Aegean religion and exploitation went hand in hand, and we cannot doubt that superstition and the awe of great magic was an essential element in mer-cantile success. In Malta we have seen the effects of that religion in perhaps its purest intensity, and Sicily and Sardinia have shown how its sepulchral ritual flourished most strongly on the main line of seaborne commerce. Now it has already appeared (p. 128) that the Western settlers on the Almerian coast of Spain had turned themselves from the first to their new country's resources of metal, and seem gradually to have entered into trading relations with the Eastern Mediterranean. When, in the middle years of the third millennium, Mediterranean trade attained its first heyday of expansion, Almeria was not slow to react to its effects, and here, as before, commercial activity and sepulchral magnificence show their maximum concentration together.   At Los Millares on the Andarax River, and Almizaraque on the Almanzora, rose great trading-citadels of Chalcolithic civilization, each side by side with a big cemetery of corbelled tombs, which combine the essential features of the Cretan tholoi and the Cycladic and Mid-Mediterranean rock-cut sepulchres.[1]   The circular corbel-roofed chambers, with antechambers and often subsidiary cells as in the Sardinian rock-tombs, are of dry-stone walling (sometimes plastered over), with three-slab or door- or window-pierced single-slab portals,[2] which may be multiplied in series down a long slab-roofed entrance-passage, for the tomb was most frequently built into a rising hillside, or else was covered, as very notably at Los Millares, with a large round cairn, making it in truth an artificial cave.   Within, burials might accumulate to the number of fifty or more; and outside, an occasional vestige of slab-wall remaining round part of a broad circle implies a sacred forecourt for ritual or dance.[3]   Thus the various elements of the Mediterranean sepulchral convention were united here in a particularly imposing form made possible by the wealth of the merchant rulers, and the magic hold of their religion over a superstitious people.

Both facts are alike attested by the contents of the rectangular stone-built dwellings in the Almerian fortress-towns, and those of the tombs, whether in Almeria or the extensions of the culture which they record in Granada and Sevilla.   The Aegean type of female stone figurine occurs, but is also simplified into flat plaque-idols of schist, and phalange-bones ornamented with the twin-eye design alluded to above (p. 127), embellished with concentric-curve eyebrows, arm-lines, zig-

---

[1] Fig. 16, *h*.   [2] As Fig. 16, *i*.   [3] Fig. 16, *h*.

zags, and chequers, embody the type afresh.[1] Shells include
Dentalium from the distant Red Sea, and ostrich-eggshell
beads and luxury- and cult-objects in alabaster, ivory, and
hippopotamus-tusk attest an Egyptian-African as well as Aegean
traffic for the gold, silver, and copper which answer them with
the riches of Spain. Though stone persists, copper was
freely in use for flat axes and other tool-types: at Almizaraque
silver was smelted from ores mined on the spot, and even
argentiferous copper-ore treated to produce both metals;
while the gold which is often found buried with the dead was
obtained apparently from native-exploited river-washings, by
barter against the magnificent flint-work in which the settlers
naturalized as Iberian the fruits of Egyptian tradition. Among
a variety of types, big tongue-like pointed blades with a
notch-flanked heel were for mounting at right angles to their
shaft as halberds, perhaps in adaptation to a Mesolithic 'pick'
tradition, and above all, barbed and tanged and leaf-shaped
arrowheads[2] were now made in great abundance, as finely as
they ever were in Egypt; the hollow-based type (above,
p. 130) is relatively rare in Almeria, but became a beautiful
speciality,[3] together with large triangular renderings of the
Early Minoan copper dagger, in the culture's westward
extension to Portugal, which we must now follow.

The Almerian corbelled tomb-type, reappearing in splendid
double-chambered form at the Cueva de Romeral at Antequera
near Malaga, and more simply as at Gor in Granada[4] or Matarrubilla in Sevilla, is no less well represented in Southern
Portugal, where the cemetery of Alcalá is the most famous in
the province of Algarve. Dry-stone work may be exchanged
for vertical slab-walling, but the long entrance-passage with
its portal sometimes repeated in series, and the circular corbel-
roofed chamber, perhaps with one or more side-niches, remain
essentially as before, both here (though pierced-slab portals
are not found at Alcalá) and up the Atlantic coast as far as
Cintra, with outliers beyond, and inland ultimately to Badajoz
and even Salamanca. And therewith the rock-cut tomb
reappears also, most notably at the great cemetery of Palmella

---

[1] Fig. 17, 2. [2] Fig. 15, 9 *a-b*.
[3] Fig. 15, 9, *c-e*. [4] Fig. 16, *j*.

near the mouth of the Tagus,[1] where the same convention of
long passage and round-roofed chamber (often duplicated in

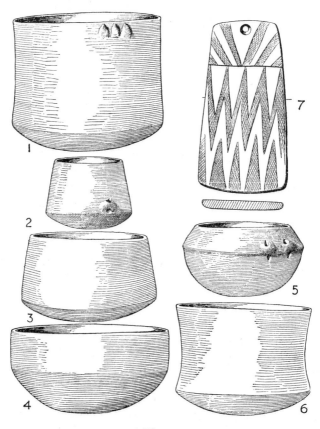

Fig. 14

POTTERY AND SLATE IDOL-PLAQUE FROM
MEGALITHIC TOMBS IN PORTUGAL

Neighbourhood of Arraiolos, near Evora, Alemtejo.
Scale : ¼.

series) not only answers to the corbelled structures, but
reproduces the essential features (including the window-entry)
seen in Sicily or Sardinia. The unity of the whole far-flung

[1] Fig. 16, *e-f.*

complex is sustained in Portugal both by collective burial-rite
and grave-goods, which include, beside the fine flint-work,
gold, and curious tanged copper arrow-points,[1] phalange-idols
and a notable series of schist idol-plaques (some of strange
crozier-like form), and cylinders, ornamented with designs
symbolizing their magic significance in hatched triangle,
zigzag, curve, and 'eye' patterns, and reflexions of eastward
contacts such as ritual adze-models in marble, of positively
Mesopotamian appearance, ivory objects among which is a
pommel-knob of the Troy II type already encountered in
Sicily (p. 152), and an Early Minoan II type of segmented
stone bead. Once again, then, initial dating should fall within
the middle third millennium, and the new trading culture and
its great religion can hardly have begun to sweep over the
Mesolithic natives of the Portuguese coast more than a
generation or so after 2400 B.C. There, as in Spain, it lasted
for centuries: as well as cave-dwellings there were substantial
settlements, and many generations used the collective tombs;
but merchant enterprise was meanwhile far from spent, and
in those tombs, Portuguese and Spanish too, appear not only
the products of Iberia and the East, but strange merchandise
of jet, callaïs, and amber from the North. However, before
pursuing so far we must pause in the hinterland of the
Peninsula.

The Chalcolithic expansion to the west was predominantly
coastwise, but its effect on the cave-dwelling folk inland was
bound to be felt, especially when its spread up the Atlantic
littoral enclosed them on yet a third side. The new culture
was not only a metal-trading one, but it was based on the
steady farming economy of the original Neolithic settlers in
Almeria, which now had its range greatly enlarged; and the
South Spanish cave-people were thus put into contact with
metal-working and agricultural life altogether. Besides
learning to use copper and improving their old industry in
flint and stone, they acquired seed and stock and began to
settle themselves in regular villages. For these the valley
of the Guadalquivir in Sevilla has become well known, most
notably in the settlement of El Acebuchal, Carmona, where

---

[1] Fig. 15, 9*f*.

with many polished stone axes and some flat copper ones, Almerian and Portuguese flint arrowhead-types and copper daggers of the distinctive 'West European' form of Fig. 15, 4, the old incised pottery of the caves is found transformed into a greatly superior fabric beautifully ornamented in horizontal and zigzag 'ladder' and hatched-linear patterns, often with white inlay, in which the old style is refined to a close rivalry with basketry models, and the 'stab-and-drag' of Boquique (p. 128) to a toothcomb technique of stamping 'hyphenated' lines.   In this ware,[1] finely polished and red to black, hemispherical and shallower bowls were made (some at Carmona even on pedestal feet) and the carinated Almerian forms answered by round-bodied splay-necked vessels, of a broad bell shape,[2] which gave rise to that most famous of West European prehistoric pottery-forms, the Bell-beaker.   Though bell-beaker ware is the Spanish analogue of the incised pottery of the Mid-Mediterranean, its originality is indisputable, and its makers' inheritance, through their ancestral cave-culture, of the ancient native traditions of the Peninsula is shown by their occasional use of schematized animal-forms [3] derived from the repertory of the old hunters' rock-paintings (p. 127) of Mesolithic and even Palaeolithic descent.   Indeed, the more easterly Spanish mountain-dwellers are to be credited with a whole cycle of rock-paintings of this Chalcolithic age, and the same animal-forms side by side with the Mediterranean 'eye'-pattern on pottery at Los Millares,[4] no less than the concordance in ornament between beaker pottery and the Portuguese idol-plaques, show that the relations between the hinterland and the coasts were not one-sided.   And while in the corbelled tombs of Algarve, Alemtejo, and elsewhere in Portugal outside the old cave-culture area, plain pottery of manifestly Almerian type (Fig. 14) reminds us that the coastal Iberians were bred from the Western Neolithic, some of the finest beaker ware known comes from the rock-tombs of Palmella,[5] and in Almeria, despite the enduring tradition of Western plain-ware, the bell-beaker even appears in the cemetery of Los Millares itself.

[1] Fig. 15, 6-8.   [2] Fig. 15, 6.   [3] Cf. Fig. 17, 9.
[4] Fig. 17, 1.   [5] Fig. 15, 8.

Fig. 15

EARLY METAL DAGGERS, FLINT ARROWHEADS, ETC., AND BEAKER POTTERY FROM MEDITERRANEAN AND ATLANTIC EUROPE

1, Flat copper axe (p. 88), Cyprus; 2, Early Cycladic dagger (p. 89), Amorgos; 3, Tanged dagger, Remedello (pp. 157, 253); 4, West-European dagger, of Ciempozuelos (Bell-beaker) class (pp. 164, 252 ff.), with No. 11 from grave of British B 2 Beaker culture (p. 268), Sittingbourne, Kent; 5, Chalcolithic tanged dagger (p. 307), Velefique, Almeria; 6, 7, 8, Primitive and developed forms of Bell-beaker, Central Spain (6, Avila; 7, Ciempozuelos), and ornamented bowl, Palmella; 9, *a-b*, Almerian; *c-e*, Portuguese flint arrowheads; *f*, copper 'Palmella point' (pp. 163-166); 10, Callaïs pendant, Locmariaquer, Brittany (pp. 163, 181); 11, Stone 'bracer' (p. 252), found with No. 4; 12, Tanged bronze dagger, British B 1 Beaker culture (p. 267), Sutton Courtenay, Berks.; 13, Bell-beaker from passage-grave of Quelvezin, Carnac, Brittany (pp. 182, 265-6).

Scales: 1-5, $\frac{1}{4}$; 7, about $\frac{1}{7}$; 8, about $\frac{1}{10}$; 9, all about $\frac{1}{5}$; 10, $\frac{1}{8}$; 11-13, $\frac{1}{4}$.

The native element thus incorporated in the trading and tomb-building civilization of the Iberian coasts was, in fact, strong enough, as we shall shortly see, to take part in not a little of its subsequent expansion. But neither seafaring nor the magic of collective tomb-burial was original to these people: their dead, when not in natural caves, they buried in pit-graves beneath a small round mound, and it was as landsmen that they were destined to make their greatest mark in European prehistory. The first stage in that destiny was the spread of their Chalcolithic culture from the primary contact-region of Sevilla, where its genesis must have begun by 2300 B.C., northward to the basin of the Tagus. Down this river, as well as directly from Sevilla, ways led to Palmella and the many other beaker and incised-ware sites of the Portuguese coastal civilization; but in the districts of Toledo and Madrid a new centre of the undiluted culture was formed, best known from the site of Ciempozuelos,[1] whence the same current spread among the cave-dwellers round the Upper Duero in Soria and Burgos. Westward and north-westward expansion, into Portugal and Galicia, followed in due course from all these regions, but within them the incised-ware and beaker folk were already fringing the North Spanish cave-culture (pp. 128, 156), and their next main movement, under way presumably about 2200, was across the Ebro and north-eastward to the further seat of that culture and its plastic-ridged and finger-printed pottery in Catalonia. And this whole stretch from North-Central to North-Eastern Spain soon became their starting-ground for the great Continental journeyings to be chronicled in the next chapter. But here meanwhile there is something else to consider, for, as we have seen (pp. 130-1), the whole East Spanish coast had been early sprinkled with Almerian colonists, and their expansion inland naturally received a fillip from the Chalcolithic advance of civilization in Almeria itself. Thus, while an inland Catalan cave like Joan d'Os, Tartareu, gives a fine array of plastic-ridged and finger-'rusticated' pottery, diversified by southern incomings only of 'ladder' and other incised work, the addition of beakers to these, as is well seen at the Aigües Vives Cave at

[1] Fig. 15, 7.

Brics, met the plain pottery and fine flint-work of Almerians pushing in from the coast. There, as is clear from a string of caves like those of Fonda de Salamó, the culture into which beaker immigrants were now likewise received was a mixed one, set up between the natives and the original Almerian colonists, wherein, despite the continuance of native cave-burials, the colonists' rite was interment in slab-cists. And while their inland push was gaining for this a firm hold throughout Catalonia, the new seaborne current of Chalcolithic culture had brought in to join it the chambered passage-tomb. A partial fusion ensued between slab-cist and chambered tomb, and this serves to introduce a new phase of our subject which is already overdue.

We saw in Sicily and South Italy (p. 152) that the Mediterranean rock-cut tomb might be reproduced by a simpler slab-built structure above-ground, where rock-hewing and the difficult technique of the dry-stone corbelled vault were each ruled out for lack of resources. There is no suggestion that these slab-tombs are necessarily a later class there—indeed, their rock-cut prototypes lasted the whole length of the Chalcolithic; they differ only as, for example, in the Cyclades (p. 149), different types of chamber-tomb do among themselves. Analogous slab-tombs answer to the rock-sepulchres of Sardinia, passing over also to Corsica, and though these are not satisfactorily dated, it is possible that such humble grave-building accompanied the spread of Mid-Mediterranean influence (p. 159) to South France and up the Rhône to the Chassey and Fort-Harrouard culture-areas, where a scatter of these tombs exists but has not been dated either. Sardinia indeed developed its own form of elongated gallery-grave, to which we shall return below (p. 194), but in general Mediterranean slab-tombs were probably buried originally in round cairns or barrows, though these are now often denuded away, and in this they resemble their greater brethren the corbelled tombs of Almeria and the Iberian coasts. An intermittent replacement of dry-stone work by slab-building in these has already been remarked (p. 160), and we must now follow this up by observing that with them, and in far larger numbers, occur tombs, under round cairns or hillocks, not only walled in passage and chamber with slabs, but with flat slab roofs both over the passage and in place of the less easily achieved corbelling over the chamber. In the Almerian extension-area of Granada, for example, the great group of tombs round Gor and Guadix includes 8 corbelled like that mentioned above (p. 161),[1] and nearly 150 slab-built structures, mostly of small size, which confirms their character as 'poor relations' in the sepulchral family. The passage may open into a polygonal slab-chamber, closest to the circular dry-stone prototype, or more frequently into a rectangular one, and this rectangular construction may also occur in big passage-tombs like the Cueva de Viera at Antequera, where the chamber is walled by four huge slabs, the front one pierced by a square window-entry, recalling (like many others in Granada)[2] those of Sicily (p. 152). There are also 'bottle-shaped' intermediate forms, with no proper chamber-doorway, and these, though as at Guadix often small, may also run to enormous size—the De Soto tomb at Triguera (Huelva) measures well over 60 feet, and at Antequera the Cueva de Menga some 70, with three central monoliths to support the huge slab roof. Such monsters are exceptional, and the normal slab-tombs of medium or small size may be assigned to the less wealthy majority in the culture's leading districts, the average size decreasing, and the relative numbers increasing, as one passes further into its poorer outlying areas. This is well illustrated in Portugal: the slab-built polygonal passage-tombs accompanying the large corbelled structures of Algarve in the south are many of them fair-sized; in the centre and up the Tagus and Guadiana into Spain, where corbelling becomes rarer, these form the great majority;[3] while in the poorer north and in Galicia, beyond the range of the art of corbelling altogether, sizeable slab-tombs like those of Barroso become rarer in their turn, giving place to small cairn-covered polygonal chambers with at most a rudimentary portico to do duty for a discarded entrance-passage.

These slab-built tombs, of whatever size or shape, are conventionally known as Megaliths, as being of 'big stone' construction, and it was formerly orthodox to believe that

[1] Fig. 16, *j*.   [2] Fig. 16, *i*.   [3] Fig. 16, *k*.

these had passed through an evolutionary history, the smallest simple-chamber forms, under the Celtic misnomer of 'dolmens', being the earliest, followed by the more developed 'passage-dolmens', and finally succeeded at an advanced Chalcolithic date by the corbelled vaults, after which degeneration led to 'long-cist' forms in which passage and chamber became indistinguishable. This evolutionary theory, well suited to nineteenth-century 'Darwinian' thought, was first propounded in Northern Europe, where the megaliths of Denmark and South Sweden do indeed display such a typological sequence, but the reasons for this, as we shall shortly see, are peculiar to that region, and twenty years ago it was already apparent that its application to Iberia presented grave difficulties. For while the 'simple dolmens' of North Portugal were claimed to be the starting-point of the whole European megalithic series, such contents as they have yielded cannot be placed earlier than those of the larger tombs, and among those it is impossible to distinguish any period-succession among the grave-goods. One can indeed say roughly that the poorer the tomb, the poorer the contents, but the explanation of this is not chronological but, as we have now seen, geographical and economic. Professor Daryll Forde, therefore, came in 1930 to the conclusion that 'the classical typology begins at the wrong end'. The long-accepted implantation of the art of corbelling from the Aegean was about the same time shown by Peake and Fleure to fit this view far better than the older one, and the result is that English scholars at any rate are now mainly aligned behind Daryll Forde's interpretation.

Let us then turn to the relation between Iberia and the megalithic regions further north. We have now one starting-point in the south-west for a long Atlantic sea-route by way of Portugal and Galicia, where the prospective adventurers were building chamber-and-passage graves ranging from big corbelled forms to medium and small-sized slab-built ones, the humblest dispensing with the passage altogether. But we have also another in the north-east, at the Catalan end of the Pyrenees and, as we shall see, beyond them, for a short or 'Pyrenean' route, across to the west coast of France, and here the burial-rite displays a fusion between the passage-grave and the simple slab-cist of the original Almerian colonists, which we have already seen (p. 147) disseminated this way as far as Brittany. We shall find reason to believe that this shorter route was the earliest opened from the Chalcolithic Mediterranean to the north-west and north of Europe, and that the 'dolmen' tomb-form which was thus the first to reach Denmark is to be derived from 'Pyrenean' sources, while the passage-grave people using the longer Atlantic route from Western Iberia reached the north somewhat later, to inaugurate there the second or passage-grave phase of the Danish and Swedish sequence. The third or 'long-cist' phase we shall find to be in large part of North European evolution, but yet including an element ultimately due to a subsequent development in the Mediterranean region of the elements already there before us.

3. TRADE, RELIGION, AND CIVILIZATION FROM THE ATLANTIC TO THE BALTIC

(Map IV and Table IV: at end)

The megalithic passage-grave was introduced among the cave- and cist-burying people of Catalonia (p. 167) by sea, and the best examples lie near the Mediterranean coast between Barcelona and the French frontier. All lie or lay under round cairns, and the tomb-forms, whether polygonal chamber with narrow passage as at Font del Roure,[1] or 'bottle-shaped' as at Mas bou Serenys, answer to those we have already encountered in South Spain and Portugal on the other side of the Almerian focus. They continued in use after the appearance of the bell-beaker, but one of the finest, Cova d'en Daina,[2] contained only coarse 'cave' and plain 'Western' pottery, and in view of the region's close connexion with Almeria there is every reason to suppose their first introduction early—perhaps as early as 2400 B.C. At Cova d'en Daina the 'bottle' is narrowed to an almost straight gallery, and this might become a plain oblong-rectangular gallery-grave like Torre del Moro, further inland near Solsona,[3] under the

---

[1] Fig. 16, *l*.   [2] Fig. 16, *m*.   [3] Fig. 18, *a*.

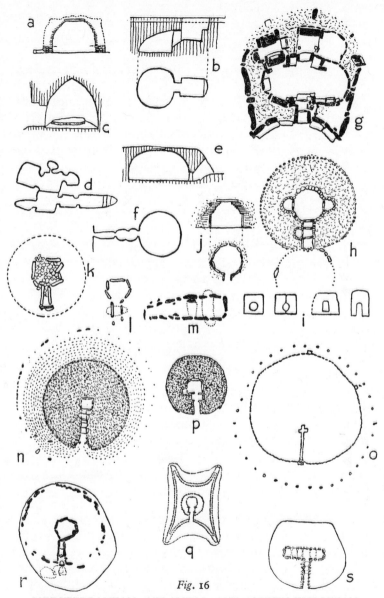

Fig. 16

MEDITERRANEAN, ATLANTIC, AND NORTH-EUROPEAN
CHAMBERED TOMBS, ETC.

a, Cretan tholos (conjecturally restored) ; Rock-cut tombs : *b*, Euboea ;
c, Sicily ; *d*, Anghelu Ruju, Sardinia ; *e, f*, Palmella, Portugal ; *g*, Maltese
temple, Mnaidra ; *h*, Corbelled passage-grave with remains of circle-fore-
court, Los Millares, Almeria ; *i*, Types of port-hole entrance, and *j*, Corbelled tomb at Gor, Granada ; *k, l*, 'Passage-dolmens', Cabecinha, Portugal,
and Font del Roure, Catalonia ; *m*, 'Bottle-shaped' tomb, Cova d'en
Daina, Catalonia ; Passage-graves : *n*, Kercado, Brittany ; *o*, New Grange,
Brugh na Boinne, Ireland ; *p*, Kenny's Cairn, and *q*, Horned cairn of Get,
Caithness ; *r*, Valla, Bohuslän, Sweden ; *s*, Hjelm, Moën, Denmark.

influence of the rectangular cist, which itself remained prevalent throughout the period. Some such cists are still the closed boxes of earlier tradition, but fusion with the passage-grave idea led to 'dolmenic' cists with an entrance open at one end, like Taula dels Llades, where the wholly plain 'Western' pottery is again consistent with a pre-beaker date. Further interaction between passage- and cist-forms could lead to the formation of a gallery of cists placed end to end, the transverse slabs being lowered to make sills or septa which separated the cists without blocking the continuity of the 'segmented' gallery. Puig Rodó near Vich is the Catalan example,[1] but when this composite but highly individual 'Pyrenean culture' spread westwards to the Basque Provinces, several other cases appear, side by side with closed and open cists and poorly rendered passage- and gallery-graves, and one of them, Arzabal, shows the strength of the original cist idea in being closed at both ends. We shall find this 'segmented-cist' form, in both closed and open varieties, further afield as we proceed.

On the Mediterranean coast the Pyrenean culture extended from the first past the east end of the Pyrenees across the French frontier, and there were analogous developments on this side of the mountain chain, though they are less well explored. The megaliths of Languedoc are thickly distributed all round the south of the French 'massif central', and though they continued to be used and made to a late date, the close parallels among them to the forms of their Catalan neighbours leave little doubt that their inception was nearly or quite as early. As in Catalonia, again, natural cave-sepulchres were still much used, e.g. in the Narbonne district, just as caves continued as the principal sites of habitation, but cave-tombs and megaliths were simply alternative forms of collective sepulchre within the same culture, and that culture's material shows it to be still based on the old Western Neolithic, with its plain and pierced-lug pottery, compounded with native 'cave-culture' elements on the one hand, and on the other now with incomings by sea. Of the latter a main source in Sardinia has already (p. 159) been suggested by the distinctive concentric-semicircle or twin-eye pattern grooved or rather

[1] Fig. 18, *b*.

'channelled', on the pottery of these regions, and this may be traced from the Mediterranean coast north-westwards, across the tributary valleys of the Garonne to the Charente district of the Atlantic littoral. In this direction, as we saw above (p. 159), it is not followed by the pointillé incised style which occurs with it in the South French caves, and its priority in association with the original current of collective-tomb civilization from the Mediterranean to the Atlantic is confirmed and explained by its evidently magical character. For from South France it appears, most significantly in the twin-eye form already noticed in Sardinia and further east at Los Millares (pp. 158, 164), not only in the fortified settlement of Peu-Richard in the lower Charente,[1] but in a megalithic tomb at Availles near by in the Deux-Sèvres, while in the same direction north-westward across Languedoc are found sculptured slabs, some tall free-standing stones but others forming part of megalithic tombs, on which analogous eyes and semicircles enter into the delineation of the same female divinity that we have found similarly portrayed on the plaque- and phalange-idols of Iberia. This corner of the Mediterranean, then, owes its importance as the start of our short or 'Pyrenean' route to the north to something more than the coastwise contacts with Almeria manifest on its Catalan side: with these, but acting principally on the French side in Languedoc, we have direct influence from Sardinia, whence prospecting voyagers brought the same religious ideas as were being diffused simultaneously and in the same fashion from Almeria.

Their route onwards to the Atlantic was, we have suggested, already marked out by the older Western Neolithic colonists as far as Brittany, and since the only form of sepulture other than simple trench- or natural cave-burial which these people knew was the slab-cist, a general similarity is natural between the South-West and West French megalithic tombs and those of Catalonia where the same was the case. The true passage-grave remains relatively rare, but both closed and 'dolmenic' cist-forms are abundant, and there are various gallery-graves among which the 'segmented-cist' idea shows itself, e.g. at

[1] Pl. V, 3.

Maranzais (Fig. 18, *c*) and elsewhere in the Haut-Poitou, and at St. Antoine-du-Rocher, nearer the Loire in Touraine, which contained only plain round-bottomed 'Western' pottery. The most famous and most highly developed segmented gallery-grave in France is that of La Halliade (p. 309 below), but its contents and its peculiar T-shaped plan suggest it to be a relatively late manifestation of what we may regard as an early-implanted idea, and the West Pyrenean megalithic group to which it belongs stands closer to the Basque province of the Pyrenean culture on its Spanish side than to the Languedoc-Charente-Loire distribution which is leading us towards Brittany. Nowhere in that distribution, from Languedoc to the Vendée and the Lower Loire, is it possible to propound a full chronological sequence of megalithic types; one can only say that the old slab-cist and the passage- or gallery-grave must have a long history of interaction during and after the latter centuries of the third millennium, while the 'camp' of Peu-Richard, with its multiple defences, the abundant industry in flint and bone accompanying its channel-decorated pottery,[1] its sandstone querns, and its remains of domestic animals, is virtually the only document for the Neolithic economy of small-scale cultivation and stock-farming which must have formed the staple of these people's existence. We shall do better to pass on to Brittany at once.

In Brittany it has already appeared that Western Neolithic colonists who buried their dead in slab-cists had settled in the country and effected with its Mesolithic inhabitants a fusion which is mirrored in the sepulchral 'long mounds' of the type of Manio (p. 147).[2] It would seem that the fresh impulse of trading-adventure from the Mediterranean reached here early, doubtless by sea from some more southerly point on the West French coast, while the land movement which we have been following up to the Loire was only beginning. For among the more imposing and 'dolmenic' cists which one would expect, as further south, to appear in this context, the semicircle pottery-design is found, at Penker-ar-bloa in Finistère, in a form of 'ladder-pattern' more Sardinian-looking than anything else in West France, while in Morbihan the

[1] Cf. the 'twin-eyed' perforated lug, Pl. V, 3.   [2] Fig. 18, *g*.

notable cairn-covered cist of Le Castellic has yielded primitive Western pottery like that of the Manio long mound, and including the 'trumpet'-lug already (p. 146) noticed in the answering Neolithic of South-West Britain. Such an early reinforcement of the Mediterranean element in the cultural mixture would naturally impel abandonment of the scattered-cist convention of Manio in favour of the concentration of collective sepulture at one spot in the mound, answering to the Mediterranean tomb-chamber. There are long mounds at Crucuny where this may have happened, and soon the long mound was being used in Brittany as an alternative to the normal round cairn to cover the regular megalithic passage- or gallery-graves which came in when the current of seaborne colonization gained greater strength. But before that the rite of unchambered long-mound collective burial was transplanted to South-West Britain, and it must surely have been the increase of new arrivals from the south in Brittany that provoked the migration of long-mound-burying folk across the Channel at just this point in the history of their sepulchral ritual, perhaps not long after 2400 B.C.

To what extent the British Neolithic A culture was already established at that time is uncertain, but in any case the bringing of the rite of concentrated collective burial in unchambered long mounds, like Holdenhurst (p. 146) or the timber-revetted Wor Barrow in Dorset,[1] can best be accounted for from this quarter and at this juncture, and in that form the 'long barrow' soon became characteristic of the British Neolithic A culture at large. Continued contact with Brittany thereafter promoted chambered forms of long barrow in the Severn-Cotswold region which are genuine megalithic gallery-graves (p. 184), but the earlier tradition remains manifest in their careful mound-revetment and at Notgrove (Fig. 18, *i*) in the curious internal dome-structure, Mesolithic in origin as we saw at Téviec (p. 68), still axially placed within as in the long mounds of Crucuny.

While this initial offshoot of the main north-bound current was spreading over the hinterland of Neolithic Britain, adventurous seamen began to explore our western coasts.

[1] Fig. 18, *h*.

There are a few long mounds from West Dorset to Cornwall with quadrangular 'dolmenic' tomb-chambers in one end, and a scatter of more in Wales, but some other such chambers had normal round cairns, and while vanished grave-goods make it impossible to say how early any of these were erected, or any of the unspecialized examples of quadrangular 'dolmens' in Ireland, the later dates which may most often be suspected need not make us deny early beginnings to this coastwise voyaging. The impulse behind it in the south began early and was continually growing, and while the occurrence of long mounds should mark the graves of adventurers of Breton connexion, activity from as far as the Pyrenean region is suggested not merely by round cairns, which may occur anywhere, but by cases of that 'segmented'-cist structure of which we have noticed and accounted for the tentative beginnings in Catalonia and West France. It is not certain if any of the few Cornish and Welsh examples of this are really early: the pair of big portal-stones which some of them have suggests the contrary (p. 196), but that the growth of the segmenting idea ran a partly parallel and related course in the British Isles and the Pyrenean region is probable from the similar ties between the two areas perceptible further afield. There are round-cairn gallery-graves of Catalan appearance in the easy South Irish landing-ground by Waterford Harbour, while in another quarter Cairnholy in Kirkcudbright, despite its late-looking portal-stones (p. 196), is likewise distinguished by its retention of the round cairn among the important segmented-cist group of South-West Scotland, inevitable landfall for voyagers up the Irish Sea. Nether Largie in Kintyre also has a round mound, but in the main this group shows the Pyrenean segmented cist locally developed to a specialized form in fusion with the Breton long mound. How near it stands to the single quadrangular cist is seen at Clachaig in Arran,[1] simply a septally divided pair of such: the number of compartments is never certainly more than four, and a good number of the tombs were enclosed in their long mounds without any sign of an entrance or passage. Of such the most famous is Beacharra in Kintyre,

[1] Fig. 18, *d.*

which has given its name to the group's distinctive family of Neolithic pottery.

This pottery consists of plain hemispherical and deep baggy bowls, the latter especially with lugs, and a related series, including also collared and shouldered forms, bearing decoration in shallow channelling and narrower grooving, with some amount of finger or tool punctuation. The designs include various forms of parallel-line pattern, most notably with alternating panels, and in a few cases, of which Beacharra is one, with the concentric-semicircle pattern. The technique and its pattern-repertory is comparable to the channelled style already familiar from South and West France,[1] while the sharper grooving is more characteristic of the answering patterns from some of the passage-graves in Brittany whose arrival was just now foreshadowed. Such passage-graves are absent from South-West Scotland, and one may thus argue that the establishment of segmented-cist-making settlers there was parallel to and not derived from that of the passage-grave settlers in Brittany. In fact, the passage-grave convention in South-West Scotland is manifest only in influence upon, and beyond in the Isles only in fusion with, the segmented-cist convention in its simple form; the Beacharra pottery is repeated at Larne on the opposite coast of Northern Ireland, and when later the strong North Irish Mesolithic population (pp. 167-8) sustained a more thorough Neolithic immigration from across the North Channel, both the pottery and the tomb-form of the immigrants turn out to be very largely of Beacharra derivation.

In the meantime the Beacharra and North Irish populations between them controlled in the North Channel the single approach to what lay beyond. The grave-goods other than pottery in their collective tombs, never abundant, yet show a material culture generally, though not in all details, similar to the Neolithic A of England, and that it was likewise based upon small-scale agriculture is shown not merely by a quern-fragment from one of their few known settlements at Rothesay, but more effectively by their geographical distribution, in which cultivable alluvium, accessible from

[1] Fig. 17, 5, 10-12.

the coast, clearly governs the choice of primary areas of settlement. The culture lasted long enough for expansion to secondary areas inland, and for the appearance in coastal regions of more specialized tomb-forms under the seaborne influence of the passage-grave convention; in fact, if its maximum initial date be put at 2300 B.C. its duration was something like 500 years in Scotland, and its Irish derivative lasted till still later. Such vitality is hard to explain if livelihood relied on no more than petty farming. We have seen that in the Mediterranean the parent culture owed its expansiveness largely to successful prospecting and trading in metals, and it is usually assumed that the spread up the Atlantic seaboard was prompted by desire to extend this exploitation to fresh fields. Brittany, Cornwall, Wales, and South and East Ireland all had metallic wealth to offer, and although working is not attested by positive evidence in these early centuries and its incidence must at first have been sparse and uneven, it is reasonable, as we shall see, to take its inception in this context for a certainty. But any lodes there may have been in Scotland and the North Channel coasts can only have been of the poorest, and something more is evidently needed to explain the economics of our tomb-building culture in these regions and its success in maintaining its individuality and its control of the 'North-West Passage' for so long.

The megalithic tombs of Northern Europe, centred in the West Baltic region and principally in Denmark, were introduced to our notice in the previous section. We saw that their serial chronology, made classic by Montelius, would not work when applied to Iberia, but the orthodox formula of dolmens first, passage-graves second, has in its Danish homeland an independent validity guaranteed, whatever some may say, by the serial chronology of their grave-goods. For, as will appear in more detail in the next chapter, the pottery distinctive of the simple dolmens has direct roots in the Ertebølle culture of the Danish Mesolithic, and attests their makers' membership of a widespread North European Neolithic culture whose typical 'funnel-beakers' may be followed both eastward into Poland and southward into a context of well-dated 'Nordic' intrusion into Danubian Europe. To make due harmony with that context, the adoption of dolmen-building by the culture's Danish branch cannot be dated later than the century 2300-2200 B.C. The passage-graves, on the other hand, not only introduce us to a pottery-series marked by radical innovation, but are tied by synchronisms of three different kinds to a date-span which cannot begin before 2100—synchronisms with the Central European Copper Age, with the Continental spread of the Bell-beaker folk from North-Central Spain, and with the great Corded-pottery culture of East-Central Europe, with its stone battle-axes and single-grave barrow-burial, which we shall soon find dominating the Continental scene. It is agreed that both dolmens and passage-graves must have reached Denmark from the West, and that by way of the British Isles; why then did they arrive in this sequence which in their Western home in Iberia does not hold good? The answer is provided by the duality of sea-routes from the Iberian region northwards expounded in the last section, and by the sequel to it now unfolding in the region of the North Channel. For the simple dolmens of Denmark[1] are not the mere 'poor relations' of passage-graves which we have seen associated with their greater kin in Portugal (p. 168): they are square box-like structures such as have been shown in Catalonia and West France to result from the impact of megalithic ideas on the simple slab-box cist. It is this 'dolmenic-cist' convention which was taken by the shorter or 'Pyrenean' route northwards, passing Brittany to the westerly coasts of the British Isles, where, expanding into the segmented cist form in frequent association with the Breton long mound, it distinguishes the first-established masters of the sea-route through the North Channel and the Isles beyond—the Beacharra people. And it is from the Beacharra cist, not from any more direct representative of the Iberian passage-grave, that the Danish dolmen draws its inspiration. Only later did the voyagers from Portugal by the 'Atlantic' route, having established themselves and their passage-graves in Brittany, gain sufficient hold on the 'North-West Passage', mainly through Ireland, not merely to influence and fuse with, but to turn the flank of the

[1] Fig. 18, *e.*

Beacharra people, and establish beyond them, in Caithness and Orkney, a strong colony to dominate the Baltic sea-route's vital turning-point at the Pentland Firth.   Only later, accordingly, did the passage-grave make its appearance in Denmark.

The Danish chronology, arrived at on wholly independent grounds, thus fits absolutely with the Western evidence.   For the whole suggested archaeology of our 'Pyrenean' route, from Catalonia and West France to Brittany and the British Isles, favours an initial date for Beacharra about 2300 B.C., which exactly suits an initial date for the Danish dolmens soon after if these are its derivatives.   And that they are appears in three ways.   The true Danish dolmen is a simple square slab-box with a big capstone but no entrance-passage: Beacharra cists only have entrances when the 'horned' façade, to be explained below, becomes added to them under what will be argued to be subsequent influence.   Segmenting is indeed unknown in Denmark; but we have seen it to be merely an optional augmentation of the cist convention, appearing only tentatively in the Pyrenean region and West France, and elsewhere, as we shall find shortly, only in combination with other features: in Scotland there may be as few as two segments, and the single cist remains the 'minimum' form throughout.   The absence of Western in favour of native Baltic pottery in the Danish dolmens shows them to be due not to a Western mass-immigration but to a conversion of the natives to the 'megalithic religion', so that it is natural to find their tomb-architecture of 'minimum' form and not fully understood. And this is exactly borne out by the fact that the majority of them have one of their four wall-slabs lower than the rest, a device to facilitate subsequent interments which can only be borrowed from the exactly similar septal-slab structure of a segmented cist.   And finally, while the round mound has been noticed in some cases as far north as Scotland and becomes normal for the single dolmen in Denmark, the more dominant Scottish long mound is there no less regularly repeated, in its original Breton oblong-walled form, especially where two dolmens are placed beneath it side by side[1]—a phenomenon itself reflecting the same 'combination-grave' idea as the

[1] Fig. 18, *f.*

segmented cist, in parallel fashion to the untidier cist-
aggregation which developed in the long-mound sepulchres
of Finistère. Reminiscences of Danish megalith-pottery in
Scotland (pp. 191, 320) and Brittany enter the picture in
due course.

Denmark indeed had no metals for the adventurers who
thus reached her coasts, but those coasts yielded a strange
and beautiful substance, amber, which must have been invested
with mystic attributes, special in virtue of its magnetic
properties, but, broadly speaking, of the same order as had
attached to precious stones and shells from the earliest days
of civilization in the Near East (p. 84), and were now likewise
credited to the turquoise-like stone callaïs, found probably
in Brittany.[1] At any rate, both amber and callaïs are found
in the chambered tombs of Iberia, whither they must have
been traded from their lands of origin down the Atlantic coast,
and we must now follow the West Iberian adventurers in
their turn along their 'Atlantic' sea-route to these same
north-western lands. The chambered passage-graves of
Portugal, with the so-called 'dolmens' which reproduce them
on a reduced scale (p. 168),[2] are so closely repeated in Brittany
that one can only conclude that a direct sea-route was established across the mouth of the Bay of Biscay. Several of the
simpler Breton passage-graves, such as Moulin des Oies,
have yielded the narrow-groove version of channelled pottery
noticed just now in connexion with Beacharra: the magic
semicircle-pattern must, as we have seen, have been already
current along the West French coast, but it is so frequent on
the incised pottery taken over from the South Spanish
cave-culture (p. 164) into that of the settlements and tombs
of the Portuguese Iberians, that these may equally have
brought it and its allied repertory to Brittany with them. In
any case,[3] in a tomb at Conguel it was stratified under a
secondary burial-pavement bearing bell-beaker ware, and as
there is only one Breton association of these two wares together,
it would seem that some time elapsed before the Bell-beaker
people became sufficiently well established in the West Iberian
megalith-building civilization to take part in its people's

---

[1] Fig. 15, 10.   [2] Fig. 16, *k*.   [3] Fig. 17, 5.

oversea adventures and come upon death in a foreign land. When that did happen, bell-beakers closely similar to those of Portugal were brought to Brittany,[1] while further points of affinity with those of North Spain and the Pyrenees may be explained partly by subsequent mediation through the Basque and South-West French extensions of the Pyrenean culture (p. 174), partly by the arrival of North Spanish beaker-folk in the northerly extension of Portuguese culture in Galicia, the last Iberian shore to be touched on the Breton voyage. The first beaker-men must have been joining in that voyage in the years after about 2200 B.C., and by that time the Breton tombs were beginning to display a rich variety of form and grandeur born of the union of the long-mound and cist and gallery-grave traditions with the passage-grave convention of Iberia.

Passage-graves like Mané-Lavarec and Kerlagard may have little slab-cists of the old sort embedded beside them in their covering round cairns, while others like Parc-Guren or the magnificent Île Longue tomb introduce the Iberian corbelled vault, over a big slab-walled chamber in a round cairn entered by a wholly slab-built passage; beside these, the purely megalithic passage-grave has its classic example at Kercado,[2] where the squarish chamber is roofed by a single great slab, the passage with smaller ones, and the dry walling of the round cairn's margin is answered by an outer ring of encircling stones. Such a chamber might, as in Iberia, be augmented by a lateral cell, as at Kermarquer, but there appears also the influence of the gallery-grave or elongated cist, often in its earlier-formed association with the long mound. An extreme example of the simple long-mounded gallery-grave is Mané-Roullarde; in cases like Mané-Lud such mounds are associated with true passage-graves with terminal chamber, but while the gallery might also be adapted to a round mound in its simple form, or bent at right angles into an 'elbowed gallery' like that of Le Rocher (Plougoumelen), there are also cases, under mounds long to oval in shape, where chambering was effected by building out transepts on either side of the gallery at or near its inner end. A good example of such a gallery-

---

[1] Fig. 15, 13.   [2] Fig. 16, *n*.

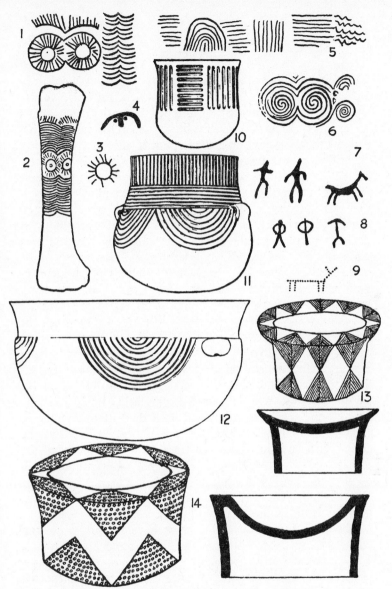

Fig. 17

ART-MOTIVES AND POTTERY ASSOCIATED WITH
WESTERN MEGALITHS

Concentric and eye-patterns and derivatives : 1, On pottery bowl, Los
Millares ; 2, On phalange-idol, Almizaraque, Almeria ; 3, On bowl, Las
Carolinas, Madrid ; 4, Painting in the De Soto tomb, Huelva ; 5, On
bowl from passage-grave, Conguel, Brittany ; 6, Spiral carving in the
New Grange tomb, Ireland. Schematic figures : 7, Painting in the Orca
dos Juncaes dolmen, Portugal ; 8, From Iberian rock-paintings ; 9, On
pottery bowl, Palmella, Portugal. Channelled ware : 10, 11, From caves,
Dépt. Gard, S. France ; 12, Passage-grave, Kervilor, Brittany. Vase-
supports : 13, 14, Stone circles of Er Lannic, Brittany.

Scales : 2, 10, 11, 13, about $\frac{1}{6}$; 12, about $\frac{1}{8}$; 14, about $\frac{1}{4}$.

grave with double transepts is Mané-Bras (Erdeven), and it is this type of structure which is most closely paralleled in the 'chambered long barrows', mentioned by anticipation above (p. 175), in the Severn-Cotswold region of Britain. In this period, when voyaging from Brittany was without doubt being intensified up our western coasts, contact with a Neolithic A population spreading over that region is to be expected, and the distribution of chambered long barrows within easy reach from the Severn Sea suggests how such advances in tomb-ritual and architecture were communicated to these natives. Such transeptal gallery-graves, in oval-long barrows, are typified at Parc le Breos Cwm in Gower, and Uley and Nymps-field in the Cotswolds: at Notgrove the type appears in combination with the old axially placed dome-structure (p. 175), now superbly stone-built and erected over a separate cist-interment,[1] while at Stoney Littleton in Somerset the grandeur of six transepts and a corbelled roof is accompanied by a septal slab in the gallery which betrays its underlying kinship with the segmented cist. There are also simpler Severn-Cotswold tomb-forms, and the group's later archi-tectural history will be noticed presently, but while the long-mound tradition maintained itself in Brittany, issuing in gigantic examples like Moustoir and St. Michel, where the closed cists within show no trace of influence from the passage-grave convention, it was that convention which dominated the Breton culture at its height, as it did the Iberian, and its further spread attests the fullest achievement of the Atlantic civilization.

Though copper axes and daggers have scarcely ever, and trinkets of gold have but seldom, been found in the tombs, which abound rather in highly polished axes of fine stones such as chloromelanite and jadeite,[2] the currency of the flat axe[3] and small triangular dagger in hammered copper is a certain assumption: such axes occur in small hoards near the West French coast, and smelting from the Breton ores must have been introduced from the south. While the region of Carnac on the Gulf of Morbihan is shown by its great con-centration of tombs to have been the main cultural centre,

---

[1] Fig. 18, *l*.   [2] As Pl. V, 6.   [3] Pl. V, 4.

both Finistère on the one hand and the Lower Loire and Vendée on the other received the passage-grave into their megalithic repertory; in time it was taken as far as West Normandy, as is witnessed by the great multiple tomb of Fontenay-le-Marmion, and though North Brittany is on the whole poorer in megaliths than South, activity on this side is well attested in the Channel Islands, above all in Jersey, which was then, like the smaller islands off the Morbihan, not yet severed from the mainland by transgression of the sea. The most imposing of the Jersey tombs, La Hougue Bie, has its big slab-roofed chamber fitted with branch cells on a cruciform plan, such as will shortly meet us in Ireland, but one feature of its grave-goods will serve to introduce us to a yet unmentioned element in the Breton culture, one derived from the inland French Neolithic of Chassey, Catenoy, and Fort-Harrouard (p. 158). We have seen how the pointillé-incised style of pottery-ornament had spread from the Mid-Mediterranean to South France and on to augment the plain-ware tradition of the earlier Neolithic further north; its most distinctive expression there is on a peculiar form of low cylindrical 'vase-support', apparently embodying the old south-eastern idea of the pedestal (pp. 93, 101), which, often with the addition of a saucer-top that made it vase and support in one, became a conventional article of tomb-furniture when westward expansion brought this culture into the ambit of the Atlantic civilization (Fig. 17, 13-14). Over a dozen were found in La Hougue Bie, and the pointillé ornament, almost invariable and (p. 316) long-lived as it was, seems in this context to have attained a ritual significance comparable to that of the semicircle pattern, which on one of them at Moustoir actually replaces it. But the style was, of course, not confined to these ritual vessels: its occurrence in varying forms on a full range of domestic wares at Chassey or Fort-Harrouard is repeated in the settlements of the West, of which the Pinnacle Rock site in Jersey is noteworthy for the stratification distinguishing an earlier occupation from a later one associated not only with a flat copper axe but with bell-beaker ware. The westward movement of Chassey-Harrouard people should thus have set in before our limiting date for

beakers.   Soon after 2200, the mingling of both thereafter
in the full blend of the Breton civilization is shown by the
well-assorted pottery of the Morbihan settlements of Croh-
collé and the fortified Camp de Lizo.   Space forbids the full
description of the people's material equipment, above all in
flint, but one element of importance is the honey-coloured
flint of Le Grand-Pressigny near Tours, which now began
to furnish a widespread trade.   It is abundant, for example,
at Fort-Harrouard, and its introduction to the West is attested
at the Pinnacle in the second phase and in the contemporary
Breton sites; we shall meet the same distinctively beautiful
Pressigny blades over wide areas of Western Europe, and in
Brittany fine examples occur in the tombs.   The pottery
includes beside bell-beakers finger-ornamented and incised
wares associable in origin with them, and while the channelled-
groove convention lasted beside the newer pointillé style, the
basic tradition of Western plain ware was maintained for
developed forms of carinated bowl, one of which is peculiar
to Jersey.

It should be added that the ritual nature of the vase-support
type and its specialization of pointillé ornament is further
shown by its association with the first distinct appearance of
the kind of ritual monument destined to have great importance
throughout North-West Europe, the stone circle.   On what
is now the Morbihan islet of Er-Lannic, and partly submerged
by the sea-transgression which subsequently cut it off, are
two circles juxtaposed, formed of stone uprights, which, like
many of the isolated standing stones of these and other
megalithic regions, had by them ritual deposits, in this case
of burnt material in stone-built hearths, recalling the fires
associated with the Téviec Mesolithic burials and the Manio
long mound no less than those of megalithic tomb-practice
and its Mediterranean original, with which were found vase-
supports[1] to a total number of 79.   A stone-enclosed circle
for ritual observance or dance may equally be seen in combination with the megalithic tombs themselves, and that in
two ways.   Remains of such circles have been noticed (p. 160)[2]
appended to the front of some of the tombs of Los Millares,

[1] Fig. 17, 13, 14.   [2] Fig. 16, *h*.

and it is a fair assumption that the area in front of a tomb-entrance, whether thus stone-delimited or not, had always a ritual importance. The alternative, of which Kercado (Fig. 16, *n*) has given us an example, was to enclose the whole of such a round-mounded tomb within a similar circle—a practice which, though it begot its own long-lived series of derivatives in the north and west of the British Isles, arose nevertheless in intimate connexion with the forecourt convention. For the forecourt, of which the yard or pit outside the .ancestral tholoi and rock-cut tombs of the Aegean and the Mediterranean is evidently the archetype, is in these circle-enclosed passage-tombs not suppressed, but given the form of a splaying-apart of the passage-entrance. This is well seen at Kercado; but a long mound could not readily be circle-enclosed in this way, and accordingly in the South British chambered long barrows the splaying alone represents the ritual area, giving the mound's end on the flanks of the entrance the form of a pair of blunt horn-like projections.[1] Its ritual importance, even in this form, is brought out by the fact that when degeneration in due course overtook the Severn-Cotswold tradition of long-barrow architecture, and its transeptal gallery-grave became as it were dismembered into a series of separate cists opening separately on to the side or rear end of the barrow, the splayed entrance between its blunt 'horns' still persisted as a ceremonial dummy. The Severn-Cotswold area was by then from the Atlantic point of view a cultural backwater; but a more drastic modification of the long mound to accommodate a fully fledged ritual forecourt, akin to the frontally appended circles of Los Millares, will soon meet us on the North-Western Atlantic coasts, where the megalithic religion was now powerfully reinforced through the colonizations undertaken by the devotees of the passage-grave.

The passage-grave family has no known members in South-West Britain, and in West and North Wales is uncommon and represented chiefly, as at Longhouse in Pembrokeshire, in the diminished form we have witnessed in the misnamed 'dolmens' of Portugal. Sometimes such tombs have had

[1] Fig. 18, *l*.

side-chambers, as probably at Plas Newydd in Anglesey, but Bryn Celli Ddu in the same island provides the leading Welsh example of a true passage-grave on the grand scale, with features including trench-set stone circles round the cairn-margin and a buried one of paired stones within, and the remains of a sacrificed ox interred in the forecourt-area. Of special interest is the ritual pit behind the chamber, covered here not by a dome-structure (cf. p. 175) but a recumbent slab, adjoining which was another slab bearing an intricate incised design, an isolated outlier of an art which is perhaps the most striking memorial of the megalithic religion, and has its three chief provinces in Iberia, Brittany, and Ireland. We have already seen (pp. 127, 164) how the rock-paintings of Southern Spain embody a tradition of immemorial antiquity in 'schematic' forms distinctive of this period, and these have their counterparts on the slabs of the Iberian chamber-tombs, no less than among the plaque- and phalange-idols found within them.[1] The extension of West Iberian civilization brought this same magic art to fresh expression in engraving on the rocks of Galicia, and simultaneously inaugurated the extraordinarily rich development which it underwent in Brittany, where an imposing number of the megalithic tombs bears similar decoration. Those of Les Pierres Plates and Mané-er-Hroëk are simply two of the most renowned on which this symbolism appears, with its schematic renderings of the human form, above all those comparable to the Iberian idols and the statue-slabs of Languedoc, of animal-forms, and amongst others of the hafted axe, whose place in the symbolism, distantly recalling the famous axe-cult of Minoan Crete, is borne out by the frequent deposit of fine stone axes in the tombs. The concentric motive already so often encountered on pottery appears in distinctive abundance at the great tomb of Gavr'inis, where it is modified in some places into a true spiral, echoing perhaps the incoming of the spiral into Mid-Mediterranean art (p. 158) which we have seen in culmination in the holy places of Malta. And the art thus manifest in Iberia and Brittany accompanies the extension of the culture and its passage-graves to Ireland.

[1] Fig. 17, 2, 4, 7, 8.

The leading Irish passage-graves are found in three geographical regions: close to the east coast, on hills rising from
the central plain, and in the north-west towards Sligo Bay.
In the first the most famous group is the Brugh na Boinne
cemetery on the Boyne in Meath, with the renowned tomb of
New Grange;[1] the second is best known from the Slieve na
Caillighe group on the Loch Crew Hills in Westmeath, but
may have outliers as far to the south-west as County Limerick;
while in the third, beginning beyond the Upper Shannon,
there have been excavations inland in County Sligo among
the tombs of Carrowkeel Mountain, but none as yet in the
coastal group of Carrowmore under the hill of Knocknarea,
on whose summit, looking out over the twin bays of Sligo and
Donegal, Queen Maeve's Cairn is probably the largest unopened
megalithic tomb in Europe. Close by it are the ruins of
another, displaying what must be half of a destroyed 'port-hole'
entrance—a version of the type we have seen in Iberia—and
the remains of a cruciform chamber-plan, somewhat as at
La Hougue Bie (p. 185), which stands out as typical of the
Irish province, above all from its employment at New Grange.
New Grange, in fact, with its arrangement of cells on this
cruciform plan round the high-corbelled main chamber, its
encircling ring of standing stones, and its huge round cairn
originally covered with white quartz pebbles, is at once typical
and pre-eminent, and both here at Brugh na Boinne and at
Loch Crew the extraordinarily rich engraving of the tomb-slabs
has the closest affinity to Iberian and Breton art, the spirals
of Gavr'inis being at New Grange superbly multiplied.[2]
Clearly the settlement of Ireland in this age of enterprise and
religion was no affair of a mere scatter of adventurers, but
a colonization by men who brought with them the full flower
of Atlantic culture; further, its affinities were not only Breton
but also directly Iberian, for Ireland has yielded a good number
of such flint daggers and fine hollow-based arrowheads[3] as
are typical of Portugal but not of Brittany, and the Portuguese
rock-cut tomb, on a small scale it is true, has been recognized
both in Galway, where further traces of the culture must
surely await discovery, and in the Wicklow Mountains, where

[1] Fig. 16, *o*.   [2] Fig. 17, 6.   [3] Pl. V, 8.

the settlers, whether or no they exploited so soon the copper ores further south to make flat axes like Pl. V, 6, probably discovered the alluvial gold which gave Ireland such an outstanding glory in the ancient West.

Passage-graves in Wicklow have been explored at Seefin and Baltinglass, and from Bray here at the corner of Dublin Bay northward to Dundalk was the coast, with the Boyne mouth in its centre, from which the colonization may be regarded as spreading, along the low ridges or eskers of glacial gravel that cross the central plain. But settlements in the plain are unknown, and though a complex of forty-seven circular stone enclosure-walls was found adjoining the Carrowkeel tombs, it is from sepulchral remains alone that the culture must stand to be assessed. The great passage-graves were no doubt accompanied as well as followed by lesser 'dolmenic' versions of their type, and that there were also non-megalithic slab-cist burials is vouched for at Moytirra in Sligo, where the associated pottery included true bell-beaker ware of Breton type. Perhaps also present there, and certainly plentiful at Carrowkeel and Loch Crew, is a cruder sort of pottery, ornamented all over with stab lines, often giving a 'rusticated' effect; in some cases the method is stab-and-drag like the Boquique technique of Spain, but the whole style is barbarous enough to recall still more closely that of the heirs of the North European Mesolithic, whether in the British Peterborough ware or its Continental counterparts (pp. 140, 201-2), and accounts cannot yet be settled here between Iberian and possible native Irish elements of North European affinities. Geographically, indeed, the Mesolithic Irish are ill attested everywhere outside the flint-bearing north-east where (p. 67) we have already noticed them, and whatever natives the oversea settlers may have incorporated, the exclusion of their passage-graves from the north-east is as remarkable as is that of the simple Beacharra cists previously described in Scotland just across the North Channel: an isolated cairn on Slieve Gullion terminates their northward distribution beyond Dundalk, and it was no doubt this vigorous north-eastern population that kept their makers' line of expansion deflected westward towards the Atlantic coast at Sligo Bay, away from

the North Channel route to the North and Denmark which
we have seen that they and the Beacharra people between them
must have controlled (p. 177). But from Sligo the barrier
could be turned, and though their traces are not to be found
in Donegal, both passage-grave and pottery reappear on the
North Antrim coast: the pottery, from sand-hill and sea-cave
sites, has been collected rather than excavated, but includes
unmistakable renderings of the bell-beaker and some very
Iberian-looking incised ornament as well as the 'stab-rusticated'
ware; and of the passage-graves there is a notable corbelled
example, Carnanmore, close to Torr Head, whence one could
set sail for the Hebrides and beyond without touching the
North Channel. And in the Hebrides the known tombs are
predominantly round-cairned passage-graves likewise, while
beyond in Caithness and Orkney a magnificent assemblage of
kindred tombs shows how their builders settled on both
sides of the Pentland Firth, and thus secured a gateway of
their own to the North Sea passage to Denmark, where their
entry into the field is marked by the appearance, among the
dolmens derived from their predecessors' cists, of the passage-
grave once more, in the century or so before 2000 B.C.

We shall find presently (p. 216) that while the Danish
passage-grave pottery belongs basically to a North German
family, it shows also numerous traits of Iberian derivation,
and the Danish-looking impressed-cord ornament of a vessel
from Doune in Perthshire, to which certain sherds suggest
parallels in Ireland, could betoken a reflex influence that may
even have reached Portugal. But the typical pottery of the
Orkney and Caithness tombs, named, after one of them in
Orkney, Unstan ware, is a distinctive variant of the Western
family in which stab-and-drag technique, as in Ireland, is
used together with plain line-incision, normally on large
wide carinated bowls recalling some Breton examples in
form, for patterns usually of alternating hatched triangles,
which are evidently the outcome of similar alternating arrangements of the concentric-curve design first seen in Scotland
at Beacharra (p. 177). The clue to what this implies is supplied
by the Hebrides, where this development opens on generically
Beacharra pottery like that of Eilean na Tighe in North Uist,

and must reflect a fusion between Beacharra folk and the Passage-grave newcomers from Ireland which is more clearly reflected in the form of Hebridean tombs like Clettraval in the same island or Rudh' an Dunain in Skye, incorporating the segmented-cist tradition of Beacharra into the passage-grave convention. The Passage-grave people thus incorporated Beacharra elements into their northern settlements when once they had intruded upon their north-western sea-route, and it is reasonable to assign to the same period those segmented cists in the Beacharra homeland in South-West Scotland which are not simply enclosed in their long mounds, but are brought to conform more closely to standard megalithic funeral-practice by having an entrance, like that of the passage-graves. But before these the Caithness-Orkney tombs beyond them must be described.

The Iberian inspiration of their architecture is not open to doubt. Indeed, recent work on the Orkney cairns has transcended the Iberian evidence by showing that the exterior no less than the passage and chamber within could be a carefully finished work of faced dry masonry. The finest tomb in Orkney, and indeed in all the British Isles, is Maes Howe, with its cruciform slab-walled chamber set about with three square niche-like cells and crowned by a high corbelled vault under its great round ditch-girt cairn. The slabs used are enormous; the 54-foot passage has portal-jambs at two points, and the resemblance, closer even than in Ireland, to the Iberian architecture of Antequera, Alcalà, and Los Millares itself (pp. 160 ff.), is repeatedly upheld both in Orkney and in round-cairned corbel-tombs in Caithness like Camster or Kenny's Cairn,[1] with their pairs of often slant-topped monolithic jambs demarcating chamber, antechamber, and passage. The Unstan tomb itself exemplifies a new tendency to lengthen the chamber—not surrounded by branch cells as at Quoyness on Sanday and elsewhere, but itself 'stall'-divided by similar pairs of jambs—transversely to form a T-shape with the passage: this T-form, side by side with the more original round, oval, or square-chambered plan, is especially distinctive of the derivative passage-graves of Denmark,[2] where the

---

[1] Fig. 16, *p*.   [2] Fig. 16, *s*.

convention had a parallel history of its own, running at times
to multiple chambering but omitting the Orkney 'stalls'.
Each province, in fact, of the whole great complex of tomb-
architecture developed its own peculiarities: in Orkney the
stalling becomes a dominant feature, and Midhowe on Rousay
there introduces us to its combination with the long cairn,
presumably derived by the culture from its Beacharra element—
the result being a sort of gallery-grave entered by a short
passage at one end, divided into no less than twelve compartments by stalls with benches between for the repose of the
dead.   Outside, the side walls are produced to flank terminal
courts, and in Orkney, and above all in Caithness, the device
of recessing a ritual circle-court into the face of the cairn
became adopted in extreme forms.   Thus the round cairn
became modified into the 'short horned cairn', the horns
running out to embrace the recess at both ends,[1] while the
adoption for passage-graves of the long cairn similarly horned
attained gigantic development, the 'long horned cairn' of
Yarrows in Caithness measuring as much as 240 feet in
length.

We have already seen how the appending of a circle-court
to the front of Iberian tomb-cairns is answered in the passage-
grave derivatives of Brittany and the British Isles by the
splaying-apart of the passage-entrance, and how the same
convention is embodied in the Severn-Cotswold long barrows
with their blunt flanking 'horns' (p. 187).   But the horns of
these northern cairns are sharp, to allow the forecourt recessed
between them to retain its full circular plan, the inward arc
of the circle forming a concave crescentic façade to the cairn,
with the tomb-entrance in the middle.   And it is this feature
which is paralleled in the Beacharra area of South-West
Scotland: nearly a dozen long-horned cairns are known on
the coasts of Galloway, Arran, and Argyll, where such a façade
fronts a segmented cist of the distinctive Beacharra type.   In
the best-known example, Carn Ban in Arran, the excavator's
plan even shows the vestige of a stone surround that must
have completed the forecourt-circle on its outer side.[2]   Thus the
ritual need of a forecourt gave rise to related forms of structure

------

[1] Fig. 16, 9.   [2] Fig. 18, *j*.

in all these different areas: while the other use of the ritual circle—to surround the whole periphery of a round passage-grave cairn—continued, as in Brittany, in its own context both in Scotland and Ireland, and gave rise there and further afield to the free-standing stone circles of the Bronze Age (p. 321), the wedding of forecourt-circle and long cairn made the horned cairn a well-defined type on our north-western coasts. Oddly enough, it has its closest parallel far away in the parent West Mediterranean region, in Sardinia (p. 167). In that region the concave façade had perhaps its own analogous history, appearing, for instance, in Malta in the third Hal Tarxien temple (p. 153), and again at Mnaidra;[1] and though the exact place of the Sardinian tombs in this history is not really known, their resemblance to those of the far north-west is striking enough to suggest that there may have been some direct connexion. They are known as 'Giants' Tombs', and while the nature of their primary grave-goods is obscure, they must presumably belong to some part of the period covered by the rock-cut tombs of Angelu Ruju, to which they are in a sense the counterparts above-ground; their long straight grave-gallery is unsegmented, and usually so narrow as to give the whole a sort of 'tuning-fork' plan, which the north-west cannot match owing to its continued retention of the big long-mound cairn already familiar. Thus the relationship between the Sardinian and north-western groups is suggestive without being sufficiently clear-cut for any definite inference, such as that the north-western horned cairns must on this account be given a priority of date over the simple unhorned variety. One can only regard them as, broadly speaking, the contemporaries of the passage-graves, and it is, in fact, the priority of the simple closed Beacharra cists that gives them their context in the sequence of events as here presented.

The coastal distribution of the South-West Scottish horned cairns reminds us that it was by sea that the whole culture's currents of vitality ran, and outliers of the horned-cairn group appear as far oversea as Pentre Ifan in Pembrokeshire and even as Ballynamona on the Waterford coast of Ireland; and both in Ireland and in Wales the more widespread feature of a

[1] Fig. 16, *g.*

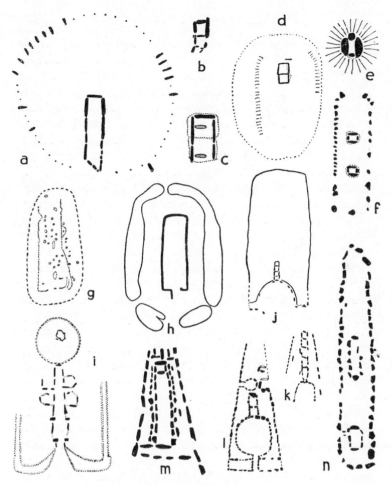

Fig. 18

CISTS, GALLERY-GRAVES, LONG BARROWS, AND DOLMENS
OF WESTERN AND NORTHERN EUROPE

a, Gallery-grave, Torre del Moro, Catalonia. Segmented cists : *b*, Puig Rodó, Catalonia ; *c*, Maranzais, Haut-Poitou ; *d*, Clachaig, Arran. Denmark : *e*, 'Simple dolmen' ; Twin dolmen in long mound, Valdygaard, Zealand. Long cairns and barrows : *g*, Manio, Brittany ; *h*, Wor Barrow, Dorset ; *i*, Long barrow with transeptal gallery-grave and inner cairn, Notgrove, Glos. ; *j*, Long cairn with segmented cist and recessed forecourt, Carn Ban, Arran ; *k*, Horned cairn of North Irish type, Cashtal yn Ard, Isle of Man ; *l*, Lobster-claw cairn, Creevykeel, Sligo, Ireland ; *m*, Wedge cairn, Labbacallee, Co. Cork, Ireland ; *n*, Huns'-bed, Emmen, Drenthe, Holland.

prominently large pair of portal-stones seems to carry on the same idea of emphasis on the tomb's façade in a shortened form, needing no built forecourt at all, which should be regarded, as again on the shores of the Solway (p. 176), as a late development. Cashtal yn Ard in the Isle of Man, with forecourt as well as big portal, marks the island's favoured position astride all routes across the Irish Sea,[1] and Northern Ireland now enters the picture as no outlier, nor any longer as a stronghold of obstinate Mesolithic aborigines, but as a new centre of Western Neolithic civilization in which the horned cairn attained a development of unique character. Geographically, the tombs cluster thickest round the well-placed 'fjord' entry of Carlingford Lough, and while simpler cist-forms, occasionally, as here at Clonlum, round- instead of long-cairned, may have accompanied as well as degenerately following (as in a remoter hinterland region like Tyrone) the main development, a standard form of horned-cairn tomb[2] has been repeatedly attested by excavation in recent years at Goward, Browndod, Ballyalton, and elsewhere in the north-east Irish counties. This is no mere repetition of that of South-West Scotland: the segmented cist-gallery combines the septal slabs of Beacharra with the lateral stall-jambs of the Iberian and Orkney passage-graves, showing that elements formerly distinct were here fused into a new unity. The pottery in these tombs belongs in good part to the Beacharra family, and the main impulse of settlement must have come from South-West Scotland as the previous situation (p. 177) would lead one to expect; but the prominence of broad carinated bowls,[3] coupled with the apparently total replacement in the collective burial-rite of inhumation by cremation, points to a secondary recruitment of population which can only, it would seem, have come across the Irish Sea from Yorkshire. This is a new suggestion; but the spread of British Neolithic A culture of Yorkshire type westward over the Pennines is attested in Cumberland not only by long-mound cairns but in the material of the lakeside settlement of Ehenside Tarn,[4] and its original inclusion of elements from Belgium (p. 144)

---

[1] Fig. 18, *k*.   [2] Like Fig. 18, *k*.
[3] Cf. Fig. 13, 3.   [4] Fig. 13, 3.

may possibly help to explain the 'Campignian' character (p. 133) of the North Irish flint-work of this period, for example at the Rathlin Island site of Ballynagard. Thus Neolithic settlers succeeded to the old hunting-grounds of the Mesolithic natives, introducing tillage and stock-farming, such as one must suppose accompanied the Continental passage-grave colonists further south against whose achievement of dominance, already here traced, this whole movement must be set. The natives fell back inland, mainly upon the valley of the Bann, where under Neolithic influence they developed the distinctive 'Bann River culture', characterized by a maturity of their old traditions of stone and flint-work in which tanged flint points are an outstanding feature. The reappearance of these in the Isle of Man, and within Ireland the evidence recently enlarged on for a specialized tradition of salmon-fishing, are individual points within the truth that here, on the far edge of Europe, native survival always remains to offset the effects of intrusive colonization. Yet the horned-cairned intruders, like the Passage-grave people, did not fail to spread west: they even reached the edge of the passage-grave concentration-area in Sligo, and there as in Donegal their tombs attest the continued ritual importance among them of the circular forecourt by a peculiar structural development: the horns become 'lobster-claws' entirely enveloping the circle, as at Creevykeel[1] or Malinmore, and finally the well-known Deerpark tomb near Sligo itself shows a confronted duplication of the plan in which the 'claws' join to surround a single circle-court in the centre. The forms of the megalithic religion had indeed a tenacious hold of its votaries' minds.

One form of Irish tomb alone remains to be noticed: the 'wedge-shaped' cairn, a long cist or simple gallery-grave entered from one end, often through a 'port-hole' window-entry.[2] Its distribution is southern and western but includes South-Central Ulster, and what little is known from excavation points to a late date; it may be a simplified derivative of the segmented cist, but it has been suggested, on the strength especially of the 'port-hole', that this type represents a direct extension by way of Brittany of a distinctive group of port-

---

[1] Fig. 18, *l*.   [2] Fig. 18, *m*.

holed long cists in North France in the Paris basin, broadly speaking east of the Fort-Harrouard culture-area, round the Seine, Oise, and Marne. The people who took to making these cists were no branch of the true Western Neolithic stem: their coarse flat-bottomed bucket-pots[1] are something quite different and seem to represent the individual expression by Late Mesolithic folk of the pot-making idea, drawn from true Neolithic neighbours with whom they at first shunned actual contact. The Mesolithic character of their flint, horn, and bone work is indisputable, and in the next chapter we shall find the same material culture characteristic of a fresh group of pile-dwellers on the Alpine lakes, before whose entry south-eastward into Switzerland from this part of France the old Cortaillod folk retreated, as we have already seen (p. 136). Here it is known as the Horgen culture, and while it may be assigned a simple version of the same sort of cist-grave at Aesch near Basel, its people escaped the main impact of 'megalithic religion' which invaded their North French kinsmen. The source of this was the south, where in the period just before 2000 B.C. new activity, centred once more probably in Sardinia but reflected likewise in the Balearic Isles, manifested itself in great underground tombs, the best known near Arles,[2] whence the Seine-Oise-Marne forms may most plausibly be derived. For the long port-holed cists there are also underground,[3] and in the chalk country of the Marne they are replaced by artificial grotto-tombs cut in the chalk, on whose walls reappears the now familiar goddess of the statue-slabs and idols. It is now generally recognized that this culture in its turn was borne westward to join in the great amalgam of Brittany: not only do the bucket-pots intrude there among the round-bottomed Western fabrics, but the tomb-form also. The long cists of Kerlescant in the Morbihan and of Le Couperon in Jersey are two well-known examples, and on the slabs of another at Tressé, Ille-et-Vilaine, are sculptured the breasts of the goddess just as on the grotto-walls of the Marne or the statue-slabs whether of Languedoc or Guernsey. It is possible, then, that the Irish wedge-cairns were brought in from this quarter, but is far from certain.

[1] Fig. 11, 11.   [2] P. 263, Fig. 22, 5.   [3] Fig. 22, 6.

And the Seine-Oise-Marne cists have what seem to be closer, and are sensibly more important, relatives in quite the opposite direction, in West Germany, and in Denmark and Sweden.[1] The latter are, in fact, a component of the third great member of the classical megalith-series of Northern Europe, introduced at the end of the previous section (p. 170). How they were brought to the West Baltic lands is a question on which we can only embark when much that intervenes has been described not only in Northern but in Central and Eastern Europe.

Thither we must now turn, looking back on a civilization in the West created first by the introduction of the Neolithic arts on village-life, handicraft, and agriculture from North Africa, ultimately perhaps from Egypt, by way of the southwest, and the reaction thereto of native cave-dwelling and Mesolithic peoples, and then by the great spread of maritime enterprise, from the middle of the third millennium onwards, from the Eastern Mediterranean and the Balkans to Sicily and South Italy, to Sardinia, and to the first landing-ground of the Neolithic cultivators in Spain, whence not only was civilization brought to the cave-people of the Spanish hinterland, but the ways of commerce and metal-working were carried by a Pyrenean and more powerfully by an Atlantic route to all the coast-lands of the north-west, accompanied by a Mediterranean-Eastern religion, the power of whose magic explains the adventurers' success, and has its monument in the amazing series of great sepulchres which we have now followed right round to the distant coasts of the Baltic Sea.

[1] Fig. 22, 7.

Chapter Six

MIGRATION, CONFLICT, AND CHANGE

I. THE NORTHERN NEOLITHIC AND THE WARRIOR
CULTURES

(Map V and Table V: at end)

OUR last view of Northern Europe as a whole (pp. 60-64) showed it still a Mesolithic world. The shore-lines of the Litorina Sea had been peopled since before 4000 B.C. by the fishing and hunting folk of the Ertebølle shell-middens, while Late Tardenoisian food-gatherers still roamed the inland heaths, and the bulk of habitable Scandinavia and Finland knew only the primitive cultures of the 'Arctic Stone Age'. But in the third millennium the Danubian cultivators were settling in parts of North Germany and Poland, while rather later the West Baltic coasts were reached by the navigators from the Atlantic. The archaeology of Denmark and its neighbourhood should show how the Northern peoples first reacted to the approaches of civilization, and in fact the centuries before and after 2000 B.C. record the development of nearly all the elements which made their culture the potent force it has ever since been in European history. It was formerly believed that a clear line could be drawn in Denmark between the native Ertebølle Mesolithic and a Neolithic civilization marked by the introduction of the 'dolmens' by sea from the West, at a date usually estimated at about 3000 B.C. The last chapter has shown that the 'dolmens' cannot be nearly so early, but we have now to realize that a mere reduction of date will not bring us to the real truth of the matter. It might be thought that the methods of geology and botany which have so clarified the Northern Mesolithic would fix definite horizons in terms of land-movement, climate, and vegetation-history, but this has not yet happened beyond a certain point. For while a steady regression of the sea from the Litorina maximum provides indeed a continuous relative time-scale on the more northerly Baltic and Norwegian coasts, the renewed encroachment which interrupted the same process in South Sweden coincides only with a fairly advanced Neolithic stage about 1800 B.C., and climate and forest-history shows a transition from the 'Atlantic' (p. 57) to the next or 'Sub-Boreal' epoch marked only by change in the composition of the 'oak-mixed-forest' which is not yet closely correlated either with land-movement or the archaeological record. Thus the conventional lower limit of the 'Atlantic' at 2500 is really only a maximum, and if the renewed sea-transgression in South Sweden be treated in conformity with that already referred to in the English Fens and Essex coast (p. 141), we should not speak of an established 'Sub-Boreal' till some 700 years later. But at any rate no sign of change in the Ertebølle culture is detectable before the middle portion of the third millennium, so that an upper limit of date not very far from 2500 B.C. may be allowed for change when it appears.

The first sign is an innovation in these peoples' bag-bodied splay-rimmed coarse pottery (p.61: Fig. 19,1). From the upper layers of a midden at Sølager in North Zealand come pieces of a number of pots with decoration,[1] not only in stab or shell-edge markings but impressions of a twisted or more distinctively a whipped cord, either curled round the thumb or applied in straight lengths, the latter tending to a parallel vertical arrangement which also appears in plain grooving. Similar finds, with greater variation, including more regular horizontal and curved cord-impressions and deep pitting as well as stab and shell-edge work, are thinly scattered between Jutland, South Sweden, and Bornholm [2] on dwelling-place sites with no direct Ertebølle context; but the clearest association with unmodified Ertebølle pottery and flint-work appears at Strandegaard in South-East Zealand, and not in a midden but among the stone footings of a rectangular log house, where occurred also bones of domestic ox—the earliest-known appearance of these marks of civilization in the North. Now it is just this peculiar style of ornament that characterizes the Peterborough or Neolithic B pottery already (p. 140: Fig. 13,7) noticed in the east of England.

---

[1] Fig. 19, 3 *a-b*.   [2] Fig. 19, 4.

Individuality here grows up in the frequency of finger and bird-bone marking along with the whipped-cord or 'maggot' and other forms of cord-impression, and the shortening and thickening of the splayed rim to project above a commonly pit-ornamented hollow neck and a carinated shoulder, which seems to be borrowed from the contemporary carinated bowls of the East English Neolithic A, in answer, as it were, to the B influence in decoration seen, e.g., in the pottery of White-hawk, Brighton (Fig. 13, 2).   That interchange, datable from about 2300-2200 B.C. onwards, implies that these B people were then already in occupation of their favourite dwelling-sites (like that of Peterborough itself) along the waterways leading in from the North Sea.   Doubtless the earliest settle-ments were submerged in the subsequent marine transgression, but since, anyhow, the culture shows no sign of admixture with what in Denmark accompanied the arrival of the dolmens by the north-western sea-route, this Baltic element in Britain must be early—roughly contemporary at least with the inde-pendent incoming of Neolithic A from Western Europe soon after 2500.   Our Late Mesolithic Halstow culture was first cousin to Ertebølle, and it may be that Neolithic B represents little more than the adoption by this old population of new arts brought by small-scale movement from their more centrally placed relatives.   To it, and to the related culture newly recognized on the Lower Rhine, we shall return below (p. 271), but its rise seems wholly parallel to the formation on a similar Mesolithic stock of analogous 'dwelling-place cultures' in all the Baltic countries.

The same sort of pottery, though with different individu-ality, marks those of Southern and Eastern Sweden, and just touched Southern Norway.   In the Swedish dwelling-places, cord-impressions are an early feature in the sequence of pottery-ornament; its main phases are the Åloppe style, with echoes of the vertical patterns soon to be seen dominant in Denmark, and successively those of Säter and Körartorp, in which regional independence is expressed in more shell-edge work, but also in replacement of the cord by a serrated 'comb'-stamp.[1]   And on the opposite shore of the Baltic in Finland,[2]

[1] Fig. 19, 3, *c.*   [2] Fig. 19, 2.

cord-impression appears only in the earliest Urjala pottery of the first sub-Litorina shore-lines, together with the same comb-stamping, which in the succeeding Jäkärlä ware ousts it and develops into the typical comb-pottery style of the middle strand-levels, reaching degeneration far on in the second millennium. This comb pottery is the characteristic ware of the vast forest tracts of Russia, and its southerly outliers overlap on the Ukrainian loess and black-earth borders with the painted pottery of the peasants of Tripolye (p. 99), but while shell-edge work accompanies it in the north and is found right down to the south also, it is South Russia which furnished the finest series of cord-impressed techniques, and their incidence can be followed from the Black Sea north-westward across the steppe and the dune country of Galicia and Poland to East Prussia and the Baltic coasts opposite the sites with which we began in Denmark and South Sweden. Those sites are earlier than the earliest in Finland and the Russian forests, and the conclusion seems inescapable that the primitive north-easterly and forest folk, learning of pottery from their neigh-bours to the south-west, adopted a simple decorative device like shell-edge work but replaced by comb-stamping the cord-impression which they did not understand and had not the spun hair or wool thread to make. It is along the belt of relatively open country from the Black Sea to the Vistula mouth that cord-impression appears as the potters' primary technique, and it may be argued that the Mesolithic neighbours of the Tripolye peasantries, settling to pastoralism and learning of pottery and spinning together, took to decking both them-selves and their pots with the same sort of twisted neck-bands. Dwelling-place sites with this cord-impressed pottery are extremely numerous in the whole steppe-region of the Dnieper, and only less so over the dune-lands further north-west towards the Baltic; and though the site at Oussatova near Odessa on which the technique has been most closely studied has suggestions of contact not with the original Tripolye culture but with its second phase nearer the end than the middle of the third millennium, yet the convention may well by then have been long established, and the Baltic evidence speaks unequivocally for an earlier date. We may conclude that in the period centred on 2500 B.C. the peasant civilizations of the Ukraine and Poland awoke their Mesolithic neighbours over a wide stretch of country between the Black Sea and the region of the Vistula to a rudimentary pastoral Neolithic culture, archaeologically best marked by this peculiar pottery-ornament, which reacted directly on the Ertebølle people of the Western Baltic and their periphery of allied groups as far west as the Lower Rhine and Britain, and eastwards became more gradually reflected among the fishermen and hunters with their comb ware in Finland and the inner forests of Russia. In the east and the whole northern periphery of this diffusion pottery was previously unknown, so that the pots appear in simple bag and basket forms and the largely horizontal schemes of impressed ornament show direct influence from basketry patterns, pitting being added from the repertory of Mesolithic wood-work. But in the Ertebølle area the existing pottery tradition was able to hand on the splayed neck to be standard-ized in the characteristic form known as the funnel-beaker (Fig. 19, 4-6; Pl. VII, 1), whose typically vertical scheme of ornament was probably inspired by the shoulder-stitching necessary on the corresponding form in leather.

The peoples of the northern periphery remained as yet impervious to the advance of the essentially Neolithic arts of food-producing. Even pot-making was very slowly diffused in Norway, and flint, stone, and bone work combined gradual adoptions from the south with long retention of old forms such as the Mesolithic tanged point (p. 57), which had a long survival from the days of the Fosna culture on the West Norwegian coast in the Garnes type of dwelling-place and corresponding sites in Sweden. Indeed, the more civilized Danish and West Baltic population later took over a form of tanged arrowhead from this tradition among their northern neighbours.

Just as the Northern hunters and fisherfolk had borrowed elements like the Lihult or Nøstvet axe (p. 61) from the Ertebølle culture, so now they borrowed from that culture's successors; more advanced types of axe and other implements were imported and translated into local materials, especially into slate, while a regular trade grew up in Danish and South

Swedish flint, and even amber. But the 'Arctic Stone Age' remained one of hunting and fishing culture: stock-farming and agriculture were still foreign to these peoples' way of life, and it is to these centuries, on the evidence of shore-line associations, that the Scandinavian hunting art already alluded to (p. 62) attained its most advanced expression in animal rock-carvings. To the oldest group, the simple naturalistic work of the Central and North Norwegian districts, now succeed related styles still marked by some naturalism in the Oslo region, but more schematic in the west and in Central Sweden; the figures, of elks and other game, at times accompanied by human forms, are rendered in pecked outline, normally on a waterside rock-face, and their bodies are often filled in with complicated markings, sometimes evidently representing internal organs (Pl. VI, B). Thus can we recognize the summer mountain hunting-grounds of the Arctic folk who in winter would return to the lower levels where their dwelling-places are most frequently found. But all this stands in contrast to the development centred upon Denmark.

There the dwellers in the log houses first revealed at Strandegaard came to adopt not only cattle-farming but agriculture, and therewith embarked upon the creation, on the old Ertebølle foundation, of a distinctive Neolithic civilization of their own. Whence skill and seed for husbandry were brought is not yet fully clear. Domestication of animals, spinning from their coats, and pot-decoration with the spun cord seem to form an interdependent complex for which the pottery evidence points to the south-east, and though agriculture is absent from that initial connexion, there were now Danubian peasant settlements in Pomerania and from Poland and Silesia across Central Germany to Hanover and beyond, and contacts here would seem to be far the likeliest explanation. The earliest signs of corn in Denmark are two grain-impressions on potsherds, one of emmer wheat from the Sølager midden, the other of little-wheat from one at Brabrand in Jutland, and both these varieties were grown by the Danubians: finds of a few stray 'shoe-last' hoes and of possibly related axe-forms point the same way, though the stone-bladed hoe or plough was never adopted in the North, where such evidence as there is suggests an original-one-piece implement of wood. Just when these particular middens were abandoned we do not know, but such grain-impressions become relatively frequent on pottery typical of the period of the dolmens. Indeed, it has often been believed that agriculture and the dolmen were introduced together, but the apparent absence of little-wheat from the Neolithic West and of all trace of Western colonization in the North, supports the contrary view here taken. In fact, the material culture of the Northern Neolithic, including the pottery which the dolmen finds exemplify, must have been fully formed when the Western navigators first made the Baltic voyage. For that pottery consists simply of the native funnel-breaker already seen developing at Sølager and Strandegaard (Fig. 19, 4), together with straighter-necked 'amphora' forms with shoulder-lugs (cf. Fig. 19, 7) and flasks most normally represented by a type having a narrow neck with a projecting collar-band (Pl. VII, 2), implying a native leather-bottle prototype with a nozzle in wood or deer-horn. Fragments of these collared flasks have been found at a dwelling-site at Havnelev in Zealand with just the same Ertebølle-like coarse ware as there was at Strandegaard—indeed, the Ertebølle tradition runs right through the age of the dolmens and passage-graves, and is expressed not only materially but in a well-defined rite of burial in a flat grave, quite independent of megalithic conventions, and evidently in being before their introduction. The conclusion that the Northern Neolithic became established as an agricultural as well as a pastoral culture soon after 2500 B.C., while dolmen burial was introduced only from about 2300 from the West, will be borne out by what we have now to see of the culture's extensions to the East and South.

Its original focus included not only Denmark but much of Schleswig-Holstein, where the Strandegaard find has probably analogues at Südensee and Ellerbek. While the leading pot-forms there undergo certain degenerations of profile and developments of ornament in the course of time,[1] eastward along the North German coast scantier early settlements are succeeded by the formation of several new local groups, that of Zarrenthin perhaps belonging to the first expansion of

[1] Fig. 19, 5, 7: cf. the Danish type, Pl. VII, 1.

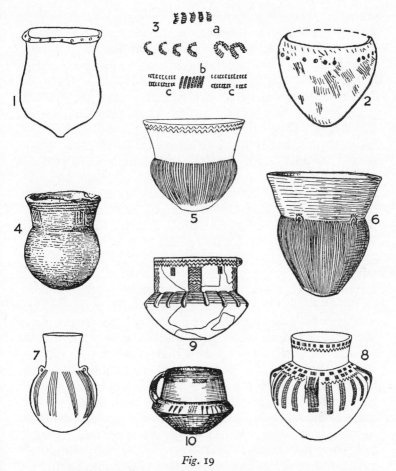

Fig. 19

NORTHERN NEOLITHIC AND RELATED POTTERY

1, Mesolithic pot from Ertebølle shell-mound, Denmark (pp. 61, 201);
2, Pot of Dwelling-place culture, Finland (pp. 202-4); 3, *a*, Whipped-
cord ('maggot'); *b*, Shell-edge; *c*, Comb-stamped impressions on pottery
(pp. 201-2). Funnel-beakers (pp. 204-8): 4, Early type, Bornholm; 5,
Schleswig-Holstein; 6, Mecklenburg. Amphorae (pp. 206-8): 7, Schleswig-
Holstein; 8, N.W. Poland; 9, Decorated bowl (Grand style) from passage-
grave, Denmark (p. 216); 10, Handled bowl of Walternienburg culture,
N. Germany (p. 217).

Scales : 1, 2, about $\frac{1}{10}$; 4, about $\frac{1}{6}$; 5-7, rather under $\frac{1}{6}$; 8, $\frac{1}{8}$.

settlement, perhaps around 2400 B.C., along the whole littoral from Mecklenburg[1] to Pomerania and East Prussia. The culture shows little trace of contact with the more transitory makers of whipped cord pottery, but seems to overlap the outlying Danubian settlements with stroke-ornamented ware in Pomerania, and while later developments created the Molzow group in East Mecklenburg and the Uckermark, and that of the attractive Gingst pottery of Rügen, it was thus early established in the East German-Polish region on its own, incorporating no doubt the local Mesolithic inheritance. Its pastoral and small-farming economy brought rapid increase in numbers and so in territory, and this independent eastern province, in its earlier or Wiorek stage, soon stretched from Brandenburg to the Niemen, and from the Silesian Oder to the Vistula beyond Warsaw. The funnel-beaker, collared flask, and shoulder-lugged jar or 'amphora' remain its leading pot-forms, with bold ornament including zigzag friezes but dominated by vertical furrow-patterns, especially in hatched stripes on the shoulder of the globular or pear-shaped jar-bodies.[2] Similar work, with regional differences of detail, distinguishes the southern province into which colonization within a short while further spread: south-eastwards up the Vistula and Bug over Galicia, and south-westwards as far as Moravia and Northern Bohemia beyond their mountain frontiers, both from Silesia, where its later growth is typified at Nosswitz, and from Saxony up the gorge of the Elbe. Westwards between the Elbe and the Harz Mountains, however, recent research has recognized a related but definitely individual culture-group, with pottery dominated rather by distinctive plain forms of jar and flask than by funnel-beakers. This is called the Baalberg culture, and it has an importance of its own to which we shall shortly (p. 219) return.

The people's small-scale cultivation and pastoralism, not unmixed with hunting, was not an economy which impelled them to concentrate on the loess soil which they thus began to encounter, like the Danubians who had settled on it first; they were content with 'intermediate' country and even sandy dunes, and thus their relation with the Danubian peasantries in Galicia and Silesia was one of contact leading to some

---

[1] Fig. 19, 6.   [2] Fig. 19, 8.

PLATE V

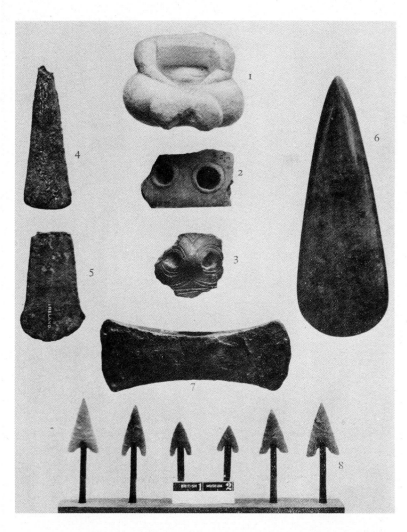

LIMESTONE STATUETTE FROM MALTA (1): CHALCOLITHIC POTTERY, AXES,
AND ARROWHEADS FROM MEDITERRANEAN AND ATLANTIC EUROPE (2-8)

Limestone: 1, Hal Tarxien, Malta (from a cast). Pottery: 2, Tunnel handle, Mnaidra, Malta;
3, Perforated lug, Peu Richard, W. France. Copper axes: 4, Herpes, W. France; 5, Ireland.
Polished greenstone axe, Breton type: 6, Canterbury. Bronze double axe: 7, Topsham, Devon.
Hollow-based flint arrowheads; 8, Ireland

British Museum

Scale in inches   See pp. 153-4, 158, 174, 184, 189-190, 215, 264-5

PLATE VI

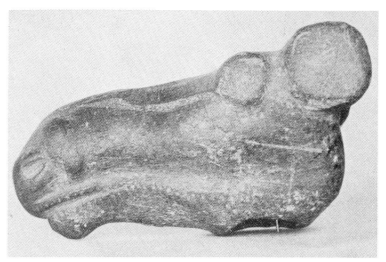

A. PERFORATED ELK-HEAD OF STONE, FROM DWELLING-PLACE SITE
HVITTIS, SATAKUNTA, FINLAND

(Length 14.7 cm.)

National Museum, Helsinki

Photo : J. G. D. Clark

B. ROCK-ENGRAVING OF ELKS AT EKEBERG, NEAR OSLO, NORWAY

Scale of 1 foot

See pp. 205, 231

degree of fusion. Indeed, in Silesia, it has been well shown how the frontier march between the two cultures, e.g. at Jordansmühl, where the debt of the developed Danubian civilization to the Theiss culture of Hungary has been described (p. 116), gave rise to exchanges in material culture which emphasize the basic contrast of North with South while demonstrating the fertility of their commingling. That contrast is as clearly shown when the 'Nordic' immigrants reached Bohemia and Moravia. Their distribution covers much ground, including regular hill-country, suitable for pastoralists and hunters, which the loess-bound Danubians had left alone; but they also intruded on the loess, especially in the Prossnitz region, and established many settlements there. At first their material seems untouched by Southern influences, and overlaps the last phase of the Moravian painted pottery which had accompanied the later Danubian stroke-ornamented ware (pp. 111, 115), but assimilation to Danubian technique was soon at work, and before long zigzag and furrowed ware and plain forms of funnel-beaker are found alongside fluted and other pottery introducing, with the so-called Baden culture, the Danubian 'Copper Age' of our next section. Handled forms become characteristic, and in general the pottery comprises a complex of groups, for which the common name 'Danordic' has been coined. The Moravian hill-site of Stary Zámek has yielded stratified evidence for a sequence of phases, in the latter part of which the fluted-pottery association is succeeded by another, which recurs, for example, in Galicia, of collared flasks with peculiar crescent-handled mugs, of affinities to be discussed presently when this 'Nordic' immigration, and that of the corded-ware people which followed it, can be reviewed in a Danubian context. But it is important meanwhile for our Northern chronology, for it is impossible to give this interruption of Danubian culture an initial date much later than 2300 B.C., and the contacts of North and South exemplified at Jordansmühl may reasonably be reckoned to begin with the last quarter of the third millennium.

In pushing so far south into Central Europe the Northern migrants were not moving blindly. Not only must their early contact with the northerly Danubian outliers have brought

them word of good lands to southward, but the trade which
we have already watched developing throughout the Danubian
basin was now already bringing small stocks of tempting
Southern merchandise to the North European plain. Copper,
early in evidence in the south-east, was, we know, attaining
a small-scale but wide circulation in the Theiss-Münchshöfen-
Jordansmühl nexus of Danubian cultures by the middle years
of the third millennium, and though only trinkets come in
witness to this from graves, it is undeniable that implements
or weapons of copper were beginning to share the same rare
but significant currency. Isolated finds of flat copper axes,
such as had long been current in the Aegean-Anatolian region
(pp. 88-9), are numerous in the whole territory of the Middle
Danube, and their distribution northward, chiefly down the
Elbe, must have begun before copper attained the development
we shall witness in East-Central Europe in the next section.
For it is only from these as models that the Northern peoples
can have devised the axe-form notoriously typical of the earlier
Northern Neolithic—the 'thin-butted axe' which reproduces
exactly the form and shining-smooth surface of copper in
polished flint.[1]   Round-bodied stone axes were indeed a
Mesolithic heritage (p. 61) which had already been improved
upon in a flint or ground-stone form with a pointed butt for
easier hafting, but the pronounced thickening of the latter's
distribution from west to east suggests that in Schleswig-
Holstein and Jutland lying nearest to the Elbe trade-route
from the south, they were early superseded by the copper-
inspired thin-butted type which was rather more slowly passed
eastward across the Danish islands to Sweden. In the new
axe the old art of grinding or polishing bone and stone was
for the first time applied to flint, and though it is not yet found
in the oldest Neolithic sites, the enormous numbers in which
it is present all over the Western Baltic and adjacent regions,
despite its known obsolescence at the end of the third
millennium, point to an early initial date, around 2400 B.C.,
which is supported by its presence with the early coastwise
movement eastward from the Oder to the Vistula. Once the
eastern group, however, was established on its own, it soon

[1] Pl. VII, 5.

took to its own simpler form of axe, with a pointed-oval body-section chipped in the old Mesolithic fashion and only the cutting-edge polished, and this type was already established when southward movement brought its users into contact with the copper-using Danubians of, e.g., Jordansmühl. For the thin-butted axe made no headway in these regions: good ground-stone axes of wedge-like shapes were there already being developed, under copper-form influence, from the old plano-convex 'shoe-last' tradition, and such attained a good distribution in Middle Germany. Thus when Middle Germany did produce a standard type in flint, it was the similarly wedge-shaped 'thick-butted axe',[1] which when carried northward, as we shall see presently, superseded the thin-butted axe in its West Baltic home. The other early imported copper weapon to be rendered in stone was the axe with perforated shaft-hole, which in a distinctive form with knob-hammer butt became widely distributed in North Central Europe, eastwards in Poland, and ultimately south-westwards towards the Alps, as well as establishing itself all round the Western Baltic. The whole shaft-hole axe family will have to be discussed shortly in a wider context, and the knob-hammer type is actually not earlier than the Danish dolmens, so that these and the other Northern tomb-forms had better be considered next.

We have said that the Northern dolmen was due to a 'conversion to the megalithic religion', by which is meant the acceptance, in the coast-lands of Denmark and North Germany where these tombs are found, of the magic power of the religion brought by the Atlantic voyagers of our last chapter, especially in its concern with the dead. Belief in a disbodied spirit meant belief in a ghost's potency for good or evil to the living, and magic proclaimed by dark strangers who could sail the whole Western sea in winged ships—for sail may well have been an unknown mystery to the Northern paddle-boatmen—would take a natural hold among a people already careful of funeral custom. Their native grave-rite—it may occur in an actual Ertebølle midden—was to lay the dead out under a spread of small stones, or between two rows of such, beneath a shallow earth covering; this was not ousted by the new

[1] Pl. VII, 10.

mode, and further, the simplest dolmens [1] may at first have
held one body only; the collective-burial idea had to gain
ground, and these box-like structures are crudely built affairs,
though a lowered sill-stone on one side, at times fronted by a
rudimentary gallery, has been seen (p. 80) to show a kinship
with the Scottish segmented cist borne out by the long stone-
girt mound, sometimes enclosing two dolmens side by side,[2]
which gained equal currency with the otherwise similar round
one; the capstones are big and were probably never covered.
But even quite small dolmens may contain five or six dead,
each deposited, to the confusion of the previous occupants,
with its grave-goods of pottery (shoulder-lugged or collared
flask and funnel-beaker), rough notched amber beads, thin-
butted axes, and occasionally a mace or a shaft-holed knob-
hammer axe of stone. The accession of the Atlantic Passage-
grave people to the North Sea route is first attested by reduced
versions of such graves analogous to those misnamed dolmens
in Portugal or the Longhouse type in Britain, polygonal in
form and sometimes with a rudimentary passage. While these
'passage-dolmens' cover roughly the same mainly coastal
areas of Denmark and Schleswig-Holstein as the simple
dolmens, and extend more sparsely south and east into
Germany, the remoter folk through Mecklenburg to Pomerania
and Rügen, in contrast to the intensive passage-grave development which ensued in Denmark and South Sweden, pursued
on their own a development of the simple dolmen into an
elongated-gallery form, tending to a position near one end of
the rectangular stone-girt long mound. The same idea was
more faintly caught in a northerly strip of the culture's eastern
area, running into Poland, where a curious extended-triangular
form of long barrow appears, known as the Kujavian grave,
with one or two interments in its broad end, each laid out flat
in the old pre-megalithic fashion, sometimes in a simple trench-
grave. Kujavian graves of this kind, containing the typical
funnel-beaker pottery, as at Rybno and Lesniczovka near
Warsaw, will have to be distinguished presently (p. 228) from
the type as taken over and augmented with internal stone
grave-chambers by the wholly different people distinguished

[1] Fig. 18, *e*.   [2] Fig. 18, *f*.

by 'globe-amphora' pottery. But here in the east the pre-
megalithic tradition remained the strongest, and simple flat-
graves, often with a spread of small stones, are widespread,
while the small-stone flanking may also persist, as in the south
at Jordansmühl. The idea of a simple dolmen appears only
in the reduced form of a flat-buried stone cist, which is only
less widespread in Poland and East and North Germany
generally. And long mounds, for instance in Mecklenburg,
may contain wholly unchambered interments. The long
mound—popularly known as the 'Huns'-bed'—had a different
history in the other direction, westwards from the Elbe to the
Ems and the Drenthe province of Holland.[1] On this coast
passage-grave influence was not wanting, so that the Huns'-bed
has an entrance in one of the long sides, giving on to what is
either in effect a passage-dolmen or a modified form of passage-
grave extended each way along the axis of the mound. In
Drenthe the latter tends to oval shape and is less often stone-
girt; there are also a few cases of closed dolmenic cists. From
this quarter perhaps came the isolated group of apparently
long-mounded megalithic tombs in the Medway valley in
Kent, for Coldrum and Addington here both suggest Huns'-
bed form, and though the former yielded a scrap of British
Neolithic A pottery and the same county contains a long
barrow of British type at Chilham, a relation with the Netherlands is suggested in between at Grovehurst, where coarse
pottery in a sort of Ertebølle tradition which recurs among
the Frisian sand-dunes was used by flint-workers making not
only British axe-forms and leaf-arrowheads, but curved flint
sickles, of a distinctive East British type [2] shared probably by
the kindred Peterborough folk (p. 140) and remotely paralleled
later on in Denmark.

   To Denmark and its passage-graves we must now return.
Intensified contact with the West in the couple of centuries
before 2000 B.C. led to the appearance not only of larger polygonal or oval-chambered tombs,[3] but next also, in the Danish
islands, of laterally expanded oblong forms of chamber running
at right angles to the passage,[4] the whole carefully built in flat

---

[1] Fig. 18, *n*.   [2] Fig. 13, 10.
[3] Cf. Fig 16, *r*.   [4] Fig. 16, *s*.

slabs and dry masonry under a big stone-girt round or long mound as before. A subsidiary cell may quite early be present, notably in Jutland, and paired tombs side by side in the same mound were a rather later island development. The culture is now much more prominent in Sweden, not only in the south but north to Västergötland and on the Kattegat coast of Bohuslän.[1] The different varieties of tomb-form are to some extent regional specializations, just as the whole complex is specialized in relation to its Western originals, but there is no sign of new Western populations: the different groups of Northerners themselves elaborated the tradition they had adopted from overseas in their own distinctive ways. Immigration, however, there was, and it came not with the Western current of trade and religion, but from the German mainland between the Elbe and Weser. The Mesolithic natives here must have been in contact not only with the Danubians across Middle Germany, but more particularly with the Rössen people, in whom the Danubian convention of stroke-ornamented pottery had taken new form in a culture of much native individuality (p. 118), and now too with the Northern Neolithic groups forming in the Baalberg area, in Saxony, and in Silesia to the east of them; the result was a fresh growth of Neolithic civilization, marked by sharp-profiled stab-ornamented pottery whose forms and angular-patterned decoration betray Danubian inspiration through Rössen models while in relation also with their eastern neighbours' work, as matured for example at Nosswitz, and, above all, strong in their own individuality. That individuality is no less essentially Northern than the Nosswitz or indeed the Danish dolmen-people's style, but from the stroke-ornament idea, helped evidently by a native basketry tradition, it created stabbed-line and zigzag work embodying feeling for horizontal as well as vertical pattern in a quite distinctive form.[2] Through these peoples' territories passed the trade-route from Central Europe to the West Baltic centre of Northern civilization, and especially when across its course to Saxo-Thuringia and the Harz Mountains a wholly different current from the east began to confront them with the new and warlike cultures now shortly

[1] Fig. 16, *r*.   [2] Fig. 19, 9 ; Pl. VII, 3.

to be described, it is not surprising to find them moving out northward to share the wealth in land and trading, and the ghostly strength in magical religion, of related folk on the northern coasts and islands. Accordingly, while simple forms of megalithic tomb became adopted far into their North-West German homeland, it is this distinctive pottery of theirs that appears in the early passage-graves of Schleswig-Holstein and Denmark, together with flasks and funnel-beakers developed from the native tradition, and in Sweden, where that tradition had scarcely a footing, it comes in with absolute dominance. With them, too, the migrants brought the thick-butted flint axe,[1] now engendered inland in Germany as above described, and while flint-working issued also in narrow chisels [2] and later in hollow-bladed gouges, the same axe-type was made in polished stone, and the old transverse arrowhead gave way before a three-sided tanged form [3] elaborated from remoter Northern tradition (p. 204). Also, along with oval mace-heads, there are stone shaft-hole axes,[4] imitating not now the knob-hammer form so much as a new presumptive copper import from the South, the true double-axe, which, already symbol as well as tool in Minoan Crete, passed from the south-east to the North apparently by Central Europe: it was either this way or from Central Europe across France that two examples, not in pure copper but an early rendering of bronze, rather later reached the coasts of Britain (p. 265: Pl. V, 7). That its divine symbolism was brought to the North with it is probable from the adoption of its form for a whole series of beads [5] among the wealth of amber buried with the dead which reminds us what was the chief object of the Northern trade.

But the most striking single testimony to that trade is the finding at Bygholm, on the east coast of Jutland, of four flat axes, three spiral armlets, and a triangular dagger of copper in a pot of the funnel-beaker class. Both the slightly splay-laded axe-forms and the armlets, foreshadowed already at Jordansmühl, will soon meet us in the Copper Age of Central Europe, and the now connected Remedello culture of North Italy (p. 157), though the midrib-grooving on one face of the

[1] Pl. VII, 10. [2] Pl. VII, 9. [3] Pl. VII, 6.
[4] Pl. VII, 8. [5] Pl. VII, 7.

dagger has parallels in the Iberian tombs of Alcalà which
bring the Western sea-route also into the picture.   These
synchronisms converge on a date not far short of 2000 B.C.,
and that it is in fact round about a century earlier (p. 248) is
confirmed by the form of the pot, which has its closest analogues
appreciably after the dolmen period in dwelling-sites contemporary with the early passage-graves.   Typical of such
sites is one at Troldebjerg on Langeland, whose inhabitants
lived by crop and cattle-farming in oblong-rectangular houses
recalling that of Strandegaard.   The culture's general distribution continues mainly coastal, shunning, for instance, the
inland heaths of Jutland, and ever within touch of coastwise
and maritime trade.   And the effect of the maritime trade
with the Atlantic West appears distinctly in Iberian influence
on the funerary pottery-ornament, which stylistic analysis,
helped by the stratigraphy of successive tomb-deposits, has
classified in a sequence beginning with a strong survival of
vertical design and even some whipped-cord work from the
dolmen period, and continuing with the blending of the
immigrant Elbe-Weser convention with this and long-distance
influence from the Iberian bell-beaker ceramic in a 'Grand
Style',[1] after which a 'Refined Style' side by side with cruder
work is succeeded by phases of degeneration.   The Elbe-
Weser tradition ran a straighter course in Sweden, and this
sequence is in the main a Danish phenomenon, but its incidence
is far from uniform.   In the Danish islands, where the passage-
graves were used for scores of successive interments, the
whole series may be represented in them, and often is; in
Jutland, on the other hand, the later styles are virtually absent,
and the tombs not only exclude developed rectangular chamber-
forms but contain far fewer burials.   Obviously the civilization
was here cut off in its prime.   And southward in Schleswig-
Holstein the burial-pottery has an even shorter history after
the Elbe-Weser immigration, answering to the absence of the
characteristic forms of Danish passage-grave, and what is
more, of the Huns'-bed developments of Mecklenburg and
the Ems or Drenthe also.   And while in Mecklenburg and the
east the funnel-beaker tradition stayed self-contained, the

[1] Fig. 19, 9.

Ems-land in the west shows only late forms of funnel-beaker [1] and collared flask together with an Elbe-Weser pottery-style dominant indeed but quite isolated from the rest of the Northern world.   Finally, the Elbe-Weser culture, south-eastwards in the middle Elbe-Saale basin, begins to take on a new and no less sharply sundered form, that of the Walternienburg group, where a heightened reliance on basketry models is shown by angular handled cups [2] and shoulder-lugged jars with stab and zigzag decoration; two stages are distinguishable in this material, of which the first overlaps the parent culture and the outgoing Rössen, and the second issues in the sequence of three further stages under the name of Bernburg—the whole running parallel with the Baalberg and funnel-beaker cultures on and beyond the Middle Elbe.   Stone double-axes and their amber miniatures here indeed recall the Danish passage-graves, but the plain thick-butted axes are made in Widra shale from the neighbouring Harz, and the collective cist-tombs not only differ, as we shall see, to a marked extent from Northern models, but are throughout alternative to flat earth-graves for a single contracted skeleton.   In fact, the Walternienburg-Bernburg people, with the so-called Havel culture which presently grew up eastward of them in Brandenburg, developed on lines of their own.   What was the disruptive force which split the Northern Neolithic into these divergent groups?

The answer is nothing less than the invasion down the Elbe of a new and warlike people.   Their seizure of the fat lands of Holstein explains the Huns'-bed folk of the barren Ems-land and Drenthe heaths as largely a refugee population, even more isolated than their Walternienburg cousins inland to the south-east from the centres of West Baltic civilization.   Pushing on, the invaders established themselves thickly in South Jutland, and spread down the centre of the peninsula, cutting off a remnant of the natives in Vendsyssel at its northern end, and squeezing out the main body from their coastal homes eastward upon the Danish islands.   The stages of their advance correspond exactly to the curtailment of the native culture just described: for a coastal settlement-trend they substituted an inland one, incorporating perhaps the remnants of the old

---

[1] Pl. VII, 4.   [2] Fig. 19, 10.

Gudenaa hunters (pp. 60-1); and though they might violate native megalithic tombs for the burial of their own dead, their characteristic burial-rite was something quite different, namely, single-interment in a contracted position in an earth-dug grave, often purified by fire, and covered as a rule by a bowl-shaped round barrow. The Single-grave people by their invasion of Schleswig-Holstein and Jutland made a clean break in the continuity of the Northern Neolithic; the history of the ensuing centuries is that of the progressive welding together of invaders and invaded in what became the unitary Bronze Age civilization of the North, but at first the cleavage was absolute, as is well shown by the contrast in archaeological material. The first single-graves contain three typical objects: a big beaker-pot with an ovoid body and a spreading neck decorated with plain horizontal cord-impressions,[1] a thick-butted flint axe [2] with a slightly lopsided cutting-edge, and a stone shaft-hole battle-axe [3] with a down-curved expansion of the blade and a slightly less drooping lobe-ended butt. A spheroid stone mace-head and an amber ring or button may complete the warrior's equipment. In succeeding generations, the practice of secondary burial in existing barrows produced a sequence, above the original earth-dug 'bottom-graves', of 'ground-graves' sunk through the barrow into the ground-surface, and 'upper-' and 'top-graves' above again ; and the types in each show progressive development, the beakers to a bent S-profile (sometimes inbent again at the rim), and then by truncation of the body to a mortar or top-hat form,[4] and the battle-axes first by reduction to symmetry of the drooping blade and butt, and then, with a buttward shift of the shaft-hole, to simpler and finally much-straightened types of weapon. We shall find this final stage coinciding with the end of the passage-grave period in the adjacent islands about 1750 B.C., but the early phase of that period which caught the first impact of invasion may be dated roundly at 2000 in Jutland, and rather earlier in Holstein, so that we have to find a source somewhere up the Elbe whence the movement will have started about 2100.

That source lay on the further confines of the Mid-German

---

[1] Fig. 20, 8.   [2] Cf. Pl. VII, 10.   [3] Cf. Pl. VII, 11.   [4] Pl. VII, 12.

Neolithic provinces so far described, on the high Middle Elbe and Saale in Saxo-Thuringia. Here were Mesolithic people who have not much to show of Danubian and Rössen influence, but who shared presumably the same contracted-burial practice as was inherited by Walternienburg and Bernburg circles, and belonged apparently to the belt of microlith-using peoples which had stretched over these regions from Silesia and Poland (p. 64). And their adoption of Neolithic culture was evidently in large part inspired from that easterly quarter. Baalberg-culture pottery (p. 208), and what became the Nosswitz type of funnel-beaker ware, in relation as it was on this side with the Elbe-Weser and thereafter the Walternienburg development, was evidently not unknown to their earlier potters; their 'amphorae' stand close to Baalberg types, and their distinctive beaker implies the same sort of prototype as the funnel-beaker itself, but in a different strain, worked on by this influence, but in its rendering of a basket-neck harking back to that peculiar device which we followed earlier from the east on to German territory, of ornament by cord-impression.[1] It is here indeed reduced to simple terms: whipped-cord work is unknown, and the impressions are merely of a two-thread cord round the beaker's neck, but even so, this derivation can alone explain it, and it was doubtless brought to Saxo-Thuringia from among those folk we saw with it earlier further east, who, if not remaining to blend with the funnel-beaker settlers in Poland (p. 208), presumably retreated before them. These lines of inception harmonize with backward reckoning from the exodus about 2100 to give the first Saxo-Thuringian corded ware a date somewhere between then and about 2300 B.C. And with the coming of copper axes along the Elbe trade-route it is natural to find its makers specializing the thick-butted flint axe and their own distinctive type of shaft-hole axe in stone.[2] But the latter's insistent uniformity —in the right hand of the buried warrior—and the fashion of the graves themselves, bespeak ideas of a hitherto unfamiliar sort, and by following our pottery clue eastward we shall get a clearer notion of these and also of the history of the battle-axe weapon in general.

[1] Fig. 20, 1-4.   [2] Fig. 20, 5.

Early as was the inception of cord-impressed pottery on the steppe- and dune-lands of Eastern Europe, it had a long life, and the history of these lands during—and after—the second half of the third millennium B.C. was one of reaction to influences coming not only from the West, as in the Tripolye culture from the Danube and the Aegean, but also from the opposite quarter. For on the east, where past the Sea of Azov and the borders of the Caucasus the steppe stretches unbroken over into Asia, a different inspiration was by now at work. Our fullest knowledge of this south-easterly region comes from the verges of the Caucasian Mountains, and there remains of extraordinary interest reveal an entirely new factor in the situation—nothing less than direct contact with the high civilization of the Mesopotamian area across the Armenian and Persian highlands. This fresh opening of connexion with the Near East calls for particular notice, though space forbids more than mention here of recently discovered Neolithic culture and its sequels in the Armenian region. The answering process on the European side of the Caucasus is first revealed in the cemetery of Mariupol on the Sea of Azov, where superimposed rows of dead, of medium or long-headed type, lay extended in a prepared bed of red clay, with abundant finery of shell and wild-animal tooth and bone ornaments, and rarer axes and knobbed mace-heads of stone. These remains point to a mainly hunting people still, unversed even in pastoralism, and with no use for pottery, but further developments have appeared at Nalčik in the Caucasian foothills between the Kuban and Terek rivers. Here the superimposed burials were grouped to the number of over 150 in a large barrow or 'kurgan', the bodies being thickly covered with red ochre in the manner already noticed in Palaeolithic times (p. 38), of which the red clay of Mariupol must represent a variant. The ornaments now include rare stone bracelets and a ring of copper; a crude stone figurine was also found, and here or in near-by settlement-sites occurred an industry in flint and obsidian, a stone axe, grinding-stones, a spindle-whorl, and round-bodied pottery. Clearly the 'Neolithic arts' are appearing, and an obsidian and perhaps even a copper trade with the South would provide a context for the growth of what next became a brilliant Copper Age civilization. Already the idea of a ritual mound for burial bespeaks a distinctive adaptation of Near-Eastern reverence for the dead to the circumstances of a barbaric clan, and in due course the princely chamber-tombs of Sumer find their counterpart in the chambered kurgans of the Caucasian Copper Age chieftains.

The most famous of these are in the Kuban valley, where pastoralism and simple cultivation are revealed together with an intensive Southern trade and an adopted metallurgy. The huge kurgan of Maikop covered a shaft-grave double-chambered in wood, wherein the chieftain's ochre-stained body lay contracted under a canopy decked with gold and silver, with rich jewellery, vessels not only of pottery but of stone, gold, and silver also—some decorated with animal scenes—and steer and lion figures in the same precious metals. Here and in the less richly furnished barrows of Tzarevskaya in the same valley the funeral equipment, with distinctive round-bodied pottery, includes not only flint arrowheads of Mesolithic derivation but copper implements of Sumerian forms, the flat dagger, the poker-butted spearhead, curved rod-pins, and shaft-hole axe and adze types which at Maikop were also combined into a double-bladed 'axe-adze'. The grave-chambers at Tzarevskaya were double cists of squared stone slabs, the partition pierced by a round window-opening like those which we have seen as tomb-entrances in the different usage of the Mediterranean (pp. 152, 160). Stone-cist graves occur not only along the Caucasus but in the Crimea, on the Lower Don, and in the Ukraine, and we shall shortly meet this type again further north-west as far as Central Europe. But in general the kurgans of the steppe grow poorer as one leaves the Caucasus behind, and in most cases the ochre-stained bodies under them lie contracted in simple pit-graves. When the rite appears among the Corded-pottery people of South Russia from the Don valley westwards into the Ukraine, these graves yield egg-shaped vessels with the typical cord-impressed ornament,[1] and in the Don-Donetz region a flat-based beaker-like type of pottery supervenes when these had been overlapped and succeeded by the peculiar form of sepulchre known

[1] Fig. 20, 7.

as the niche- or catacomb-grave, where the grave-pit under
the barrow opens laterally into a cave-like excavation exactly
like the rock-cut tombs of the Early Aegean (p. 149). This
remarkable feature opens a case for South Russian connexions
not only with Mesopotamia but with the Aegean cultures, and,
in fact, not only do copper beads here copy Early Cycladic
phallic ornaments, but there is much in the splendid material
of Maikop itself to point to correspondence with the treasures
of Early Minoan Mochlos and of Troy II. That correspondence implies a relationship of obvious importance for these
cultures' chronology, and as far as the Caucasus is concerned,
though erroneous belief in a low date for Troy II has led some
scholars to place the Kuban Copper Age wholly after 2000 B.C.,
the Anatolian datings now established (p. 107) cannot fail to
join the Minoan in re-establishing an initial date for it a good
500 years earlier. The Sumerian types represented were all
established by 3000 and had thereafter a considerable life, but
without going in detail into a difficult controversy it may be
reasonably claimed that, while Mariupol and Nalčik are not
later than the early third millennium, the Kuban Copper Age
flourished around and shortly after 2500, so that the pit-grave
kurgans of the steppe may be dated from after that limit, with
the catacomb-graves in turn beginning on the Don and
Donetz a little before the disuse of their Aegean prototypes
towards the end of the millennium.

Evidently in filling out the picture Mesopotamian, Aegean,
and Anatolian archaeology will all have their part. Indeed,
Tepe Hissar in Northern Persia has produced in its third
culture-layer close parallels both to Kuban metal-forms and
Early Minoan pot-types, and particular interest attaches to
new discoveries in Copper Age Anatolia, which have a close
bearing on South-Eastern Europe. The detailed discussion
of the 'royal tombs' of Alaca Höyük is here impossible, but
two types of especial European interest may be singled out,
the hammer-headed pin (cf. Fig. 20, 10) and the shaft-hole axe.
The former is absent from the Kuban culture proper, but its
abundance at Alaca is answered both in copper and bone in
the so-called Kuban-Terek stages which prolonged it. The
Kuban-Terek graves are roughly the Caucasian equivalents

of the stone-cist, pit, and catacomb graves of the main South
Russian area; they run in date from something like the same
upper limit through three stages: the first, of simple pit-
graves, with pottery and flint-work much as in the great Kuban
sepulchres; the second taking up wooden grave-linings and
also (with an occasional catacomb-grave) flat-stone cists; and
the third carrying both these forms later in independent
development. The hammer-headed pins in the first are of
bone only, in the second also of copper, and in the third of
bronze; but on the steppe only the bone form appears—
mainly in pit-graves, once in a catacomb. And, while it has
not been found west of the Ukraine, a bone copy occurs as
far away as Frejlev on the Danish island of Laaland, in a
passage-grave with pottery of about 2100-2000 B.C.[1] Somehow,
then, by that date, the steppe was in touch with the Northern
Neolithic, and with this striking fact in mind we must next
consider the shaft-hole axes.

Their general ancestry may be called threefold: perforated
implements of antler, first appearing in the Upper Palaeolithic,
had long been current in the Mesolithic of Northern (p. 61)
and doubtless likewise of Eastern Europe, and shaft-hole
antler axes lasted well into the Metal Age all round the Black
Sea. On the other hand, perforated stone implements,
beginning with simple and widely diffused Mesolithic and
later mace-heads, were in the Near East brought early enough
to plain-axe or axe-hammer forms for these to be current in
the Danubian Neolithic (p. 123), while Mesopotamia, with
its lead in metallurgy, was establishing their manufacture in
copper. In metal the shaft-hole needed no thick encircling
body or supporting butt, and thus the plain Sumerian pattern
as brought to the Kuban, whether true axe or transverse-
bladed adze, is just a flat blade with a simple shaft-hole behind
it; but while such copper chopper-axes, together with the no
less Mesopotamian double-axe (p. 215), were soon adopted in
the Early Aegean world, the stone form had some centuries'
start, and was developed into a shapely-bodied hammer-butted
weapon apparently under the influence of the contemporary
axe of antler. In West Anatolia this series begins as early as

[1] Fig. 20, 10.

Troy I and the first two towns at Thermi, and runs on through the third millennium. In due course, influence from this quarter on Danubian Europe introduced there an analogous form which the beginnings of metallurgy in the Carpathian region (p. 104) brought into being in copper: examples come from Tordos, Csoka, and Lucska north of the Upper Theiss, and stray not only over Rumania and Hungary but to Bohemia and Jordansmühl. The chronological horizon is thus the eve of the full Danubian Copper Age, around 2400 B.C., and it was the rendering of these weapons in stone that produced the knob-hammer axe which we have already (p. 211) described in North-Central and Northern Europe.[1] Probably about the same time the simple chopper type in copper was introduced into Rumania and Hungary from the Aegean, just as further east it had reached the Kuban; but there, too, the knob-hammer was known, for from the Kuban grave of Vozdviženskaya comes an example in which the features of the stone rendering are translated back into copper. The Caucasus, however, receiving as it did the direct influence of Sumerian metallurgy, transmitted to Europe also axes with the specifically Sumerian features of a projecting shaft-tube and a drooping splay in the blade (engendered originally by hammering the metal out and then conventionalized in casting): such occur sporadically in the southern half of Russia, occasionally in kurgans, and joined in influencing the makers of axes in stone. Thus from the Kuban-Terek area northwards appears the Pjatigorsk type of stone knob-hammer axe, with just this droop of the blade, and also another feature regularly met with where the influence of a metal prototype is strong, namely a lengthways ridge copying the 'seam' left along the junction between the two halves of the mould in which a copper weapon was cast. When, as will shortly be seen, the distinct culture-province of Fatyanovo was formed in Central Russia, its battle-axes retained both seam and blade-droop, with a flat hammer-butt,[2] while the shaft-tube occurs in various other stone types. The metal chopper type combined with native antler weapons in engendering the straight-backed group of East-Central and also West Russia, and is more distinctively

[1] Fig. 20, 11.   [2] Fig. 20, 12.

followed by the South Russian type with only a short offset behind the shaft-hole. Lastly, the copper 'axe-adze' creation of Maikop reappears to the west, and was not only taken up in the Anatolian-Aegean area before the end of Early Minoan II, to have a long subsequent life there, but was introduced in strength into Rumania and Hungary, where it became typical of the Copper Age to be described in the next section (Fig. 21, 1).

The appearance of the copper axe-adze in Troy and the Aegean should be due to the same culture-contact across the Black Sea as brought Aegean elements—including, one may add, some distinctive stone idols—to the Kuban and South Russia; but in Rumania and Hungary the context suggests something more drastic, namely an actual invasion of warriors from the steppe. Related Ukrainian and Galician finds come from sites of the Tripolye culture, and occurrences at Cucuteni, Erösd, and the Gumelnitza site of Vidra suggest that the whole nexus of Painted-pottery peasant civilization described above (p. 96) in South-East Europe was overrun and interrupted by invaders, after which its resumption will be seen below (p. 235) to take a differentiated form implying just such a break in continuity. And in Hungary, mainly round the upper Theiss where entry from the east would be easy, a string of barrows covering the ochre-stained contracted burials typical of the steppe now suddenly appears, one of which has yielded a typical copper axe-adze. It seems, then, that the invaders swept across the black-earth and loess territory of the Painted-pottery peasants to settle in the Hungarian plain and in Rumania, where the context of similar barrows will be further discussed below. Their axe-adzes, compared with the original Maikop invention, have a perfected beauty of form which again probably owes something to antler models, the blades gently drooping, in the manner already cited, on either side of a shaft-hole normally with a low tubular projection (Fig. 21, 1). The copper hammer-axe already current became by assimilation simply a hammer-butted variant of the same type,[1] and such copper battle-axes are scattered from Russia across Central Europe and northwards even to South Sweden.

[1] Cf. Fig. 21, 2.

Naturally the metal forms are rare away from ore-bearing regions, and as in Eastern so now towards Central Europe there begins to appear a whole series of analogous battle-axes in stone, which in relation to the older-established knob-hammer series represent the refinement of a warrior weapon specialized under the influence and prestige of the copper axe-forms.

The same influence appears in West Anatolia, where the stone weapons of Troy and Thermi, already very similar, now more closely recall European pattern, and rise to magnificent perfection in the great hoard of ceremonial battle-axes of semi-precious stone, with crystal haft-knobs of the type already noted in the Mediterranean (p. 152), from the third period of Troy II, shortly before 2300 B.C. Other treasures here in Troy II include precious ornaments, gold basket-earrings with looped-wire bodies, gold spirals, and distinctive pins, which became models for types of the ensuing period in Danubian and Central Europe. Its Continental no less than its Mediterranean connexions were, in fact, close, and it has been suggested that the battle-axes attest South Russian invaders here too, who arrived to dominate the rich Trojan civilization, only to share its downfall when about 2300 the fortress-city was sacked and burnt, in circumstances to be discussed below. Similar precious axes survived, long treasured, to be buried in a much later hoard—for so it must surely be explained—at Borodino near the South Russian border of Rumania, but the type appears already well defined in a Donetz grave at Lugansk, which, though a catacomb, was early enough to contain pottery related to the round-bodied vessels of the Kuban. The globular Kuban types had, in fact, themselves been introduced on to the steppe, in common with the kurgan burial-rite, and in the Ukraine they came to share the traditional cord-impressed ornament with the egg-shaped pots of the pit-graves. Both stone battle-axes and globular pottery were, then, current in South Russia by 2300 B.C., and we are next carried north-westward by the fact that exactly the same sort of pottery is abundantly found in Volhynia and Galicia, whereby it emerges in Poland as the globe-amphora which we mentioned there earlier in this section.[1] The globe-amphora, in fact, suggests an invasion of steppe-folk, passing from the east across the territories of cord-ornament tradition north-westward from the Black Sea and mixing with their inhabitants, and, furthermore, reaching not only Poland but still further west into Central Germany. There, beside the Baalberg-Nosswitz nexus of the Northern Neolithic, the Corded-ware people of Saxo-Thuringia were beginning in the century or two before 2100 to mature the individuality they owed to their admixture of Eastern-derived with Northern elements (p. 219), as beyond them were the Elbe-Weser people their different but no less distinctive character, which on their easterly marches by the Middle Elbe basin was starting to take on the special features of the Walternienburg culture. Even remnants of the old Danubian civilization (p. 118) had here not quite died out, and it is possible to detect Danubian as well as Northern Neolithic elements in the culture which the arrival of the Globe-amphora immigrants from the east created out of this situation, with the Harz Mountains as a western boundary. This may be distinguished as the Globe-flask culture,[2] and when the Corded-ware exodus from Saxo-Thuringia down the Elbe about 2100 sundered the Walternienburg people from their brethren to the west and north, it came to share with them the territory from the Elbe-Saale junction to the Havel-land, where it and the Walternienburg-Bernburg-Havel tradition lasted side by side and in close relationship into the dawn of the Bronze Age.

Battle-axes are not generally found in Globe-amphora graves, but the simplified boat-like type which became general from South Russia to the Baltic, as well as further east, is related at once to the Pjatigorsk knob-hammer form diffused from the Caucasus, and to the copper weapons already discussed, so that while one cannot really speak of an 'invasion of battle-axe folk' from South Russia to Germany and the North, the migration of the Globe-amphora people at least shows the North in contact with the whole culture of the steppe-area where the battle-axe was becoming the warrior's favourite weapon. And since the North was already developing the knob-hammer axes described earlier in this section, the

[1] Cf. Fig. 20, 9.　　　　[2] Fig. 20, 9.

rise of new battle-axe types in the regions thus in touch with
one another is a natural sequel. That specialized by the
Corded-ware people of Saxo-Thuringia is termed the faceted
battle-axe (Fig. 20, 5) from the facets in which its surface was
ground: next to this stand the weapon of the Single-grave
invaders of Jutland,[1] and the related forms diffused elsewhere
over the Continent as we shall shortly see. From the boat-
like type in Poland sprang the 'boat-axes' which further
invasions took respectively to Sweden[2] and Finland, while
across the line of its eastward distribution the kindred
Fatyanovo culture of Central Russia was specializing its own
type as already described.[3]   Truly the Globe-amphora people
acted as potent leaven.

Their eastern origin has long remained unrecognized, and
is still contested, but not only is their distinguishing pot-form,
with its big round body, small perforated ears, and short
upstanding stamp- or cord-ornamented neck, as close to the
steppe and Caucasian vessels as it is to those of the Walternienburg people in whose orbit they formed the German
'Globe-flask culture': other considerations point the same
way. For their thick-butted axes they remained fond of the
banded flint of Galicia, where the type must first have met
them, and their funeral custom included not only single contracted burial in pit-graves but the flat-stone cist of South
Russia also, which, while merging in Germany with its Northern
counterpart (as made by their Walternienburg neighbours),
yet reproduces the window-pierced partition of Tzarevskaya
in the famous barrow of the Baalberg, and again among the
Corded-ware folks near by in Saxo-Thuringia. In Middle
Poland, indeed, the Globe-amphora people tended to adopt
the Kujavian grave-type of the Funnel-beaker folk, though
modifying it by the introduction of stone chambers (p. 212),
but in the main their work was to naturalize in North-Central
Europe the grave-rites of the steppe. Since their contact with
the Corded-ware people was close, it is natural to find the
latter making not only simple flat-graves but typical pit-graves
under barrows, which remained absolutely distinctive of these
people wherever—e.g. to Holstein and Jutland—expansion

[1] Pl. VII, 11.   [2] Pl. VII, 13.   [3] Fig. 20, 12.

Fig. 20

CORDED WARE AND OTHER POTTERY, STONE BATTLE-AXES, AND HAMMER-HEADED PIN

1-4, Saxo-Thuringian Corded Ware and amphora; 5, Facetted stone battle-axe; 6, Stone battle-axe, Yverdon, Lake Neuchâtel (pp. 219-31, 249); 7, Egg-shaped corded pot, pit-grave, Kharkov, Ukraine (p. 221); 8, Corded beaker of early Single-grave type, Jutland (p. 218); 9, Globe-flask (globe-amphora), Central Germany (p. 227); 10, Bone hammer-headed pin from passage-grave, Frejlev, Lolland, Denmark (pp. 222-3); 11, Stone knob-hammer axe, Central Europe (p. 246); 12, Fatyanovo stone battle-axe, Central Russia (p. 224).

Scales: 1-4, 6, $\frac{1}{4}$; 5, 7-9, $\frac{1}{6}$; 10, $\frac{1}{3}$; 11-12, $\frac{1}{5}$.

subsequently took them. In the last centuries of the third millennium the opening up of the whole stretch of territory between the Elbe and the dune and steppe-lands south-eastward resulted in the mingling of corded ware of absolutely Saxo-Thuringian type with the bag and globular pottery of those lands themselves. Evidently there was direct Saxo-Thuringian expansion back in this direction: overflowing, as will shortly be seen, into Bohemia and Moravia, it entered Silesia and Poland, mixing not only with the Globe-amphora but the Funnel-beaker people too, and passed on to Volhynia and the Ukraine. In the Kiev area a regular centre of corded ware and its hybrids arose, of which the pit-graves of Stretovka and Jackovica are respectively the best earlier and later representatives. The stone battle-axe was now the dominant weapon from Germany to the Black Sea in a nexus of warrior cultures animated by movement from both directions, and the influence of the corded beaker was taken up in the flat-based pottery of the Don-Donetz catacomb graves, while those graves themselves were introduced to the Polish loess country of Kielce and Sandomierz.

In this region of Poland the mixture of Globe-amphora, Corded-ware, and Funnel-beaker elements took a particularly fertile form in what is known as the Złota culture. All three traditions are manifest in the pottery, side by side at first (the funnel-beaker kept for domestic use) and then blending; crescent-handled pottery recalling Moravia and Galicia (p. 209) appears too, since the culture ran a parallel course to the Danubian Copper Age, but in its initial phase, around 2100 B.C., this area witnessed the start of the northward movements of invasion which carried the 'boat' type of battle-axe and round-bodied cord-ornamented pottery to the Baltic, just as at the same time (p. 217) the Saxo-Thuringian warrior invasion carried to Holstein and Jutland the battle-axes and corded beakers of the Single-grave culture. It is often said that the Fatyanovo culture of Central Russia also originated with a migration from Poland, but its pottery lacks the Corded-beaker element prominent at Złota, and is far more purely in the Globe-amphora tradition, while we have already seen how directly its drooping-bladed battle-axes point to the south and the Caucasus. In fact, recognition of west-to-east connexions across the Russian forests, attested, e.g., by the spread of 'boat-axes' (p. 227), leaves the actual origin of the Fatyanovo people to be accounted for in the main by movement straight from the south, by which a group of steppe warriors brought the battle-axe, corded globular pottery, and ochre-burial to dominate the primitive comb-ware population of forested Russia. The tradition so set up there had a long life, and played a leading part in the Russian Bronze Age and even later; but the distinct invasions of the Baltic lands from Poland had a different though analogous history. Round-bodied corded pottery appears first on the southern Baltic coast in East Prussia, and the island of Bornholm has produced not only derivative pot-forms but boat-shaped battle-axes which take us further oversea to the 'Boat-axe culture' which thus invaded the south of Sweden. The course of its development there must be described later, but Pl. VII, 13 shows its highly specialized form of boat-axe, with metal-derived 'seam' and shaft-tube, and the round-bodied pots which with this and the thick-butted flint axe characterize its earth-dug single-graves look to Poland, not only in their shape but the wave-like arrangement of their earlier cord-ornament. Finally, east of the Baltic a similar movement passed up the coast to Finland, where fringed-pattern corded pottery, distinct from the Swedish but looking also to Poland, and a separate boat-axe development, attest the invaders' arrival at a period answering to an advanced stage of the native comb ware (p. 203). The pottery-traditions fused in the hybrid Kiukais style, and inland and in neighbouring Karelia the idea of the battle-axe, in time entered into the animal art of the Arctic hunters, to produce the strangely beautiful beast-headed axes and axe-like sculptures in fine stone which have sometimes been found in their dwelling-sites and places of animal sacrifice (Pl. VI, 1: p. 205).

The movements of the warrior cultures into Central Europe, and beyond it to the west and south, were no less far-reaching than these northerly invasions, and the problem of their ethnic identity and language is of fundamental importance for prehistoric and later European ethnology. But this will be best appreciated in the fuller setting of a fresh section.

2. PEOPLES, MOVEMENTS, AND METAL-WORKING

(Map V and Table V: at end)

The whole phenomenon of the warrior cultures, with their single-graves, their corded pottery, and above all their battle-axes, has been invested with a crucial importance for the disputed origin of the Indo-European or Aryan group of languages, and also of the 'Nordic Race'. The physical type encountered in the Single-graves is undoubtedly in general tall and long-headed as the 'Nordic' should be (p. 51), and it is no less true that linguistic evidence, when it becomes available, reveals Aryan-speaking peoples distributed roughly wherever those cultures of the Neolithic occur or spread. And the intensive study of the Indo-European (or Indo-Germanic) languages has, broadly speaking, shown that the primitive group of dialects lying behind them must be native to some part, or all, of the territory, of rather varied physical character, stretching between the Baltic and at furthest the North Sea on one side and the Black Sea and the Caucasus, or the Caspian, on the other. Those dialects must have had some connexion or contact with Finno-Ugrian and Uralic speech to the east, and also with Caucasian and Near-Eastern tongues to the south, from which various words were borrowed before the wider separation into the distinct language-groups of which Germanic, Celtic and Italic, Illyrian and Thracian, and Greek are, with Slavonic, the principal European representatives. The Sumerian words both for 'copper' and for 'axe' play a part in this connexion, and both in material and spiritual culture the conception of a northerly Eurasiatic element joined with southerly Near-Eastern incomings seems fundamentally implied by Aryan linguistics. It is obvious how well this general outline fits the prehistory of this territory in the third millennium. An acute controversy has indeed raged between those who would place the original 'Aryan homeland' in North and North-Central Europe, and those who would have it between there and the Caucasus, often specifically in South Russia. But we have seen that while the Globe-amphora migration did proceed from South Russia to North-Central

Europe, the Corded-ware people of Saxo-Thuringia were simply an outstanding group within a great belt of Neolithic peoples in which cord-impressed pottery had been adopted before warrior culture had made its mark, and they thereby take their place not only beside the pastoralists of the Ukraine but the dwellers in the Baltic North. The underlying unity here is not Neolithic but Mesolithic: it was the microlithic cultures, the eastern counterpart of the western Tardenoisian (p. 64), that provided the basic affinity between the Black Sea and the Baltic, and behind again (pp. 30-2) lies the Upper Palaeolithic unity of the East-Gravettian hunters.

The origin and diffusion of the 'Nordic Race' is a matter for thinking on broad lines, and to realize that the earliest stage of Aryan language now recognizable goes back to the outgoing Mesolithic is to understand that no 'Aryan homeland' can be as narrowly delimited by the prehistorian as has sometimes been wished. While recent attempts to equate the Aryan-speakers of the Neolithic with the Danubian peasants or the Comb-ware peoples of the north-east seem unlikely to win acceptance, it would be rash to suppose Indo-European speech limited on all hands to our warrior cultures, though their possession of it is open to no reasonable doubt. Their significance is the combination of Aryan speech with a vigorous, warlike, and essentially masculine material and spiritual culture, resulting from the impact of Near-Eastern influences upon a native heritage none the less important for its partial cloaking by the archaeological poverty of Mesolithic remains. The glorification of the individual warrior by barrow-burial with his battle-axe and his drinking-beaker is typical of the whole attitude to life to which the richness and flexibility of Aryan language later gave the highest expression in the 'heroic' epics. With the rise of the warrior cultures a new element was thus let loose into European civilization. We have seen something of its initial action in the east of Europe, and in the whole related nexus of the Northern Neolithic: its effects in the south-east and in Central Europe and beyond, now await our attention.

The warrior invaders whom we have already (p. 225) begun to follow into South-Eastern Europe found Hungary in possession of the Theiss culture, which southward to the Danube and beyond embraced the tradition of the Körös and Vinča groups in a form not very dissimilar from that taken by the kindred elements in contemporary Macedonia and Thessaly (pp. 106, 114). With the Danubian 'crusted ware' there was handled pottery of Aegean or Anatolian inspiration, and these characters were now apparently caught up in part into the formation of a peculiar and from its wide but thin distribution evidently half-nomad culture, created by invaders in partial union with the Nordic elements which had pushed down towards the Danube higher up with the funnel-beaker pottery of the Northern Neolithic (p. 208). The Austrian name for this is the Baden culture: in the Danube valley its handled pottery, with fluted body-ornament, runs to the crescent or 'ansa lunata' handle-forms already noticed by anticipation in Moravia, Bohemia, and Galicia, where these south-eastern adaptations, as at Stary Zámek (p. 209), were crossed with the Nordic funnel-beaker ware, and may be accompanied by Northern thick-butted and knob-hammer axes. There is further variation in the South Austrian mountains, but here and everywhere very high handled vessels are typical,[1] often very similar to those of the Grey Minyan ware we shall soon encounter in Greece, and these characterize the culture throughout Hungary, where its hut-pits appear on various sites at the end of the Theiss culture and herald the ensuing true Copper Age. Southward in West Rumania an invading element is more clearly attested by the association, with crusted and handled pottery, of corded ware, including whipped-cord ornament of evidently Eastern derivation, in what is called the Coțofeni culture, which had its centres in Western Wallachia and the Maros valley, but extended east to the Alt and west into Serbia. Here the invaders also maintained the Eastern rite of barrow-burial, sometimes with stone-cist or stone-lidded graves and occasionally with ochre-staining as in Hungary (p. 225); stone battle-axes may occur in this context, and at Decia near the Middle Maros a cemetery of ochre-graves has yielded Eastern-looking knobbed stone mace-heads and a copper axe-adze. The pottery here has lost

[1] Fig. 21, 14-15.

cord ornament, but similar ware accompanied the axe-adze already mentioned at the Painted-pottery site of Erösd in the Alt valley (p. 225), lying in the topmost stratum above the main occupation, which its users evidently brought to an end. It is this and the analogous finds at Cucuteni and the Gumelnitza site of Vidra that point, as already observed, to the breaking of these earlier Painted-pottery cultures by the Eastern invaders, and both on the Alt and in the Wallachian plain, mainly east of the Coțofeni area, the result was the distinctive Schneckenberg culture, represented also above the Gumel-nitza A horizon at Glina near Bucharest. In this handled and also corded pottery was adopted, and it is immigrants from this direction that seem, passing on into the Hungarian plain, to have joined in transforming the Theiss culture into that of the Hungarian Copper Age to be presently described.

On the Alt the Schneckenberg culture lasted on into the ensuing Early Bronze Age, when its handled pottery becomes assimilated to the Perjamos type noticed below (p. 293), but in Wallachia its survival was shorter, and it was the painted, or more distinctively graphite-ornamented, pottery of Gumel-nitza[1] that maintained itself into the second millennium, Gumel-nitza B lasting from after the invasion about 2200 till succeeded, perhaps about 2000, by Gumelnitza C. The same survival of the old peasant civilization distinguishes Bulgaria, where 'tells' or settlement-mounds like Tell Ratcheff near Jambol carry the graphite-ornament tradition on to quite a late date. And north-eastwards in Moldavia, the invasion-period was succeeded by the renewed Painted-pottery culture of Cucuteni B. Here, on the old site re-fortified, the old pottery-style appears in a new form, its patterns mostly in black on a whitish, or less often a reddish slip ground, and far more sophisticated and compact, the spirals regulated and geometricized; the pot-forms too stiffened into deep-shouldered or biconical-bodied jars and cups with neatly formed necks, and flat open bowls, though the hollow support (p. 101) still survives. There is again a distinctive series of mainly erect female figurines, both plain and ornamented with painted designs, and while copper is rare, bone and antler, flint and stone

[1] Pl. VIII, 3.

industries still predominate, the stone axes including hoe-like forms but in the main square-sided and thick-butted. Beyond, from the Black Sea to the Galician loess-lands, an analogous new phase of Painted-pottery culture appears, its earlier stage connected at Horodnycja in Galicia with the Zališčyky stage of the older series (p. 99), but appearing after a gap at Schipenitz in the Bukovina, and reaching further maturity at sites like Bilce in Galicia and Petreni in Bessarabia. Schipenitz B has pottery answering largely to Cucuteni B, though particularly rich in the curious 'binocular vases'[1] beginning to appear already at Zališčyky, which seem really to be double kettle-drums for accompanying dances; the ornament shows an even wider range of beautifully stylized patterns, in part panelled but still owing much to the spiral tradition, and in their complexity and variety as fine as any abstract art in Europe. We are here in the last centuries of the third millennium, and around 2000 the culture's consummation in Galicia is marked at the site of Koszyłowce, whence a typical painted jar and other pottery are illustrated in Pl. VIII, 1-2; white ground-slip, white and red panels, red hatching, and black debased-spiral designs are typical, still beautiful, but now approaching an artistic standstill.

This whole development is one with that of the Ukraine, where the renewal of the old Tripolye culture as Tripolye B is attested on a good number of sites, especially in the Kiev region, where the peasants lived in rectangular pit-dwellings (the Russian 'zemljanki') with a sunken 'stove'-place, and made also, besides earth-dug ovens, rectangular structures ('ploshchadki') whose remains are always found burnt, without as yet any agreed explanation. The Tripolye B settlements yield, with figurines, painted pottery much as in Cucuteni B or Schipenitz B, with angular forms, including 'binoculars', and two-colour painting in which spirals have been reduced to circle-and-tangent patterns, accompanied by stylized animal or other figures. Copper is rare, bone, flint and stone plentiful, the axes recalling Cucuteni B but including 'shoe-last' hoe-forms. Food-remains show that, as throughout this civilization, the people were mainly grain-cultivators and breeders

[1] Cf. Fig. 8, *e*.

of oxen, sheep, goats, and pigs. A small percentage of horse-bones also occurs, but one does not know if the horses were tame or wild. However, the eastern Przewalski type of horse appears on the silver-ware of Maikop (p. 221), and an introduction of horse-taming with the warrior culture from the East is usually accepted. The Corded-ware warriors of North-Central Europe, and, e.g., the Swedish boat-axe people, are proved horse-breeders, and the breaking of horses of European breed grew over Europe until in the Late Bronze Age they became a potent instrument of domination. But there is no reason to assume the Asiatic practice of riding was brought in so early. The horse in Europe was a draught animal before he was ridden, and, as in the Near East and the Aegean, the warrior's first recorded use of him is in chariot-harness. But however they used their horses, 'warrior' folk were still flourishing on the steppe in the neighbourhood of the Tripolye B peasants, and coarse pottery of cord- and comb-ornament type found in the peasant settlements as far west as Cucuteni, Schipenitz, and Koszyłowce shows that the peoples overlapped: near the Oussatova settlement, too (p. 203), 'warrior' kurgan-finds include, with a copper dagger, a painted Tripolye bowl. The mainly late stratigraphy of the coarse ware at Cucuteni is not everywhere repeated, but it seems scarcely open to doubt that it was by the warrior folk that the Painted-pottery cultures were again and finally extinguished. The later kurgan-graves with wooden linings or coffins, corresponding to the third Kuban-Terek stage along the Caucasus (p. 223), are spread widely over the steppe and lead into the Russian Bronze Age; one of these in the Kiev area was built above a burnt 'ploshchadka', and we may conclude in general that at some time after 2000 B.C. (pp. 235-6) the culture they represent finally triumphed throughout the steppe and its borders.

But westward and southward the original warrior invasions had a different sequel. We have seen how in Central Europe their semi-nomadic mode of life entered in the Baden culture into a material setting of largely Danubian-Aegean origin or derivation; the Schneckenberg and Coţofeni cultures show them definitely dominant in an analogous conflation, and in the latter especially the intrusive corded pottery was here and

there carried deep into the handled and crusted-ware province
of South-Eastern Europe. Southward on the Aegean, civilization was in palpable correspondence with that province; in
Thessaly crusted ware and other derivatives of Neolithic
tradition lived on, subject to encroachment from the Early
Helladic civilization of Central Greece, now advanced from
Boeotia to the Spercheios valley, and to infiltration from the
north and Macedonia, where the 'Early Macedonian' culture
was undergoing regional development from its Trojan-
Anatolian initiation (p. 107). Developed forms of pot-handle,
conspicuous in Thessaly, are typical of Macedonia, which
remained also in partial contact with the Bulgarian version of
Gumelnitza to the east, as it was with the Middle Danube to
the north. And the whole North Aegean was open to touch
with the region centred upon Troy, whose influence stands
over against the southerly civilization of the Cyclades and
Crete. On the Greek mainland, the third phase of Early
Helladic culture in its northern areas, in the centuries just
before 2100 B.C., comes to differ somewhat from the older
pattern: there is 'light-on-dark' painted ware, for instance,
at Eutresis in Boeotia and Hagia Marina in Phokis, which,
seemingly of different implication from the 'dark-on-light' of
the Cyclades, recalls Macedonia in suggesting Trojan connexions. And we have already seen in the third phase of
Troy II evidence for intrusion by powerful people from the
steppes, which was followed by the city's sack and destruction
about or not long after 2300. It would then be no surprise
to find that sequel echoed further round the North Aegean on
its European as well as its Asiatic side. And echoes there seem
to be. At the end of the Early Helladic III occupation at
Eutresis appears a copper axe-adze of intrusive look, and some
pieces of corded ware, with Coţofeni or Schneckenberg
parallels, which are repeated at Hagia Marina; and with these
must be considered the wide distribution of Northern-seeming
barrows, in and beyond Macedonia, in Thessaly, and as far
south anyhow as Drachmani in Phokis, where, though in general
many such barrows may belong to later periods, one contained
a contracted burial with plain pottery accompanied by a bronze
knife and a painted pot of a kind marking the beginning of the

Middle Minoan or Middle Cycladic I period in the islands, about 2100 B.C. Furthermore, there are barrows also in North-West Anatolia, some of them datable in the earliest Bronze Age of about this time, and it is from about 2000 B.C. that Anatolia witnessed the first rise of the Hittites, a people under whose ensuing rule, along with many purely Near-Eastern tongues, a dialect with unmistakable Indo-European affinities was in official use in the second millennium. That an element among the Hittites, whether or no responsible for this 'Našili' dialect, entered Anatolia from the north-west has often been suggested, and we have now to realize that these same centuries saw the entry of a new civilization, of distinct form but from roughly the same quarter, into mainland Greece.

Its arrival is marked by the abrupt destruction of Early Helladic settlements, and its main characters are three; rectangular instead of oval houses, contracted burial in stone-cist graves, and material including stone shaft-hole axes with knife-weapons in bronze, decorated clay spindle-whorls, and pottery which agrees with the bulk of these features in pointing to a close connexion with Troy, not only in its cruder domestic forms, but above all in the fine silver-grey fabric, high-handled, angular-bodied, and attesting for the first time in Greece the potters' wheel, which is known as Grey Minyan ware.[1] The name was bestowed by the excavators of Orchomenos in Boeotia, where Greek tradition located a really much later Minyan dynasty of rulers, and at this site the new culture appears, on the burnt ruin of its Early Helladic predecessor, in its purest and primary form, characteristic of the focus it established here in Central Greece. The origin of this pottery in the Troadic area—whence its analogues in the Baden culture of the Danube (p. 234) must also have been inspired—may now be regarded as certain; its colour probably imitates Trojan silver-ware, and among the culture's other features the rectangular houses may be singled out as the *megaron* type distinctive of Troy II, and credited with a Northern origin likewise apparent in its parallel earlier appearance at Dimini and Erösd (p. 102). In the generations after the fall of Troy II, then, while a remnant on its site peopled the feebler villages of

[1] Fig. 21, 16-17.

Troy III and IV, this new culture, compounded of Troadic elements with the Northern incomings already reviewed, seems to have attained compact formation in the North Aegean, appearing on the coasts of the 'Early Macedonian' province, and was then brought by direct invasion to Central Greece. With their centres at such sites as Orchomenos and Eutresis, the immigrants spread it both northward to the Spercheios valley to fade out in Thessaly, and southward to Korakou by the Isthmus and into Argolis, where its grey ware was less skilfully imitated, and rendered also in local yellow-buff clays. Its influence, weaker in West Greece, extended in due course to the Cyclades, whence came the island matt-painted pottery convention to accompany the mainland grey, and to confirm its chronology as Middle Helladic, the counterpart of the Middle Cycladic and Minoan civilizations which began their first period about 2100, their second about 1900, and their third about 1700 B.C. And there seems now little doubt that this is the context of the implanting in Greece of the Greek language: these Middle Helladic invaders, with their links with the Aryan-speakers of the European continent cast now anew in an Aegean mould, have, if anyone, the right to be called the first Greeks.

Their coming made a cleavage, despite the go-betweens of Cycladic trade, between a Continental Greece and an island world in which the Cyclades passed more and more under the domination of Middle Minoan Crete. Middle Cycladic pottery, matt-painted at first in a geometric style with Early Cycladic memories, developed gradually a curvilinear style under Minoan influence, and in Middle Cycladic III polychrome naturalistic work in the Cretan manner begins to look forward to the Late Minoan achievement of the sixteenth and fifteenth centuries; though native traditions were never swamped, centres like the Melian town of Phylakopi reflect unmistakably the growth of Minoan ascendancy. Crete itself, renewing its relations with Egypt, where an interlude of invasion and disunion was ended towards the close of the third millennium by the Middle Kingdom, giving Middle Minoan culture an upper dating-limit about 2100, underwent changes which brought this new culture's focus of strength from the east to

PLATE VII

NEOLITHIC POTTERY, AMBER, TOOLS, AND WEAPONS FROM NORTHERN EUROPE

Denmark, dolmen types : 1, funnel-beaker ; 2, collared flask ; 5, flint thin-butted axe. Denmark, passage-grave types : 3, angular cup ; 6, three-sided tanged flint arrowhead ; 7, amber double-axe head ; 8, stone shaft-hole axe of related form ; 9, flint chisel ; 10, flint thick-butted axe. Holland : 4, funnel-beaker from Hun's-bed, Drenthe. Single-grave types, Jutland : 11, stone battle-axe ; 12, mortar-shaped beaker ; Sweden : 13, stone boat-axe.

British Museum

Scale 1 : 5   See pp. 204, 206, 210-1, 214-5, 217, 218, 228, 231

PLATE VIII

PAINTED POTTERY FROM KOSZYLOWCE, GALICIA (jar, height 18⅝ in., and bowl),
AND GUMELNITZA, RUMANIA

British Museum and National Museum, Bucharest

Scale about 1 : 6

See page 235-6

the centre of the island, to Knossos near the northern and
Phaestos near the southern coast, where the twentieth century
saw the erection of palaces, the centres alike of power, commerce, and religion. The black-ground polychrome 'Kamares
ware' was then just passing its early peak of excellence, and the
trading of Middle Minoan pottery to Egypt and Syria well
reflects the culture's orientation to the full maturity of East
Mediterranean Bronze Age civilization. Growing mastery of
the alloying of copper with tin appears in the skill with which
the Minoan bronzesmith used his tougher metal, especially for
round-heeled daggers longer and stronger in midrib and
riveting, and for the elongation of the broad-tanged type into
the long and beautifully tempered rapiers which we shall find
when in due course Minoan culture broke into the Helladic
mainland. And precious metal-work, like pottery, betokens
all the sophistication of a civilization which can no longer be
called prehistoric, but has attained a maturity completed not
only by the essential prominence of engraved seals in all the
transactions of life, but by the emergence of an actual system
of writing. And this gave place to a regular linear script
when, after a mysterious disaster had overwhelmed Knossos
and all the palaces and villas of the centre of Crete about
1700 B.C., a brilliant restoration brought in, with the third
Middle Minoan period, the island's Golden Age. Meanwhile
the mainland, though well enough versed in the metallurgy of
bronze, was quietly continuing in the relative barbarism of
Middle Helladic culture, in which we have seen that incomings
from inland Europe played their part in a blend first compounded in the region of Troy. Exactly analogous, north of the
Balkans, was the blend resulting from the similar incomings
into the Hungarian plain. We have seen the Theiss culture
intruded upon by Eastern barrow-builders, and equally, while
the Baden culture was moving among the sedentary peasant
Danubians, the impact of what in Rumania was the Schneckenberg culture upon the Theiss tradition. The result of that
impact was the Hungarian Copper Age culture known by the
name of Bodrogkeresztur.

Bodrogkeresztur and Pusztaistvánháza are this culture's two
leading cemetery-sites, and though the latter seems somewhat

the later, their material well represents the period. The dead lay contracted in flat-graves, the men on their right, the women on their left side, and from these and the associated settlement-sites (at Bodrogkeresztur overlying a Theiss-culture occupation) comes a pottery-series in which, but for slight echoes of Jordansmühl and the funnel-beaker, the types represent a development from Neolithic modes in which the Theiss tradition played the leading part.[1] Tall hollow-pedestal pots are prominent, the old Danubian bowl is now flat-footed and handled as well as lugged, and the dominant form is a cylindrical-necked mug with a round body and two little handles just under the rim. While surfaces are mostly plain and polished, incised decoration in the old manner still occurs, though any kind of painting has died out completely. The late Theiss-culture site of Tiszaug helps to represent the transition to the new level, and there is analogous material at Lengyel (p. 115); at the same time, the Balkanic correspondences which we have noted do not drop out of mind, and though the Aegean-Anatolian element in Hungary may in the past have been overstressed, there can be no doubt of trading-connexions with that quarter (a Grey Minyan sherd is even reported from Cucuteni B). While obsidian, flint, and stone industries remain in prominence, the now established prevalence of copper-working is an indisputable debt to the south-east, and flat axes, daggers, knives (Fig. 21, 7), awls, axe-adzes and axe-hammers (Fig. 21, 1-2) were freely manufactured, as probably were chopper-axes, by casting in that metal. Among copper ornaments the double-spiral (p. 115) retained its popularity, attested also at Jordansmühl, and when, after the beginning of the second millennium, the Danubian Early Bronze Age begins, pins, basket-earrings, and the like still embody the traditions of the treasures of Troy II (p. 226). If the fusion of elements that produced the Bodrogkeresztur culture began as early as 2200 B.C., its maturity in the following centuries led, through a transition from the Pusztaistvánháza stage represented at the Konyár cemetery near Debrecen, to an inception of Bronze Age civilization which we shall presently find datable about 1900.

[1] Fig. 21, 8-10.

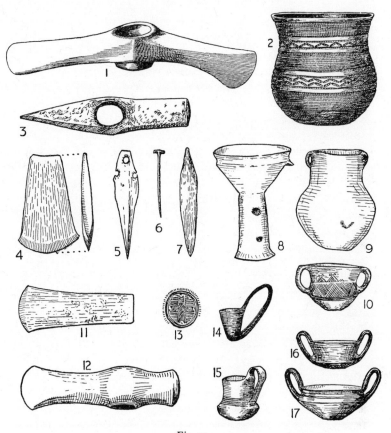

Fig. 21

IMPLEMENTS AND POTTERY OF THE DANUBIAN COPPER AGE
AND ITALY, AND MINYAN WARE FROM GREECE

1-3 from Hungary: 1, Copper axe-adze (pp. 225-42); 2, Bell-beaker
(pp. 250, 256), Erd, Budapest; 3, Copper axe-hammer (pp. 224, 242),
Kiskörös; 4-6 from Alpine lake-dwellings (pp. 246-9): 4-5, Mondsee;
6, Vinelz; 7, Copper knife, and 8-10, Pottery, Bodrogkeresztur Culture,
Hungary (pp. 241-2); 11-12, Flat copper axe and stone battle-axe from
grave of Remedello Culture, Guardistallo, Pisa, Italy (p. 250); 13,
Incised white-inlaid design on Slavonian pottery (pp. 246, 337); 14-15,
High-handled pottery of Baden Culture (pp. 234, 239), Hungary; 16-17,
High-handled vessels of Grey Minyan ware, Greece (p. 239).

Scales: 1-2, $\frac{1}{4}$; 4-5, $\frac{2}{6}$; 6, 11-13, $\frac{1}{4}$; 7, $\frac{1}{3}$; 8, $\frac{1}{7}$; 9, $\frac{1}{10}$;
14-15, $\frac{1}{8}$; 16, $\frac{1}{11}$; 17, $\frac{1}{9}$.

Further west the same progression followed a somewhat different course. The mixed cultural areas of Moravia, Bohemia, Austria, and the Upper Danube flanked the region of lake-dwelling civilization in the Alps, and while the Michelsberg culture (p. 137) had been carried from South Germany as far east as Bohemia, it will be remembered that in the Eastern Alps, as on the Upper Neckar, sites like Schussenried and the second settlement at Aichbühl show a conflation of the same 'Western' element with a derivative Danubian tradition analogous to that of Jordansmühl (p. 137). Beside this we have now to set the primitive but important Horgen culture (p. 198), which, from Mesolithic origins apparently somewhere in the east of North France, was established in Switzerland, perhaps about 2200 B.C., in a series of lakeside pile-dwellings which on Lake Neuchâtel overlie the remains of their Cortaillod predecessors (p. 136), and are represented on the Lake of Zürich by that of Horgen itself. We have, in fact, reached the Alpine and westerly zone of Central Europe whose 'Westernization', in contrast to the Danubian territories to the east, and now, too, to the Northern Neolithic on its side also, received due emphasis in an earlier section (p. 137). Here now the East began in turn to make its influence more strongly felt by the introduction of copper-working, while a new hand was taken by warrior invaders from the Saxo-Thuringian north. On this course of events we must here briefly dwell. But it will lead us to the redressing of the balance by the most far-reaching of all the Western currents in European prehistory, the spread of the Bell-beaker people from North-Central Spain.

The Horgen people with their coarse, ill-baked, bucket-like pottery[1] and plentiful bone and horn work evidently stand for an aboriginal reaction to West European Neolithic culture, and the crude gritty ware, plain but with occasional simple plastic ornament which became much developed at a rather later stage, puts them on the same plane as the aboriginal cave-folk whom we have noticed (p. 156) round the North Mediterranean and as far inland as Central France. At the same time, their well-built pile-dwellings, good flint-work, and antler

[1] Fig. 11, 12-13.

axe-sleeves improved from the Cortaillod pattern (p. 134) by
a projecting 'heel' to safeguard the wooden haft,[1] are not to
be disregarded, and the whole element in West and Central
Europe of which they represent a part lived to form a basically
important substratum in its later prehistory. Their pile-
dwellings are known eastward as far as Lake Constance and
Württemberg, and while there was contact here with the
Schussenried-Aichbühl group of lake-dwellers in which
Danubian had blended with Western-derived Michelsberg
culture (p. 244), there were also direct Michelsberg inheritances
in the important though mixed culture which their overflow
into the South-German-Austrian region set up, in conflation
with the mixture already effected between Danubian and
immigrant 'Nordic' (p. 209). This is known as the Altheim
culture, from a Bavarian example of the hill-top type of
settlement which characterizes it no less than the lake-dwellings:
another case is the Goldberg near Nördlingen, on which the
earlier Rössen and Michelsberg settlements have already been
described (pp. 119, 137). The timber houses here were rectangular, yet not of the log-cabin type, but sunk-floored
squarish structures with wattle-and-daub walls whose supports
probably curved in upwards to a dome-like roof in a manner
suggesting the influence of a round-hut tradition, a convention well reflecting the mixture of cultural elements
involved. There are analogies at the Horgen pile-settlement
of Sipplingen, and again at Dullenried where the material
is contemporary with Altheim. Altheim pottery combines
the bucket shapes of Horgen, developing the plastic ornament
which in Switzerland belongs to that culture's progress
into a corresponding 'Upper Neolithic' stage, and a strong
'Nordic' or funnel-beaker element, as well as a tendency
to incised decoration, recalling Schussenried, which reappears
among the pile-dwellings further east on the Attersee and
Mondsee in Austria, in the furrowed technique already noted
in the commingling of 'Nordic' with Danubian (p. 209).
Further again to the south-east, the pile-settlement of Laibach
Moor in Carniola, with the same plastic-ornamented coarse
ware, yields more elaborate incised and white-inlaid ornament

[1] Fig. 11, 10.

on its finer fabrics, which while recalling those of Hungary, still have 'Nordic' reminiscences; and yet beyond, in the so-called Slavonian culture of sites like Sarvaš and Vučedol on the Lower Drave in Jugoslavia, on the borders of West Hungary, and even on and beyond the Save, the same Alpine-Danubian-Nordic blend appears in a further form, mingling now with the Danubian-Balkan currents already cited in previous contexts. Slavonian pottery is richly ornamented, in a technique not so much incised as excised, giving a fretwork effect enhanced by white inlay,[1] and though, as we shall recall presently, this culture seems the latest of the whole group, yet the Balkan-Aegean and even Cypriote adaptations which have been recognized among its potters' products bring home the fact that here all along its eastern fringes the Alpine region lay open to influences of civilization from the south-east, just as on its other side we have seen it open to the Western world. And in this period, at the turn of the third and second millenniums, those influences had their most important manifestation in the spread of metallurgy in copper.

The importance of copper-working in the Hungarian Bodrogkeresztur culture has already been stressed; essentially, that culture was simply the Hungarian equivalent, with the ores of the Transylvanian and Slovakian mountains at its disposal, of the mixed cultures we have been describing: both north of the Danube, where among sites contemporary with Jordansmühl the Moravian cemetery of Košir, and the Bohemian fort-settlement of Homolka, each help to reinforce the bridge between Hungary and Altheim, and south of it in the Mondsee and Slavonian areas. Stone and flint, with horn and bone, were indeed still everywhere prominent, and the Mid-European stone knob-hammer axe was in full use throughout these mixed-culture regions, but before 2000 B.C. the currency of imported copper objects began definitely to be supplemented by the discovery and working of copper ores in the Eastern Alps themselves. At the Mondsee and Attersee, as at Laibach, copper slag and crucibles plainly attest this new native industry, which produced flat axes, riveted daggers,[2] awls, and spiral ornaments, and copper-workshops are similarly

---

[1] Fig. 21, 13.   [2] Fig. 21, 4-5.

revealed further west not only at Altheim, but also in Switzerland, first of all in the settlement at Niederwil, and then more abundantly on a number of pile-dwelling sites, above all at Vinelz and Locras on the Lake of Bienne. This establishment of a Copper culture in the Alps evidently owes its primary inspiration to Hungary. But there is another factor to be considered, which here re-enters our narrative from early in the last chapter (p. 157), namely the influence of the closely analogous Copper culture of North Italy, with its type-site at Remedello.

The same South-Eastern Aegean civilization which exerted its stimulus on the Hungarian Copper Age has there been seen in the form of long-range activity direct from an Early Minoan source, and the result was that in the outgoing third millennium the Alpine region could be penetrated by the trade and industry in copper from both these quarters at once. To the square-tanged Early Minoan dagger-form[1] the Remedello culture added longer flat-heeled midrib daggers as current in the Aegean in these later centuries, and flat dagger and axe types answering exactly to the Hungarian,[2] while similar dagger-forms and triangular tanged arrowheads were beautifully made in flint, copper-working was clearly in the forefront of North Italian industry, which furthermore we shall find closely analogous to its counterpart in East Spain. This may already here be witnessed in the half-moon-shaped ornament of thin silver (a type whose importance in Spain and the West will shortly emerge) from a Remedello grave at Villafranca, and the use of silver at Remedello itself for a crutch-headed pin. The imitation of this pin-type in bone at Vinelz,[3] and the appearance of the half-moon ornament in copper in a contemporary grave at Velvary in Bohemia, help to show how Italian and Hungarian influences blended in forming the Copper culture of Central Europe, for to the Hungarian element manifest in the copper-work of Vinelz and its like the Velvary grave adds copper spiral armlets, a type early enough established in the Danubian area to appear in simple forms among the copper trinkets of Jordansmühl (p. 242), and now definitely a feature of the Hungarian industry. Finally, the influence of the metal trade

---

[1] Fig. 15, 3.   [2] Fig. 15, 11 ; cf. 4-5.   [3] Fig. 21, 6.

through Central Europe on the civilization of the North, already (p. 210) attested in the spread of flat copper axes and their rendering in the Northern thin-butted axes of flint, and in the copper prototypes of the Northern shaft-hole axes of stone, is, now that Central Europe had so strong a copper industry of its own, more strikingly manifest still. For this is the context of the discovery at Bygholm in Jutland, in a pot representing the Northern funnel-beaker type as current in Denmark in the early Passage-grave period (cf. Fig. 19, 5), of the now famous hoard already mentioned (p. 215), of three such copper spiral armlets, four flat axes, and a triangular dagger. And if the dagger has its closest analogues not in Central Europe or Italy but in the chambered tombs of Iberian Alcalà (p. 161), where similar flat axes too were current, this only shows that the Western current of seaborne commerce met in the North the landborne one whose two starting-points, Hungary and Italy, were now joined in Central Europe. As a dating-point the Bygholm hoard could hardly be bettered: the copper types entirely agree with the pot-form for a date just before the invasion of Jutland by the Single-grave people from the Elbe and Holstein, that is, round about 2100 B.C. The trans-European trade-route so signalized became an axis of outstanding importance to the Bronze Age and later civilization of the Continent.

The parent stock of the Single-grave invaders in Saxo-Thuringia, whose expansions we have already followed not only north but east (p. 230), did not fail to extend their swarming, which in 2100 they were just beginning, south and south-west along this route also. The force behind this general explosion from the Elbe and Saale must have been prodigious, and it diffused the virile aggressive culture, which we have seen begotten by Eastern influence on native strength, over Central Europe far and wide. It has sometimes been said that these Corded-ware people were mere nomad fighters, but a whole series of excavated settlements, at Bottendorf, Doberschau, Schelditz, and soon south-westwards at Neusetz in North Bavaria and Haldorf and Schulzenberg near Kassel, shows them living solidly on the land in good timber dwellings: their warrior prowess was soundly based on Neolithic economy, and they expanded not as destroyers but exploiting conquerors. Bohemia and Moravia, as we began to see above (p. 230), early underwent their invasion; westward and south-westward across Germany the story was the same as far as the Rhine, the Black Forest, and the passage to the Swiss plateau: Bavaria and Upper Austria received the same experience, and their outliers may be traced south-east down the Alpine march already described on to Jugoslavian territory. Their material traces are easy to recognize: the single-grave with its contracted corpse, most characteristically under a round barrow, the faceted stone battle-axe or derivative (Fig. 20, 6), the tall cord-ornamented beaker, not now with its original straight-splayed neck but a softened S-profile, the ornament less careful and rich than originally in their homeland, and with it a round-bodied jar or amphora recalling variously the globe-amphora and the Baalberg or Nosswitz jars of the Northern Neolithic (p. 219), with which their contacts were so close. By these distinguishing marks we can recognize their diffusion in groups, contemporary with those of Silesia, Poland, and beyond already noticed (p. 230), not only over Bohemia and Moravia but further into Slovakia and even just into North Hungary, and not only to the Rhine, which will be discussed separately below, but from South Germany and Austria over all the Alpine fringes. There typical corded ware occurs in most of the pile-dwelling sites just considered, south-eastward to the Mondsee and even Laibach, and westward to Vinelz and such other Swiss sites as Crufensee and Utoquai near Zurich, and others again on Lake Neuchâtel, where with pottery developed from the native 'Upper Neolithic' it occurs overlying the pure Horgen levels—an indication of its relative lateness borne out by its absence from a relatively (p. 247) early copper-working site like Niederwil, and its presence on sites of the full Altheim culture like the Goldberg. In fact, in all these regions the culture arrived late, probably after 2000 B.C., and lasted to become a major element in the Mid-European Bronze Age (p. 299).

It should be added that on the Italian slopes of the Alps, where an early echo of Cortaillod (p. 136) was succeeded by a more strongly attested form of Lake-dwelling culture with plastic-ornamented pottery answering to the Swiss 'Upper Neolithic', there is little to show for copper-working, and only a limited encroachment of corded ware (at Lake Varese); though the easterly sites of Fimon and Arquà will later start us on the question of a Transalpine-Balkan influence manifest in exaggerated pot-handle forms, this North Italian Lake-dwelling culture was evidently true Alpine in its basic elements. On the other hand, the more potent Remedello culture beyond it incorporated something more definite from the North, betokened by the 'warrior' stone battle-axe. Examples, related to the Central European weapon of the Corded-ware people, have occurred in its graves as far south as Guardistallo in the province of Pisa[1] and Rinaldone near Viterbo, and thus it would seem that warrior intruders from the North made their way into this Chalcolithic province and penetrated with it right into Central Italy. It will later appear probable that here we have the Italian counterpart of the 'Minyan' invasion of Middle Helladic Greece, and that the end of the third millennium was the date of the first introduction into both peninsulas of Indo-European speech and its essential implications. But meanwhile Italy has next to be considered in connexion with another current, moving the opposite way and different in kind—which must form the final subject of this section.

Civilization on the shores of Spain gave rise among the cave-dwelling people of the southern interior to a distinctive form of Chalcolithic, or copper and stone-using culture, characterized in material by the pottery bell-beaker (p. 164: Fig. 15, 6-7). The spread of this Bell-beaker culture from South to North-Central Spain was going on from about 2200 B.C., that is, simultaneously with the beginnings of Copper Age civilization—it might equally be called Chalcolithic also—in Central Europe. And of the latter's two cultural roots, both the Hungarian and the Italian themselves engendered from the same ultimate Mediterranean-Eastern sources, the Italian was itself in a contact with Spain which we have already recognized (p. 247). That contact was probably not effected overland by South France, which was a recipient rather than an inde-

---

[1] Fig. 21, 11-12.

pendent propagator of Chalcolithic culture, so much as by
seaborne traffic through Sardinia, which we have seen cause
to reckon from the start as a centre of West Mediterranean
civilization rivalling both the Italian on the one hand and the
Spanish on the other (pp. 156-8). Thus when the Bell-beaker
people established themselves in both the hinterland and the
coast of Northern Spain, and also, we must here add, as
participants in the parent Chalcolithic culture of its south-
eastern coast in Almeria—for excellent bell-beakers appear in
the chamber-tombs of Los Millares itself (p. 164)—the way
was open for their oversea expansion across to Sardinia, and
thence south to West Sicily, and, more effectively, north to
the Tuscan coast of Italy and beyond. Simultaneously, however, their entry into the Pyrenean culture of Catalonia opened
to them South France—accessible indeed from Sardinia also
(p. 158): in fact, the barrier of the Western Alps seems to
have divided their northward movements into two streams,
with this one centred on the valley of the Lower Rhône, as the
Italian was on that of the Po. Thus, from a date to be reckoned
about 2100 B.C., typical bell-beaker pottery, with finger- and
plastic-ornamented coarse ware, as we have seen them in Catalonia and the Pyrenees (pp. 128, 166-72), was introduced to the
cave-dwellings and cave and megalithic tombs of Languedoc,
and this first overland expansion of the beaker folk out of
Spain now brought copper there into more effective though
still rare currency. In the stratified caves of the Narbonne
region the Beaker level directly overlies that of the pointillé-
incised and channelled pottery discussed in the last chapter
(p. 173), and is followed only by the local equivalent of a
Bronze Age horizon: beaker material is well seen at the Grotte
de Falaise, and a fine beaker-bowl may be cited from the
dolmen of Boun-Marcou. And east of the Rhône beaker
pottery is likewise represented in the analogous caves and
megaliths which its bringers will have found similarly in
use among the inhabitants. Developments in this region
must await notice in our next section. Meanwhile, there is
strong reason for believing that the major force of the Bell-
beaker immigration here did not thus remain caught up in
this southern environment, but travelled northward up the

Rhône without much delay, to create, by a road whose stages are not yet fully marked, a fresh centre of the culture about 2000 B.C. on the Middle Rhine. We shall return to the Rhineland beakers soon: our concern first must be with the other stream of the people's movement, east of the Alpine barrier in North Italy.

The notables among them, who in Sardinia, as had happened already in Almeria, were received into the mercantile Chalcolithic culture, were buried at death in the great rock-cut tombs of the families to which they had presumably become allied, and their typical equipment stands out in the material (p. 156) found in the collective sepulchres of Angelu Ruju—regular East Spanish bell-beakers with horizontal bands of diaper and zigzag pattern in fine comb-stamping, barbed and tanged flint arrowheads and the archer's stone wrist-guard or 'bracer', stone buttons with a V-shaped boring, and the copper awl and, above all, the dagger of the form they had standardized from the Early Mediterranean pattern in Central Spain, the short flat triangular-bladed dagger characteristic of sites like Ciempozuelos (p. 166), with hafting-tang broadened into a slanting-sided tongue (Fig. 15, 4). The leading types occur also in the upper stratum of the Cave of San Bartolomeo (p. 126), equally in the context of the Sardinian island culture with which their own Spanish traditions had so much in common (p. 157), though a polypod form of bowl is distinctively Sardinian. The context is very similar when some of them passed over to West Sicily, as represented in the Cave of Villafrati near Palermo, where similar bell-beakers accompanied incised pottery akin to the native Sardinian (p. 126). But here, as in Sardinia, the immigrants are distinguished from the 'Mediterranean' native stock by the short round skull-type suggestive of inland Spain.

In the other direction, the north-westerly coasts of Italy have already been seen (pp. 157-9) to have been brought into some connexion with Sardinia. And though neither the Ligurian nor (despite contrary assertion) the Tuscan cave-dwellers have left any direct traces of Bell-beaker penetration among them, Tuscany at least must have been traversed by Beaker folk if it was indeed from Sardinia that they intruded themselves, probably rather after 2100 B.C., into the Remedello culture-province. That province's commercial importance, initiated originally from Minoan Crete and connected by the trade already witnessed with Sardinia and Spain, attracted them just as had Sardinia and Almeria, and just as did Brittany, for example, their cousins along the Atlantic sea-route: wherever, in fact, we find colonies of the Bell-beaker people, they are in cultural centres where trade, and especially that of copper-working, opened the most inviting possibilities. Thus to sherds of beaker at Remedello itself we have to add regular Bell-beaker burials at Santa Cristina, also near Brescia, with flints, a flat copper axe, and a 'Ciempozuelos' copper dagger, and another with three bell-beakers at Ca' di Marco not far away; and a new dagger-type hybridized between this and the culture's own Minoan-derived form becomes commoner than either. Once established here, the Beaker merchant-venturers found immediate access to the trade-route across the Alps to Central Europe, where the prospect of markets and supremacy was far greater than within the bounds of the already well-grown Remedello civilization, and to Central Europe accordingly we must next follow them. The western passes, from the upper Po, the hinterland of Liguria, over to the west of Switzerland, have indeed nothing to show of them: instead, there is a poor but well-marked group of small contracted-burial cist-graves in South-West Switzerland, best known from the cemetery of Chamblandes, and traceable across the Great St. Bernard by Aosta from the Ligurian region, to which their 'Mediterranean' long skull-forms and Mediterranean shell ornaments alike refer their origin. This Chamblandes culture would seem to be one of natives of the somewhat obscure North-West Italian Neolithic migrating before the progress of maritime incomings already observed there (pp. 131-2, 157); at any rate, it not only kept the Corded-ware people out of South-West Switzerland (there are even outlying cists in their territory at Opfikon and Birseck), but made the whole West Alpine region on this side a negative one for Bell-beaker folk. It was in the east, by the already growing trade-route over the Brenner Pass, that the Bell-beaker people penetrated to Central Europe.

While the influence of their pottery-ornament may be detected among the easterly Italian-Alpine lake-dwellers, and the neighbouring cave-dwellers round Trieste, it was the Danubian regions of civilization, across the mountains and down the valley of the Inn, at which they directly aimed, and accordingly the distribution of their remains now shifts, in the years just before 2000 B.C., to the Upper Danube, Moravia, and Bohemia.

They appear there as something absolutely new and foreign to all preceding traditions. At the same time, settlements are scarcely known, and the material comes almost uniformly from earth-dug graves (sometimes, but not often, grouped in a cemetery), containing a contracted skeleton, the skull invariably short and round, with rather prominent brow-ridges, as in the culture's Southern provinces and home-land. This is accompanied by a bell-beaker, other pottery, V-bored stone buttons, flints, worked as in the Mediterranean by fine pressure-flaking and including arrowheads often enough to show, as does the archer's stone wrist-guard or 'bracer', that the principal weapon was the bow; often, too, by small copper awls or needles, and less often by copper daggers, which, however, in the majority of cases conform absolutely to the 'Ciempozuelos' type. While in Bavaria on the one hand, and East Moravia on the other, the form and ornament of the beakers often have a late look, the Danubian series as a whole may be said to begin with vessels really identical with types encountered in Mediterranean territories, and this is pre-eminently true of Bohemia, where in the already mixed cultural environment the newcomers evidently settled thickly, multiplied, and extended their connexions in every direction.[1] The finely red-surfaced beaker is covered in horizontal zones of neatly comb-stamped ornament, diapered or zigzag-lined less often than simply hatched; it is occasion-ally given a handle like the plain jugs, with affinities both Danubian and Italian, which occur in association, and the other pottery includes plain bowls and dishes for which relations may also be claimed in Mediterranean lands—notably a polypod bowl-type which can best be referred to Sardinia (p. 252)—and coarser pots, on which plastic ornament

[1] Fig. 21, 2.

may make its now ubiquitous appearance, that suggest some incorporation of the country's existing populations.

Into the blending patchwork of originally Neolithic elements which were destined to pass into the dominant Early Bronze Age civilization of this most central area of Europe, the Bell-beaker people thus entered as in many ways the most potent element of all. Their strongest concentration was in the Bohemian basin of the Upper Elbe, where of their beakers alone nearly 300 have in all been discovered, and while the Neolithic traditions of agriculture and pastoralism were now mingled as the economic basis of Central European life in general, they were here ideally placed for the major contribution which they made to the growth of long-distance trade. As well as Slovakian or East Alpine copper, and Slovakian or Bohemian gold, notably in wire spirals, probably ear-rings, Baltic amber is found in their graves, and as the same ear-ring type is known from Baltic passage-graves, they were evidently promoting the existing commerce with the North as an amber trade—from Svodobne Dvory near Könniggrätz comes an actual trader's hoard of such merchandise. And among out-lying examples of the bell-beaker itself, Denmark has produced a definite though late-looking specimen from a passage-grave at Bigum in Jutland, where it lay in a secondary position with a mortar-shaped beaker evidently intruded by the Jutland Single-grave invaders in the 'upper-grave' stage of their culture (p. 218) —a synchronism plainly determinable at about 1900 B.C.

Less far afield there are some important bell-beakers in Silesia, which may be correlated likewise with the Marschwitz and Oder cultures whose emergence from the Corded-ware family at this time we shall describe in the next section, and this way Bell-beaker emigrants passed eastward into Southern Poland, spreading along the loess to Sandomierz and even into the Bukovina, and radiating influences still further east and south-east into the Ukraine, to be perceived in the pottery of the niche- or catacomb-graves already (p. 222) dated from shortly before 2000 onwards on the Don and Donetz. Into Hungary the flourishing Copper Age civilization did not allow them to penetrate far, though outliers from near Budapest and Szentes have left a beaker still as purely Medi-

terranean in type as Fig. 21, 2; in relation to the Mid-European
Copper culture their value lay rather in the extension of its
relations outwards, and above all to the north and west. Of
capital importance, therefore, both for Northern and Western
contacts, was their colonization of Saxony, effected from
Bohemia along the mountain-gorge of the Elbe.

That the Saxon Bell-beaker province was a direct and early-
founded offshoot of the Bohemian appears clearly from its
pottery, especially the admirable form and decoration of the
beakers, on which horizontal-zone ornament in the Bohemian
manner is absolutely dominant: the associated plain jugs and
bowls, polypod vessels, dishes, and coarse pots agree, and the
province may be considered established by 2000 B.C. From
the Elbe westwards, however, where the old homeland of the
Corded-ware folk—still surviving in many districts—had
stretched from Saxony into Thuringia, this pure Bohemian
character loses itself in a mixed group in which it is found
competing with features derived from a different Bell-beaker
province in the Thuringian Saale region. It was from this
mixed group, opposite the corner of the Harz, that the contacts
were effected with the North: its beakers, plump in form, are
variously decorated, the all-over Bohemian zone-ornament
hybridizing with the Thuringian province's distinct convention
of grouping the zones in two broad and often panelled bands.
This convention, together with decoration on the bowls,
notably big stone bracers, and a probable association with
point-butted axes of West European type in fine polished stone,
shows that while the Saxon province looks south-east to
Bohemia, the Thuringian looks south-west, by way of allied
groups in Lower Franconia and Hessen, not to Central Europe
but to the Rhine. And the Bell-beaker culture of the Rhine
had come from the south apparently not by way of North
Italy, but west of the Alpine barrier (p. 251), direct from South
France. Therewith we must begin a fresh section; but we
are taking leave of Central Europe with most of the pre-conditions now fully formed for the creation of the Bronze Age,
which the next chapter will find opening in Hungary about
1900 B.C., and soon afterwards in the Bohemian centre of what
is known as the Aunjetitz civilization.

3. TOWARDS A BRONZE AGE EUROPE

(Map V and Table V: at end)

The route taken by the Beaker people from South France to the Rhine is actually obscure. The most northerly beaker in the Rhône basin comes from a stone cist at Cranves in Savoy, but this is simply an isolated outlier of the group that remained (p. 251) caught up in the now essentially megalithic civilization of South France. The latter's reactions northward will appear shortly; meanwhile it would seem that the Rhine group migrated speedily away from the influence of megalithic observance, so that in their earth-dug graves there are pure zone-ornamented beakers very close to South French models, while their more distinctive tendency to banded ornament occurs already at Saint-Vellier in Provence. The line of the Rhône and Saône to the bend of the Rhine at Basel may yet yield intermediate finds, and the first signs of the Rhenish group appear in Upper Alsace and Baden, notably in the burials at Feldkirch near Freiburg. The associated pottery here, and at a newly found settlement-site further north-east at Nähermemmingen near Nördlingen, includes plastic and finger-ornamented coarse ware just as in South France (p. 251), and this may also be the context of plastic and channel-ornamented pots from Frankenthal and Rüssingen in the Palatinate, while not only the beakers but splay-walled bowls, polypod at Griesheim near Darmstadt, flat-based at Alsfeld in Oberhessen,[1] may be incised in good banded 'ladder-pattern' of positively Iberian character. The settlers' main concentration was along the Middle Rhine above and below Mainz, and it was from here that the Hessian and Franconian groups spread out to reach Thuringia and mingle with the Bohemian colonists from Saxony. However, none of this was a mass-migration taking exclusive possession of the land: on the contrary, another movement was just at this time in progress in the reverse direction, from Saxo-Thuringia to the Rhineland— that of the Corded-ware people, whose thrust this way, contemporary with their other movements already chronicled

[1] Pl. IX, 2.

from about 2100 B.C. (pp. 218, 248), now comes from p. 249
once more into our picture. The whole stretch of country
between the Middle Rhine basin and the Elbe thus became by
2000 B.C. a patchwork of the two cultures, with the remnants
of the Michelsberg and other Neolithic populations for substratum. Round barrows with typical advanced corded ware
and faceted stone battle-axes occur here just as in Thuringia
and further south round the Main and Neckar, but, for instance,
one near Fulda contained a Bell-beaker secondary burial, and
Michelsberg pottery and point-butted 'Western' stone axes
may occur in them likewise.

Now, while east of the Rhineland a unitary culture did not
emerge from this mosaic until the ensuing Early Bronze Age,
the unifying conditions of the narrow Rhine corridor brought
a genuine mixed culture into being a clear stage sooner, from
around 2000 B.C., interspersed among its two component
cultures themselves. Its distinguishing pots are known as
Zoned-beakers: the Corded-ware and Bell forms coalesce in
a usually tall shape with a slack neck-curve and a somewhat
angular body, the zoned ornament of the Bell tradition persisting in a coarsened form, and its technique invaded by cord-
impression, no longer confined to the neck as in pure Corded-
ware, but covering the whole vessel in horizontal lines. Plain
cups and mugs may occur too, and cord-impressed sherds
have been found with much finger-tip coarse ware in the
fortified hill-camp of the Dietzenley near Gerolstein; that
such fortification was due to Michelsberg example is suggested
by the occurrence of zoned-beakers in the great Michelsberg
stronghold of Urmitz (p. 137). Burials may often be under
round barrows, and lower down the Rhine in North-West
Germany, and above all in Holland, round-barrow finds
become of predominant importance. Here the Bell-beaker
folk spread in moderate strength, followed and accompanied
by the Zoned-beaker people in considerably greater numbers;
Rhineland Corded-ware peters out in rare outliers, but
gives place instead to a different element, sprung from the
same Saxo-Thuringian root on another and more northerly
line. This was a branch of the same migration which created
the Single-grave culture of Schleswig-Holstein and Jutland

(p. 217), which, turning south-west instead of north from the Lower Elbe, spread gradually across Hanover to appear on the flank of the Beaker peoples moving down the Rhine. The result, reached by about 1900 B.C., was once more a patchwork, but one blending, as did that on the Middle Rhine, into a continuum, with one centre of gravity, the Rhenish Beaker elements preponderating, in Central Holland, and another further north in Drenthe and Groningen, dominated rather by the Jutland-related 'Single-grave' element. Throughout the continuum the round barrow is distinctive, but there is also a subtler factor of unity to be recognized, contributed by the pre-existing native population. This factor, quite different from anything on the Middle Rhine, will best be approached when we take up the story of the Low Countries again below in connexion with the ensuing Beaker invasions of Britain; meanwhile, we have to remember that the round-barrow immigrants found the Northern megalithic culture of the Huns'-beds (p. 213) still existing in the 'Ems-land' of Hanover and Drenthe, and must now observe also that southern outliers of it became caught up in a fresh cross-current of megalithic culture of quite different origin.

It is noticeable that on the more southerly reaches of the Lower Rhine, before it touches the Dutch border, there is a marked thinning-out of the Beaker finds, suggesting that Beaker settlement here was soon disturbed, leaving the Dutch province in some degree of isolation from that of the Middle Rhine. On the other hand, West European point-butted axes are here quite plentiful, and the natural supposition of an intrusion crosswise from the West finds support in the presence, across the river here in Westphalia, of a new and distinct group of megalithic tombs. For these are unmistakably of Western and not of Northern type. They are long cist or gallery graves, from nearly fifty to well over sixty feet in length, built of big limestone slabs, sunk in an excavated trench into the ground and covered by a low long mound. The entrance is typically at one end, where the slabs give place to a screen of dry-stone walling, easily removable for the insertion of successive interments, for these are of course collective tombs, and the numbers of skeletons found run from some score up to as many as 200. Inside the entrance an antechamber is frequently separated from the main gallery by a partition-slab, and within there may be small-scale slab-partitioning of grave-places, which at Ülde near Lippstadt takes the form of genuine segmenting as in Atlantic regions (p. 172). The distribution of these underground long cists is thickest in Westphalia on and south of the Upper Lippe; it runs on also southward into Hesse-Cassel, and it is in that region, as is best known from the great cist of Züschen near Fritzlar, that the entry from the antechamber is most often found to be by a circular 'port-hole' pierced in the partition-slab, a feature we have already encountered in the Mediterranean and the West (pp. 152, 160). In the more northerly Westphalian area the distribution marches with that of the North-West German Huns'-beds, and this contact led to hybrid cist-forms with a Huns'-bed build of entrance in the middle of one side (p. 213). The skeletal types represented are throughout distinctly mixed, and so are the grave-goods: the Northern contact brought in outlying collared-flask and Bernburg elements (pp. 208, 217), and in the Züschen cist collared flasks lay with a tall zoned-beaker; but quite strange to the German Neolithic, and attributable only to the immigrants who introduced the cist-type to this mixed population, are simple flower-pot mugs, and bigger, rather bulging pots with slightly flaring rims, in coarse plain ware, with rare plastic- or finger-decoration; the same is true of transverse arrowheads of flint. There is in fact only one quarter whence cist-type, arrowheads, and anything like this pottery can have been brought, and that is the Seine-Oise-Marne region of North France. There we have already (p. 198) observed the grafting of Neolithic elements upon a native Mesolithic tradition, to produce a culture which survived the departure (p. 244) of the Horgen emigrants to Switzerland to adopt from the south an underground long-cist type of megalithic tomb positively identical with that which we are now discussing. The long buried gallery, the port-hole entry from the partitioned antechamber, the great number of interments, are features which there can be no mistaking:[1] the point-butted axes and the transverse arrow-

[1] Fig. 22, 6.

heads are no less typical, while the strange West German pot-
forms can well be in part at least derivatives from the bucket-
like North French type.[1] An intermediate shape occurs in the
natural cave-tomb of Vaucelles in Eastern Belgium, and it
must have been this way, round the forested barrier of the
Ardennes, that the North French colonists travelled to Westphalia about 1900 B.C. A possible reason for their migration
would be disturbance caused by the arrival of advanced bands
of Corded-ware people on their eastern border: though there
is no positive evidence, some of the round barrows of East
France may quite conceivably indicate such a vanguard for
the warrior invasions to be considered in the next chapter.

In any case, the matrix of the Seine-Oise-Marne culture
stayed fast throughout these centuries, and its continued
occupation of this whole North French area explains in the
first place the isolation of the Rhineland Michelsberg culture
from its relative the Chassey-Harrouard culture further west
(p. 158), and in the second the failure of the otherwise ubiquitous Bell-beaker folk to make any impression of their own
in the gap between. A beaker sherd indeed turned up among
the native pottery in the cist of Les Mureaux (Seine-et-Oise),
but this only reminds us that Beaker folk were included in the
megalithic civilization of South France, whence the cist-type
will be seen to have most probably come. We must, then,
turn back for a space to the developments in West Mediterranean lands already mentioned by anticipation on p. 178,
which will account for its emergence and its introduction to
the backward people of the Seine, Oise, and Marne. The
importance of Sardinia in the West Mediterranean became
further manifest on the reception of Bell-beaker folk into its
mercantile population. Not only does the island type of
polypod bowl attest a Sardinian element in the Bell-beaker
colonization of Central Europe (p. 254) and even (p. 257) the
Rhine, but the more permanently accessible eastern region of
South France seems to have received afresh Sardinian attention
of a different kind. The possibilities of an earlier implantation
of megalithic tomb-building in Provence have been seen
(p. 167) to be somewhat imponderable, but when this region

[1] Fig. 11, 11.

was overrun by Bell-beaker colonists (p. 251), we find not only 'dolmen' forms of megalith but rock-cut tombs of distinctive type, which have no immediate counterparts further west, and may be more plausibly connected with the Sardinian tombs of Angelu Ruju (p. 155), though the long narrow chamber lacks their multitude of subsidiary cells. A very similar but even more Sardinian-looking form of tomb appears in the hitherto uninhabited island of Majorca, where the groups of such cave-tombs, notably at Llucmajor and at San Vicente near Pollenza, display the same elongated chamber, sometimes with lateral rock-benches which may be 'stalled' into grave-places like cairns in Orkney (p. 192), but sometimes also with subsidiary cells, on occasion paired inside the entrance, which opens, most often from a rectangular forecourt, into an ante-chamber giving on to the main gallery by a 'port-hole' opening in the rock partition. And one Majorcan site, at Felanitx, has yielded an incised sherd of a vessel like the Sardinian polypod bowls. But the bulk of the pottery is plain fabric unmistakably related to the developed ware of Almerian Spain, where, as the next chapter will show us, the great age of Los Millares and its corbelled vault-tombs was terminated by the re-emergence of the old plain pottery (p. 129) to complete dominance, in a civilization which cast off the megalithic tomb-ritual in its transition to the Bronze Age. With this transition—an affair of some three centuries, beginning about 2000 B.C.—we may reasonably connect the withdrawal of emigrants to share with Sardinians a colonization of Majorca in which the ancient rites were still maintained. We shall find the resulting mixed Sardinian-Almerian character typical of the Balearic Bronze Age when we return to it later on. Meanwhile the family likeness between the tomb-types assigns to the same stage of events the development now in question in South France, though, as this still falls within the period of Mediterranean bell-beakers, it must have begun relatively early—in fact, probably before 2000 B.C.

While the region shows a wide scatter of 'dolmen' or cist-forms, of which that at Cranves (p. 257) is an outlier, the rock-tombs compose a famous group of five near Arles.[1] In the

[1] Fig. 22, 5.

forecourt, entered as in one Majorcan case by a stepped-down approach, may be merged either the paired subsidiary cells, as in the Grotte des Fées, or, as in the Grotte Bounias, the antechamber, but the access to the main chamber is characteristically of 'port-hole' type; the whole is covered by a low circular mound, and circular or oval mounds may survive round the 'dolmen' tombs of the same culture. The burial-rite was of course collective, and the material includes bell-beaker and other pottery, leaf-shaped and barbed-and-tanged flint arrowheads, small stone axes, a bronze derivative of the 'Ciempozuelos' type of dagger (cf. Fig. 15, 5), V-bored buttons, numerous beads, many of callaïs, a few of copper, and in the Grotte de Castellet a bead and a strip of gold. Evidently the culture lasted from the Bell-beaker period into the ensuing Bronze Age, as further west did the related Chalcolithic of the Pyrenees, Languedoc, and beyond (p. 172), with its derivative 'dolmen' tomb-forms, stretching over to the Atlantic coast. And in due course Sardinia entered upon its own Bronze Age, maintaining both rock-tombs and their megalithic equivalents above-ground—the 'Giants' Graves' already mentioned in connexion with the horned cairns of the British Isles (p. 194) —to which, furthermore, a Balearic counterpart arose in the elongated 'navetas' of Minorca. But meanwhile we are dealing with the mainland, and there the Arles tombs must stand initially—that is, from 2000 B.C. at latest—for an active centre of civilization; and that this was the source whence the religion they imply reached the humble Seine-Oise-Marne population seems the inevitable conclusion from the similarity which unites them in turn with its distinctive sepulchres. Those sepulchres, whether subterranean long stone cists or the chalk-dug grottoes of the Marne (p. 198), need not here further be described: their gallery-form, antechamber, and 'port-hole' entrance-type[1] all speak compellingly for this Southern derivation, and with their great numbers of broad-headed dead occur not only the bucket-pots and the varied abundance of flint-work, antler axe-sleeves, bone, and stone, shell and tusk ornaments, which distinguish their culture, but also Grand-Pressigny flint[2] and fine stone axes from the West,

[1] Fig. 22, 6.   [2] P. 186.

and occasional callaïs and amber beads, which testify to their makers' share in Western Europe's long-distance trade, and lastly, rare small objects of bronze attesting their duration for some centuries into the second millennium. To their eastward and north-eastward offshoots we shall return again; we have already observed (p. 198) that which went westward to join in the megalithic civilization of Brittany, and the situation in Brittany must now once more engage our attention.

The complex megalithic civilization had now reached its peak. The successive groups of settlers had created a culture, based ultimately on Neolithic economy but owing its main material wealth to the trade of the Atlantic seas, in which every activity was overshadowed by what we have called the 'megalithic religion' and its extravagant cult of the dead. We need not here recall the complicated morphology displayed among the tombs (pp. 174, 181, 198) by the traditions of the multiple-grave long mound, the cist, the gallery-grave, and above all the passage-grave introduced by the dominant merchant-colonists from Iberia. Their distribution is crowded along the South Breton coast from beyond the Loire mouth to Finistère, with extension as far as Guernsey and what is now Jersey, while in North Brittany the incoming of the Seine-Oise-Marne settlers by land brought a counterweight, with an inshore bias answered by their inland and eastward trade-connexions, to the southern maritime belt with its centre of gravity at Carnac in the Morbihan. From the date of their appearance, about or soon after 2000 B.C., the commerce of land and sea thus met in the peninsula on equal terms, and fine stone axes could now pass, like Grand-Pressigny flint, eastward overland to the Rhine, while the sea-trade to the British Isles and the Baltic was bringing in their metal and amber to be concentrated and distributed, like the axes, callaïs, and native metal, southwards to Iberia and eastwards over the Continent as well. The seaborne Western contributions to Baltic civilization have been noticed (p. 211), and Brittany in return has, for example, produced two approximations to the Northern collared flask and a Northern-like knob-hammer axe; but further, stone copies of the Minoan double-axe seem here and from the Seine basin eastwards, as

(p. 215) in the North, to have been inspired from inland Europe, where, as well as an occasional true specimen in metal, big copper currency-ingots of double-axe form were evolved; one comes from the Swiss Copper Age pile-dwelling of Locras (p. 247), and their distribution between North-Central Germany and West-Central France suggests a trade centred among the Beaker peoples of the Rhine, with Brittany as a western terminus, whence perhaps the British double-axes of p. 215.

The bringing of Brittany into these extended trade-connexions by land as well as by sea, which seems largely due to the incoming of Seine-Oise-Marne people thither from the east, must have diluted the solidarity of the Breton culture. The acceptance of the newcomers into its prevailing amalgam is shown by the occurrence of, e.g., bell-beakers and Breton bowls in their tombs, as at Kerlescant, and of their bucket-pots, as at Quelvezin, in Breton passage-graves; and such a fusion must have been countenanced by the religious system which so evidently dominated the country's life. That this had a potent centre at Carnac can hardly be doubted when one considers the extraordinary magnificence of its megalithic remains: not merely the great concentration of tombs, but the world-famous 'alignments' or avenues of standing stones, which, taken in addition to the stone circles previously discussed (Er Lannic, p. 186), must signify a growth of ceremonial which could draw together a whole great people under the spell of the religion dominating its life. Their huge extent, no less than their disregard of the old Neolithic long mound of Manio (p. 147), should assign them to this advanced stage of the culture's history. The religious domination must have maintained not only observances but also tabus as governing factors in the social system; such ritual restrictions are an inevitable assumption for an amalgam of peoples who are shown by their varied tomb-architecture and tomb-furniture to have kept up original distinctions within the whole. And among them a peculiar status must, it would seem, have been reserved for the Bell-beaker people. Their distinct origin was never forgotten: their distinctive pottery remained always constant,[1] and though here, as further south, it may appear

[1] Fig. 15, 13.

anywhere, yet it can hardly be accident that in the whole
extent of the colonization described in the last chapter along
the Atlantic coasts of the British Isles no Bell-beaker burials
are known from the colonists' collective tombs.   Something
prevented the Beaker people from taking the prominent share
in oversea settlement beyond Brittany in the manner so characteristic of them elsewhere, and it seems reasonable to suggest
that any deliberate exclusion must have been backed by a
religious sanction.   But in following their progress from
Sardinia and South France to North Italy, Central Europe,
and the Rhine, we have already seen that the Beaker folk were
perfectly capable of discarding the megalithic religion; they
were not native to it, but rather sojourners within its gates.
And just as in Central Europe and the Rhineland they appear
reverting to their old Spanish burial-rite of the earth-dug
grave, often beneath a round mound (p. 258), which became
easily assimilated to the round-barrow burial of the Corded-
ware or Single-grave folk whom they met there, so here in
Brittany there seems to have come a time when, in some
crisis perhaps of the situation created by the incorporation of
the Seine-Oise-Marne element in the amalgam of culture, a
body of Beaker people revolted against the system which there
controlled them, and 'walked out'.   In some such way, it is
allowable to suggest, came about the initial Beaker immigration
into the Wessex country of Southern Britain.

The immigrants' distinguishing beakers, well-made, reddish-
surfaced vessels with zonal ornament normally in fine comb-
stamped technique and a reasonable elegant S-profile, are
closer than any other British group to the Continental Bell-
beaker model; [1] they form Type B I in the standard classification of British beakers, and are distributed with fair compactness from Hampshire towards the Upper Thames, and the
Bristol Channel (on which one was found recently with a
typically Breton piece of finger-nail coarse ware).   The focus
of this radiation is at the Christchurch entry, the long-
flourishing ancient port at the mouths of the Stour and Avon,
and here near Bournemouth and inland on the Downs of South,
Central, and North Wiltshire are their main concentrations.

[1] Pl. IX, 1.

How the Beaker man, distinguished by his big build and broad skull, was buried crouched in an earth-dug grave is well known, and may be illustrated from this Wessex group by a grave on Roundway Down near Devizes, in this case under a round-barrow mound, which need not always be present. With a typical beaker there was a barbed-and-tanged flint arrowhead, a stone bracer, a tanged copper blade resembling the Iberian 'Palmella point' (p. 163), and a broad-tanged copper dagger enlarged from the old Ciempozuelos type;[1] similar finds come from barrows at Mere and Winterslow, and the 'Western' character of this B1 Beaker group is altogether clear. Further, for all their discarding of megalithic collective burial, the immigrants did not shake off the Breton practice of building both stone circles and alignments. That our southern standing-stone circles such as Stanton Drew near Bristol, associated with avenues, are their work, may be argued from the recent discoveries at the most famous of them all, at Avebury, where it has been shown that in its original form the monument consisted likewise of standing stones only, approached by the similarly built West Kennet Avenue, at the foot of four of whose stones have been found burials, two with B1 beakers and a third with a bowl of related character. The nature of the population on whom the newcomers impinged is revealed in the upper ditch-levels of the old Neolithic A camp on Windmill Hill (p. 142), where beaker pottery occurred along with Neolithic B or Peterborough ware, the hall-mark of the Baltic-related Eastern contribution to the British Neolithic. Following the stage of their influence upon the A folk, noted on p. 144, the Peterborough people seem to have reached Wessex not long before the Beaker immigration; in Wiltshire they have a site e.g. at Winterbourne Dauntsey, and, like the Beaker folk, they are in evidence at the near-by flint-mines of Easton Down (p. 140), while their pottery's intrusion at the West Kennet long barrow is paralleled (at the megalithic tomb of Bryn yr Hen Bobl) in another settlement-area they reached in North Wales. There, while scattered settlements were made elsewhere further north, they developed a great stone-axe industry at Graig Lwyd on Penmaenmawr, whose products

[1] As Fig. 15, 12.

were traded far and wide, and by way of the Severn basin and
the Cotswolds came to Wessex from the north-west: at
Avebury examples occur at their same horizon on Windmill
Hill, and again with their pottery in a settlement-site directly
anterior to the West Kennet Avenue.

At what date thereafter, then, did the Avenue builders with
their B1 beakers arrive? The Breton situation suggests after
2000 B.C., and this suits the Neolithic chronology in Wessex,
where, further, a clear margin is wanted before the fresh
immigration of the A Beaker folk from the opposite direction,
which we shall shortly find occurring not long after 1800.
About 1900 is therefore acceptable, and this is borne out by
the fact of the culture's mutually exclusive distribution with
another to the east of it, which stretches from the Sussex
Downs to East Anglia, with outliers spread away to the northward. This relationship points to coincidence in time, and
1900 B.C. is equally the date required for the eastern culture,
which is also the creation of Beaker immigrants, but this time,
as was foreshadowed above, from Holland and the Lower
Rhine. Their beakers, the B2 type, derive directly from the
Zoned-beaker group that we have there described (p. 258): in
some cases the S-profile comes close to that of the B1 class,
but more distinctive is the squat ovoid-bodied form with ugly
short neck [1] which the Zoned-beakers tended from the start
to assume in Holland. Associated in the typical crouched
inhumation-graves are barbed-and-tanged flint arrowheads,
stone bracers,[2] and very rarely [3] metal daggers of the Ciempozuelos family. The immigrants seem to have superseded the
local Neolithic in Sussex—certainly at Whitehawk (p. 144)—
and Kent, and settled along the Essex and Suffolk coastal belt,
finding but a single river-gap for a slight penetration through
to the inland chalk ridge beyond the broad barrier of the East
Anglian forested boulder-clay. Northward, a thin scatter on
the Norfolk coast and the Lincolnshire Wolds leads on to those
of East Yorkshire, and along this line a few obtained a footing
among the long-barrow Neolithic populations, while others even
reached the Forth and still further up the coast of East Scotland.

In all this B2 Beaker distribution the most interesting area

[1] Pl. IX, 3.   [2] Fig. 15, 11.   [3] Fig. 15, 4.

is that of the Essex coast, for it will be recalled (p. 141) that
this coast has only been brought to its present line by a very
considerable transgression of the sea, which has drowned the
former shore-belt far enough for remains of Neolithic occupation to be found not merely under patches of a foot of peat,
but beneath a widespread sheet of soft marine clay of a proved
depth of ten feet, lying wholly below present high-tide mark.
And the Neolithic A and B remains so submerged are exceeded
both in quantity and importance by those belonging or related
to the B2 Beaker culture, so that the sea-transgression provides
a limiting date for the arrival of its bearers from the Continent.
Obviously, before the submergence the coastal flats on both
sides of the Narrow Seas ran out much further: the actual
configuration of the ancient shore-line is impossible to re-
construct with accuracy, but inevitably the passage for boat-
loads of immigrants must have been much easier than it is
to-day. The recent work of the Fenland Research Committee
has thrown a clear light on the corresponding transgression
into the Cambridge Fen basin from the direction of the Wash.
Above the Lower Peat, in which the Neolithic A horizon
previously noted (p. 141) was found at Peacock's Farm, Mildenhall, the incoming salt water deposited a silt-bed of blue
'buttery clay' no less than six to seven feet thick, above whose
surface the eminences, large or small, of the region's original
sandy landscape were left as islands in a surrounding of oozy
estuarine mere. This in due course freshened and cleared to
allow willow-scrub to open the formation of an Upper Peat,
which gained with renewed subsidence till the tops of sand-
hill islands like those examined near Mildenhall were completely covered. Now, pollen-analysis of this Upper Peat
assigns it to the climate-period known as Sub-Boreal, the drier
successor, as indicated at the beginning of this chapter (p. 201),
to the Atlantic which accompanied Late Mesolithic and earlier
Neolithic times, as represented here in the Fens by the Lower
Peat. We have already seen that conditions do not allow of a
uniformly datable horizon between Atlantic and Sub-Boreal,
but compared with the latter's oncoming of drier average
climate, the incoming of the sea is a more definite affair, and
among various possible correlations for our south-eastern

submergence the most interesting archaeologically is that which may be suggested with the second Baltic transgression, following well after that of the original Litorina Sea at 4500-4000 B.C. (p. 56), traceable at the Jära Bank at Limhamn in South Sweden. For the intermediate shore-line thereby submerged has yielded remains datable down to and within the period of the Northern passage-graves, and the date in the early part of the second millennium thus given for the submergence accords well with the limit provided by the drowned Beaker pottery for the transgression on the Essex coast. And just as the Jära Bank transgression was followed by a partial recovery associated with remains of the Northern Stone-cist culture, which directly succeeded that of the Passage-graves (p. 199), so in the Fens the post-transgression Upper Peat is associated with occupation of the surviving sand-hill tops by people of the contemporary British culture, that brought in by our third and last wave of Beaker immigrants, the A Beaker people. These came also from the Lower Rhine-German area, but they have a distinctively blended character, and to understand both them and their B2 Beaker predecessors better we must next revert to that area again. There and in Britain alike we shall find the date indicated for their migration is about 1800 B.C., so that archaeology and natural sciences are here combining to define a very closely-dated series of events. It may be added that one of the quite numerous Lincolnshire long barrows, at Skendleby, with peculiar structural features in turf and timber derivable from the stone-built Severn-Cotswold group (p. 184), was erected by Neolithic A folk actually after B2 Beaker people had arrived in the district, while the Yorkshire Neolithic A (p. 145) no less certainly survived into Beaker times.

The B2 Beaker class as a whole has been seen to derive directly from the Zoned-beakers of the Lower Rhine region and especially Holland. But its Essex coast representatives introduce features of plastic neck-ridging and finger-ornament, which take us over to a distinct, though here partly associated type of pot, bigger than a beaker and with a cylindrical neck on an ovoid body,[1] known as the Bell-urn (*Glockenurne*). This

----

[1] Pl. IX, 5.

is well known in Holland and the Lower Rhineland, often in
Zoned-beaker associations, and is now recognized as the contribution to the Beaker amalgam there of the native population
whose importance was foreshadowed above.   It is the outcome
of the primitive potting-tradition, responsible also for our
Peterborough (Neolithic B) ware, which we watched in the
dawn of the Northern Neolithic originating from the influence
of an East European cord-impressed convention on the rude
fabric of the Mesolithic peoples centred in the Ertebølle
culture.   With cord-impressed or finger decoration prevailing
along with such plain work as spread to Grovehurst in Kent
(p. 213), this pottery of the Neolithic fringes around the Lower
Rhine survived till its makers became caught up in the Beaker
culture—as they were further north in that of the Huns'-bed
megaliths, into which, as at Bronegger in Drenthe, their bell-
urns may intrude.   But while the original pot-forms must
have been round or point-bottomed, as among their Baltic
(p. 201) and Peterborough relatives, the bell-urn shows, both
in its shape and the horizontal zoning of its ornament, the
influence of the bell-beaker.   And though the genuine Bell-
beaker people cannot be proved on local evidence to have reached
Holland in advance of their Zoned-beaker relations, yet it was
their pottery, and not the zoned-beakers, that combined with
the native ware to produce new and distinct ceramic styles.
In Holland we thus have first the bell-urn—to which their
own coarse ware (p. 259) should also have contributed plastic
and finger-tip ornament—and with it next a new form of bell-
beaker, known from its Mid-Dutch region of incidence as the
Veluwe beaker, in which the same ovoid body and cylindrical
neck are adapted to a broad squat form to suit bell-beaker
size; these beakers occur plentifully in the round-barrow
burials of the Veluwe and occasionally further afield, and are
recognized to have lasted throughout the Early Bronze Age.
Their ornament, though its included panelling may be a debt
to the Huns'-bed people's ideas, is regularly zonal in the
Bell-beaker manner, and in particular displays the 'ladder-
pattern' component which, as we know (p. 157), goes back
to that manner's Southern region of origin.   And finally we
are confronted on the pre-submergence Essex coast with a

distinct class of ware displaying the same 'ladder-pattern', which, while associated with plastic, finger-printed, and rusticated ornament, is rendered, together with angular panel-patterns, in the 'channelled' shallow-grooving technique like-wise native to the South (p. 173), whence it is known as Grooved ware. Clearly this is a parallel manifestation to the accompanying bell-urn; but the prevailing Grooved-ware form is a splay-sided bowl no less clearly derived from the Rhineland Bell-beaker repertory, as instanced above (p. 257) from Alsfeld,[1] and therewith, as in the related Veluwe style, we are left in no doubt about the proportion of Bell-beaker to native element. And though native convention got also into the Zoned-beaker group which produced our Essex coast B2 beakers, yet not only does the Grooved ware there come from a distinct occupation-site, at Lion Point, Clacton, but it is also found spread inland—and more surprisingly also, as we shall later see (p. 321), in the far north—unmixed with and largely outside the district of any B2 beakers. Indeed, it is often associated instead, and very naturally, with its part-relation Peterborough ware: not only near Peterborough itself, but up the Thames (wooden paddles found near the Clacton site suggest how its makers travelled), whence the Kennet valley leads west to Avebury. At Avebury it occurs not merely in the B1 Beaker association of the West Kennet Avenue (p. 267), but also in association again with Peterborough ware in the directly anterior settlement (p. 268) which the Avenue cuts across. It looks, then, as though the Grooved-ware people first arrived somewhat sooner than either B Beaker movement. Their flint implements attest both hunting, in a peculiar class of derivatives from the transverse arrowhead traditional in the Northern Neolithic, and agriculture, in the curved flint sickles already noticed (p. 213) with their Kentish relatives at Grovehurst. Their contribution to our spiritual culture will appear shortly.

We have, then, to preface the B Beaker immigrations with one of Grooved-ware folk, derived from native groups in Holland parallel by descent to the British Peterborough stock, but strongly intermixed with Bell-beaker people. In Wessex

[1] Pl. IX, 2.

the B1, in Essex the B2 Beaker immigrants overtook them, the latter shortly before the great subsidence, to spread both south-west and north in a distribution of their own. Following in turn, and after the subsidence, we next have the A Beaker immigration. The A beaker[1] is a tall vessel, with an out-slanting or cylindrical neck sharply offset from its ovoid body, as in the Veluwe or Bell-urn types. The rim is occasionally inbent, but the ornament is still very much in the bell-beaker manner, though enriched with some individuality. Its associates include similarly ornamented handled mugs, and coarse pottery, in which rusticated ware abundantly proclaims its affinity with the Bell-urn group already discussed. Its distribution differs markedly from the B2 beaker's: its makers' first main landings seem to have been round the Wash, and it is virtually absent from the south or east of the East Anglian forested boulder-clay which sunders the Narrow Sea coasts from the Cambridge region and the chalk ridge which leads thence along the Chilterns to the Upper Thames and beyond. This way the newcomers reached the Wessex chalk, and occasionally even further west; by various routes some penetrated to South, Central, and North Wales, but in the Northern Midlands they concentrated much more thickly on the upland Derbyshire limestone (having from the Wash settled where the B2 people had more sparsely preceded them in Lincolnshire), and above all in East Yorkshire. From Northumberland they reached South-East Scotland, but direct settlement by sea further north found its main centre in Aberdeenshire, whence there was some still further diffusion —while venturers from the North Wales group scattered along the West Scottish coasts. Throughout the North the culture's chronological centre of gravity is late, a fact reflected in the form of the beakers, in which the ovoid body grows at the expense of the neck, thus producing the short-necked C Beaker forms, among which signs of fusion with the prior B2 tradition may appear in various ways. All this then belongs properly to the Bronze Age, and will be dealt with in the next chapter; but we must first scan the primary evidence from further south for an assessment of the culture's character and origins.

[1] Pl. IX, 4.

First of all, the burial-rite is typically contracted inhumation under round barrows, whose abundance at once recalls those of this period in Holland and North-West Germany. The latter indeed have very marked peculiarities of structure. Within the covering mound of sand, the actual grave was enclosed in a timber structure, broadly speaking of one of two kinds: either a ditch-bedded round or polygonal affair of logs laid upon each other, with a domed sod-and-branch or log roof, or a ring, single or double, of upright posts, their tops encircling the brow of the mound.[1]　Later[2] a multiple ring of such posts might be relegated to the rim of a mound built of sods and so independently stable. The domed log type is best represented in the Veluwe, the post-barrows in the North, and just as both stone and wood grave-enclosures have been seen (pp. 221-3) to occur in the kurgan barrows of the East-European steppe, and recur in the Corded-ware culture of Central Germany and its Jutland offshoot, so in Holland the same idea reappears in these specialized forms, each representing an earthed-up house for the dead, answering to the round hut-form which at Nähermemmingen (p. 257) and in Bavaria characterizes the Bell-beaker people, and was doubtless one of their contributions to the Dutch cultural blend. In the derivative British barrows an internal dome, e.g. of flints or clay, may correspond to the Dutch domed log structure, but post-barrows are less manifest, though there is one on Calais Wold in Yorkshire, and a later development will meet us presently. However, Britain has a remarkable series of evidently ceremonial circles, in which one may see a ritualized similar round house not earthed up for the dead but open to the sky.[3]　They are regularly surrounded by a ditch, and outside it a large bank should have accommodated spectators of rites conducted in the space within, to which one or two causeways give entrance. The Arminghall monument near Norwich is a leading simple example, with posts in horseshoe formation, and the pottery found there is a form of the rusticated ware of which we have seen something with grooved ware and B2 beakers, but which makes a very definite contribution also to A Beaker material. So the whole series should be

---

[1] Fig. 22, 3.　　　　[2] Fig. 22, 4.　　　　[3] Fig. 22, 1, 2.

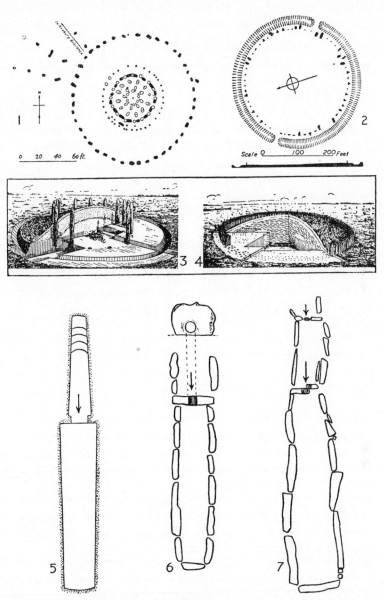

Fig. 22

BRITISH 'HENGE' MONUMENTS (pp. 274, 321)

1, The Overton Hill Sanctuary, Wilts. ; 2, The Ring of Brodgar, Orkney.

DUTCH PALISADE-BARROWS (p. 274)

3, Langedijk I, Friesland ; 4, Wessinghuizen III, Groningen.

ROCK-CUT TOMB AND LONG STONE CISTS (pp. 262, 282)

5, La Grotte Bounias, Arles, S. France ; 6, Long Cist of Villers-Saint-Sépulcre, Oise, N. France (with elevation of port-hole entrance-slab) ; 7, Long Cist of Skogsbo, Västergötland, Sweden. The arrows in 5-6-7 mark the port-hole entrances.

connected with these eastern Dutch-derived Beaker cultures. In Wessex, where the closest concentration of these monuments is found, it would seem to be eastern Beaker folk, joined to Peterborough people, who diversified the Avebury complex of monuments with the timber-circle Sanctuary on Overton Hill; [1] it is unembanked indeed, but excavation indicates that it was soon converted into a stone-circle monument of the same Breton-derived type as the rest of the complex, to which it was linked by a duplet extension of the West Kennet stone Avenue. And at the now famous Woodhenge near Amesbury, with its developed profusion of the eastern grooved and rusticated pottery together with the B1 Beaker ware proper to Wessex, we may see a clearer sign of the fusion of Dutch-derived and Breton-derived religious practice which bore greater fruit in the refashioning of Avebury itself, as excavation is now brilliantly revealing, into a majestic combination of the stone-circle and embanked types, the huge new circuit enclosing the bulk of the primary circle-complex (p. 267), and also covering the adjacent end of the West Kennet Avenue. The results of such fusion throughout Britain await us in the next chapter, culminating above all at Stonehenge.

In any case, it was the A Beaker people whose arrival in Wessex from the north-east set a seal on that region's cultural amalgam, just as they did, for instance, on the Upper Thames, and more powerfully in East Yorkshire; while up to Aberdeenshire their dominance became as nearly absolute as in Derbyshire or in their original settling-grounds round the Wash, and the northernmost of their Welsh outposts intruded with the Peterborough people (p. 267)—and beyond them here and there over West Scotland—into the megalithic tombs of the old Atlantic settlers. This far-reaching achievement implies an opening-up of new land-routes across Britain, already in part begun through the Yorkshire Neolithic A migration to North Ireland (p. 196) and the Neolithic B settlement in North Wales, which inevitably left the remoter northern tomb-builders of Scotland isolated from the Atlantic-Baltic trade. But it was just at this time that Ireland, with the horned cairns and their 'lobster-claw' derivatives (p. 197), with the wedge-

[1] Fig. 22, 1.

cairns (p. 197), and, as throughout Atlantic Europe, with 'dolmen' degenerations of all sorts, was passing its megalithic tomb-tradition into a Bronze Age in which Irish wealth in metals became more than ever a leading factor in Baltic and indeed all West-European commerce. With that we shall be concerned in the next chapter, but it is with the A Beaker colonization that the land-routes of Britain finally superseded the northern sea-passage as the middle term between Atlantic-Irish and Baltic-Continental worlds, and we must not leave these potent colonists of our island without a closer assessment of their composition and its date.

What, then, are the leading types of material accompanying their pottery? The barbed-and-tanged flint arrowhead with enhanced barbs, and V-boring applied not only to buttons but to 'pulley-ring' pendants, are elaborations of familiar Bell-beaker traits.[1]   But the absence of bracers shows a decline of specialized archery, and instead the hand-to-hand stone battle-axe weapon of Eastern and North-Central Europe makes its appearance in a boat-like axe-hammer form [2] which is only like a sundered variant of what some of the Jutland or North-West German battle-axes became (p. 218) in the later stages of their history. Evidently the North-West German branch of the Corded-ware invaders from Saxo-Thuringia, the twin of the Jutland Single-grave culture, has taken a strong hand in the A Beaker blend, as the tall shape of the beakers—also their occasional inbent rims (p. 218) and the absolute dominance of barrow-burial alike attest. And a British distribution based not on the Narrow Sea coasts but on the Wash suggests, as it does in the Anglo-Saxon case of over two thousand years later, a starting-point lying away north of the Rhine-mouth passage to our south-eastern shores—in fact, close to just the area strongest (p. 259) in Jutland-related as against Rhine-land Corded-ware elements at this period. Thus, exactly as in the B2 migrants Bell-beaker folk were compounded with the latter, so they are here with the former, with the native contributors of bell-urn and rusticated ware common in a measure to both blends; and though archaeologically the A Beaker migrants cannot be seen ready blended at any

---

[1] Fig. 23, 9-11.   [2] Fig. 23, 10.

starting-point, yet the great sea-transgression of precisely this time, by inevitably drowning an extended Frisian coast, should explain this, just as, with no room left in the hinterland, it explains why they had to migrate. And one further element in their archaeology, their daggers, will help us to confirm this date of about 1800 B.C. for their migration, and link it with the developments in Northern Europe with which we must end this chapter.

The Bell-beaker people's broad-tanged copper daggers on the Ciempozuelos model had no long vogue on the Continent, and before the Beaker phase was over in the Middle Rhine the currents of trade already emphasized had brought in another type of dagger, adopted equally by the Beaker folk in Moravia and Bohemia. This was a variant of the type current in the Hungarian-inspired Copper culture of Central Europe and the Alps (p. 242), with a short triangular blade and a round heel fixed to the haft by two rivets.[1] Now, copper daggers were readily imitated in Central Europe in flint; only, since the coppersmith's rivets could not be reproduced, the concomitant round heel was not adopted, and the flint dagger had to be hafted, as a specimen, e.g., from the Vinelz pile-dwelling (p. 247) shows, by running the body of the blade tang-like back into a thong-bound or wooden grip. Throughout and especially round the periphery of the Mid-European metal culture exquisite flint daggers on this principle were made: the North Italian series is particularly fine, as are the Grand-Pressigny flint weapons of the West, and the Western tradition of fine flint-work introduced by the Bell-beaker immigrants began in due course to enable an analogous response to the inspiration of the metal dagger to be made further north. It is with these that the flint daggers of the British A Beaker folk are to be classed: the fine pressure-flaking practised in all the Beaker cultures is nowhere finer than in theirs, as their arrow-heads and great multitudes of round scrapers and other tools everywhere show, and applied to the dagger it produced a lancet-like weapon (Fig. 23, 7), normally with a broadened convex-edged blade in imitation of a tendency which became marked on the round-heeled metal daggers, evidently to lengthen

[1] Cf. Fig. 23, 6.

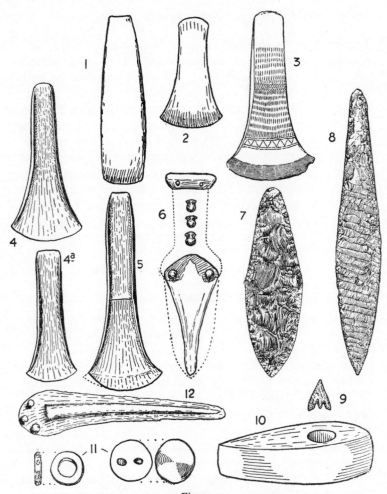

Fig. 23

METAL AND FLINT AXES AND DAGGERS, ETC., OF
WESTERN AND NORTHERN EUROPE

1, Copper axe, Lugarico Viejo, Almeria (p. 307); Flat bronze axes, Britain:
2, Round Barrow, Butterwick, Yorks. (p. 325): 3, From deposit in Round
Barrow, Willerby, Yorks., ornamented (p. 325); 4-5, Flanged bronze
axes, N. Europe (p. 325): 4, Pile type, and 4*a*, N. German Falkenwalde
type, from the Pile hoard, S. Sweden; 5, Tinsdahl type, S. Sweden;
6, Round-heeled bronze dagger (p. 278), with remains of handle, from
Round Barrow of A Beaker Culture, Helperthorpe, Yorks.; 7, Flint
dagger of A Beaker Culture (p. 278), from Round Barrow, Lambourn,
Berks.; 8, Lancet-shaped flint dagger of early Cist period, Denmark
(pp. 280-3); 9-11, Barbed and tanged flint arrowhead, stone axe-hammer,
and jet button and ring with V perforations, A Beaker Culture, Britain
(p. 277); 12, Bronze halberd, Co. Wexford, Ireland (p. 329).

Scales: 1-3, 6-7, $\frac{3}{10}$; 4-4*a*, $\frac{2}{9}$; 8, 12, $\frac{1}{5}$.

the life of a blade which had to be kept sharp by repeated edge-grinding. For the round-heeled metal type was itself current among them also,[1] and, thus introduced in Britain into the orbit of Irish-Atlantic metal-supply, became developed as a specific type of the British Early Bronze Age. Northern Europe, with no near-by metal-supply, remained virtually restricted to the flint dagger [2] for many centuries yet. But the adoption there of the dagger as a universal type of weapon, and of the pressure-flaking technique which alone could encompass it in flint, constitute a real revolution in habits and in craftsmanship for a people hitherto devoted to the axe, and to the surfacing of flint-work by grinding and polishing. And this revolution dates from roughly the same period as the A Beaker immigration into Britain. That that immigration is not earlier than around 1800 B.C. follows not only from the dating of the rest of the series of events already set forth, but from the impossibility of any sensibly earlier habituation at its starting-point to the round-heeled metal dagger-type, which to its B2 predecessors of around 1900 was still unknown. That it is not later will be confirmed in the next chapter from the chronology of the ensuing Wessex Bronze Age; and thus the association we have claimed for it with the North Sea and Baltic transgressions of the eighteenth century B.C. seems scarcely to admit of denial. What then was the cause of the parallel revolution in Northern Europe?

Though there was there no true Bell-beaker invasion, the sporadic infiltration attested at Bigum (p. 253) was only one aspect of a process consisting mainly of northward movement originating in the North German half-way house between the Baltic and the Bell-beaker and metal-using civilizations further south. The expansion of Corded-ware peoples from the Saxo-Thuringian centre where their descendants, in close contact with the Bell-beaker settlers, still lived, had created the Jutland-related group of Single-grave folk in the west, on and beyond the Elbe as we have seen, and in the east a Silesian group and the Złota culture of Poland (p. 230). Roughly within the Corded-ware belt so formed, the Bernburg and Havel cultures (p. 217) were still maintaining their individual

[1] Fig. 23, 6.　　　　　[2] Fig. 23, 8.

developments of the Northern Neolithic tradition, intimately
related to the Globe-flask culture alongside them (p. 227),
which in turn, while its Polish counterpart had entered fully
into the amalgam of Złota, was the neighbour not only of the
surviving Baalberg group—and now of another Northern
Neolithic branch, related to the Silesian Nosswitz, with a
site at Britz outside Berlin—but also, of course, of the Corded-
ware centre itself in Saxo-Thuringia. That centre's reception
of influence from the Saxon and Thuringian groups of Bell-
beaker people was shared more strongly further east by its
Silesian branch, in union with the heirs of the Nosswitz folk
and the Danubian-inspired civilization of Jordansmühl. This
union is represented by the Silesian Marschwitz culture: its
pottery jugs, Danubian in their close form-relation to the
Hungarian series but yet typically cord-ornamented, and its
metal pins and trinkets, thick-butted flint axes, and locally
developed fine battle-axes of stone, are associated in its many
contracted-inhumation graves with elements of clear Bell-
beaker derivation, the stone bracer and the Ciempozuelos
type of dagger imitated in flint. And the Bell-beaker people,
with their eastward spread now across Southern Poland (p. 255),
further influenced a new culture which arose about this time,
in partial succession to Złota in Little Poland and more
centrally in East Germany on the Lower Oder. Here the
Corded-ware element is fundamental, but its battle-axes are
poor, and its beakers degenerate affairs, often ledge-handled,
and accompanied by simplified 'flower-pot' vessels closely
recalling the mortar-shaped beakers of the later Jutland single-
graves (Pl. VII, 12); but from Silesia, where the culture mingles
with the Marschwitz, northwards, the flint dagger was likewise
adopted by these people as their own. And this adoption was
not confined to the east. The Oder people's lancet-like form
of the weapon has a distribution balanced on the west among
the Single-grave folk on both sides of the Elbe—in Hanover,
where it approaches the starting-point of the cognate A Beaker
type's introduction to Britain, and in Holstein, whence its
introduction to their relatives in Jutland was part of the wider
movement we are now to witness.

For it was now not only in Jutland that these Single-grave

folk had invaded the old territories of the Passage-grave people. At a date which the S-form of the beakers and the simplified battle-axes shows to be rather after 2000 B.C., groups of them from the Lower Elbe and Holstein had begun to invade the Danish islands, where they were reinforced not only by minor incursions of their Boat-axe cousins from South Sweden (pp. 228, 231), but by adventurers of the Oder culture from the opposite N. German coast. So when, a little later, the flint dagger began to spread among the populations that had sent off these colonists, its extension in their wake was a natural sequel. Thus the final triumph of Single-grave over Passage-grave people was before long followed by the beginning of the flint dagger's dissemination round the Baltic, at this time about 1800 B.C., when the sea-transgression already noticed (p. 270) must have reinforced the restlessness of a warlike folk with expanding-room still before them. The other hall-mark of the period in these regions is burial in stone cists. In North Germany, where the long history of megalithic burial had put dolmen-derivative cist-graves into relation with the flat-stone cists brought in by the Globe-amphora invaders (p. 228), cist-burial was widespread, and one-man cists are common in the later single-graves of Jutland. And when the invasions of the Danish islands brought such cists over into contact with the megalithic tradition of the subjected Passage-grave people, the result was a fusion which made single and small-scale collective burial in various types of stone cist the joint rule— though there are still barrows and many flat-graves also— throughout West Baltic lands during the two centuries and more from 1800 or 1750 B.C. when even secondary burials in the old passage-graves gradually died out, and invaders and invaded, with the flint dagger as their typical weapon, grew together into a united people that laid the foundation of the great Germanic civilization of the Bronze Age.

But one strange anomaly remains to be recorded. On the Middle Kattegat coast of West Sweden, and over a considerable hinterland, the stone cists have no place whatever in the Northern series prevailing elsewhere. The Skogsbo cist in Västergötland is a typical example.[1] They are long, for the

[1] Fig. 22, 7.

most part subterranean gallery-tombs for multiple collective burial, with an antechamber partitioned off by a slab typically pierced with a 'port-hole'—faithfully reproducing, in fact, the West European type of the Seine-Oise-Marne people described above. We have seen in Westphalia and Hessen (p. 260) that this was brought by migrants from France to West Germany: is it deniable that a further compact migration, leaving no traceable tombs upon its way, took these folk from homes either there or actually in France itself, where aggressive warrior peoples (p. 261) threatened their existence, overland to the coast and thence by ship to the seclusion of West and West-Central Sweden? It is at least undeniable that the Swedish cists have no otherwise intelligible explanation, and that their pottery most closely resembles the Seine-Oise-Marne bucket-type (Fig. 11, 11), while lancet flint daggers [1] show them to date from within this same period, the latest in which the French and West German cists can very well have been in use. And even in North-West Germany and Denmark, where stragglers from such a migration might have been caught up, the dagger period's simple pots, though conventionally derived from the mortar-shaped beakers of the Single-graves,[2] have an unmistakable Seine-Oise-Marne look about them. There should, then, be a West European element in the Northern Stone-cist culture, and at that one must at present leave it. But this whole culture's life and achievement falls really outside the limits of this chapter, for it is the contemporary of the full Early Bronze Age of Europe at large. And it is now time to gather together the variegated threads of the transition we have been so long following, and set the fabric of Bronze Age civilization at last before us in initial completeness.

[1] Fig. 23, 8. [2] Pl. VII, 1-2.

Chapter Seven

THE BRONZE AGE AND THE EUROPEAN
ACHIEVEMENT

I. THE MEANING OF THE AGE AND ITS INCEPTION IN
CENTRAL EUROPE

(Map VI and Table VI: at end)

BY the opening centuries of the second millennium, the period which our survey of European prehistory has now reached, the civilization of the Near East was already ancient. The third chapter of this book ended with the exposition of the cardinal fact that from beginnings at least as early as 5000 B.C. two thousand years of growth had led up to a commencement of dynastic history, both in Mesopotamia and Egypt, at a date when by far the greatest part of Europe still remained in Mesolithic barbarism. Even Anatolia in 3000 B.C. had a long period of Chalcolithic culture behind it, and while Troy and Thermi were already in their beginnings as centres of settled and organized life, Minoan Crete was only just taking shape, and on the European mainland the dawn of civilization was breaking slowly in the form of peasant cultures which did little more than reflect the long-established primacy of the Orient in a new setting. But that new setting meant new opportunity. Neolithic civilization was not created in Europe by the unaided efforts of immigrant Orientals: it was a complex reaction by Europe itself, in which Oriental impulse was blended and transformed into a diversity of essentially European cultures. We have seen how manifold was the process of blending and transformation, as indeed was the impulse itself. The results have been displayed as Aegean and Mediterranean, Balkan and Danubian, Western, Northern, and East European cultures, each with true individuality, and each drawing upon native energy and tradition and native opportunities of environment and its resources. Furthermore,

284

as the successful exploitation of environment enabled populations to grow and the exploited territories to expand, these cultures have come into ever greater contact with one another, have overlaid each other, and have become cross-fertilized and cross-bred, so that the culmination of the Oriental impulse in the propagation of metallurgy did its work in a Europe in large parts of which the mingling of peoples and cultures was liberating a maximum of initiative, and promoting all the vitality of competition. The immediate climax of that process was the establishment of Bronze Age civilization, and before entering upon our record of its achievement we must pause to consider just what a Bronze Age means.

The metal on whose service Near-Eastern civilization had been built up had initially been copper. The antiquity of its discovery, of the recognition that from seemingly unpromising greenish substances, malachite apparently first, and then the oxidized ores to be found in surface lodes in certain regions, reduction by heat could extract a generally serviceable metal, has been touched on above (p. 73), and the revolution thereby brought about in human life indicated, with the momentous sequels it implies. With the fact of the Oriental civilization thus made possible as our background, we have watched the metallurgy of copper making new homes in Europe, and have begun to see something of the results. The issues involved were not only industrial, but intellectual and social no less than commercial and economic. In the first place, the original implicit recognition that shapeless ore, liquid molten metal, and cold metal moulded in any shape desired, were all forms of the same substance, had been an intellectual feat which deserves to rank among the foundations of scientific thought. In the second, the elaboration of the smith's technique, by constant experiment and invention, turned the product of thought into a skilled craft—a 'mystery' into which the layman could not penetrate, but which made its masters indispensable to him and his whole society. Maintained therefore, as we remarked above (p. 85), out of society's surplus of subsistence production, the smiths became privileged specialists, passing on their knowledge only within a limited circle of apprenticeship. Their contribution to society's resources in return was a form of wealth not only uniquely precious, as most obviously in the case of gold and silver, but in that of copper uniquely serviceable. Worn or broken implements had no longer to be thrown away: in copper they could be recast in the same or different forms, limited in range only by technical bounds which the craftsman was constantly seeking to extend. Metal was thus not merely a precious possession: it was capital. Its supply thus became a vital matter in society's economics. Ores were difficult to find, and confined to certain regions, to which access had to be maintained with care. Prospecting, and the establishment and security of trade-routes, became consequently essential. And two things followed: first, the growth of organization with the community had to take on special characters, culminating in adaptation for warfare as the ultimate sanction for protecting coveted wealth; secondly, the territorial growth of civilization as a whole had to adapt itself to an economic geography concerned not merely with the old primary considerations of food and water, but with the distribution of mineral resources.

A great deal of this has already been seen in action in the European prehistory of the third millennium. The civilization first engendered in the Orient had passed on its primary characters to Europe inevitably ahead of its specialized development of metallurgy, and we have shown how 'Neolithic' culture is simply the product of the time-lag between the one and the other in any given region. As a matter of fact, in many provinces of Neolithic culture men were throughout acquainted with metal objects, though they seldom possessed many, and still less often left those they had for archaeologists to find in their settlements or graves. Or during the lifetime of a Neolithic culture metal objects were introduced by trade from without and gave rise to imitations of their forms in stone or flint, or new forms in which their influence is seen combined with that of traditional work in native materials. But gradually, in one region after another, metallurgy itself arrived to establish new homes. We have seen this happen, for instance, in Spain: we have seen something of it in Italy: and we have watched the formation of a Copper Age culture in Hungary whence the smith's craft spread right into Central

Europe. And the result of the period's whole complex of processes, compounded as it was of so many activities, of migration and land-winning as well as of trade, and of trade not only for metal, but for other sought-after substances, whether precious in themselves like amber or, as with metal's still dominant competitors stone and flint, for their utility, was the vivid patchwork of Europe in the opening of the second millennium. On first acquaintance this patchwork seems almost desperately confusing—a welter of cultures often not even geographically distinct, but interpenetrating one another in a fashion only in part to be explained by the physical geography of their environment. But if one can look past the multiplicity of appearance, and bear with the many and various group-names it has made necessary in archaeology, the underlying shape of things in the Europe of the twentieth century B.C. is not really difficult to discern.

The Danubian, the Western, and the Northern Neolithic civilizations have all to a greater or less extent overspread each other's original bounds, and together with that, the vigorous expansion of what we have called the Warrior Cultures has spread a new element among the peoples of Europe from Russia to the Rhine and Britain, and from Greece and Italy to Scandinavia. The Bell-beaker people, spreading in a rather different manner from the Iberian Peninsula over much of Central as well as Western Europe, represent a distinct form, unique in its individuality, of the Western contribution to the amalgam. And the Warrior Cultures rank in a sense with the Northern, but are differentiated by the radical modifications they owed to the Eastern steppe, with its Caucasian and Anatolian further contacts. Thereby they became equipped in a fashion likewise unique for their greater destiny—that of linking the greater part of Europe together by a common increment in material and spiritual culture, by a common factor, it would seem, in language, and by an unevenly spread, but everywhere in some sort palpable, common contribution in blood. Meanwhile, throughout, the strength and significance of metallurgy was growing, as we have said, and already before the end of the third millennium it was rising towards a dominant position in Central as well as Southern

Europe and in favoured regions in the West. The Bell-beaker people added to its potency in their own way, and in the two centuries after 2000 the Beaker invasions of Britain, and the analogous Northern movements which created the Stone-cist culture round the Western Baltic, may rank as preconditions for the bringing of the north-west and the north of Europe respectively within the same cultural orbit as the centre, while the old Atlantic sea-route yet afforded its own connexion with the Mediterranean. Already by then the trans-Alpine route between Central Europe and Italy and the Adriatic has begun to show its promise of importance, again, in part at least, in connexion with the Bell-beaker people, while the links between the Danubian and the Aegean worlds have by no means lost their significance, with Greece now passing under a new people in whose Middle Helladic culture Aegean-Anatolian elements were blended with an obscure but vital contribution from further north, relating them somehow with the Warrior newcomers to the Danubian basin and still further afield. In short, the drawing together of Europe into a nexus of cultures alive, in however varying degrees, to a common rhythm of civilization is becoming possible. In that rhythm Oriental impulse and native response will harmonize in a positive and original measure, the cultural individuality of the Europeans. Thus we approach the Bronze Age; but meanwhile one important aspect of the matter recurs at this point for mention, the European climate.

At the beginning of the last chapter we spoke of the transition from the fairly warm but moist 'Atlantic' climate of later Mesolithic times (p. 57) to the 'Sub-Boreal' epoch of still warm but relatively dry conditions, and saw that this process cannot be very closely tied down to dates. The change in the composition of 'oak-mixed-forest' vegetation which does most to indicate it in northerly latitudes is assigned an upper dating-limit about 2500 B.C., and thereafter with the increasing dryness conditions far more favourable to human activity began to make themselves felt. It is against this background of change, gradually thinning and contracting the dense forests which had so dominated the economy of Mesolithic man, and so sharply delimited the distribution of the early Danubian peasantries, that the whole kaleidoscope of human movement and intercourse in the centuries before and just after 2000 must be set. Barriers of really dense forest shrank, lightened, and wide tracts formerly wooded became park-land, or even sometimes open heath, while unencumbered steppe-land extended its borders, so that travelling, and equally grazing and agriculture, found a widening range of opportunity and encouragement. At the same time barriers of mountain became easier to traverse, and the importance of great passes like the Brenner across the Eastern Alps ranks perhaps among the most momentous results of the change to Sub-Boreal climate. However, the change was not a simple matter of universal gradual improvement. For on the one hand, in some regions the dryness might intensify to drought, and on poorer soils within the North European plain, and eastward as one passes further away from the maritime and deeper into the orbit of Continental conditions, an increasing precariousness of agriculture may have been as potent a stimulus as any to the migration of peoples; while the traditional nomadism of pastoral steppe-folk would be likewise affected, and many have seen in Sub-Boreal drought a prime cause of the expansion of the Warrior Cultures. In any case, on the general balance of gain and loss pastoralism was more favoured than agriculture by the change, and the old days of more or less exclusive contrast between dense forest, Danubian tillage, and food-gatherers' 'bad-lands' came to be replaced in the Bronze Age by a less diversified landscape more widely favourable to pastoralism than to any other element in food-producing economy. On the other hand, in the West, where wind and wet from the ocean were in all periods the dominant climatic factors for man, the Sub-Boreal epoch, like the Boreal before it, was never really dry enough to thin down forest-growth by mere restriction of rainfall: on the contrary, in its exposed and upland regions, it was the storm-favouring Atlantic age that had kept the tree-line down and promoted peat-forming moorland, whereas the reduced storminess of the Sub-Boreal now let upland forest grow at the moorland's expense, while the dense forest on lowland clays remained intractable, and on the lighter soils the change

favoured pastoralism rather than agriculture without essentially
altering the total area available to human enterprise. Thus
the Sub-Boreal amelioration of climate was offset at the
Continental end of the scale by excess, and at the oceanic by
defect, of the factors making at the mean for improvement
of conditions for man. But taken as a whole, it was a
momentous, if gradual, shift in the balance between man
and his environment. And man's response was far-reaching,
and falls roughly into two stages. The first is the great phase
of movement, conflict, and intermixture that we have already
followed through the later centuries of the third millennium
and the opening of the second. The second, supervening
upon that and gathering the harvest of its struggles, was the
Bronze Age that we have now to approach. By the time it
had reached its climax, European civilization was in all
essentials founded.

Bronze is an alloy of copper and a metal not yet here
mentioned, tin. Serviceable as copper not so alloyed may be,
it yet has three main disadvantages: it is relatively soft, so
that the blade of an axe, for example, needed constant
hammering-out if used for cutting hard wood; its melting-
point is rather high (1084 degrees centigrade for pure copper);
and for chemical reasons it is not easy to cast successfully,
because the gas-bubbles which it generates when molten tend
to produce a 'blistered' casting. The presence of an alloying
metal can produce a metal at once harder, with a lower
melting-point, and, owing to chemical reaction, less prone to
'blister'. Now the discovery that tin, mixed with copper in
a certain percentage, gave these desirable results can scarcely
have come about through its prior recognition as a distinct
metal. The first step was the lighting upon ores which contained some amount of tin as a natural impurity: such ores
were, we may believe, exploited by Near-Eastern metallurgists
who came to recognize their good qualities without at first
understanding to what they were due. The percentage of
tin in them was not very large, and their metal must have
been regarded as just a superior sort of copper; before the
second millennium there is no proof of deliberate production
of bronze at its standard percentage of 90 per cent. copper to

10 per cent. of tin. But there need be no doubt of the realization that some ores—those, in fact, containing tin—were better than others; the metallurgists of Troy II, to take an exceptional example, sometimes used copper alloyed with tin in proportions varying up to as much occasionally as 10 or even 12 per cent., and before the third millennium neared its end it may be considered certain that Anatolia, with the Asiatic Near East generally, had become aware of the separate existence of the two metals, and was proceeding by experiment towards the standardization of bronze. Tin-containing copper ores, or actual tin ore for smelting together with copper, must have been watched for by prospectors in search of new sources of supply. And since in Crete and the Cyclades, as we have already mentioned (p. 241), bronze-production begins with Middle Minoan times, and in mainland Greece simultaneously (p. 239) with the incoming Middle Helladic culture, one may suppose that in the century or so before 2000 B.C. the existing copper resources of the Aegean world were supplemented by a discovery of tin somewhere reasonably near at hand. In fact, the only certainly recorded tin-working in Greece, behind Crisa, the ancient port of Delphi on its bight in the Corinthian Gulf below Parnassus, have yielded potsherds which, taken with those occurring on the site of Crisa itself (now Maghoula), may imply the metal's discovery here perhaps by precisely the required date. Thus the legendary landing of Minoan Cretans at Crisa, which Greek tradition came to connect with the founding of the shrine of Apollo at Delphi, may really echo a Minoan tin-trade: in fact, it may have been Crisa's monopoly of Aegean tin that founded the fortunes of the Delphic sanctuary.

But well before this, as we have previously seen, commerce in metals had begun to ply along the Western sea-route, and Aegean-Anatolian trade had for a large part of the third millennium made known copper in Danubian Europe, where native copper-working was now being extended westward and north-westward from Hungary, and connexions were in the making with the corresponding metallurgy of Mediterranean and Atlantic lands. Inevitably there will have followed an extended search for European tin. And inevitably, as earlier in the Near East, its first discovery should be looked for in combination with copper that will have attracted attention in any case. Now, tin occurs with copper in North-Western Spain, and in due course, as we shall see below, Iberian metallurgists discovered it, just as it was discovered in fairly close proximity to copper in Brittany, and, greatly outweighing the neighbouring copper-supplies, in the famous tin-streams of Cornwall. There is also evidence for an independent discovery of the tin of Etruria, within the Chalcolithic culture-area of Remedello in Italy, which will have supplied the smiths of the Bronze Age that supervened there, and even possibly, as Sir Arthur Evans has urged, have been drawn on by Minoan Crete. But nowhere in these regions is there proof of priority over inland Europe. There the copper now long familiar in our narrative could be obtained on both sides of the Lower Danube between the Morava and the Wallachian plain, along the Maros in company with the gold of Transylvania, and beyond both in North Hungary east of the Theiss and above all west into the Slovakian Mountains; we have seen the evidence for the first opening-up of the rich deposits of the Eastern Alps, and observed the contemporary presence of copper objects in Bohemia on the edge of the metalliferous mountains that stretch westward into Middle Germany. But, since there is no evidence of ancient knowledge of the local tin on the edge of the South Hungarian Banat, the Bohemian-Middle German region is the only one of all these where the first tin of the Mid-European Bronze Age can be sought. For there and there alone the metal is to be had in quantity, from the Bohemian Erzgebirge west to the Thuringian Hills round the upper waters of the Saale. And in the centre of that belt, in the Oelsnitz district of the Vogtland, the copper ores in which it is also rich have the tin-stone occurring with them in natural combination. The superiority over pure copper of a metal containing up to 3 per cent. of tin would in any case attract notice, and since the brown spots of the tin-stone are easily detectable in the ore, the recognition of the independent presence of tin was bound to follow. Thereupon could ensue the establishment of standard bronze. Thus localized by the facts of mineral geography, the event can be fairly closely dated in archaeological terms, and thereby we shall obtain the first fixed point, outside the Aegean area, in a chronology for our European Bronze Age.

The first bronze objects found in the Bohemian region adjoining these tin-bearing mountains are pins for fastening the dress, of a distinctive type known as knot-headed,[1] which, as we shall see directly, is of Near-Eastern derivation. They occur in graves, as at Velka Ves in Bohemia and Opatovice in Moravia, of a culture in the main analogous to the Silesian Marschwitz (p. 281), in which the mixed elements of the region's Copper Age (p. 244) were developed in a form closely similar to that of contemporary Hungary. Since the ensuing civilization of the Bohemian Early Bronze Age is known as the Aunjetitz culture, this prior stage has been called Pre-Aunjetitz (or Proto-Aunjetitz). It follows from our previous findings that its date, like that of its Marschwitz associate, is somewhere in the early second millennium, but these pins, and its Hungarian affinities in general, can fix its chronology rather more closely. Those affinities are most easily appreciated from its pottery, in which handled jugs recalling Fig. 24, 4-6, are prominent; this type of jug is, in fact, a leading characteristic of the initial Hungarian Bronze Age culture, often called Tószeg A from the earliest occupation in the great settlement-mound of Tószeg near the Middle Theiss, typified at Nagy Rev close by, and further south at Oszentivan and at Pecska and Perjamos by the Lower Maros over the present Rumanian frontier. The last three settlements have produced bronze knot-headed pins, and Oszentivan also a rendering of the equally Eastern roll-headed pin. The cultural tradition of the Hungarian Copper Age is still strong there, and at Perjamos the Copper Age type of spiral armlet (p. 247) appears at a low level in bronze: these ornaments may, in fact, be accounted the earliest true bronzes in Danubian Europe, and the recurrence of the knot-headed pin in the related Bohemian-Moravian culture points to their direct connexion with the discovery of tin on the marches of Bohemia and the Vogtland. Metallurgists acquainted with Aegean-Anatolian bronze were then not only settling in Hungarian copper-working centres

[1] Fig. 24, 1, *a*.

but penetrating to their counterparts in Bohemia and bringing the tin discovered there into use in both areas in the first bronze made in inland Europe—devoted to ornaments among which the knot-headed pin stands out, as introduced by the same craftsmen from a contemporary Near-Eastern model.

The principle of this pin [1] is to provide a loop for a thread, to secure its hold of the dress, by a multiple coil of its wiry upper end, finished off by winding round the shaft; the device had long been known in the Near East, and appears in Cyprus and at Troy II, but the form it assumes in Europe may be dated by its occurrence in the time of the Middle Kingdom in Egypt, that is, about 2000-1750 B.C. And that its European appearance is fairly early within that period is argued by the evidence of another Near-Eastern bronze type, the so-called ingot torque, a penannular neck-ring of thick wire with flat-hammered ends rolled back into loops (Fig. 24,3). This also turns up in Egypt, but its best-dated occurrence in the Near East is a hoard found in the floor of a Middle-Kingdom stratum at Byblos, the well-known Egyptian trading-station on the coast of Syria. The Byblos hoard not only shows these torques were traded as bulk merchandise, but allows them a date about 1900-1800 B.C. And of a number of identical torques found in Danubian Europe, one occurred in an upper level at Perjamos, and others in graves not far away at Ó Beba where were also knot-headed pins, imported Mediterranean shells, and some gold ornaments including flat-ended ear-rings again of Near-Eastern inspiration. These torques indeed gained currency in Middle Europe not only for wear, but as a convenient unit form for metal as bulk merchandise (whence the 'ingot' in their name), and the Byblos hoard is answered by a good few such in the Danube basin, notably between the tin district and the Slovakian and East Alpine sources of copper. It would be unjustifiable to put the start of this practice in Europe too far away from its date at Byblos, and since it seems that the use of bronze began with the smaller-scale production attested by the pins, 1900 may be accepted as a date for the earliest appearance of these, on sites like Perjamos in the Hungarian region, and

[1] Fig. 24, 1, *a*.

simultaneously in Pre-Aunjetitz Bohemia and Moravia. Then by 1800 the ingot torque may be considered regularly current, with the maturity of the Hungarian culture, and therewith the full Aunjetitz civilization of Bohemia begins to usher in the Early Bronze Age of Central Europe generally.

We shall find this chronology confirmed by later findings, just as it well suits those of our previous chapter. The validity of its basis in these Near-Eastern type-datings is confirmed by further evidence for the underlying assumption of active Near-Eastern-Danubian trade relations at this time. The hook-tanged 'Cypriote' dagger is indeed only a doubtful case of intrusion into Central and even Western Europe. But gold ornaments do reveal Near-Eastern influence, and among them not only the simple form of ear-ring already mentioned and the little coiled hair-ring related to it, but also a curiously lame borrowing from the magnificence which remoter Eastern forms of ear-ring had assumed in the treasures of Troy II. The big hooked-basket shape of the Trojan models was not copied, though it does reappear in the British Bronze Age of the West: the Central European goldsmiths were content to reproduce the decorative wire coils, which the Trojans had liked to solder on to them and they could not, as separate ornaments—not for the ear at all, but probably, like the little coiled rings just noticed, for the hair. These impoverished adaptations of the antique became popular in the Aunjetitz and related cultures: they may be termed lock-rings (Fig. 24, 2), and we shall presently find them also as exports in Northern lands. The same is true of the pins, to whose more direct adoption from Near-Eastern sources the knot-headed type has already introduced us. With it the roll-headed pin came in forms both simple and specialized by broadening the roll-topped head into the 'racquet' type;[1] to these already ancient Near-Eastern variants Central Europe added one simplified into a simple disc-head form, and altogether it is clear that a pin-fastened costume became with the Early Bronze Age the leading European fashion—a spontaneous native reaction to initial Near-Eastern influence. Lastly, the period's pottery in most of Danubian Europe continues the

[1] Fig. 24, 1, c, d.

Copper Age tradition, not least in its Eastern and Aegean reminiscences (pp. 234, 242), but in a new standardization of forms which we shall best appreciate in considering the various cultures singly. At least the metal types appearing together with the bronze industry have validated our conception of its origin, and therewith of its chronology.

The mainly Hungarian culture of Tószeg A and Perjamos was firmly founded on old Danubian traditions, handed down through its Copper Age predecessor, but it is a curious fact that cases of the same site occupied continuously from that age into this are nowhere yet on record. The new Early Bronze Age settlements were substantial affairs, normally close above the flood-plains of big rivers. The old agricultural basis of economy remained—even the stone 'shoe-last' hoe may still be found, and stone axe-hammers remained current, reminding us of the previous period's cultural admixtures, as does the Bell-beaker type of stone bracer found at Nagy Rev; flint and bone were yet in use, while flat axes and daggers presumably began to be made in the new bronze. Tószeg A and Nagy Rev may rank as typical for most of the Hungarian plain: their pottery is dominated by the handled-jug type, in fine brownish ware, seen in Fig. 24, 5, *a-c*; the handled dish (*d*) is also notable, and there are coarser domestic vessels with roughened surfaces and sometimes finger-printed bands, while the fine ware is normally smooth, but for occasional small body-ridges and nipples. In the more southerly region typified at Perjamos, the jugs,[1] sometimes two-handled, have the handles starting from the flaring rim instead of half-way down the neck as more often at Tószeg, and in general Perjamos pottery is closer to Aegean-Anatolian, even Minyan, type than further north where standardization was more purely from the Copper Age tradition. Further east we have noticed the survival of the Schneckenberg culture on the Alt (p. 235) to join hands with the Perjamos group, and while in the north of Hungary there are barrows which suggest the survival of less civilized warrior people on the fringes of the Danube basin throughout this period, other cultures grew up in various parts of Rumania, that of Monteoru on the edge of the Carpathians

[1] Fig. 24, 4.

and over much of Moldavia, superseding the last of the
Painted-pottery culture of Cucuteni B; that of Otomani in
West Rumania nearer to Perjamos; and later the still rather
obscure Witenberg culture of Transylvania. The Monteoru

Fig. 24

EARLY BRONZE AGE POTTERY AND ORNAMENTS
FROM CENTRAL EUROPE

1, Bronze pins : *a*, Knot-headed ; *b*, Bohemian cast version ; *c, d*, Roll-
headed and racquet ; *e*, Bulb-headed perforated ; *f*, Trefoil (pp. 293-5, 301).
2, Aunjetitz gold lock-ring (p. 295) and 3, Copper ingot-torque (p. 294),
Saxony. 4, Perjamos jug, Oszentivan, Hungary (p. 296); 5, *a-d*, Tószeg
A pottery, Nagy Rev, Hungary (p. 296); 6, Aunjetitz mug of early form
(p. 300), Saxony; 7, Aunjetitz mug of (p. 300) developed (carinated) form,
and bone crutch-headed pin (p. 301) from grave, Weissensee, Saxony.

Scales : 2, ½; 3-7, ¼.

and Otomani cultures may be dated perhaps from about
1700 B.C., and we shall meet them again below; their importance here is simply that of reminding us that side by side
with the great Tószeg-Perjamos-Aunjetitz complex other less
advanced groups were existing round the Danube basin, in

which traditions of the previous period were kept alive in
distinctive forms, to emerge further on in the Bronze Age
to a more widely spread importance. Thus the high-handled
decorated pottery of Monteoru looks back to the later third
millennium, and the culture must rank as an easterly relative
of that which in the Middle Bronze Age comes out in the
Rumanian-Hungarian borderlands of Vattina as a product of
the old warrior-culture tradition of our last chapter (including
actual Corded ware), matured as a neighbour of Early Bronze
Age Perjamos. Similarly the Otomani culture of that same
neighbourhood has indeed its similarities to Perjamos, but in
its richly decorated pottery it reminds one once more of later
Bronze Age developments in Hungary, and its case seems very
similar to that of the Slavonian culture of the Drave and Save
country to the south-west, where we have already (p. 246) seen
Balkanic and Corded-ware elements fusing in a group distinguished by decorated pottery, and destined to spread its
influence far afield over Hungary when the Bronze Age got
beyond its Early stage. So we should picture the progressive
peoples centred in the Hungarian plain as in large measure
ringed round by cruder folk, off the best land and probably in
the main pastoral hillmen, among whom the 'warrior' elements
of the later third millennium were not yet embedded in the
settled tradition of Danubian civilization, but remained to
merge with it in the ensuing period of Bronze Age maturity.

Something of the same kind can be said of the Aunjetitz
centre of progress in Bohemia, so closely related to the
Hungarian, and its neighbours in various directions. The
centre of gravity of the Aunjetitz civilization was the heart
of Bohemia along the Moldau and the Upper Elbe; it had
provinces northward and westward in German territory, which
will be considered presently: eastward, from the start, of
course, it embraced Moravia, but its settlement-area stopped
short at the Slovakian Mountains: southward it reached and
just crossed the Danube in Lower Austria, but got no further,
and not only Upper Austria, but the whole hill-country of
Southern Bohemia, lay outside its borders. Like its Tószeg-
Perjamos sister in Hungary, it was primarily a civilization of
the loess plains and river-lands, the thousand-year-old home

of Danubian farming, and now the focus of Middle Europe's strongest cross-currents of culture and richest highways of trade. In it the varied upshot of those cross-currents was caught in the civilized setting of the Danubian tradition, fertilized anew as it was by commerce and industrial progress, and the result made the Aunjetitz territory the cultural centre of the major part of Europe. But all around it were cultures in which the legacy of the preceding centuries, dominated in one form or another by the powerful contribution of the 'warrior' element, remained to a greater or less extent in control, and these were during the Early Bronze Age penetrated by its influence only to emerge in the Age's ensuing maturity as its counterweight in the balance of Europe that was then achieved. In the mountain region south of the Upper Danube we have to reckon with a continuance of the Laibach and Mondsee cultures (p. 245), under a share in the dominance of the Corded-ware people which becomes ever more pronounced as one goes westward into Switzerland and Bavaria (p. 248). In Upper Austria and the South Bohemian hill-country, as over the Bavarian border to the west, the Corded-ware people were still in the ascendant, attested, as ever, by the distinctive round-barrow burials. And on the opposite side its Moravian fringes were edged by Bell-beaker groups as yet unabsorbed into its main body, and by a peculiar outgrowth apparently from some part of the Corded-ware complex, distinguished by pottery ornamented not with cord but with textile impressions, the so-called Braided ware; these both recur south of the Danube by the West Hungarian border, and with them there, and also both further west and north-east into Slovakia, there also appear important groups surviving from the ubiquitous Baden culture of the preceding period (p. 234). And in these regions there are furthermore three distinct Early Bronze Age cultures not of the true Aunjetitz or Tószeg stamp. In West Slovakia the Mad'arovce or Veselé culture is differentiated by a domination of its blending by a Baden element, recognizable in the big handles of its pottery, and by one of Corded ware. On the marches of West Hungary south of the Danube, the Wieselburg or Gáta culture is again distinguished by its pottery, and may include connexions with the Braided-ware people: it has been quoted as analogous to the Otomani culture on the opposite marches of Hungary, though its divergences from the Aunjetitz norm, like the Baden element of Mad'arovce, recall rather the character of Perjamos. Lastly, Lower Austria south of the Danube begins its Early Bronze Age with yet another outcome of the previous period's admixtures which lacks the specific increment distinctive of Aunjetitz, and was only gradually influenced thereby: this is called the Böheim-kirchen (or Unter-Wölbling) culture, and its composition answers to that of the Mad'arovce culture of Slovakia. Thus the mosaic of the period around 2000 took some time to fuse, under Aunjetitz influence, into a greater unity; and while these three cultures presently become virtually Aunjetitz provinces like those soon to be described in Germany, the less accessible highlands where we have seen the Corded-ware invaders more absolutely dominant never followed suit, but developed in time, in antithesis to Aunjetitz, the Barrow cultures which rose in the Middle Bronze Age to counter-balance it. And now we must look more closely at the Aunjetitz civilization itself.

It takes its name from a great cemetery south of Prague, in Czech called Únětice, and the major part of our knowledge of it comes from graves. The body is laid in a closely contracted position, usually on its right side facing south, sometimes covered by slabs. The grave-goods include in the first place pottery; the prevalent jugs, following on those of the Pre-Aunjetitz stage, answer in general[1] to those of Tószeg A, but develop[2] an angular or carinated body, as sometimes in the B I stage of Tószeg to be described below: the broad-rimmed dishes are matched there also, and in general, though some forms may copy Aegean stone vases, Aunjetitz pottery may be said to combine the blended traditions of the preceding period with a standardizing element ultimately south-eastern, but more directly inspired from Hungary. The domestic ware comprises a fairly wide range of jars, bowls, and amphorae, and it is not difficult to recall from it how many elements both Northern and Western had now met in Bohemia on the

[1] Fig. 24, 6.   [2] Fig. 24, 7.

old Danubian substratum. Physically, however, the people show little variation in skeletal type, being as a rule moderately-sized and rather long-headed. Their settlements include some hill as well as valley sites, and the primary economy was pastoral as well as agricultural; but industry and trade are, of course, outstanding. While stone and bone tools remained plentiful, bronze casting made rapid progress. The flat axe of the Copper Age now begins to be superseded by the type with lateral flanges[1] to keep it securely bound in the cleft-crook wooden haft which must by now have come into use. The dagger is standardized in the round-heeled triangular form already noticed (p. 278) from its wider diffusion and imitation.[2] Ornaments become more varied: the pin types already described were augmented by a characteristically Bohemian solid-cast rendering of the knot-headed form,[3] by another[4] with vertical thread-hole in a globular head, by single and multiple ring- and trefoil-headed forms,[5] and finally by a crutch-headed type.[6] These pins were exported and imitated widely, as were other Aunjetitz bronzes; but before considering the long-distance connexions so demonstrated, the culture's own northerly and westerly provinces remain to be noticed.

In the west one became established in the plain of the Bavarian Danube, known after a type-site at Straubing, in which with a slightly weaker equipment of Aunjetitz metal-forms the pottery follows up the Pre-Aunjetitz tradition in its own way, keeping to the pouch-bodied instead of the carinated jug, not so chary of ornament, and with peculiarities of bowl-form. In the north-east in South Silesia, on the other hand, the culture's Marschwitz basis was more thoroughly overlaid with classic Aunjetitz convention. Round the Middle German arc between these we have direct Aunjetitz penetration from Bohemia at work in the matrix of Bell-beaker, Baalberg, and Corded-ware cultures, with the Bernburg culture also concerned, and Globe-flask and Oder culture elements within sight too, that we last saw there in the previous chapter. In Saxony the Aunjetitz tide set in strongly, but in addition to its carinated- and handled-mug pottery[7] the assort-

---

[1] Cf. Fig. 23, 4-5.   [2] Cf. Fig. 23, 6.   [3] Fig. 24, 1, *b*.   [4] Fig. 24, *e*.
[5] Fig. 24, *f*.   [6] Cf. Fig. 24, 7.   [7] Fig. 24, 7.

ment of other forms betrays Corded-ware and even Oder culture contributions; the territory stretching east to Silesia and the Middle Oder, known as the Lausitz, will presently be revealed as of peculiar importance for its cradling of what from these Early Bronze Age beginnings grew, in the Middle Bronze Age, into a self-standing Lausitz culture, destined after the period covered by this book to expand as one of the most powerful forces in the whole prehistory of Europe. Westward into Thuringia, the blend was somewhat different: while any Bernburg contribution affected rather the Lausitz, and the Globe-flask people held still to their own individuality, the Bell-beaker people combined readily with the Aunjetitz advance, and the warriors of the Corded-ware tradition played a potent part in giving this Saxo-Thuringian province a character of its own. Their greater chieftains were interred in mighty barrows, which will engage attention more than once again hereafter (pp. 328, 365), with martial weapons of distinctive types; and secondary burial in older barrows, most notably perhaps at the Baalberg (p. 228), stresses the continuity with Neolithic times. Thuringia covers indeed the great mining region centred in the Vogtland, and the metal industry and trade gave it the closest connexion with the culture's Bohemian centre; copper-mining extended also as far northwest as the Harz, but in that direction a further Corded-ware element asserts itself, in a form not dissimilar from the Marschwitz contribution in Silesia. Lastly, further south in Thuringia, a distinct 'Arnstadt group' is recognizable for its preponderance of Bell-beaker elements.

We saw above (p. 256) that these had there combined Bohemian-Saxon with Rhineland origins, and it is not surprising to find analogies now between the Arnstadt group and the distinct culture which came into existence during the Early Bronze Age as the successor to the Beaker cultures of the Rhineland itself, considerably more remote from Aunjetitz influence. This is called the Adlerberg culture, from a cemetery near Worms; it is plainly the work of descendants of the Beaker peoples, and with it we reach the western edge of the main orbit of Aunjetitz civilization. The West, with its individualities now accentuated by its possession of the resources for metal industry of its own, calls for treatment in a new section. We may take 1750 B.C. as a limiting date for the formation of the more outlying Aunjetitz provinces, and for the Adlerberg culture, and thus Central Europe entered on the second quarter of this millennium with its Early Bronze civilization fully shaped. In the Alpine lands that civilization was slow in forming, in the west as in the east, and the change of lake-levels due to the Sub-Boreal climate restricts continued recourse to the evidence of lake-dwellings. But across the Alps we have seen the way open into Central Europe from Italy, and Italy had an Early Bronze Age civilization of its own (p. 334), based on the old Remedello culture in the fusion we have already suspected with 'warrior' immigrants from over the mountains (p. 250) as well as with Bell-beaker people, which maintained the closest connexion with Central Europe, and contributed with it powerfully not only to the enrichment of the Bronze Age in the West, but above all to its ultimate creation in the Baltic North. This too, then, must next engage our attention.

2. THE WEST, THE NORTH, AND THE CHANNELS OF TRADE
(Map VI and Table VI: at end)

There were really two major zones of Bronze Age civilization in the West, each with a metal economy based on its own sources of copper and tin, with precious metal besides. The south-western consists mainly of the Iberian peninsula, the north-western embraces North-West France—above all Brittany—and the British Isles. In between, the use of metal for long continued to make little headway, so that while we shall find important incomings from Central Europe into France on the east, much of the country, especially the old megalithic regions of the south and west, remained until a late date with an economy that can only still be called Chalcolithic. To take the Iberian zone first, the peninsula has been seen to be one of the richest and longest-known metalliferous regions in Europe. But whereas the abundant copper—and the precious metal—of the south formed the chief economic strength of the civilization we have seen centred in Almeria, tin is only to be had in the north. Its chief abundance is in the north-west (p. 292), where its discovery by the people of the megalithic tombs, bell-beakers, and rock-carvings noticed above (p. 188) may have been due to its occurrence together with the copper they were already exploiting, as in Central Europe, or in the North Portuguese rivers where they probably conducted washings for alluvial gold. But there is little to show for any early importance of North-West Iberian bronze, and in fact the Almerian south long maintained in its Bronze Age the use of the unalloyed copper it had so much closer at hand. There appears, however, to be a little tin together with copper in the hinterland of Catalonia in the north-east, where we have seen an Almerian element early encroaching into the so-called Pyrenean culture (p. 166), and the first recognition of the value of tin-alloyed bronze may have been promoted on this side of the peninsula through contacts with bronze-using centres further east. Since the Aegean let its old sea-trade with the Iberian West languish altogether with the rise of Middle Minoan civilization at the end of the third millennium (p. 152), it is more natural to look for such contacts with North Italy, where Spanish connexions in the Remedello culture (p. 247) had been reinforced by the expansion of the Bell-beaker people, by way of Sardinia, here at just about that time (p. 253). The Italian Bronze Age succeeded to Remedello on the strength of its own tin supply; its bronze output soon reached markets not only northward across the Alps but westward to the Rhône and South France, and since South France has produced also some Early Bronze Age objects of Spanish type, there may have been Italian-Spanish connexions this way, even though indirect. In any case, even apart from the Bell-beaker people, there was a certain background of cultural parallelism between the Spanish and the Italian Chalcolithic. Mention has already been made of the fine flint-work which characterized both cultures (pp. 161, 247), and among the finest Iberian flint weapons are those triangular blades fashioned for hafting at right angles to a wooden haft which are conventionally known to archaeology as halberds. This type of weapon probably descends from very ancient beginnings in the south and west, in deer-antler

PLATE IX

BEAKER POTTERY FROM BRITAIN AND THE RHINE AREA

1, B1 Beaker, Cholsey, Berks. (height 6 in.) ; 2, Bowl, Alsfeld, Oberhessen (height 4¾ in.) ; 3, B2 Beaker, Felixstowe, Suffolk (height 5 in.) ; 4, A Beaker, Figheldean, Wilts. (height 7¼ in.) ; 5, Bell-urn, Lion Point, Clacton-on-Sea, Essex (height 10¼ in.)

1, 3, 4 *British Museum :* 2 *Alsfeld Museum :* 5 *Hazzledine Warren Coll.*

See pp. 257, 266-273

PLATE X

1. . THE FOLKTON CHALK DRUMS

Scale 1 : 4

See p. 378

2-5. FOOD-VESSELS OF YORKSHIRE AND IRISH TYPES

2, Alwinton, Northumberland (height 4⅝ in.); 3, Goodmanham, E. Yorkshire (height 4¼ in.);
4, 5, Northern Ireland (heights 4 and 3½ in.)

British Museum

See pp. 319-20, 322-3

picks and their stone and flint-bladed equivalents such as we have already connected with the derivation, in a sense a parallel process in the east and north, of the shaft-hole axe (p. 223). And whether or no flint blades were mounted in this way in Italy, the Remedello culture certainly had among its copper weapon-types one which seems to be the local counterpart of the metal halberds that are now to meet us in Iberia.[1] The continuation of the halberd in use into the Italian Bronze Age is attested by its depiction in the famous rock-carvings of the Monte Bego, close behind the Riviera coast on the French frontier, and by a number of actual bronze halberds, and while the paramount influence here was the trans-Alpine diffusion of the weapon in its Irish-derived form, to be discussed shortly, North Italy has yet produced one example (from Frosinone in Tuscany) answering to the Iberian type. But this is little enough: obviously in the main Italy and Iberia drew apart in the Early Bronze Age; and since, of the intermediate islands, we have already seen that Sardinia, connected as it was with South France, did no more than cross contributions with Spain in the purely insular megalithic culture of the Balearic group, the Iberian Bronze Age can really only be considered in isolation—an isolation only otherwise modified by certain Atlantic connexions with the North-West along the old-established sea-route.

The reduced character of these latter connexions, compared with the rich long-distance sea-trade of the previous centuries, must rank with the parallel interruption of the Eastern Mediterranean trade as dominant causes of the Iberian isolation. And the reason is not far to seek: the opening-up of the overland trade-routes across Central Europe, and the rise of Hungary, North Italy, and the whole great Aunjetitz province to a controlling position upon them, drew off the commerce of the North, and most of that of the North-West, away from the Atlantic West into the heart of the Continent, whence the Aegean and the Near East could be reached by way of the Balkans or the Adriatic, so that Iberia was thrown largely upon its own resources. And it is likely that the Sub-Boreal improvement of climate which made the opening-up

[1] Fig. 25, A 1.

of the European land-routes possible led in Spain to a good deal of desiccation, which will have upset primary food-production even in the coastal plains and made the always arid inner Spanish plateaux in part virtually desert country. Now the prosperity of coastal Iberia, and its potency of influence inland, in the Chalcolithic Age had been closely bound up with the dominance of the megalithic religion. Fertility, economic and commercial wealth, had been associated with the mysteries of the great tombs, and in the cult of their sacred dead must have lain the magical guarantee of the enjoyment by the living of the bounties of divine Nature. If Nature began to change her ways, and riches for the tomb-builders and offerings for their dead no longer flowed in from the traffic of three seas, the sanctions of the old religion would lose their hold. And, in fact, with the rise of the Bronze Age the corbelled tombs of Los Millares and their like, and their megalithic counterparts spread over much of the peninsula, became deserted. The magnificent hypertrophy of Mediterranean religion for which they had stood died away, and in its stead the old Almerian rite of simple cist-burial reasserted itself in a new form: six thin slabs, or a big earthenware jar, held the contracted corpse, and the graves were scattered among or beneath the houses of the living. The leading settlements were strong hill-top villages defended with stout stone walls, and from their houses—each usually a huddle of rectangular rooms with stone foundations—and their graves come material remains which enable one to trace something of the nature and course of the culture.

From its original south-eastern focus the Chalcolithic Almerian civilization had spread not only round the coasts but in the east up the Ebro, into Aragon, and right on to the central plateau of Spain, where its arrival, late in the third millennium, seems to have put a partial end to the Bell-beaker culture and may well have helped to stimulate its people into their great overland migrations (p. 251). But with the coming of the changes of which we have spoken, its main vigour shrank to its homeland in Almeria itself, which became the chief centre of Bronze Age culture. The initial stage of transition from the Chalcolithic is held to be represented there by the settlements of Lugarico Viejo and Fuente Vermeja, to which correspond further north a number of sites in the Albacete province, while in the Portuguese West, probably after a longer survival of megalithic culture, as at Alcalá (pp. 161, 248), a variant of the same is adduced in the cist-graves of Castro-Marim and Quinta da Agua Branca. The implements of this stage are predominantly pure copper,[1] and the unalloyed metal continued in use, side by side with a bronze containing never more than a quite small percentage of tin, throughout the fully developed culture which is reckoned to have supervened about 1700 B.C. The type-site of this in Almeria is the fortified hill-settlement of El Argar, which is answered by neighbours such as El Oficio and Fuente Alamo, and by the middle of the second millennium it is thought that the El Argar culture, in a varied degree of dilution, extended over the greater part of the peninsula. The dilution comprehended a survival of degenerate megalithic tomb-form in much of Portugal and the north-west, and with it in Galicia a continuation of the old rock-carving art (p. 188) in an extremely conventionalized form to which we shall find close parallels in Britain. There is also in West-Central Spain and near by in Portugal decorated Bronze Age pottery in the Bell-beaker tradition, while in the north the Pyrenean culture long maintained both megalithic usage, in harmony with that of South-Western France, and its own traditions of pottery-making, including decoration in which the old plastic and finger-tip ornament (p. 128) remains prominent. On the fringes of its Almerian penetration in Catalonia, such ware has been found mixed with El Argar types at the mining site of Riner, together with stone moulds for casting axes in what the presence of tin with the local copper ore entitles us to consider was bronze. The axes of the El Argar culture tend to a well-splayed blade, but remain flat, with scarcely a hint of the flanges elsewhere now developing. Awls, arrowheads (the archers wore stone bracers in the Bell-beaker manner), and triangular daggers with two to four hafting-rivets[2] were also made: the dagger became at times elongated into a simple short flat sword, but the most distinctive weapon is the halberd

---

[1] Fig. 23, 1 ; and cf. Fig. 15, 5.   [2] Fig. 25, A 2.

above mentioned.[1] For these a broad butt and a tapering blade with a strengthening midrib are the two main characters, which appear in varying proportion: the result is a normally symmetrical weapon fixed at or nearly at right angles by stout rivets to a wooden haft of which its butt often bears tell-tale traces. Among metal ornaments silver becomes prominent, not only in plain ring-forms but in attractive simple diadems with an upward projection in front, sometimes found worn by the buried dead; there are beads of stone, shell, and wire, rarely of imported callaïs, and in one case of an Egyptian faience which will be used in its wider context below (p. 346) to show that the culture was still flourishing after the middle of the millennium. In fact, it probably lasted to near its end; but throughout, its traces of contact with the outside world are sparing, and though its typical smooth dark pottery, round-bottomed save for some pedestalled forms, and comprising mostly simple or carinated bowls, runs sometimes to handled shapes which have been compared with Aunjetitz, the El Argar civilization as a whole kept to itself, and despite the slight Atlantic connexions we shall shortly notice, Spain did not play any extensive further part in European affairs in general until after the period covered by this book. But the type of culture which the El Argar Iberians developed was in no sense discordant with those of the rest of Europe, and it remains an essential, though secluded, part of the European scene.

We have said that the Pyrenean culture maintained both its megalithic usage and its distinctive pottery. The stone-cist form of grave which was so early introduced there (p. 167) and had been augmented in the megalithic gallery-grave, is now represented with the waning of megalithic tradition by forms as simple as had ever been, in which bronze ornaments and arrowheads and El Argar types of pottery bespeak advanced date; as one goes west into the Basque country, the culture gets poorer and El Argar influence dwindles, while native material is supplemented rather by bone and stone ornaments like those of the megaliths of South-West France. The latter, situated where their builders could be reached by

[1] Fig. 25, A 1.

influence not only from Spain but by the Rhône from Italy and Central Europe, may contain along with their wealth of native material objects from that direction which can date their long survival more strikingly: trefoil-headed pins[1] of quite late Aunjetitz and North Italian types occur sometimes, as well as arrowheads and the El Argar dagger-type in copper and poor bronze; there is native tin in the Cevennes as well as copper, but flint and stone remain predominant, for tanged arrowheads and daggers, often of very fine workmanship, while bone phallic beads and slate palettes, taking one back to the days of seaborne Aegean contacts in the third millennium, occur among the wealth of barbaric ornaments together with these other evidences of long survival through the second. The tombs themselves are of various degenerate 'dolmen' forms, continuing the tradition whose implantation in Languedoc we have recounted earlier (p. 172): the alternative form of collective sepulture in natural caves remained current also, and cave habitations are overwhelmingly common everywhere, with coarse finger-tip pottery and often polished stone axes. Whether the peculiar polypod bowls of the gallery-grave of La Halliade, south-west toward the Pyrenees (p. 174), are contemporary with the bell-beakers also found there, or are secondary introductions of this later date, is unknown: their remarkable shoulder-groove, interrupted by substantial lugs, oddly recalls the 'groove and stops' embellishment of the British food-vessel pottery to be discussed presently, but the possibility of a connexion is highly conjectural, and the bowls may well be as early as the beakers and so make it chronologically hopeless. Really, the whole mountain region between the Rhône and Loire valleys and the Atlantic remained throughout the second millennium a cultural backwater, distinguished from the far more estimable culture of contemporary Spain by its backward retention of a debased megalithic religion, and its Chalcolithic poverty of material equipment.

Very much the same seems to be true of the south-western slopes of the Alps. But between runs the Rhône valley, already long established as a channel of communication into inland Europe, open to contact south-eastward with Italy

[1] Fig. 24, 1, *f.*

over the Alps, and north-eastward giving on to the Swiss
plateau, which in turn connects eastward with the Brenner
route connecting Italy directly with the Aunjetitz province
of Central Europe. And from the middle Rhône to West
Switzerland a new province of Early Bronze Age culture now
came into existence, formed, as its variation of grave-form
between small megalithic and small single-cists suggests, of
a combination of outlying Western megalith-folk with the
Swiss cist-people of Chamblandes (p. 253) and such further
relatives of theirs as are known from Savoie, together under the
unifying influence of a contribution from the Aunjetitz
direction, and open also to one from North Italy, to which
they were in part connected by ties of origin. In Savoie,
indeed, a cist-grave at Fontaine-le-Puits, richly furnished with
a whole armoury of flint arrow- and dart-heads, fine greenstone
axes, and copper weapons including a dagger and a flat axe,
marks an antecedent stage closely parallel to Remedello.

When the new culture supervenes, its bronze products may
occur in Swiss lake-dwellings, and an actual Early Bronze
Age stage of the Lake-dwelling culture, still imperfectly known
from sites like Morges on the Lake of Geneva, may be recognized as contemporary with it; but it was itself essentially not
a lake-dwelling affair, and may be distinguishably named the
Rhône culture. Ingot torques, knot-headed, roll-headed, disc,
and trefoil-headed pins, proclaim its connexion with Aunjetitz,
and the independence of main types of tool and weapon shows
it to have run parallel to the Aunjetitz and contemporary
North Italian cultures. It produced its own variety of flanged
bronze axe, side by side with those of Aunjetitz and the
distinctive Italian form with a notch in the butt,[1] and more
remarkably made a third with Aunjetitz and Italy in producing
a dagger with a cast bronze hilt—the three original types so
created forming not a derivative series but an interrelated trio.
These bronze-hilted daggers (Fig. 24, B) will be considered
again in connexion with the coming of the Bronze Age from
Central to Northern Europe: they multiply as the period
proceeds, but their invention by the connected bronze-workers
of Aunjetitz, Italy, and the Rhône culture cannot have been

[1] Fig. 24, C 2.

long after 1800 B.C., when, of course, blades of the same triangular form for riveting to non-metal hilts were also current. It was, then, through the Rhône culture that elements from the Italian-Aunjetitz cultural axis reached the cave and megalith folk of Languedoc and the south-west, and that process lasted long, as is shown by the bronzes of the caves of Durfort, Les Buissières, and their like in the Gard region, and was felt as far west as the Gironde. But this was not all. Directly north of the Rhône-culture area, where the Jura takes up its mountain line from South-West Germany, the uplands of Franche-Comté were now being peopled by a warrior Round-barrow and Single-grave folk. Just the same thing was happening in Alsace and in Lorraine, and in time spread over into Burgundy. The origin of these vigorous and evidently pastoral folk is not open to doubt: they were born of the warrior Corded-ware peoples whom we have watched overrunning already so much of Central Europe, and who were there forming what we have recognized as the potential counterweight to the Aunjetitz mode of civilization. No corded pottery is associated with them in France, but the barrows and single-graves themselves are typical of the whole 'warrior culture', and with their inhumed dead the grave-goods sometimes include the same bronze triangular daggers and trefoil-headed pins as we have been considering. Their relationship to the Rhône culture is, in fact, just that of their kindred further east to the Aunjetitz and Hungarian civilizations; and one may add that on the Rhine they must have connected intimately with the related people of the Adlerberg culture. The difference, however, was that here on the outer fringes of the Central European economic system their material culture was greatly impoverished; indeed, the archaeological finds that do anything to reveal their chronology are few and far between before a time well on in the Middle Bronze Age. But the preceding centuries had seen the growth of a trade across these regions between the Rhine lands and the West. And there now not merely fine stone axes and Grand-Pressigny flint, but a wealth of copper, tin, and gold, was known to be controlled by peoples of an ancient and probably decaying Atlantic civilization, famous for the magic of their megalithic tombs and sanctuaries, and altogether as inviting to stout adventurers as Montezuma's Mexico. The next thing we find is a sudden invasion of dagger-armed, barrow-building warriors in Brittany.

The Breton barrows take the form of great stone cairns, containing a closed grave-chamber sometimes roofed with the corbelled vault long native to the country, but essentially as different from the old megalithic tombs as were the barrows of the Single-grave folk of Jutland. The grave-goods include a special form of beautifully worked barbed-and-tanged flint arrowhead in great abundance,[1] one or two flat or slightly flanged bronze axes,[2] and from two up to eight triangular daggers of the same metal,[3] with the fine grooves (though not the engraved ornament) of the Rhône and related weapons, and hilted, not indeed save in one poor example in cast bronze, but in wood, with the same distinctive central indent and with similar bronze rivets. A variant with a midrib is probably due to subsequent influence from the British Isles (p. 318), but peculiarly characteristic is a small tongue projecting from the base of the blade into the hilt.[4] The invaders, then, dominated their new country's resources of copper and tin, and the skill in flint-work (Grand-Pressigny flint is often used) and the building-labour of its people. But their graves are never intruded among the old megalithic sanctuaries, and their rite seems to have become modified in face of the alien mysteries of the megalithic religion. Though some of their burials are by inhumation, as one would expect, yet the ritual fire, which had been a widespread adjunct to inhumation-burial, became now extended—as happened sometimes in the megalithic religion itself—to the actual cremation of the corpse; a development which became more and more widespread in the European Bronze Age as time went on. In any case, the aloofness of a ruling caste stands out clearly in their shunning, unlike the Bell-beaker folk and even the Jutland Single-grave people, any frequent contact with megalithic tombs, and admitting into their own none of the offerings of fine stone axes and even none of the pottery traditional among the

---

[1] Fig. 25, D 4.   [2] Fig. 25, D 3.
[3] Fig. 25, D 1-2.   [4] Fig. 25, D 1.

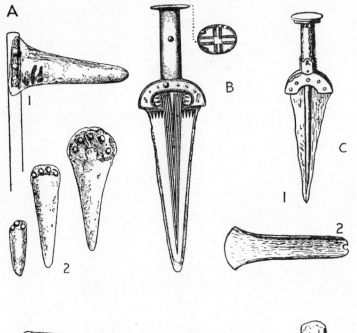

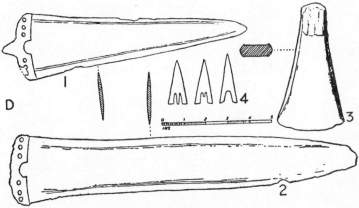

Fig. 25

EARLY BRONZE AGE WEAPONS FROM SPAIN, THE RHÔNE
VALLEY, ITALY, AND BRITTANY

A: Bronze halberd (pp. 305, 329) and 2, Bronze daggers, El Oficio, Almeria:
   Spanish El Argar Culture (pp. 307-8).
B: Bronze-hilted dagger of Rhône Culture (pp. 310-12), La Guillotière,
   Rhône, France.
C: 1, North Italian dagger from lake-dwelling, Polada; 2, Italian notch-
   butted flanged axe (pp. 310, 335).
D: 1-2, 3, Bronze daggers and axe, and 4, Flint arrowheads, from grave
   at Remedon, Côtes-du-Nord, Brittany (p. 312).

Scales: A-C, rather over $\frac{1}{5}$.

natives. Their own pottery, when it is found, appears in handled vessels new to Brittany, but not wholly unrelatable to those which became current in the Adlerberg and ultimately the more extended Barrow cultures of the Rhineland and Central Europe, save that it tends to high-shouldered forms and the broad ribbon handles may be as many as four in number. Ornament, when present, is in incised zigzags or hatched triangles as on the Rhône, Italian, and Central European daggers, and a similar sherd accompanies an isolated burial much further south at Singleyrac in the Dordogne, with a bronze-hilted dagger, flat axe, and Aunjetitz-like spiral ornament, which suggests a related lesser intrusion from the same easterly source in that direction also. The St. Menoux barrow in the Allier may be compared with its two daggers and globular-headed Aunjetitz pin: in fact, it is unknown how far groups of these invaders may not have scattered themselves over France: the Breton group is simply far outstanding for the wealth it drew from its unique territory. Therewith gold does not fail to appear: the wood hilts or leather sheaths of as many as eight of the known Breton daggers are ornamented in an extraordinary pointillé technique of studding with hundreds of tiny gold nails. It would seem that this amazing embellishment was suggested by the pointillé ornament of the later Chassey Neolithic (p. 158) and Breton pottery, which we have seen embodied in a special form on the ritual 'vase-support' vessels of the Breton megaliths (p. 185). Thus, at a date which their culture's freedom from Central European sequels shows to be as early as our derivation of its bronze types will reasonably permit, warrior adventurers from far inland took possession of Brittany. The date can hardly be much later than 1750 B.C.

Their conquest of a land where the spiritual and social tradition of megalithic culture must have had such a firm hold can hardly have been easy of adjustment. To dominate while incorporating so little of that tradition must have involved religious and intermarriage problems and all the stress of a clash of cultures; also the land was small and densely populated, while yet commanding easy access to other lands overseas. It need thus be no surprise to find evidence for a secession, within a generation or two of the initial conquest, over to South-West Britain, whither the Beaker people had seceded, we believe for some similar reason (p. 266), nearly two centuries before. For the evidence is unmistakable. Spreading out over the Wessex chalk from the entry-port already signalized (p. 266) at the Christchurch river-mouths, a series of richly furnished graves, under round barrows as distinctive in their way as the Breton cairns, forms the most brilliant memorial of the Early Bronze Age in all Britain. The barrow-type so introduced is the bell-barrow, surrounded by a berm and embanked ditch, which became varied as the disc-barrow, with a small central burial-tump surrounded by a greatly enlarged berm which the embanked ditch in turn encloses. And the leading bell-barrow burials, as in Brittany sometimes inhumations but more often—and for the first time in the British Bronze Age—cremations, and as in Brittany with the deposit sometimes laid on a plank of wood, are accompanied by triangular bronze daggers initially identical with the earliest Breton type. Furthermore, in two famous cases the hilts of these, at Normanton in Wilts of wood, and at Hammeldon Down in Devon of amber, are studded with exactly the pointillé ornament of tiny gold nails just noticed in Brittany. Flanged as well as flat bronze axes appear also: occasionally the barbed-and-tanged flint arrowheads reproduce the Breton type; and while not more than one or two pottery vessels recall the Breton handled forms, two wholly new types of ritual pottery augment the case for the culture's origin in Brittany with a most significant implication. These are the initial members of the small-sized series known as 'incense-cups' or pygmy cups, which runs a long course through the sepulchral practice of the British Bronze Age: one, called from its surface-covering of applied knobs the grape-cup,[1] reproduces a type evolved in the later Chassey-Breton ceramic across the Channel and adopted into ritual use there in the megalithic tombs, while the other, known from the Wiltshire finding-place of the finest specimen as the Aldbourne cup,[2] corresponds in its burnished surface and fine white-inlaid incised and pointillé ornament very closely to the later Chassey

---

[1] P. 331: Fig. 26, 5.　　　　　　　[2] Fig. 26, 1.

and Breton 'vase-supports' of which the same is true (p. 314), and also preserves some memory of their form in its peculiar waisted, splay-rimmed shape, and the perforations which usually pierce its sides. The precise ritual use of these cups is unknown, but their preservation of the ornament of their Breton counterparts at once emphasizes the evidently magical character (p. 185) which alone can explain its otherwise inexplicable duration from the third so far into the second millennium, and gives a clue to the situation which brought about the Wessex culture's secession from Brittany. For this megalithic magic was just what the invaders who remained behind there would have nothing to do with, and one can easily see that those of the invading caste who—perhaps in the second generation—stooped to intercourse with the dreaded superstition of their subjects, might be driven out to seek their fortune in a less rigorous land. And a date about 1700 B.C. for this well suits the situation in Britain.

That they found the fortune they sought has already begun to appear from the wealth of their grave-goods, and will appear still more forcibly when the rest of it, especially its gold and amber, comes to be described. And that Wessex was less rigorous has begun to appear also in our account (p. 276) of the way in which its varied Neolithic and Beaker peoples were combining in a fusion of religious practice symbolized by Avebury, the Overton Hill Sanctuary, and Woodhenge. The predominantly Beaker culture responsible for that fusion was not at all ousted by the newcomers: their relations with its people seem to have been simply those of an upper class, which justified its social dominance by so extending long-distance trade connexions as to bring Wessex into a position of European importance, as a commanding *entrepôt* between the West and the whole sphere of influence of the Aunjetitz civilization. To see how this happened, we must review the situation throughout the British Isles. But first, the tale begun in the Avebury complex and Woodhenge demands its culmination, and it is hard to believe that that culmination is not to be found in the central glory of prehistoric Wessex, Stonehenge. The history of Stonehenge seems to begin with some unditched stone structure of unknown plan, which was followed by the ditch-enclosed circle of uprights known after the discoverer of their empty and silted-up sockets as the Aubrey circle. Together with flints and antler picks, its ditch has yielded a piece of the grooved ware already (p. 276) signalized at Woodhenge; but the monument so assignable to the same phase as Woodhenge and the refashioned Avebury complex was itself thereafter refashioned.[1] The lintelled circle of sarsen stones, with the great horseshoe of sarsen trilithons within it, was laid out from four 'station'-points and erected inside the Aubrey circle, while thereafter again these were supplemented with the most astonishing feature of the whole monument, the circle and horseshoe of 'blue stones' proved to have been brought from the Presely Mountains in far-distant Pembroke-shire. The earthwork Avenue that runs up the 2360 yards of easiest gradient to Stonehenge from the river Avon, whatever its time-relation to the Aubrey circle whose ditch-entrance it fits so oddly, is most readily explained as the 'sacred way' up which the blue stones were borne from the last stage of a journey made from Pembrokeshire by water. It is disputed when this was, but beaker pottery overlies the full silting of the Aubrey ditch, and the enormous concourse of Bronze Age barrows round the great monument shows that in these centuries it was a hallowed centre to which the honoured dead were brought for burial from near and far. And whoever brought the blue stones so many hundreds of miles to augment its sanctity, the Early Bronze Age civilization which so venerated it effected, under the supremacy of the immigrants from Brittany, precisely such a union between East and West as that act would fittingly symbolize. What East and West each meant we may now consider.

The arrival of the immigrant upper class in Wessex from Brittany fell something under a century after that of the A Beaker people from the opposite quarter (p. 270), who were thus at this time, about 1700, still in the morning of their vigour throughout their widespread areas of distribution. That the new Wessex culture did not itself achieve a wide spread is, then, not surprising; but in the west it came in a measure to Devon and the vicinity of its presumed sources

[1] Pl. I.

of tin and copper in Cornwall (p. 292), while the bronzes and
superb flint arrowheads of the Breach Farm barrow in
Glamorgan show it also in a measure at work in South Wales,
and eastwards we shall shortly notice an outlier of it at Hove
in Sussex. Perhaps its strongest outlying group was that
which travelled up the Icknield Way north-east into Norfolk,
where among various relatable barrows that at Cressingham
stands out for its wealth of typical Wessex grave-goods, and
beyond this it exerted some influence in East Yorkshire,
where derivatives of its grooved and sometimes midribbed
bronze daggers[1] intrude into the area of the flat round-heeled
daggers typical (p. 278), as in Derbyshire and indeed Wessex
itself, of the A Beaker people already in possession. But its
chief home remained Wessex, and while in the south-east the
B 2 Beaker folk (p. 268) remained firmly seated, it was the
A Beaker people who dominated most of the good settlement-
areas of Eastern Britain, just as they maintained a good place
in the Wessex amalgam, and could throw out offshoots to
Wales and elsewhere far into the west. We saw above (p. 273)
that their main eastern areas were the whole circuit of the
Wash and further inland down the Icknield Way, the Derbyshire limestone, the East Yorkshire Wolds, Northumberland,
and South-East Scotland, and a big region in and somewhat
beyond Aberdeenshire. Here in the north their beakers take
on the shorter neck and enlarged ovoid body of the so-called
C type. But the B2 Beaker people must not be left out of
account, and it is especially important to remember their
proved association (p. 272) both with Grooved-ware and
Neolithic B (Peterborough) elements, from which the A Beaker
folk remained far more aloof. This is notable both in Wessex
and in the 'pool' of cultures round the Upper Thames:
A-B Beaker fusion in Derbyshire and East Yorkshire is only
slight, and in Scotland the B Beaker element, which, with
Neolithic B, had preceded the A element on the Forth and
Tay (p. 268), lived on to evolve its own distinct form of the
C type just mentioned, as indeed it did in Aberdeenshire also.
Its Neolithic B companion fades out, but the tradition both
of this and of Grooved-ware seem certainly to have contributed,

[1] Fig. 26, 4.

together with a Beaker element which appears certainly to be more B than A, to the new and distinctive form of pottery which before the Early Bronze Age was outspread over large parts mainly of Central and Southern Scotland and mainly of North-Eastern England—that known as the 'Yorkshire Vase' or 'B' type of Food-Vessel (Plate X, 2).

The problem of the origins of the food-vessel is still far from fully solved, and this is not the place to discuss it at length. But these flat-based, broad-bodied pots, with their angular shoulder, short, often hollow neck, and everted rim with a peculiar (and usually decorated) internal bevel, are in any event to be ascribed to some sort of interaction between beakers and other forms of pottery. And that the beakers in question are less A than B, or more strictly B2 beakers, is clear from their preference for horizontally banded as against panelled decoration, and, outweighing the A beaker's notched comb-stamping, for the incised and above all the cord-ornament technique in which the B2 beaker is so strong (especially in bands of repeated chevrons). At the same time the other forms involved include Neolithic B, as neck and in part rim and shoulder form shows as well as whipped-cord, finger-print, and other such decoration; the ornamenting of the bevel inside the rim, in particular, can only be derived from this source. But, to say nothing of bowl-forms belonging to the Beaker culture (polypod types (p. 257) included), grooved ware must be included also, as appears in types prominent especially in Scotland whereon hollow neck and angular shoulder are replaced[1] by shoulder- and collar-mouldings in a field of ornament running to 'ladder-pattern' and to plastic work. Here also the influence of wooden vessels, on which in the last resort the whole idea of the food-vessel form may be based, comes out strongly in the decorative device of rows of alternating tool-impressed triangles, to simulate chip-carving or fretwork, leaving a zigzag of clay standing out between in what is termed False Relief,[2] which begins to appear on bell-beakers in Catalonia and Central Europe and was perhaps here derived from Bell-beaker wood-work through the Grooved-ware people. Finally, the pottery of the megalith-

---

[1] Cf. Pl. X, 3.   [2] Cf. Pl. X, 4-5.

builders in Scotland may have supplied, e.g., stab-and-drag and whipped-cord motives: one famous Scottish food-vessel from Doune in Perthshire even attests influence from the Danish Passage-grave people (p. 191). But the actual course of multiple interaction which produced these results is still somewhat mysterious. In particular, the distinctive grooving of the angular shoulder, and its interruption—often extended also to repetition on the neck—by lug-like stops, properly (but not always) pierced to take a suspension-cord, is a feature for which, since a Pyrenean origin seems impossible (p. 309), no satisfactory derivation can at present be found at all. And the origin of the vase food-vessel will probably remain mysterious so long as our knowledge remains practically confined to sepulchral pottery and covers so little of the domestic ware of settlement-sites. Sepulchral finds, mainly from round barrows like those of Yorkshire, and the stone-slab 'short cists', with or without barrow or cairn, of Scotland, do at least tell us something about its relative chronology. In Scotland it is partly at least contemporary with beakers: further south there may still be an overlap, but in Yorkshire barrows food-vessels are definitely later than beakers. And in distribution the food-vessel is partly overlapping, partly peripheral, and partly exclusive to the beaker. It looks at present as if Scotland may have the most to contribute to the solving of the food-vessel problem, especially the Forth-Tay region where Neolithic B and B Beakers are known to have been neighbourly—though there are parts of the north of England where the same may prove true, and even further south, as on the Upper Thames or round the Fens, a sort of food-vessel pottery, compounded of Neolithic B with seemingly B Beaker and some Grooved-ware elements, stands out here and there in contrast to the A Beaker ware, and lives on, keeping alive above all the tradition of cord-ornament, to achieve a fuller emergence in the Middle Bronze Age. And Scotland also had its Grooved-ware element: it may be traced not only in its contributions to the food-vessel family just noticed, but more strikingly in the far north in the pottery of the extraordinary stone-built hut-settlements which follow the period of the megalithic tombs in Orkney. It is impossible here to describe in full the renowned settlement of Skara Brae. But the kinship of its plastic-encrusted and grooved pottery to the grooved ware of the last chapter (p. 272) is unmistakable, and the recent discovery at Rinyo, not far away, of the priority of an analogous settlement to a beaker, of late C form derived from the A Beaker series centred in Aberdeenshire, gives the culture a date in the Early Bronze Age which sets it and the food-vessel question in clear perspective to one another.

That the old megalith-builders also contributed to the North British Bronze Age is best seen from the developments of megalithic architecture itself. In the Nairn, Ness, and Upper Spey valleys an evolution may be followed from a sort of passage-grave surrounded by a stone circle to ring-cairns surrounding a central burial-hollow which are simply a specialized form of the old stone circle-court of the megalith-builders (pp. 160, 193) surviving the total disappearance of the passage-grave within. And this so-called Clava type has its place within a great range of apparently Bronze Age stone circles situated mainly in the Highland zone of the British Isles, in which the megalithic tradition appears now in, now out of combination with the embanked type of circle-monument that we have seen associated with the Beaker peoples in the south of England. In the English West Country, in Wales, in the north of England, Scotland, the Isles, and Ireland, one form or another of stone circle seems characteristic of Bronze Age and even sometimes of later religious practice. And while the simple ring of standing stones descended from those of the megalithic tomb-builders has a widespread prominence, yet the influence of the embanked type extended far—from, for example, the Derbyshire monument of Arbor Low to the magnificent Rings of Brodgar and Stennis in Orkney ;[1] and though the whole subject of British stone circles and their dating is still in many respects obscure, it is plain that contributions brought by the Beaker peoples across the Lowland zone interacted very widely with the megalithic traditions of the Highlands and the west. Where burials have been found at the centre of stone circles, these may, notably in Scotland, be accompanied by food-vessels; and though the cup-and-

[1] Fig. 22, 2.

ring carvings which, whether on stones in a monumental or sepulchral context or simply on moorland or mountain outcrop-rocks, belong certainly to the same complex, are beyond doubt the outcome of the megalithic rock-carving tradition, yet the Bronze Age brings everywhere a break in burial-rite with the megalithic past which is no less certainly the contribution of the Beaker peoples from the Lowlands and the east.

That break is the abandonment of collective for single burial. And though the food-vessel has often been ascribed to a 'native' reaction against the immigrant Beaker influence, yet it is no less a Single-grave phenomenon than is the beaker. While the intrusion of Bronze Age culture into the megalithic world begins with secondary Beaker burials in megalithic collective tombs (p. 276), these burials are themselves single, and the ensuing change-over from megalithic tomb to Bronze Age round cairn- or barrow-covered cist-grave, however long features of megalithic architecture may cling about it, is abrupt in the superseding of collective by single burial. Many single burials may be deposited in the same barrow or cairn, and a woman or an infant may share the interment of a man, but collective burial in the old megalithic sense none the less disappears. This is especially clear in Ireland, where in contrast to the broken potsherds of the old collective tombs the food-vessel deposited entire with the Bronze Age single burial symbolizes a change which must have come into the world of megalithic tradition from outside. And these Irish food-vessels are themselves no less novel. While forms of the vase type intrude considerably into Ireland from the north-east, as do a restricted number of actual beakers, the distinctive Irish or A type[1] is not a vase but a bowl, a round-bottomed, more or less hemispherical vessel, with a good deal of decorative resemblance to the vase-form, but yet with features such as radial ornament on the base which seem to look back to the Palmella bowls of the old Bell-beaker people of Western Iberia whence the earlier megalithic civilization of Ireland was in part at least inspired. In date the Irish food-vessel seems to belong largely to the Middle Bronze Age, and its full discussion will therefore fall outside the scope of this book.

[1] Pl. X, 4-5.

But it must here be plainly said that, so far from providing the inspiration for the vase type of Great Britain as has often been maintained, it seems on the contrary to be the result of a native Irish reaction, incorporating elements derived from the still little-known pottery of the Irish Passage-grave culture (p. 190), to an immigration from Great Britain, in the main from South-West Scotland, of people who brought with them, along with an occasional retention of the beaker, the vase type of food-vessel already fully formed as we see it in North-East Ireland, and therewith the new rite of single burial which they owed to the Beaker element in their composition. The appearance of Irish bowl food-vessel types in South-West Scotland, and their influence even as far as Yorkshire, will therefore represent a backwash: the primary movement was in the opposite direction.

But if Ireland was the receiver, not the giver, of the cultural impulse manifest in the food-vessel, she had an established primacy of her own in the working of metals. And the copper for flat axes and the gold for ornaments, which we have seen reason above (p. 190) for regarding as initially the discoveries of her megalith people, now come, with the addition of probably Cornish tin to equip the bronzesmith, into a real pre-eminence in the Early Bronze Age economics of the greater part of North-Western and Northern Europe. In bringing this about, Great Britain, with the fertile mixture of Eastern and Western, Continental and Atlantic, immigrant and native elements in her Early Bronze Age cultural range, played the part of an essential intermediary. And from the food-vessel people of the North, in whom that mixture has appeared at its subtlest, we may most fittingly let the narrative begin. The leading ornament found in Scottish food-vessel graves is a peculiar type of multiple-string necklace of lignite or jet beads. The idea of such necklaces, ultimately Oriental, appears early in Danish amber, and jet was no doubt Britain's substitute for that precious substance, to which the North Sea trade of the megalith people must have provided the main introduction. But the form taken by the Scottish necklaces must surely be explained from the opposite quarter. The leading ornament of the corresponding period in Ireland was the crescentic collar of sheet gold known as the lunula (p. 347: Fig. 27, *b*, 5). Its precise antiquity is unknown; but the identity of its doubtless talismanic engraved ornament with motives found on the idol-plaques of Iberian megalithic tombs (p. 163) points to an ultimately Iberian inspiration, with which the presence of Iberian types of lunula, e.g. in Galicia, agrees, though their exact date be unknown: the old Atlantic sea-route need not be thought wholly abandoned in the Early Bronze Age, and genuine Irish lunulae occur in North-Western and Mid-Western France as well as once in Wales and again in Cornwall, where at Harlyn Bay, near Padstow, two were found with one of the flat axes to be noticed directly. Eastward, their distribution reaches Belgium, Hanover, and finally the islands of Denmark, between which and their Irish homeland there are three from Scotland, the homeland of the answering jet necklace, itself occurring occasionally in Ireland as well as spreading sporadically south of the Border. Obviously lunulae and necklaces may be considered twin manifestations of the same originally Western idea. And the Baltic and Atlantic limits of the lunula distribution show the extent of an Early Bronze Age trade in Irish gold which is manifest in other forms of sheet gold-work also. The graves of the powerful immigrants from Brittany into Wessex are rich in it,[1] in a variety of ornament-forms of which the most interesting are perhaps the gold mountings for discs of amber.[2] For the Wessex people were rich in Baltic amber no less than in Irish gold, and when we realize that their graves may contain handled cups of amber (one from Clandon in Dorset, another actually from the Hove barrow (p. 366) in Sussex) as well as of native shale, and that there are several Wessex examples of the Scottish necklace-type made in amber, it becomes clear that they made a strong magnet on one flank of an Irish-Baltic trade whose richest exchange was in gold and amber. The part played in this by the poorer populations of South-Eastern and Eastern England is shown by the fact that it is in their territories that the less precious Baltic imports of flint axes and daggers are most liable to occur. But the more direct routes between Ireland and the Baltic lay across North

---

[1] Pl. XI, 1-6.   [2] Pl. XI, 1.

England and Scotland, and here the period's basic metal comes into the picture with the distribution of the Irish type of flat axe in copper or bronze.

The distribution of flat axes in the British Isles is thickest in Ireland, especially North-East Ireland, and spreads over South and East Scotland and North-East England, Wales, and much of the south. The simple primitive type, however early its beginnings (p. 190), occurs occasionally in Early Bronze Age associations,[1] but the peculiarly Irish development of well-formed axes with engraved surface-ornament is known from a barrow-find at Willerby[2] to be as early as a quite early stage of the Beaker culture in Yorkshire, which the trade in them must have reached over the Irish Sea and the Aire gap across the Pennines, while further north a secondary centre for their distribution is attested by the quantity of specimens, and also of stone moulds for their manufacture, on the coasts of North-East Scotland. And directly across the North Sea there is an answering concentration of similar axes in Denmark and South Sweden, where various associated finds show that the amber-traders of the Stone-cist culture acquired them as they also acquired the rather different version of the type current in the Aunjetitz civilization of Central Europe. And not only this: metal-workers in due course actually settled in South Scandinavian territory and produced the derivative type best known from the remarkable hoard found at Pile in South Sweden,[3] in which examples are associated with armlet, axe, and dagger types, including a bronze-hilted dagger, imported from the Aunjetitz province. If the first metal-workers came from Ireland or Britain, as the Pile axe-type suggests, Central Europe turned out to be their best source of raw material, and therewith soon the Aunjetitz form of axe with cast flanges (p. 301), which with its North German variant the Falkenwalde type[4] was reaching them in the period represented by the Pile hoard, issued in a Scandinavian imitation of its own, named from a noted find in Holstein the Tinsdahl type.[5] And the Tinsdahl hoard contained also, with bronze ingot torques and globular-headed pins, a type of weapon new to these

---

[1] Fig. 23, 2.   [2] Fig. 23, 3.   [3] Fig. 23, 4.
[4] Fig. 23, 4, *a.*   [5] Fig. 23, 5.

pages, the socketed bronze spearhead, which equates its date with the very end of the Early Bronze Age in Central Europe, towards 1500 B.C. In approximately the century before that date, then, these influences from the metal-using lands to the west and south at last engendered a true Bronze civilization in Northern Europe. Its flowering thus followed to coincide not with the Early, but the Middle Bronze Age of those lands, and before we follow so far, there is more to be said of their Early Bronze Age commerce and its influence upon the North while the age of the stone cist and the flint dagger was there still running its course.

The close connexion already emphasized in this period between Central Europe and North Italy brings Italian flanged axes into the picture as well as the Aunjetitz type, and the Falkenwalde variant which grew up on the northern margin of the Aunjetitz province in Germany. In the Fjaelkinge hoard in South Sweden, for example, the notch-butted Italian type[1] appears together with Central European forms (and also an Irish-British one). And though the Italian bronze-hilted dagger (p. 310) does not itself occur in the North, its Aunjetitz equivalent, with slightly ogival blade normally decorated with grooves and engraved ornament, was taken from its Bohemian centre northward as well as south, and in time gave rise on the North European plain to new types: one found in the basins of the Oder and the Elbe in several variants, of which one has blade and hilt cast together in one, and another commonest in Mecklenburg and Rügen in which this is a constant feature—a somewhat inferior weapon with a plain midribbed blade known from a Mecklenburg hoard as the Malchin type. These belong to the full rise of the Northern Early Bronze Age towards the middle of the millennium; but rather earlier, while the Stone-cist peoples of the North were still only imitating the Southern daggers in flint, their relations with the Aunjetitz province are betokened by their importing and imitation of Aunjetitz types of ornaments. The gold lock-rings mentioned in the previous section have been found in several Danish and South Swedish cist-graves, and among the bone pins which are there so abundant a leading

[1] Fig. 25, C 2.

place is taken by imitations of Aunjetitz bronze originals, which occasionally turn up as imports themselves. Thus the dating of the Stone-cist period from between 1800 and 1700 B.C. to a gradual overtaking by a true Bronze Age beginning nearly two centuries later is entirely confirmed. And it should be added that for Sweden at least these centuries mark a turning-point in the absorption of the old Dwelling-place cultures (p. 202) by the settled farming civilization of the Stone-cist peoples. Thus the pre-conditions for a unitary Northern Bronze Age were fulfilled in the supremacy of this amalgam of Stone-cist populations, wherein the varied traditions of megalith folk, Single-grave and Boat-axe people, and now even Dwelling-place natives, were brought on to a common plane of culture, with a material equipment rich in the flint-work of which the developed forms of dagger, with their wonderful hilt-shaping, were the most consummate expression, but conversant with metal types imported both from west and south. And important as was the Western trade-route from the British Isles, the overland route from Central Europe and the Mediterranean stands out as the dominant feature of Continental Bronze Age geography.

The way across the Brenner Pass from Italy and the head of the Adriatic to the Danube and so to Bohemia reached the West Baltic shores down the valley of the Elbe, which a more westerly route from higher up the Danube in Bavaria also entered by way of Thuringia and the Saale. And from lower down the Danube, Moravia, and Silesia, the Vistula route to the Eastern Baltic became (though in a less degree) opened up to a similar traffic, which in due course brought into being a distinct province of Early Bronze culture centred upon East Prussia, where with imported Aunjetitz or derivative bronze types the flanged axe took on a distinctive splay-bladed 'Eastern' form. These routes were not in themselves new: they had been highways since Neolithic times; but the greatly increased tempo of Bronze Age trading-activity brought them an importance which was in effect new, for that activity was born of the fact that now the staple of material equipment was a metal whose constituents only favoured regions could supply, and whose manufacture only skilled workers could encompass, but which could under those conditions be produced in quantities great enough to supply the ever-growing demand of distant as well as home markets. And it is the distribution of the bronze goods themselves which attests both the amount of the activity and the course of its long-distance channels. Above all, the great increase in the numbers of smiths' and merchants' hoards, and their concentration in the centres and along the routes of trade, enables archaeology to record at once the geography and the chronology of the process. This on the one hand: on the other, the native wealth of the shores of the Baltic, east and west alike, in the amber which was more than ever prized in the centres of metal-using civilization, furnished an inexhaustible article of exchange which made the transcontinental traffic unique in its kind, and has earned its main artery the accepted name of the Amber Route.

The controlling position of the Aunjetitz civilization astride of the main Amber Route and its subsidiaries, running north and south, and equally of communications running east and west, has been made sufficiently clear. But in the latter direction, in addition to the westward line into France through the territory of the Rhône culture, and parallel to the North Sea route between the Baltic and the British Isles, it came to command yet another artery of traffic with the West, to Britain and Ireland, by way of the Lower Rhine, from the distinctive province of Aunjetitz territory, to which attention was above drawn (p. 302), in Saxo-Thuringia. In the great barrow-graves of the Saxo-Thuringian chieftains, as at Helmsdorf and Leubingen, and in the country's no less notable bronze hoards like those of Dieskau and Neuenheiligen, appears a wealth of weapons, implements, and ornaments among which are several prominent additions to the Aunjetitz repertory already described. As well as flanged axes, bronze-hilted daggers and big triangular dagger-blades, ingot torques, armlets, pins, and other ornaments in bronze and gold also, and a long narrow type of double-axe which adds to the total of native developments, there are not only Baltic amber beads, but examples of the Irish-British flat-axe type unmodified by Northern imitation, and lastly a splendid series representing that remarkable Western weapon that we first touched upon in dealing with the El Argar culture of Spain—the halberd.

The Saxo-Thuringian halberds and their like are indeed very different from the Spanish, but we have earlier seen reason to believe metal-working introduced from Iberia into Ireland, and it was from Ireland, likewise the source of the flat axes already discussed, that the halberd achieved its main distribution over Continental Europe. The precise origin of the Irish halberd family[1] is still obscure. Non-metal prototypes may have been contributed not only by Iberia, where flint halberd-blades occur at Los Millares and in Portuguese 'dolmen'-tombs, but also by the native Mesolithic of at least North-East Ireland; all that is certain is that Ireland is richer (mainly in and around its central plain) in metal halberds than any other European country, that of the six types into which they have been divided the three more primitive-seeming are confined to the island, and that these are sharply distinguished from the Spanish type by the growth of a stout midrib to the blade, and by the possession of a projecting haft-plate, in some cases rather like that of an Early Minoan dagger, only with four rivets, but tending to the more rounded form standardized in the types that extend outside the island to Great Britain and the Continent, where instead of the copper normal for Ireland they were rendered in bronze. How early the halberd idea was in Ireland first rendered in metal is still unknown: it is this extension to the Continent that supplies all really reliable evidence of date. While the most developed Irish type, with a graceful slightly down-curved blade and three rivets,[1] occurs no further afield than Great Britain (mainly Scotland), the main distribution is supplied by the straight-bladed type of which that was a development. In Scotland the halberds extend from the south-west to the north-east and east like the flat axes, in England they cross the Pennines to the Yorkshire coast: both these may be considered starting-lines for the North Sea voyage to Scandinavia, for in Denmark, South Sweden, and North Germany there is a concentration of them answering closely to that of the Irish-British flat axe and its imitations,

[1] Fig. 23, 12.

and clearly the two have here a common history, the date already defined for the axes being given for the halberds by the associations they reached by trading down the Amber Route into the Aunjetitz province, above all in Saxo-Thuringia. By about 1600 B.C., the upper limit for the issue of all this commerce in actual metal-working in Scandinavia, the Saxo-Thuringian smiths had not only adopted the halberd, but were matching it with the bronze-hilted dagger by encasing its haft partly or wholly in a cast bronze sheathing, with an ornamental head which may be either riveted to or cast in one with the blade. These splendid and doubtless ceremonial weapons, represented in the Dieskau find and abundantly elsewhere in Saxo-Thuringia, East Germany, and the borders of Poland, were traded eastward even to Lithuania, northward back along the Amber Route to the Baltic shores, and southward to the Danube. And in token of Saxo-Thuringia's westward contact with the British Isles, three of the rich Early Bronze Age graves of Wessex have yielded miniature versions of them in the form of pendants in which a tiny bronze blade is set in a haft of gold or amber or both, perforated at the butt for suspension.[1] That this contact was not merely by Scandinavia and the North Sea, but direct by the Rhine and the Netherlands, is not only suggested by Central Europe's non-dependence in workmanship upon Scandinavia, but apparent in the distribution this way of halberd-blades close to Irish models—hinting at an up-Channel trade direct from Ireland to the Rhine—or recalling the renderings of Irish imports to be found in Wales and Southern England, showing some assimilation to the prevalent type of bronze dagger already discussed (p. 278). Further, the halberd could reach Central Europe by way of Brittany and across France to the territory of the Rhône culture; it is with this spread of the distribution that we have to connect the Irish derivatives in Italy (p. 305), while down the Danube we reach those of Austria and Hungary. The association of one in a Late Aunjetitz grave at Feuersbrunn in Lower Austria with a flanged bronze axe brings back the reverse side of the picture— the Aunjetitz influence in Britain, attested, more directly

[1] Fig. 26, 13.

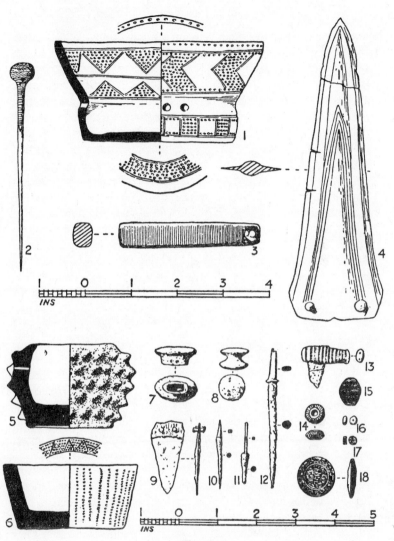

Fig. 26

GRAVE-GOODS OF THE EARLY BRONZE AGE IN WESSEX
(pp. 315 ff.)

1, Aldbourne cup ; 2, Aunjetitz globe-headed bronze pin ; 3, Whetstone ;
4, Grooved bronze dagger—from grave at Camerton, Somerset. 5-6,
Cups (5 grape-cup) ; 7-12, 14-17, Amber, bronze, and shale objects ;
13, Halberd-pendant with bronze blade and handle sheathed in gold ;
18, Gold-mounted amber disc—from grave at Manton, Wilts.

than by the halberd-pendants, in the Aunjetitz pins, occasionally [1] found imported into Wessex (and more widely imitated in bone), and on a far greater scale by the introduction of this type of bronze axe itself, with the boldly cast flanges explained above (p. 301) in sharp contrast to the mere hammered margins of the native flat type. The contrast extends also to distribution, for the cast-flanged axe, naturalized as it became in the British bronze industry, obtained its main hold in the south and east, as against the flat axe with its focus in the west and north, and the opposed and yet overlapping regions covered by the two types in the British Isles well illustrate the complementary roles of our Lowland and Highland Zones.

Britain, no less than Central Europe, has still more to show of the achievements of trade in the civilization of the Bronze Age. We shall find not merely the Danube lands involved, but the Aegean and Egypt. But this will best be seen against the fuller background that remains to be sketched in the third and final section of this chapter.

3. ITALY, HUNGARY, AND THE BALANCE OF CULTURES: MYCENAE
AND CRETE, EUROPE AND THE ORIENT

(Map VI and Table VI: at end)

Although, in considering its relations to the West and North, we have been tending to treat Central Europe as a single economic unit, yet, as became clear in the first section of this chapter, its Early Bronze Age was culturally an affair of some complexity. In Hungary Tószeg, and further south Perjamos, in Bohemia (with Moravia) Aunjetitz itself, stand for a civilization enriched by industry and commerce but basically founded on the tradition of Danubian agriculture, and centred on the river-lands and rich plains of loess. The amalgam which this comprised, of course, included the Northern elements, Corded-ware and other 'warrior' folk, Bell-beaker people, and the rest, that had entered the Danubian scene in the preceding centuries, but held them assimilated in an even whole. Therewith, however, we have seen (p. 299) cultural groups, mainly south and west of Aunjetitz and

[1] Fig. 26, 2.

Tószeg, in which this assimilation had been less even, so that one or another such element—e.g. that of the Baden culture—may be still seen in a measure preponderating, and so restricting a full growth of Early Bronze Age maturity. The Corded-ware warriors not only contributed to these, but in the upland country fringing the Upper Danube and other big river-valleys, and away over West-Central Europe to the Rhine and beyond the borders of France, they maintained an absolute predominance of their own cruder culture, attested as ever by round-barrow burials, in antithesis to the more progressive amalgamated civilization of Aunjetitz type. Further north in Germany likewise, the Saxo-Thuringian and neighbouring Aunjetitz provinces, themselves strong in the same element, were fringed by the Stone-cist and Barrow cultures of the North European plain, which did not give way to the formation of a true Early Bronze Age before the centuries directly preceding the middle of the second millennium and the establishment of actual bronze-working on the shores of the Baltic. And south-eastward again (p. 298), the plains of Hungary were bounded by Otomani, Witenberg, and Monteoru peoples in Rumania, and on the other side by Slavonian-culture folk, who were slow in attaining Bronze Age status, and maintained traditions compounded of Balkanic and 'warrior' elements in a conservatism contrasting with the progressiveness of the Central Danubian basin. Finally, between the Slavonian culture down the Save and Drave and the Aunjetitz borderlands towards the Upper Danube, the continuance of the Laibach and Mondsee lake-dwellers, again with a Corded-ware element in the ascendant (p. 249), is probably only one aspect of a situation still obscure for lack of evidence. But there is more to claim our attention beyond.

On the other side of the Eastern Alps, the North Italian lake-dwellers—basically Alpine as they were—have been seen (p. 250) to show something of the exaggerated-handle development of pottery common to the Balkans and to the Baden culture of the preceding period (p. 234)—the same that contributed so much in survival to the Mad'arovce and especially the Böheimkirchen culture in the Aunjetitz borderlands just mentioned. This feature seems to have its earliest context in the easterly sites of Fimon and Arqua, while in the more westerly lake-dwellings, e.g. of Lake Varese and of Lagazzi, Polada, and Cataragna near Lake Garda, the handles are simpler, and the better-class pottery has more in common with the direct development from the Remedello stage which seems fundamental in the Early Bronze Age of North Italy generally. Though examples of the bronze daggers and axes described above (p. 310) may occur in these lake-dwellings,[1] the North Italian settlements of this period were in the main villages of round huts, in the tradition of the Neolithic huts of Reggio-Emilia (p. 157), with floors somewhat hollowed in the ground. The heart of the Remedello culture had been in the province of Brescia, and here and in the neighbouring districts of Mantua and Cremona the ensuing Early Bronze Age is represented by hut-village sites such as Cella Dati, Calvatone, and San Pietro in Mendicate. These still have flint and even stone-axe industries as well as bronze, and in their pottery the exaggeration of the handles may be seen in apparently gradual development into horned or crescentic forms characteristically Italian,[2] especially at Calvatone where the occupation seems rather late in the period. Decoration, always slight on Remedello pots, is still fairly restrained, though incised ornament is now more in evidence. Further east and across the Po, similar hut-villages, like Monte Castellaccio in Eastern Emilia, and a number more under the edge of the Apennines round Bologna and Imola, display a culture of much the same kind, but here, where the mountains begin, the Early Bronze Age marks the rise of a distinct province of Italian culture, which embarked on a different history from that which ensued in the Po valley. It is best named the Apennine culture, and in what may be called phase I of its development, answering to the period of the Early Bronze Age sites already mentioned further north, its main strength—as far as is yet known—lay in the north-east and east of Central Italy. In these regions the Chalcolithic counterpart of Remedello had been little more than a continuation of the Neolithic, and phase I of the Apennine culture shows the same continuity lasting into the Bronze Age. In

[1] Fig. 25, C 1.　　　　[2] Cf. Fig. 27, *a*, 4 (p. 347).

the Marche, for example, where the phase is plentifully represented,[1] the stratified village-site of the Pianello di Genga shows two successive occupation-levels belonging to it directly overlying two of the Neolithic-Chalcolithic culture from which it had grown. A similar continuity is demonstrable for the population of the Vibrata valley (p. 157), and on the west of the Apennines a long Bronze Age occupation, with a starting-point marked by an inhumation-burial with a typical Remedello dagger, is attested in the hut-sites and caves of the Monte Cetona in Etruria. And throughout the Apennine culture the burial-rite remains true to the ancestral tradition of inhumation.

So far, then, Bronze Age Italy has shown three cultural groupings—the Alpine slopes with their lake-dwellings, the Po valley with its hut-villages, and the similar villages and the cave-dwellings of the Apennine culture—to which a fourth is added by the still persisting cave-dwellers of Liguria (p. 157). All, it is true, shared a common bronze industry. It is represented most prominently by hoards, many of them apparently not merchants' stock but votive deposits in the ground, perhaps buried for the use of the dead, but not, as in the Remedello period, with their bodily remains. Its leading types are the triangular dagger,[2] with bronze-hilted examples occurring from the Alps and the Po to Etruria and the mid-eastern coast, and even further south; the notch-butted flanged axe;[3] and a noteworthy development from it expanding to a broad semicircular blade like a flat spoon. And these represent native Italian production, diversified only in proportion to its own export-trade (pp. 310, 326) by trans-Alpine imports and derivatives. Among the latter we have already noticed the halberd (pp. 305, 330), yet the Monte Bego rock-carvings which attest its use among the Ligurians (p. 305) include equally axes, daggers, and other forms of general Italian distribution, while sickles, and more strikingly scenes of men ploughing with yokes of oxen, show that the people who resorted to these mountain fastnesses for the rites that these carvings presumably imply, came in time at least to share an agricultural life which the Age made equally

---

[1] Fig. 27, *a*, 1-3.   [2] Fig. 25, C 1.   [3] Fig. 25, C 2.

common to the whole peninsula. But the Ligurians, like the lake-dwellers, form none the less a distinct grouping within the whole. And the Po valley and Apennine peoples indeed began the Bronze Age on a common footing, of Neolithic-Chalcolithic foundations with the added element of 'warrior' battle-axe folk whose importance as intruders into the Remedello orbit has already been stressed (p. 250). But the two drew apart as the Age went on. The Apennine people became distinguished by their development of decorated pottery,[1] which, if the period of the sites above noticed be called phase I of the culture's growth, represents in its maturity a phase II, or Italian Middle Bronze Age. And by then its geographical distribution is impressive. Already in phase I, perhaps, its material is found as far south as Leporano on the coast of the Gulf of Taranto, and phase II finds the culture stretching in virtually perfect uniformity from the northern edge of the Apennines right down the east of Italy to that coast and the whole region of Apulia, while on the west the Monte Cetona is now answered by the Grotta di Pertosa and other cave-sites as far south as the province of Salerno and even beyond. It thus came to succeed not only to the Chalcolithic of Central Italy, but also to that of the south, with its distinct Neolithic substratum, its incised and painted pottery, and its collective tombs, discussed in an earlier chapter (pp. 126, 152) and bracketed with the 'Siculan I' Chalcolithic of Sicily. Sicily indeed remained a world apart, but the mature Apennine culture united all of peninsular Italy for which we have any evidence in a distinctively Italian Bronze Age civilization, based mainly on long-standing native foundations to which the Mediterranean-facing south contributed no less than the Apennine country proper. The Monte Cetona continuity is unbroken: the Vibrata valley occupation goes on likewise, and it is the same in the Marche, where, for example, the complement to the phase I material of the Pianello di Genga is the richly developed pottery of Filottrano in the next valley. Further down the coast at Coppa della Nevigata, the continuity lasts into still later times, and in Apulia the Chalcolithic importance of Molfetta and Matera (p. 126) is renewed in

[1] Fig. 27, *a*, 1.

PLATE XI

BRONZE AGE GOLD FROM BARROWS IN WILTSHIRE (1-6) AND CORNWALL (7)
1, Gold-mounted amber discs ; 2, gold plating of shale cone ; 3, gold-plated bone disc ; Normanton. 4, Gold lozenge-plaques, Normanton (Bush Barrow). 5, Gold plating of shale cone and pair of gold capsules ; 6, oblong gold plaque, Upton Lovel (Golden Barrow). 7, The Rillaton gold cup (height 3½ in.)

British Museum

Scale 2 : 5   See pp. 324, 378

PLATE XII

GOLD MASK (1, height 10¼ in.) AND INLAID DAGGER (RESTORED : 2, scale 1 : 3)
FROM SHAFT-GRAVE V, MYCENAE, AND LATE MINOAN I PAINTED VASE
(3, diameter, 8 in.)

British Museum, 1-2 from electrotype reproductions of originals in National Museum, Athens

See pp. 352, 355

Bronze Age occupations from which the decorated phase II pottery is well and typically represented. Older tradition here is manifest in the so-called Apulian 'dolmens', megalithic degenerations of the older collective-tomb idea now said to belong exclusively to the Bronze Age; the burial-rite here, in the answering rock-tombs at Matera, and in fact wherever known within the culture's orbit, is inhumation always; and it seems clear that the Bronze Age united the south and all the rest of peninsular Italy together in a cultural solidarity of the greatest importance for its subsequent history.

The characteristic technique of the decorated pottery is sharp incision set off with white inlay;[1] its double-line band-patterns, most prominently of zigzag form, are filled with stab or linear markings; and the whole convention reminds one a good deal of the other side of the Adriatic, where the analogous tradition of Slavonian ware (p. 246) blossomed exceedingly in this same period, and achieved, as we shall see directly, a great expansion over Mid-Danubian Europe. In fact, it is probable that the Apennine culture was not a little influenced from that quarter; in the modelling of its pottery the most striking feature is the culmination of the exaggerated-handle convention which Italy shared with the Balkans in forms surmounted by extraordinary horned, crescentic, or voluted projections, the typology of which is in large measure specifically Italian in detail,[2] but represents the culture's distinctive development of an idea originally common to Italy and the Balkans through the trans-Adriatic connexions of which we have spoken in the earlier context of the third millennium (p. 126). The simpler handle-forms of the Early Bronze Age are easier to parallel on the east of the Adriatic, and North Italy here calls for especial notice: those of the hut-village of Marendole in the Veneto, for instance, have been used to suggest connexions by way of Istria with Bosnia round the head of the Adriatic rather than across it. But the individuality of the mature Apennine developments remains, and is easily intelligible when one considers the length of the culture's self-contained life. Sites with developed pottery, it has been noted, show a decay and even atrophy of the stone-

[1] Fig. 27, a, 1.   [2] Fig. 27, a, 2-4.

and flint-working earlier represented, that must stand for a considerable lapse of time; and the same inference may be drawn when their bronzes, for example at the Scoglio del Tonno site at Taranto, run on to an advanced stage of type-development in which the flanged axe has given place to a winged form, the triangular dagger to a short sword, and the Aunjetitz-like pin to the latter-day innovation of the brooch. These types belong to the later centuries of the second millennium, outside the limits of this book, and it is probably safe to place the chronological centre of gravity of the Apennine culture's phase II towards 1300 B.C., or midway between the final stage of the Italian Bronze Age and an initial date around 1500.   Phase I will then occupy the preceding centuries, and since at its opening about 1900 this Early Bronze Age has been seen at its strongest not in the Apennine area so much as in North Italy, we have to conclude by discussing what there corresponded to the mature Apennine culture of phase II. Therewith we approach what has long dominated the Bronze Age archaeology of the Po valley, and has involved furthermore the hypothesis of a fresh invasion from beyond the Alps—the famous question of the Terremare.

A Terramara (the name is dialect for the 'black earth' of ancient settlement-refuse as used by the local peasantry for fertilizer) is a big low oblong mound of occupation-débris, which may be several dozen acres in extent; such are known in considerable numbers mainly in the lower part of the Po valley and south of the river, and the example always quoted as typical is that of the Castellazzo di Fontanellato, excavated in the nineteenth century by Professor Pigorini. Surrounded by a wet moat and a sloping-fronted, timber-backed rampart, the settlement was of trapezoidal plan, divided up by a grid of lanes, and consisting of blocks of dwellings erected on piles, interrupted in one place by an earth mound moated off and supposedly religious in purpose. Outside was a cemetery, again moated off and also with a pile substructure, where the remains of the dead, not inhumed but cremated, were buried in close-packed cinerary urns. The material remains show the inhabitants to have been agriculturalists and stock-farmers, traders who could import Baltic amber, and craftsmen and bronzesmiths whose metal-work seems to have been the main inspiration of the phase II bronze industry throughout the peninsula. The structural features thus made out in full at the Castellazzo site were claimed by Pigorini and his followers to be more or less universal Terramara characters: their regularity of plan was used to argue the Terramara to be the prehistoric prototype of the Roman camp as described by Polybius, and the 'Terramaricoli' ancestors of the Romans; and it was further sought to show that these invaders of the Po valley spread in time through Italy as the proto-Italic forefathers of the Romans and all other speakers of Italic languages in historic antiquity. The pile construction was accounted for as derived from a lake-dwelling tradition recognized as inherent in the invaders' culture and an important clue to their origins, the result of their migration to the plains of the Po being, in fact, a sort of lake-dwelling without the lake. The first thing to be said about this is that there are no Terremare outside the Middle and Lower Po valley: in particular, the old description of Scoglio del Tonno as 'the Terramara of Taranto' is wholly unjustified by the facts. The second thing is that the true Terremare vary considerably in form and feature. The classic ensemble of Castellazzo is really unique: Castione dei Marchese approaches it perhaps most closely, but Montale, for instance, has a more or less circular plan, bounded by an untimbered earth bank and no moat, no grid of lanes, and open spaces probably for animals in the middle; and all the rest diverge or fall short in one way or another. A third point is that even in the Po valley hut-villages of the old sort might still exist as well: the Santa Caterina site near Crema has been called a 'rudimentary Terramara', but it may rather be a hut-village showing Terramara influence, while the Castellaro settlement at Gottolengo not far away has huts both round and square, but no other structural feature save a simple boundary-bank of earth, and in date seems to last into phase II of the Bronze Age from phase I. Similarly, as has always been recognized, the contemporary persistence of true lake-dwellings is shown, principally in the important group on Lake Garda, by the bronze types there represented, which answer to even the latest Terramara products and were no doubt obtained from Terramara sources. The latest types in question take one on to near the end of the second millennium, when the universality of the Italian bronze industry, attested as far away as Scoglio del Tonno already, bears witness to its success in the Terramara people's hands: the earliest types obtained in genuine Terremare include triangular daggers, flanged axes, and, e.g., trefoil-headed pins corresponding to Late Aunjetitz forms of towards 1500 B.C., while socketed spearheads answer to those of the Middle Bronze Age not yet here considered in Central Europe, and an abundance of the same period's tanged bronze sickles reflects the importance of the metal in the service of the staple industry of agriculture.

Thus, though their implications may, like their uniformity, have been much exaggerated by Pigorini and his school, the Terremare have their importance. They must stand for a distinct group of population, emerging into phase II of the Italian Bronze Age towards 1500 B.C. apparently from a fusion—for it is hard otherwise to explain the presence of the pile-structure convention in such prominence on well-watered but unsubmerged land — of hut-villagers and lake-dwellers, who were in any case close neighbours one of another. But, since fusions so peculiar and so lasting do not take place without stimulus, some dominating element is required in addition, and one can scarcely fail to connect this, whatever it was, with the regular Terramara practice of cremation and 'urnfield' burial, which makes such a complete break with the hitherto seemingly general Italian habit of inhuming the dead. Since at this time we shall now find cremation beginning to spread into great importance in the east of trans-Alpine Europe, it looks as if immigration from over the mountains supplied, if not the Terramaricoli *en masse*, at least the unifying force that created the Terramara culture. Now, Terramara pottery is not, like that of the contemporary Apennine culture, characterized by rich incised decoration. It shares, indeed, the exaggerated-handle tendency, but develops it a good deal on individual lines—in particular, concentration on the horned or crescentic-projection model produces a magnificent growth of the so-called *ansa lunata* which becomes absolutely distinctive.[1] But the shallow cups so graced, the pedestalled vessels, the bowls, and the splay-walled or biconical urns of the Terremare have scarcely more incised ornament than the earlier Bronze Age pottery of North Italy; and while applied-strip decoration may recall Neolithic coarse-ware convention (p. 156), the finer ware runs rather to furrowed ornament and especially pinched-up warts or knobs protruding from the body of the pot. Fondness for plastic work is also seen in clay animal models and figurines, and knobbed and other ornament appears regularly on the whorls which weighted the spindles of the Terramara womenfolk. Individuality in handle-modelling, wart-ornament, and figurines thus all show a certain plastic sense, outweighing that of linear pattern, which may count in the ascertainment of their origins together with their cremation-rite, the innovations apparent in the structure of their settlements, and lastly the presence among their abundant bone and horn work of the curved and per-forated cheek-pieces of bits which show that they commanded the power of the horse. We have already spoken of the breaking of the horse in prehistoric Europe (p. 237), in con-nexion especially with the spread in the centuries preceding the Bronze Age of the 'warrior' peoples who contributed so much to its civilization. Now the bridle-bit, a revolutionary improvement on nose-rope and halter, meets us for the first time. This is a specifically European invention, and the earliest occurrence proved for its unmistakable horn cheek-piece is in Hungary, in the settlement-mound of Tószeg, and in the second occupation-layer—Tószeg B—which there overlies that of the Early Bronze Age already described.

Now, this Tószeg B culture belongs to the centuries before and immediately after 1500 B.C., the same period as covers the rise of the Terramara culture in North Italy. Indeed, the marginal palisading revealed by the Tószeg mound in this period, in which the houses were regular timber-supported affairs in the megaron tradition (p. 239), has often been compared to Terramara structure. And though the East Hungarian province which Tószeg represents was still faithful to inhumation-burial and so cannot of itself sponsor the

[1] Fig. 27, *a*, 4.

Terramara cremators, yet it must have some place in the picture. West of it, in the West Slovakian Mad'arovce culture, and still more in the Böheimkirchen culture across the Danube in Lower Austria and the West Hungarian border, the Early Bronze Age has been seen to be strong in survival from the Baden culture: its peculiarities of handle-modelling, and also a tendency to wart-ornament, were thus handed on there to the pottery of the period now in question. And though these borderers on the Aunjetitz province also practised inhumation, and probably indeed the barrow-burial of the Corded-ware 'warrior' element in their composition, yet further into West Hungary the cremation-rite already attested for the Baden culture (p. 234) in its prime is found accompanying the same sort of pottery-tradition (e.g. at Lovasberény) in the same phase of the Bronze Age as Tószeg B, having doubtless had a continuous survival through the intervening centuries. And if the West Hungarian pottery of this period [1] is still not identical with that of the Terramara immigrants, yet an origin for them between here and the confines of North Italy is at least as probable as geography and comparative archaeology can at present make it. For pottery, cremation-rite, and the all-important horse can all be accounted for better in this quarter than anywhere else, and lake-dwellers like those of Laibach could be brought as well on this as on the Italian side of the Alps into fusion with a dominant strain connected largely with the Baden people, but also with the 'warrior' groups who had reached not only Laibach and the Drave and Save but also Italy itself (p. 250) before the Bronze Age had begun. Finally, an exodus into North Italy from these regions would accord well with the part we have now to see them playing in the opposite direction of the Middle Danube, and set the Italian scene in harmony with the cultural geography of trans-Alpine Europe in general. For to the south the same or kindred elements had been cast in the more Balkanic mould of the Slavonian culture, characterized by the richly incised and white-inlaid pottery paralleled above not in North but in Apennine Italy: the resulting blend differed accordingly from the Apennine culture in practising cremation, and in

[1] Fig. 27, *a*, 5, 7, 8.

this middle period of the second millennium it showed its vigour by expanding north, north-east, and east until the whole Middle Danube basin had felt the influence of its advance. In Western Hungary and its borderlands these people's cremation-rite was already, we have suggested, shared by their more northerly neighbours. But their expansion is none the less attested by the spread of the distinctive white-ornamented pottery; and with mobility everywhere here stimulated by the new factor in horse-power, the pressure from the south is just what would drive out some of those neighbours in emigration westwards into Italy, just as it pushed others eastwards beyond the Danube toward the Theiss, and brought the frontier of West Hungarian cremation culture close against Tószeg and the inhuming civilization of East Hungary. Thus while in North Italy the migrants produced, in fusion with what they found there, the new culture of the Terremare, the West Hungarian culture was left to be more and more transfused by the expansion from the south, which brought white-ornamented pottery into increasing prominence until it issued in the baroque style of what is known as Pannonian ware in the full Middle Bronze Age.

The same expansion took cremation in 'urnfields' and very similar pottery into North-East Serbia, the province typified in the urnfield of Kličevac, while in Slavonia itself and the intermediate regions along the Save and the adjacent Danube a rather different version of the same culture may be named after that of Bijelo Brdo. And across the Danube eastward we have the Vattina group, in which similar elements are fused with a much stronger inheritance from the southern or Perjamos province of the East Hungarian Early Bronze Age civilization, and furthermore pass over into the Transylvanian region where the Otomani culture (p. 297) had now reached its later stages, and beyond again a clearly analogous character is borne by the Monteoru culture (p. 297) across the Carpathians. Monteoru must link up with contemporary happenings on the South Russian steppe, but our concern here is with developments from Early Bronze Age civilization as such, and since the kurgan people of the steppes and the forest folk beyond them had no true Early Bronze Age we shall not pursue them further. The Hungarian situation, on the other hand, is of crucial importance to our theme, for it shows us a period of movement and redistribution of forces in the centuries covered by Tószeg B, in which the Early Bronze Age contrast between the progressive civilization of the central areas, with its main line of life east of the Danube along the Theiss past Perjamos and Tószeg, and the marginal regions of poorer, less polished, and more conservative culture fringing it, gives place to a balanced whole compounded, in whatever variety, of elements from both sides. In appreciating this balance, we are striking the keynote of the Middle Bronze Age for a large part of Europe, and in the region of the Middle Danube it came into being through the expansion of the marginal peoples towards the centre, traceable archaeologically in the spread of decorated pottery and of cremation-burial in urnfields. The resulting establishment of the urnfield culture-groups we have named belongs to the Middle Bronze Age, after about 1400 B.C., when at Tószeg the B occupation-period had given place to Tószeg C, in which ornamented pottery is a prominent feature and cremation had nearly ousted the old inhumation-rite of the province; but it is the B period that is important as the age of transition. At Tószeg itself it may be subdivided into a B1 stage, when the Tószeg A tradition was still strong, with the typical jug developed to an angular body like the advanced forms of the Aunjetitz province nearer the centre of Europe, and a B2, when plastic wart-ornament and its accompanying furrow-designs, together with the high modelled handles of the Baden tradition, have come in in greater prominence, and the white-inlaid incised ware now well distributed in West Hungary begins to make some showing also. It is, however, doubtful how far this stratified succession at Tószeg can be applied as a rigid chronology elsewhere, and it is perhaps enough to say that the B period as a whole in Hungary may be reckoned to last until about 1400 from a beginning not usually put later than 1650 B.C. It is thus, broadly speaking, the contemporary of the developed Aunjetitz culture in Central Europe, where the initial A1 stage answering to Tószeg A may be said to give place to an A2 about the same time, with a B period beginning from around 1500, when the same re-dressing of the cultural balance sets in there also, as we shall see directly. Meanwhile, one must note that the transition in Hungary from the A stage through the phases of B is not amenable to closely accurate dating, especially in the south where the A tradition of Perjamos and its like was strong, and the burial-rite remained inhumation even when high-handled and furrowed pottery came in, as is shown by the unbroken series of graves in the great cemetery of Szöreg.[1] Both at Szöreg and Oszentivan (p. 293) the typical two-handled Perjamos jug may last well into B, when it appears at Tószeg too, so that until the Szöreg settlement-site is stratigraphically explored, the dating of graves by such long-lived pottery-types cannot be pressed too far.

But the graves of this rich South Hungarian district round the town of Szeged are of crucial importance. For in four graves at Szöreg and one at Oszentivan, associated with pottery in the main of Perjamos tradition, have been found little segmented beads of faience.[2] There are also found star or rectangular beads of the same material, among a wide range of ornaments, including also Mediterranean shells, and scientific examination of this faience has shown it to be identical with that of the selfsame form of segmented bead in Egypt, whence it thus appears the beads were imported. Further, segmented faience beads of this type have been found in roughly contemporary Aunjetitz graves in Moravia, at Němčice and Jirikovice, and another at Leopoldsdorf in Lower Austria, in an inhumation-grave with two gold lock-rings of Aunjetitz type, but pottery that assigns the whole to the Wieselburg culture, with its Bell-beaker and Baden traditions (p. 299), and further points, in its white-inlaid ornament, to the influence from the Slavonian culture-area already discussed. In this period of transition from Early to Middle Bronze Age, then, imported beads from Egypt were circulating widely in the Danube basin; and this is not all. We have already spoken of trade-routes from the Aunjetitz province to the West, as well as the Amber Route to the North (p. 328): close to that by the Lower Rhine to Britain, at Exloo in the Drenthe province of Holland, has been found a necklace comprising

[1] Fig. 27, *a*, 6.   [2] Cf. Fig. 27, *b*, 2.

four of these beads and twenty-five of more or less the same shape in tin, as well as fourteen ordinary beads of amber. Here are Western or Central European tin, Northern amber, and Egyptian faience all together, and the Western ramifications of the faience bead-trade are attested by eight from a grave of the Spanish El Argar culture (p. 308) at Fuente Alamo in Almeria, by one (of doubtful associations and relative age) from the megalithic tomb of Parc-Guren at Carnac in Brittany, and, far outweighing all in number, by at least forty from England, to say nothing of a number more from the British Isles, mainly Scotland, of different composition and apparently later date. The latter include star forms as well as segmented, and also a quoit shape which recurs in England in normal faience in pendant form [1] and in occasional association with normal segmented beads. Rarer varieties include spherical or near-spherical forms, and a few beads of blue glass have been reported also, which call to mind a few others from Central Europe, notably one from an Aunjetitz grave at Melk in Austria, and others, greenish and of pinched-circle shape, from another such grave at Polep in Bohemia. The associations of the British bead-finds are primarily in graves of the Wessex culture, most notably that at Aldbourne in Wiltshire that has given its name to the type of 'incense-cup' it also contained (p. 315), and a high proportion of the whole number have occurred in or close to Wiltshire; but they also occur further afield, and also many must be of rather later date, as accompanying cremation-interments in the large cinerary urns that we shall presently find characteristic of the ensuing Middle Bronze Age in Britain, after (some even considerably after) about 1400 B.C. Thus it would be a mistake to suppose that this bead-trade was closely circumscribed in time and so can be used as a narrow chronological horizon. It would be natural to date the Aldbourne grave and its like rather before than after 1500 B.C., and the same may be said of perhaps most of the Hungarian and Central European finds, despite the allowance above made for a late survival of associated pottery-types. And though it is theoretically possible to reduce the dates of all such finds to a common low level, yet

[1] Fig. 27, *b*, 3.

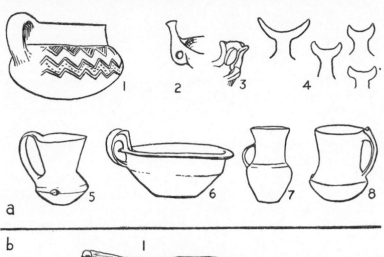

a

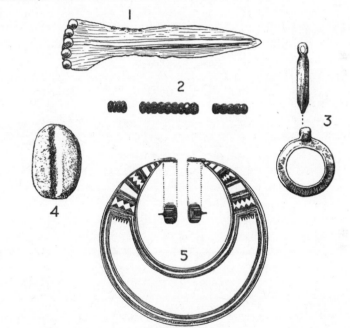

b

Fig. 27

a, SKETCHES OF ITALIAN AND HUNGARIAN BRONZE AGE
POTTERY

1, Cup with incised white-inlaid ornament, Filottrano, Marche, and 2-3,
Examples of handles, Apennine Culture (pp. 334 ff.); 4, Forms of crescent
handle (*ansa lunata*), typical of North Italian Terremare (pp. 340-1);
5-8, Hungary, Bronze Age B (pp. 341 ff.); 5, 7-8, West Hungary; 6, Szöreg,
E. Hungary (outlines only).

b, 1, BRONZE HALBERD FROM SHAFT-GRAVE VI, MYCENAE
(pp. 350, 352)

b, 2-5, FAIENCE, STONE, AND GOLD TYPES FROM THE
BRITISH ISLES

2, 3, Faience (pp. 345-8): 2, Segmented beads, Wilts.; 3, Ring-pendant,
Sussex; 4, Stone arrow-shaft smoother (p. 350), Wilts.; 5, Irish gold
lunula (p. 324), found in Wales.

Scales: 1, $\frac{1}{8}$; 2-3, $\frac{3}{5}$; 4, $\frac{3}{10}$; 5, $\frac{2}{5}$.

the British evidence requires in any case a spacing-out of dates, and those earlier than the mean need not be ruled out any more than those later.

Thus the evidence so far points to a trade persisting over an appreciable time in the middle and after-middle centuries of the second millennium. And related bead-types in bone, jet, and gold, as well as the tin specimens already noticed, and the spiral-tubular bronze beads frequent in Central Europe, have a wide enough distribution in time and space to make one take a broad view of the whole matter. For indeed the segmented-bead form in general has a very long history in Egypt and the Near East generally, from long before until well after the period we are discussing, and we can only say that production rose to its height under the Eighteenth Dynasty, from just after 1600 B.C., and that the bluish glaze-colour, and far more critically the large perforation, normal to the European finds, are recorded from Abydos with a scarab of Amenhotep III (1412-1376 B.C.), and also from among the great numbers of segmented beads from Tell el-Amarna (1380-1350), whence the resemblance to Wiltshire specimens has been confirmed by spectrographic analysis. Finally, as closely similar beads have been dated 1200-1150 B.C. at Tell Duweir (Lachish) in Palestine. What, then, is the historical context of the connexions that the European bead-finds imply between the centre and west of our continent and the orbit of Egyptian civilization? For a satisfactory answer it is natural to turn to the Aegean, and in the first place to Minoan Crete, inevitable half-way house between the Orient and Europe.

We last took leave of the Minoans (p. 241) when their Middle Minoan civilization had established contacts with Egypt and Syria, attested there in exports of its Kamares pottery such as have been found in Egyptian Middle-Kingdom associations of between 1900 and 1800 B.C. at Harageh, Kahun, and Abydos, and at Ras Shamra in Syria in the same period, while not long afterwards the inland-Syrian painted ware of Tell Atchana bears further witness in its direct Middle Minoan inspiration. By this time, about 1700, however, the disturbance of the Near East by invasion of Mesopotamia from the east and north, and the expansion into Syria of the Hittite power from Anatolia, had penetrated to Egypt, where Asiatic intrusions broke up the Middle Kingdom, and after an interval of discord led to the alien rule of the Hyksos, the so-called Shepherd Kings. In this period before the restoration of native power in the years before and after 1600, which with the Eighteenth Dynasty created what is called the New Kingdom, it was probably this upsetting of Egypt that turned Minoan activity more definitely towards the north, not only now to the islands of the Aegean but to mainland Greece. Already before the disaster (p. 241)—probably one of internal warfare within the island—which overwhelmed Knossos and the central Cretan palaces at the end of Middle Minoan II about 1700, Minoan ascendancy in the Cyclades was making contact with the mainland attested in the association of Kamares pottery with the mainland Minyan (p. 239); this phenomenon at Phylakopi in Melos is followed by the more widespread appearance of imitated Kamares ware, which occurs with the genuine product just off the mainland coast at Aegina, and Cretan influence coming this way from Melos and Thera, and more directly to the Laconian coast of the Peloponnese, led towards the end of the brilliant century of Middle Minoan III culture to a sudden and dynamic transference of Minoan brilliance to mainland seats of power. And soon the coming of the New Kingdom restored the prospects of Cretan trade with Egypt: when, at the same time about or just after 1600, the Middle Minoan III centres suffered the consequences of an earthquake, the Temple Repositories of Knossos included among their minor contents a variety of our segmented faience bead-type, and in the Late Minoan civilization which followed, one of the leading products of Egyptian importation and inspiration was a great wealth of faience objects, among which the type has now been found, as well as the spherical or near-spherical and other forms of bead represented equally in Crete, in tombs upon the mainland.

This, then, appears to be the historical context of the traffic through which Egyptian faience beads reached Central and Western Europe, whether from the Aegean across the Balkans to Hungary, or along the main Amber Route by sea to the head of the Adriatic, and so from North Italy over the Alps. All that we have said of Bronze Age trade-routes in this chapter therefore culminates in this, that from at least about 1600 B.C. onwards Europe was connected, through the Aegean, with the Orient in a commerce of a new order of significance, transcending whatever we have seen of the kind in earlier periods. A single Egyptian trade-product can now appear simultaneously in the Aegean, Hungary, Moravia, Spain and Brittany, Holland, and above all in Britain. And the Baltic amber which, with a distribution of its own almost as wide and far more abundant, was the chief precious commodity traded southward across Central Europe in the opposite direction, appears in abundance from about this same date of 1600 in the Aegean world. Further, we saw earlier that the European bronze halberd might be treated as a ritual weapon and so enter the class of precious objects of exchange, and the same period has produced two halberds in Greece: one, from a grave with Minyan pottery of about 1600 at Sesklo in Thessaly, recalls to some extent at least Hungarian pattern, while the other [1] has had closer parallels to its curved edges, straight midrib, and arrangement of rivets quoted from North Italy, and even from the far-away home of the type in Ireland. The rivets of that halberd are conical-headed in the North European manner, but they are capped with gold, and the place of its finding was the focus of the whole movement that transplanted Minoan splendour to the Greek mainland—the acropolis of Mycenae, overlooking the plain of Argos. It was in the sixth of the famous shaft-graves, in the sepulchral treasure which also included a stone shaft-smoother of a type well known in the North and Britain; [2] as for amber, beads of it were found in three of the others, in the fifth as many as a hundred, in the third thirty, with also two spherical beads of faience. The link between Europe and the Orient has become cast in the new mould of Mycenean civilization.

It is not our purpose here to attempt even a summary description of the material remains of Mycenean culture. Their magnificence is famous, their detail and abundance demand volumes rather than paragraphs. But regarding

[1] Fig. 27, *b*, 1.   [2] Fig. 27, *b*, 4.

Mycenae as we must regard it here, from the point of view of the European Bronze Age as a whole, two aspects of its greatness stand out. The first we have already approached: Mycenae as the meeting-point of East and West. Of the importance of that we shall have yet more to say, for it covers more than the precious merchandise of faience and amber. But to appreciate it better we need to consider the second: Mycenae as the seat of an essentially European culture—that is, essentially European in a sense in which Minoan culture in Crete was not. True, from the time of the earliest shaft-graves, around 1600 B.C., its rulers were steeped in Minoan taste, drew heavily on Minoan resources of craftsmanship and material equipment, and in short could not have been what they were but for Minoan Crete as their neighbour. It is, indeed, often said that Mycenean civilization was founded by Cretan colonists. But, in fact, all the original seats of that civilization—Mycenae itself, Tiryns, and Orchomenos are the foremost—were already centres of Helladic settlement, and the continuity between Middle Helladic and Mycenean or Late Helladic times is manifest in the unbroken maintenance across the dividing line of the former's Minyan and matt-painted pottery-fabrics; furthermore, the shaft-graves of Mycenae were dug within the precincts of the Middle Helladic cemetery of the place, and are themselves simply more or less aggrandized versions of the cist-grave typical of Middle Helladic times. One need not believe their occupants were primarily Cretan rulers of a Minoan colony in Argolis, though at Thebes clay bath-tub coffin-burials in the Cretan manner show that Minoan colonists were not altogether lacking. But neither, on the other hand, need one suppose that all the Minoan material on the mainland came there as plunder, and that all the Mycenean copies of Minoan work were made by captured slaves. Rather it would seem that the Helladic lords of Mycenae, controlling the vital trade-route over the mountains between the southward-facing Argive plain and the ways leading from the Isthmus and Gulf of Corinth to the north and west, and moreover with important deposits of copper— to say nothing of the quite probable tin of Crisa (p. 291)— not far away, were strong enough for a political and commercial arrangement with the Cretans, securing trade and hegemony together as mainland partners of Minoan power. The regal culture thus inaugurated imported and copied Minoan material of all kinds to make the magnificence which Schliemann so dramatically revealed to the world, while keeping an essential measure of its own individuality. In nothing is this more clearly shown than in the stelae which served the shaft-graves as gravestones, for they are adorned with sculpture in relief, an art unknown to Crete and here appearing for the first time in Greece. And the charioteering figure of the most famous shows at once how early the Myceneans had adopted the 'heroic' style of warfare that had revolutionized tactics in the Near East, and with what originality they turned a Minoan tradition of draughtsmanship to the new medium of the sculptor—the idea of which had perhaps reached Greece, like the war-chariot, from Hittite sources in Asia Minor. Two centuries later, sculpture at Mycenae reached its climax in the famous Lion Gate of the citadel.

The earliest shaft-grave is the sixth, the same that contained the bronze halberd, and from this at about 1600 the series covers roughly a century—the Late Helladic period I, answering to Late Minoan Ia in Crete. Of their abundant treasures it need be further recalled here only that the renowned gold death-masks include bearded faces,[1] contrasting sharply with those of the clean-shaven Minoans, and that the scenes chosen for the rich embossed and inlaid work show a fondness for subjects of warfare and the chase that differs significantly from the peaceful and religious interests of Minoan figural art. The bronze weapons themselves [2] are almost all of pure Minoan type, riveted daggers like that inlaid with the well-known lion-hunt, superb rapiers over three feet long which are simply beautifully proportioned and finely tempered elongations of the tanged and mid-ribbed type of dagger, and spearheads with a rolled-over form of socket secured by a terminal ring, a type soon rendered as the true hollow-cast socketed spearhead before long adopted into the Middle Bronze Age armoury of Italy and Central and Northern Europe. (The contemporary British evolution of the socket

[1] Pl. XII, 1.   [2] Pl. XII, 2.

from a collar-ring round the haft-hold of a tanged spearhead, adapted from the dagger, was probably indebted to this same source.)   Thereafter the form of royal sepulchre changes.   Already in the sixteenth century ordinary Mycenean families were burying their dead in rock-cut chamber-tombs, such as had been general in the Aegean area in Early Minoan times and had had a continuous history since, at least in Crete, where the chamber to which the entrance-passage or dromos leads in from the hillside is normally rectangular.   On the mainland it now may more often be round, and when the Mycenean rulers decided, about 1500—perhaps, but not certainly, with a change of dynasty—to renounce shaft-grave burial in favour of an aggrandized stone-built version of the chamber-tomb type, this round form gave their architects the opportunity to apply the old principle (p. 148) of the corbelled vault, and so produce the 'beehive'- or tholos-tombs which throughout the fifteenth century and after remained the regular form of sepulchre for the ruling house in all Mycenean centres, as the ordinary chamber-tomb remained that of their subjects.   In Crete, a recent discovery near Knossos has disclosed a true tholos-tomb apparently assignable to Middle Minoan III; but as a rule royal and common tombs alike remained rectangular, with apparently a post-and-beam roof save in the case of especial magnificence represented by the stone barrel-vault of the royal tomb of Isopata.   In the period of the earlier fifteenth-century tholos-tombs the Mycenean mainland had reached the high-water mark of its Minoanization in material culture;   this was the half-century of the Late Minoan Ib phase in Crete, and by now all over South and East-Central Greece the Mycenean culture with its Minoan-inspired splendours was diffused, among a long series of centres of princely power—in Argolis, not only Mycenae and the neighbouring Prosymna (whence come the segmented faience beads noted above), but Dendra and the rock-acropolis of Tiryns in the plain below; in Laconia Vapheio, where the tholos-tomb yielded the famous gold cups with their embossed bulls; in the west Messenian Pylos, and Pylos in Elis at Kakovatos, where the sepulchral treasures abounded in a superfluity of amber which well shows that here was the great port for the Adriatic and trans-continental traffic with the Baltic north; on the east, Aegina, Attica with the Athenian acropolis and the tholos-tomb at Thoricos, Chalcis in Euboea, Boeotia with its centres at Thebes and Orchomenos; and furthest north, even the Pagasaean coast of Thessaly with its early tholos near Volo. And when the palaces of the Mycenean rulers are revealed by excavation, they are seen to be no copies of the labyrinthine Cretan palace-plans of Knossos or Phaestos, but have as their central feature the pillared megaron, the 'great hall' with its central hearth as portrayed in the Homeric poems, which for all its glory of wall-painting and sumptuous interior decoration yet seems the lineal descendant of those which, whether at Troy, in Thessaly, or beyond in Danubian Europe, we have already seen repeatedly built in simpler form by other peoples of European breed and non-Mediterranean derivation (pp. 102-5, 239). Female costume at least was in Minoan fashion, with open-breasted jacket and flounced skirts, but showy gold ear-rings and hairpins suggest a taste still somewhat barbaric compared with Minoan refinement. And for all the Minoanization pre-eminently displayed by its ruling class, the Mycenean world never adopted the organized complexity of Cretan life, the abundance of official and personal seals, the writing-tablets, and the systems of linear script: seals are beautiful but rare, and associated only with great personages like those buried at Dendra, Prosymna, and (though only a few impressions survive) Mycenae; of writing, the only traces come later in a few vase-inscriptions from Mycenae, Tiryns, and Orchomenos. On the other hand, the final development of that same complexity drew Crete, or at least its dominant royal house, to overtop the Minoan-Mycenean balance of culture reached by the Aegean world in the earlier fifteenth century.

Up to about 1450, the lords of Knossos seem to have divided the supremacy of the island with other palace-rulers, and fortresses could be manned by rivals in military power one against another. But suddenly in the middle of the century the great palace of Phaestos in South Crete was sacked and destroyed, the princely seat of Hagia Triada was burnt down, and ruin, or anyhow, as at Gournia in the east, stagnation, overtook all the centres of the island civilization that may be reckoned competitors with the hegemony of Knossos. Knossos stands in unique contrast. Abounding already in wealth and armed force, the great palace now reveals in every significant aspect the prosperity and majesty surrounding an assured and absolute monarch, the priest-king of the throne-room which Sir Arthur Evans has made so famous, and the judge surely whose memory survived in the Greek legends of Minos the ineluctable lawgiver. With their new-created government script, his officials supervise administration and revenue: if the whole of Crete acknowledges his rule, his fleet must command the seas whose commerce ministers to his wealth; the commercial and diplomatic relations of the island with Egypt, attested in unprecedented plenty by the archaeology of both countries from the coming of Late Minoan and New Kingdom times, are above all concentrated under his hand, with the trade of Syria and Cyprus, and the closer hegemony of the Aegean. How the history of art in Crete, from the fresh and versatile brilliance of Middle Minoan III and the rich and tasteful maturity of Late Minoan I,[1] reflects the character of the Knossian supremacy of Late Minoan II in the grandiose 'Palace Style' of the studios and ateliers bound to the service of the court, it is beyond our scope here to illustrate. What we must not overlook, however, is the cleavage which this centralization of Cretan culture made with the Greek mainland, where art and craftsmanship continue in the main unprogressively in the Late Minoan I tradition. For the sequel to the great half-century of the Palace rule of Minos was twofold. Upon Knossos there fell sudden and ruthless destruction, which put an end once and for all to the proud imperialism of its rulers. And on the mainland, from the same moment, Mycenean culture entered upon a new era of expansion which carried its outposts during the next two centuries all round the Eastern Mediterranean, westwards to Sicily and South Italy and northwards beyond Thessaly to Macedonia, while in Greece itself its leading centres reached the climax of their greatness, displayed nowhere more magnificently than in the

[1] Pl. XII, 3.

new-built palace, the fortress wall with its Lion Gate, and the huge tholos-tomb called the Treasury of Atreus, which together make its grandest memorial at Mycenae itself.

The date of the Fall of Knossos, closely fixed by material synchronisms with the known chronology of Egypt, stands in round figures at 1400 B.C., and it is not too much to call it the turning-point of European prehistory. That it was the Myceneans of European Greece, strong enough now in their own ships, and with the power of their own wealth behind their martial prowess, who rose against the Minoan despot and delivered the blow that brought Knossos down, cannot indeed be proved outright. But the belief fits strikingly with facts as well as probabilities. How Egypt reacted is clear from the way in which evidence of her especial relations with Crete ceases at this time in the reign of King Amenhotep III, while the faience with his cartouche at Mycenae seems significantly answered by his reception in Egypt of Mycenean pottery, followed as it was by two centuries of the ware's importation and use throughout the Nile valley. The effect in Europe was that Mycenean civilization became supreme in the Aegean, standing now in its own right as the head and front of the achievement of the European Bronze Age. And in the tale of Theseus who 'slew the Minotaur' and freed his country from the oppression of Minos' tribute, a great over-throw of Knossos by their countrymen has come down to us as one of the most ancient memories of the Greek people. That overthrow symbolizes the winning of mastery in its own house for European civilization as against the Orient. With it the span of this book in time reaches its end. But it remains now to review the European scene of 1400 B.C. as a whole. And we shall find that the inception of the Middle Bronze Age at this time was in the main the emergence of a cultural balance, which we have already begun to see appearing, and of which the Mycenean achievement, unique as it remains, yet faithfully emphasizes the essential poise. It is the balance of the foundations of Europe.

Chapter Eight

PREHISTORY AND THE FOUNDATIONS OF
EUROPE: EPILOGUE

(Map VI and Table VI: at end)

THE attainment of the cultural balance that made the Middle
Bronze Age has already been sketched for the region of
Hungary and the surrounding territories, as also for Italy,
since there it appears that the process belongs to the two
centuries, or rather more, preceding our horizon of 1400 B.C.
At that horizon the Hungarian Middle Bronze Age may be
reckoned as completing its maturity, represented by period C
in the history of the stratified site at Tószeg, and characterized
throughout its area by a prevailing funeral-rite of cremation
and burial in urnfields. In North Hungary alone a Barrow-
building people seems still to have persisted from earlier days:
for the rest, there mediated between those earlier days and
the Urnfield period the development coeval with the Tószeg
period B, which consisted, as we have seen, in the expansion
of the less civilized peoples, above all those of the Slavonian
borders of the south-west, who in the Early Bronze Age had
fringed the Central or East Hungarian civilization of Perjamos
and Tószeg A, till a more or less even balance of culture was
created throughout the whole region. This process was,
then, the contemporary and counterpart of the rise of Mycenean
culture in Greece, and the resulting balance corresponds
likewise with the Mycenean supremacy in the Aegean world
that ensued upon the Fall of Knossos. Only it must be added
that between the Danube basin and the orbit of Mycenae the
peoples of Macedonia and the hinterland of Thessaly and
North Greece remained with but little to show of Bronze Age
progress; indeed, this blank in the map of progressing
civilization had a historic sequel that will come out at the end
of our story. And further east, where the picture cannot in

357

the present state of knowledge be so clear, the Monteoru culture north of the Lower Danube has to be set off against a long survival south of it of the traditions of Gumelnitza (p. 235), which in the culture revealed by the 'tells' of Bulgaria made contact with the Macedonian Bronze Age on the one hand, and lay open on the other to the influence of Troy, where quite early in the second millennium—as early, it now appears, as about 1900—the Sixth city had arisen upon the Fifth, and made a counterpart in the region of the Straits to Helladic development in Greece, with which indeed its relationship was close. From the imported and imitated Mycenean pottery among its relics, and from the massive stone walls with which it was fortified, Troy VI has long been believed to be the city celebrated in the *Iliad*; but the excavations of recent years have shown that its end came about 1350 B.C., a good century and a half before the traditional date of the Trojan War, soon after 1200, so that the Homeric city remains to be equated with its successor Troy VIIa, to which Troy VI gave place, apparently, as the result of incursions from the still obscure south-eastern corner of neighbouring Europe.

How much remains to be explained in that south-eastern corner, and further round the east and north of the Black Sea past the Monteoru area, is at present hard to estimate, but there was evidently a long continuance of the old culture of the kurgan-builders on the South Russian steppe, and in that connexion one may recall to mind the famous Bessarabian treasure of Borodino (p. 226), in which socketed spearheads and a gold-inlaid dagger and pin, all of silver and of Mycenean and Hungarian affinities respectively, lay together with battle-axes of precious stone like those of the 'burnt city' of Troy II, which had seemingly been treasured as sacred objects throughout the intervening centuries. And beyond, in Central Russia, the parallel survival of the Fatyanovo culture (p. 230) and the unbroken continuance of the simple life of the Comb-ware people of the forests (p. 203) ultimately admitted the civilizing influences attested in the extraordinary hoards of Galich and Seima, mainly of copper objects which suggest that these influences came from the south-east to bear upon the secluded traditions of the east of Northern Europe, in which the animal art of the elk-head stone axes of Finland (p. 231) had lived on to meet them; but that lies outside the confines of this book. The period of significant links between these eastern regions and Central Europe had passed away with the rise of the latter's self-sufficiency in a Bronze Age civilization to which their steppe and forest dwellers remained alien, and the situation scarcely changed till the eastward expansion of influence from Late Bronze Age Europe, and the dynamic irruption of the Scyths from the steppes westward into Hungary after the European Iron Age had dawned.

On the other side of the Hungarian region the mountain valleys south-west of it long maintained the traditions which had proved so potent a leaven in its Middle Bronze Age development, and across the Adriatic we have seen how the rise of the Terramaricoli, and the maturity of the Apennine culture south of them, made of the Italian Bronze Age a balance of cultures analogous in its way to the Hungarian, and with the lake-dwellers on the north and the Ligurian cave-dwellers on the north-west making a firm basic pattern for what supervened in the peninsula's Late Bronze and Early Iron Ages. And the renewal of sea-connexions by the south and by Sicily with the Aegean, which led to the decisive incomings of the Etruscans and of Greek colonization, began in the centuries after 1400 with the spread this way of Mycenean influence, while not only Siculans but Sardinians joined in the sea-roving activity of the Eastern Mediterranean. For these sequels and those of Italy's northward connexions across the Adriatic and the Alps, the home of the Italic peoples of history was thus prepared by the well-laid balance of her Bronze Age civilization. Now we have to turn across the Alps to the parallel Bronze Age civilization of the great Aunjetitz province and its peripheral cultures in Central Europe, and see how there too the Middle Bronze Age came in with a new cultural balance, analogous in formation, though different in constitution, to that already witnessed in Hungary.

To deal first with the south-eastern and southern borderlands of the Aunjetitz province proper, round the Austrian reaches of the Danube (pp. 299, 332-3), the change from the mature

Early Bronze Age—Bronze Age A2—to the Middle Bronze Age—B—is marked by the replacement of the southernmost true Aunjetitz outliers, and of the Wieselburg culture beyond them, by a new cultural unity, in which the Mad'arovce culture of Western Slovakia on the one side, and the Böheim-kirchen culture further up the Danube on the other, joined hands over the intervening region. These two cultures were precisely those that, despite Aunjetitz influence, are shown by their pottery to have maintained most strongly the survival of earlier elements, more particularly, as we have already (p. 333) recalled, that of the Baden culture. But, unlike their West Hungarian relatives among whom the survival carried the practice of cremation-burial (p. 342), the burial-rite of this new unitary culture was inhumation under barrows, the old hall-mark of the Corded-ware people, and it would seem that it was the descendants of barrow-builders of that stock in Slovakia, and perhaps North Hungary, and probably in Austria itself too (doubtless taking in the Braided-ware folk noticed on p. 299), whose resurgence brought about the whole unifying movement and imposed their burial-rite upon the resulting culture. Their barrow-building convention was in Austria seemingly already fused with the Baden tradition in Bronze Age A. Further west, in Bavaria, the corresponding process was simpler: the rise to absolute dominance of the descendants of the Corded-ware barrow-builders who had fringed the loess-land Straubing group of Aunjetitz civilization (p. 301) during Bronze Age A, with a Bronze Age B culture in which, despite the incorporation of Aunjetitz borrowings, their own individuality stands clearly out and barrow-burial is charac-teristic. The new culture probably contained within itself also the heritage of the Altheim culture-group on which the Corded-ware warriors had originally (p. 249) impinged. The spread of this Bavarian barrow culture carried it into Western Austria to march with the more easterly one just described, and by further expansion the two between them brought into the same orbit the uplands of Southern Bohemia, where a barrow-building population thus entered on the first stage (that of Krtenov-Smedrova in type-site nomenclature) of its development, over against the Aunjetitz civilization which still persisted in the richer lands of the centre and north of Bohemia and Moravia. The next stage, that of Chodoun-Zeleny, shows these people taking possession of the westerly lowland regions of Budweis and Pilsen, and this may be reckoned to have preceded by about a century the third and decisive stage at which they invaded the whole heart of the Aunjetitz province and finally assimilated its culture to their own. That began not before the end of Bronze Age B, about 1300 B.C., so that by the mean date of our survey at 1400 the two cultures were in the penultimate phase of their co-existence, the equilibrium preceding fusion. It is in these later centuries of the Aunjetitz culture's life that the faience beads noted above attest its connexions with the Orient, and the Amber Route by which its people forwarded the product of their Baltic trade to the Mycenean world was in its heyday. The dividing-line between Bronze Age A and B here in Central Europe may, in fact, fairly be put about 1500 B.C., which date will then make a starting-point for the rise of these barrow-building peoples to the Middle Bronze Age culture which throughout the Mid-European region is often known *par excellence* as the Barrow or 'Tumulus culture'. Therein the originally barbaric neighbours of the Aunjetitz civilization came to balance its heritage with their own, on a level answering to that of the Urnfield cultures in Hungary, whence indeed they were considerably influenced, especially in their bronze industry— the development of which, however, falls outside our present scope.

North-east and north of Aunjetitz Bohemia the culture's Saxo-Thuringian province shared its continuance from Bronze Age A into B, and in its graves and settlements, from the metalliferous region of Middle Germany (p. 292) to the Elbe and so across the south of Brandenburg to the Oder and beyond, its pottery-development can be followed into full maturity; meanwhile the bronze industry represented in its chieftain-burials and hoards carries on the history of the flanged axe, the triangular-bladed and bronze-hilted dagger, and the metal-shafted halberd as outlined in the last chapter, with the cast bracelets, the spiral armlets, and the rest of its repertory of types. That its products were traded to the

Baltic and Scandinavia we have seen (p. 326), and eastward their distribution reaches Poland and even Lithuania, in the quarter where we have already indicated a distinct East Baltic culture-province as emerging in this period, to establish its full individuality after the middle of the millennium from the Lower Vistula to the Gulf of Riga and the edge of the great country of the Comb-ware people. But the most important north-easterly region of development within the Aunjetitz orbit was not so far afield. The native elements in the Saxo-Thuringian culture already noted had their counterparts likewise in Brandenburg; and on the east the basin of the Oder displays in especial prominence the strength of the Northern and 'warrior' compound, which had kept its Neolithic character so long in the Oder culture of p. 281, in the Bronze Age that further south in Silesia, and in South-West Poland, shared the full character of Aunjetitz civilization. From about the middle of the second millennium onwards, the region of the Lausitz and the Middle Oder, from the confines of Saxony over those of Silesia and Brandenburg, witnessed the rise from these beginnings of a new and dynamic civiliza-tion, that of the Lausitz culture. Already in its Early Bronze Age it displays its own characteristics, a prominence of knob-or wart-ornament on its pottery, and in its burial-custom some instalment already of the cremation which later became its invariable rule, and a marked partiality for barrows as against flat-graves on the Aunjetitz model, the funeral-deposit within enclosed in encircling piles of stones. Thus from the Silesian and adjacent Aunjetitz groups, and a strong Northern Neolithic and Warrior combination alongside them on the Middle Oder and expanding in union with them, the Lausitz culture developed with its own cultural balance comprised within itself, resolving the old Silesian antithesis between Northern and Danubian in a unique solidarity of barrow-building warrior tradition and civilization of the Aunjetitz type. Archaeological description of the initial Lausitz material will not here be attempted: its place is the introduction to a narrative of European prehistory in the Late Bronze Age, for some two centuries after the term of this book the Lausitz people pushed out over all Central Europe and beyond in a great expansion, whose force reached from the Balkans and the Troad to Spain and the British Isles, besides exerting the strongest influence upon the civilization of the North. The point here is that the foundation of their later achievements was a cultural unity which presents our formula of a balance of elements in a strength and compactness so far unparalleled in this survey of Bronze Age Europe.

The ethnic identity of the Lausitz people has long been a matter of controversy. The great majority of German scholars have followed the lead of Gustaf Kossinna in identifying them with the Illyrians of later antiquity, who will have reached the classic Illyria between the Danube and the Adriatic as a result of the subsequent expansion just mentioned. But three other views have been put forward. A prominent Polish school, formerly supported in Czechoslovakia, has made of the Lausitz folk the ancestors of the Slavs. But though it is true that the Iron Age culture in Poland can claim continuity with Lausitz beginnings, and that it was from this direction that the Slavs of history made their appearance in post-Roman Europe, the idea of Slav 'nationality' for the Lausitz culture in its Bronze Age homeland has really no substantial support: the prehistoric origins of the Slavs must yet lie eastward beyond the focal region of Bronze Age civilization identifiable within the scope of this book. It is, in fact, better to side with more recent opinion and decline to equate the Lausitz people outright with any ethnic group recognizable through language, while agreeing that, whatever view be taken concerning the Slavs, the Lausitz expansion was an important factor in the formation of the peoples later known as Illyrian. This is the more reasonable since the branch of the same expansion that went in the Late Bronze Age into Hungary, and on south-eastward into and beyond the Balkans, must be connected with the formation of the Thracian peoples and their Phrygian relatives across the Straits, while on the other hand the contemporary western movement by which the Lausitz people brought what are known as the Urnfield cultures into Central and Western Europe had unquestionably a profound effect upon the ethnic constitution of the Celts. With the Celts we shall be concerned very shortly; meanwhile, the fourth view of the Lausitz people is that of Carl Schuchhardt, who sees in them a section of the Germanic race, only creating the Illyrians by expanding southward and fusing with the great mass of the Danubian population whom he would regard as 'proto-Illyrian' since Neolithic times. It is true that in the Northern Neolithic and warrior-culture elements in their composition the Lausitz folk can claim kinship with the Germans. But the culture as a whole is none the less essentially the offspring of Aunjetitz civilization, whereas from before the beginning of their Bronze Age onwards the ancestors of the Germans formed an absolutely distinct cultural and ethnic grouping, separated from the Lausitz and Aunjetitz provinces by the latter's fringe of peoples across the Middle Elbe and Brandenburg—among whom the Globe-flask folk of the Havel area (p. 227) preserved an individuality of their own that has recently been detected far on into the Bronze Age. The Germanic frontier of the Early Bronze Age ran from the Baltic coast near the mouth of the Oder past Mecklenburg and the north-west of Brandenburg round to the North Sea near the mouth of the Elbe: behind it, the whole of Schleswig-Holstein, Denmark, and South Sweden formed the core of the Germanic territory, with the further parts of Sweden and Norway lying within the same orbit beyond.

Remoter Scandinavia, indeed, was yet through these centuries continuing in the tradition of the 'Dwelling-place' hunting culture described here in an earlier chapter (pp. 62, 204-5), permeated gradually by the civilizing influence of the South, importing implements of flint and more tardily of bronze, but expressing the individuality of its own craftsmanship in its own stone, horn, and bone, and most distinctively on beautiful weapons of ground slate. But while Finland belonged to the East European world where battle-axe invaders (p. 231) had sunk their warrior culture in the deep matrix of the Comb-ware folk, by fairly general consent Finno-Ugrian in speech, the Scandinavian Dwelling-place population shared origins with that of the West Baltic shores where their common Mesolithic inheritance had first been raised to the starting-plane of civilization; with civilization's spread, however gradual it was, all Scandinavia short of the dim sphere of the Lapps was Germanic by natural destiny. And of the nature of Germanic formation over the whole West Baltic region, to Southern Sweden from the Elbe mouth, there is no doubt whatever. It was the product of the impact of the warrior Single-grave invaders, narrated in our sixth chapter (p. 217), on the megalith-building representatives of the Northern Neolithic. How the antithesis of Single-grave and megalith peoples, manifest throughout the Passage-grave period, was modified with the ensuing of the Stone-cist period, has been duly seen (pp. 280-3). And with the rise of a native Northern Bronze Age, the fusion of the two sets of people into a single whole could proceed to the accompaniment of a common material culture.

Burial-customs, indeed, for some time continued to reflect the old division, especially in Schleswig-Holstein and parts of Jutland, the original stronghold of the Single-grave people, stone-packed barrow-burials in their unmistakable tradition contrasting with stone cists—though, as we have seen, for example, in the Danish islands, not all stone cists represent the practice of the former megalith-builders. Throughout, inhumation was the prevailing rite, though cases of cremation occur here and there to foreshadow its universal adoption, as in the Lausitz culture, later on. The earlier Northern Bronze Age, indeed, shows the beginning of more than one new departure in the cult of the dead. Enormous barrows like those of the Saxo-Thuringian chieftains, at Helmsdorf covering a big stone cist with a wooden roof, at Leubingen a regular timber-built mortuary house, are not exactly paralleled, but the mortuary-house idea—the provision for the dead of a virtual replica of his earthly dwelling—spread on the edge of German territory lower down the Elbe together with the rite of cremation: at Gottorf near Hamburg and Baven in Hanover, and again at Grünhof near Lauenburg, such timber houses, used perhaps for cult purposes during their builders' lifetimes, were burnt with their bodies laid within, and the ruins covered by a barrow. The bodies were probably deposited in them in tree-trunk coffins, and inhumation (and more rarely burial after cremation) in such coffins was already starting to be practised in Schleswig-Holstein in the beginnings of its Bronze Age—as at Schafstedt in Dithmarsch—and became more frequent rather later there, and especially in Jutland, among the descendants of the Single-grave folk (the coffins being often piled round with stones in their distinctive manner). It is probable that the coffin originally represented a dug-out boat, and that the idea of a voyage by water to the next world, well attested in Scandinavia in the later Bronze Age and again in the Iron Age down to its famous culmination in Viking times, is here to be recognized at its first beginning, inspired, it may well be, ultimately from Egypt, through the Baltic connexions with the South now passing along the Amber Route. The same rite of boat- or coffin-burial appears simultaneously in Britain in the middle centuries of the second millennium, when the North Sea trade-route was flourishing as already described, penetrating the Wessex culture along the south coast, where the burial at Hove noted above for its Scandinavian affinities (p. 324) was of this type, but more prominent on the east coast, especially in Yorkshire, where the Irish route over the Pennines (p. 325) reached the sea. The classic example is the Gristhorpe coffin-burial near Scarborough, but the recent discovery in the great barrow of Loose Howe on the Cleveland Moors of a primary burial with no less than three boat dug-outs must henceforward stand at the head of the series, and serve to show how the same rite took hold among the seafarers on both sides of the North Sea between about 1600 and 1400 B.C.

Thus the Germanic Bronze Age began under strong influence from the South, to which indeed, but for the contributions above noted from the West (pp. 325-8), its bronze industry was wholly due. The initial stage of that industry's development, corresponding, as we have seen, to the later Aunjetitz culture of Central Europe, forms its period I, and the rapid and brilliant maturity which ensued with period II is linked by reliable synchronisms with the Middle Bronze Age represented by the latter part at least of the Central European period B and the whole of C, and the corresponding period C in Hungary. Its establishment may thus be reckoned completed by our limiting date of 1400 B.C., and though our survey must stop short of its description, we have here again, as with the

Lausitz culture, to emphasize that the Germanic civilization that created it owed its strength to the steady poise of its foundations in the equilibrium finally perfected, in the transition from the late-lasting Northern Neolithic, out of the former opposition between the Single-grave and megalithic peoples. Like the Lausitz folk, then, the Bronze Age Germans had their own well-laid cultural balance, but with them the original kinship between their two main ethnic ingredients was close, going back probably to the great North European unity of Mesolithic times (p. 233), so that their solidarity could become uniquely thorough, and their strength the biggest single historic force wholly matured on European soil.

West of the Elbe, on the heaths of the Ems-land and Drenthe, the complex of Single-grave and Beaker cultures, formed as above described (p. 259), lasted on into the Middle Bronze Age without assimilation to the Germanic province of culture. Despite its incorporation of the old Huns'-bed megalith folk, its affinities were rather with the Rhineland, and shared rather with the Beaker folk of Britain than with the Germans towards and beyond the Elbe mouth. In fact, Holland and North-West Germany are to be reckoned with the territories of the Tumulus cultures whose rise into the Middle Bronze Age has already been partly described further south. Their history in Bavaria and beyond was repeated on the Swabian uplands of Württemberg, where the Bronze Age barrow folk look back to Corded-ware origin and on to a potent sequel in the Iron Age; it was repeated again in the whole region of Hessen towards the Middle Rhine and the territory of the persisting Adlerberg culture (p. 302) along the Rhine itself; and again further south-west in Alsace, where the great barrow-concentrations of the Forest of Haguenau answer closely to those of Württemberg; and leads us over into France on the one hand by Lorraine, on the other by the Jura and the uplands of Burgundy. The irruption in these quarters of barrow-building warriors of Corded-ware stock into France has been sketched above (p. 311), and it was in the period round about 1400 B.C. that their emergence to full Bronze Age status—that of the 'Bronze Age III' of the French chronology of Joseph Déchelette—begins to be perceptible. Their westward diffusion is indeed obscure, but the group that had created the brilliant Breton culture (p. 312) was now in its heyday, and further south the Middle Bronze Age of the Charente comes to show marked affinities to that of the Rhine. In all South-West and much of Central France, it is true, the old Chalcolithic culture still clung to its caves and degenerate megaliths, while in the south the same conservatism was modified both from North Italy and slightly from Spain, and more strongly by the Rhône culture (p. 310), the maturity of which from far down the Rhône up into Switzerland probably falls within the Middle Bronze Age. The balance between Chalcolithic and true Bronze Age cultures in France was on the whole loosely formed, and much play has been made with the conception of the Chalcolithic peoples as Ligurian on one side, Iberian on the other. The Ligurian question depends for solution on too much later prehistory to be approached here, and the extent to which the Spanish contributions to French Chalcolithic culture justify the name Iberian is again a matter that can hardly here be argued. To the outline of that culture's formation attempted above (ch. V and pp. 250-1) there is nothing significant to add now, but it will be remembered that the Iberians proper in Spain are to be identified with the creators of the Almerian civilization of the coast, and the ultimate supremacy of their Bronze Age El Argar culture over the hinterland of the Peninsula cannot have been such as to eliminate the basic difference between the coastal and inland populations. It must rather have been once more an affair of cultural balance, and along the Pyrenees the individuality of the Chalcolithic is believed to have its ethnic counterpart in the Basques, whose immemorial tenacity of race and language goes back through prehistoric time quite probably direct to the distant days of the Palaeolithic. At least we can say of the equivalent of the Middle Bronze Age in the South-West that in the Spanish El Argar culture, the currents issuing from Central Europe by way of the Rhône, and the tenacity of Chalcolithic traditions between them, there was a quiet equilibrium which proved fully ready to support the fresh impacts of civilization that came in the later centuries of antiquity, and to vindicate in the Late Bronze and Iron Ages

the importance of Spain and its natural wealth both in connexion overland with the rest of Europe, and by sea along
the old link with the Aegean and the East through the Mediterranean, and up the Atlantic coast to the North-West and
the British Isles.

Of activity along these sea-routes in the Middle Bronze
Age there is not much sign—the faience beads of Fuente
Alamo (p. 346) are an isolated phenomenon, and the development of shorter trade-routes across the Continent by land had
caused a decline in seaborne trade that was not arrested till
the resurgence of navigation in Late Bronze Age times,
stimulated at least in part by the Phoenicians. And by land
the most that one can say is that the outposts and influence
of Central European culture running out south-westward
across France pointed the way for the migratory movements
that took this path to the Pyrenees and Spain subsequently.
But those movements, when in the Late Bronze and Iron Ages
they came, were migrations of the Celts, and in their coming
Central Europe, as it were, repaid Central Spain for the great
Bell-beaker contribution to the European culture-pool of a
thousand and fifteen hundred years before. Who, then, were
the peoples that emerged from that pool as the Bronze Age
ancestors of the Celts of later times? If the Lausitz folk and
the Germanic peoples had great destinies of expansive power,
the Celts are fully entitled to a place between them, for their
movements into Spain were only part of a history of expansion
which in the later centuries before the Christian era carried
them into Italy, over all Danubian Europe, and into Asia
Minor, and westward to their homes of longest national
survival in the British Isles. And whereas in Spain, as in
Italy, they were never more than a vigorous minority in an
essentially alien land, the question remains how far the Celts
who from North France and the Lower Rhine came in the
Late Bronze and Iron Ages to invade the British Isles may
have been treading paths already trodden by their own kin
within the centuries covered by this book. It is a difficult
question to answer; but the position can at least be clarified
by considering the peoples who went to make up the Middle
Bronze Age civilization of these islands in due relation to the

progenitors of the Celts on the Continent.   How, then, in the first place were the Continental Celts engendered?

The centre of gravity of the expanded Celtic world of the Iron Age comprised, broadly speaking, South-West Germany (with the Swiss plateau) and Eastern France, and it is here too that linguistic evidence, headed by that of Celtic river-names, points to the most ancient currency of Celtic speech, with the important modifications that the greater weight lies on the east rather than the west of the Rhine, and that as well as South-West also North-West Germany is to be included. Now, in the earlier prehistory of these lands of the Rhine basin we have above pointed out the importance of the great movement of 'Westernization' in later Neolithic times, which replaced their original Danubian culture by the Michelsberg representative of the Western Neolithic (p. 137).   Thus the substratum for the Bronze Age became predominatingly Western instead of Danubian as it was in the Aunjetitz province further east.   At the same time, we must not lose sight of the aboriginal element, descended, no doubt, from Mesolithic times, that seems recognizable in the long-lived tradition of finger-printed coarse pottery.   Before the Bronze Age opened, there had been two major additions to these basic constituents: the Bell-beaker folk from the South-West, and the Corded-ware warriors from Central Germany.   The former spread all down the Rhine and well away to the east of it, while the latter fused with them in the Rhine valley and as far as Holland and the north-west of Germany, and also spread west and south-west to form the Barrow cultures of the east of France, to enter into the formation of the Rhône culture, and to run out still further west, most notably to create the Early Bronze Age culture of Brittany (pp. 310-14).   Till towards the end of the second millennium, no further intrusions into any part of these territories are to be detected.   On their Alpine side, they marched with North Italy and the recruitment-areas of the immigrants responsible for the Indo-European essentials of Italic language: philological connexions between Italic and Celtic tongues are close, and as well as their Indo-European essentials, substratum contributions may also need allowing for from Western Neolithic and aboriginal sources common to both sides of the Alps. On the east, their frontier is clearly that dividing the Aunjetitz area from the Tumulus cultures that from Bavaria and Thuringia westwards grew up outside its immediate orbit. And it is, in fact, in those Tumulus cultures, formed on a Western and aboriginal Neolithic substratum by the mixed Corded-ware and Beaker peoples, that the prime element in the Celts is to be sought, running south-west to include the people of the Rhône culture, west to the outlying group in Brittany, and north to include the mixed Beaker and Barrow peoples of the Lower Rhine, Holland, and North-West Germany, where between the Weser and the Elbe ran their frontier with the Germanic population of the Northern lands.

Both these two wings, the Breton and the Northern, are of especial importance for Britain. When intrusion did come to disturb the West European Tumulus-culture area towards the end of the second millennium, it was that of the Urnfield peoples of the Late Bronze Age, with their main impulse in the forceful expansion of the Lausitz folk (p. 362). Indeed, it is often held that until this Urnfield contribution to the West had been made, it is improper to consider the Celts as a fully formed entity: the Tumulus peoples of earlier Bronze Age times can be called no more than proto-Celts. But, to take first the Northern or Lower Rhenish wing of their distribution, this was reached by the Urnfield movement late and in considerably modified form; and since it was from here that, in the Late Bronze Age and later, Britain received some of her most important drafts of Celtic immigrants, it is needful to realize that those immigrants seem to be drawn—to start with at any rate—rather from a Lower Rhenish population set in motion by the Urnfielders' approach, than from one already altered by their admixture. Further, the contemporary advance of the Germans from the Elbe towards the Weser and the Rhine should also have set the Tumulus population here in motion; and in the Late Bronze Age immigrations of Celts into North Britain, and above all Ireland, there is a good deal to suggest an origin in this quarter rather than anywhere further south or west, without anything specifically referable to a contribution from the Urnfielders. So it becomes highly relevant to recall that the composition of these Lower Rhenish and North-West German Tumulus folk, blended, as we have seen, of Beaker, Corded-ware, and Single-grave people on a substratum closely akin to the Bell-urn and Neolithic B elements in Britain (pp. 271-2), can hardly be taken as anything but virtually identical with that of the Beaker immigrants who passed over to Britain in the early second millennium from this very quarter. In other words, if the Rhenish Tumulus people were Celtic or proto-Celtic, the same should be said of the Rhenish Beaker immigrants into Britain—that is, in any case, the B2 and A Beaker peoples of our sixth chapter (pp. 268, 273). Similarly, if the Rhône culture and their neighbours are Celtic or proto-Celtic, the same should hold good for the Early Bronze Age invaders of Brittany, and if for them, then also for the dissident group of them who crossed over to make the Early Bronze Age culture of Wessex (p. 316). Bronze Age Britain, then, should be admitted Celtic to a like if not the same extent as the Continental West of the Tumulus cultures. For, as well as the Beaker immigrants, we have considerable affinities with the Continent in Neolithic substrata: on the one hand, in the Western people of our Neolithic A; on the other, in those of Neolithic B and their counterparts on the other side of the Narrow Seas, whose kinship may be supposed to go back to Mesolithic times. And if abroad the history of the spread of Celtic civilization westward is mainly that of the 'Celticization' of the Western and aboriginal peoples who had clung so long to Chalcolithic culture and the megalithic religion, the analogous process in the British Isles did not wait for the Celtic immigrations of the Late Bronze and Iron Ages: it was an affair in the first instance of the Bronze Age—begun by the northward and westward roving of groups of the Beaker folk, and maintained by the people we know from the food-vessel and its derivative classes of pottery, into and through the Middle Bronze Age. This will become clearer if we consider briefly the formation of the Middle Bronze Age in the British Isles and the cultural balance which it so distinctively represents.

The Age has long been regarded as one of fusion between the descendants of Beaker immigrants and Neolithic natives, and though both have turned out to consist of more complex population-groups than was formerly suspected, the period was certainly one in which these groups settled down in unity together. The commonly accepted symbol of this is the cinerary urn wherein the cremated remains of the dead came to be deposited, for the most part under barrows in the Early Bronze Age tradition introduced by the immigrants. But whereas the rite of cremation in the south of Britain is apparently the contribution of the Breton invaders of Wessex, responsible also for the practice of placing a pygmy offering-cup in the grave, yet the urn itself is simply the adaptation for cinerary use of a type of domestic vessel, the South British equivalent of the Northern food-vessel, of quite independent origin. That origin was doubtless mixed, and it is not yet possible to give an account of it in detail, but it seems clear that the old decorated bowls of Neolithic B, with their cord-impressed and other ornament, had most to do with it, as is suggested not only by the modified survival of that ornament on their upper portions, but by their distinctive overhanging rims. Intermediate forms certainly exist—a good example comes from Icklingham in Suffolk—and these are probably of Early Bronze Age date, contemporary with beakers, so that we must picture their makers existing side by side with the Beaker folk and only gradually drawing together with them in Middle Bronze Age cultural unity. Grooved ware (p. 272) probably also played a part: one sort of urn has an upright instead of a slanting form of overhanging rim which seems foreshadowed at Woodhenge, and it is possible that even Neolithic A traditions of form and fabric have also to be reckoned with. Beaker conventions themselves exerted influence, seen both in fabric, ornament, and the form most obviously of the lower body and flat base, as in the parallel case of the Northern food-vessels, but the over-hanging-rim urn perhaps displays rather more than they do of the reaction of native or earlier-arrived elements to the Bronze Age civilization created by the Beaker and Wessex immigrants. Overhanging-rim pots actually appear in at least two cases with inhumation-burials of the Wessex culture, but the balance which soon supervened is well witnessed by the regular use of this mainly native-bred type for the immigrant rite of cremation, often with its accompanying pygmy vessel, under the immigrant round barrow, far and wide over Britain. Indeed, for some elements in this balanced culture we have to go back to the Mesolithic. The Neolithic B culture whose heritage comes out so strongly in the cinerary urn always carried a very Mesolithic character (p. 140), and its derivatives of the old transverse arrowhead, and the other Mesolithic traits that run through the Early Bronze Age on its native side—perforated stone or antler hammer-heads, the bone-worker's technique of edge-grinding applied to knives or scrapers of flint, even a lingering attachment to microliths, as in the Early Bronze Age of the Mendip Hills—all these suggest that in the Middle Bronze Age a really Mesolithic substratum was still fairly close to the surface. Again, late in the Early Bronze Age a tanged bronze blade derived from the grooved dagger was mounted in Britain as a spearhead, secured by a collar-ring in which we have suspected a debt to the socket-ring of early Mycenean spearheads (p. 352) but which was adapted in a quite original fashion, and soon, as is shown by the celebrated hoard from Arreton Down in the Isle of Wight, was itself transformed into a hollow-cast socket. In Middle Bronze Age metal equipment the spear so perfected was dominant from the first, and this, coupled with the now apparent rarity of settlement among the old pastures and small-scale tillage of the chalk Downs, has suggested a return to hunting as one of the main supports of life, with 'fishing and hunting grounds by the rivers and amid the scrub' which, though actual settlements of this period are yet hard to find among them, would certainly support a Mesolithic habit in the cultural pattern of the Age, enhanced to some not yet closely gauged extent by climatic factors (cf. p. 289).

And there is another, and a more obvious, aspect of the period's harmony of old and new, its compromise with the megalithic religion, arrived at already in its essentials in the beginnings of the Bronze Age, as we have seen above (p. 276), but maintained not only where Middle Bronze Age barrows continue the great concentration round the unique cult-centre of Stonehenge, but far and wide where the circle-monuments discussed with Stonehenge above (pp. 274, 316-17) stand, broadly speaking, throughout the Bronze Age for the potency of a religion in which the skyward and sunward worship that seems everywhere to accompany Indo-European language was closely blended with the earthward veneration enshrined in megalithic observance. The stone circles of Highland Britain and Scotland, and pre-eminently those of Ireland, must be reckoned essentially a Bronze Age phenomenon, and with them we must not forget the cup and ring-marked stones and rocks (pp. 321-2) in which there survived so long the ancient rock-carving tradition of the West.

But to all this Highland Zone the usage of the cinerary urn spread only by degrees. Whereas in the south segmented faience beads are found with urn-burials exactly as in the earlier urnless graves of the Wessex culture, and the dividing-line between Early and Middle Bronze Age may be put at about our limiting date of 1400 B.C., in the north we have to allow for food-vessels, which, though originating, as we have seen, during the Beaker period, yet in East Yorkshire only come in with the beaker's sepulchral disuse, and last for some considerable time before the dominance of cremation was finally sealed by the adoption of the urn—which often in the north is simply a food-vessel enlarged to the size necessary for cinerary use. We have already said what is feasible of the origin of food-vessels (p. 319), and it now appears that the vase type native to the north of Britain is in a sense an analogous development to the overhanging-rim vessel which in the south became the cinerary urn. It emerges earlier as a distant sepulchral form owing to the Highland Zone's greater rapidity of fusion between natives and Beaker folk, as against the Lowland south where the imposed dominance of the latter gave the beaker a more absolute supremacy, and it survives longer owing to the Highland slowness in adopting the urn habit which the south created. Thus the northern food-vessel cannot be kept out of a Middle Bronze Age starting at 1400 B.C. But from its Early Bronze Age start, and throughout, the food-vessel, like the beaker, was essentially an attribute of the immigrant or round-barrow rite of 'Single-grave' burial as opposed to the old collective sepulture of the megalith and long-barrow people. And thus, no less than a British beaker, a British food-vessel in a megalithic context attests the intrusion of the 'single-grave' idea, the contribution of what we have called the warrior cultures of the Continent, into the domain of megalithic cult and civilization, just as when Continental single-grave pottery is found, for instance (p. 218), in a passage-grave of the megalithic cult in Jutland. In other words, like the beaker in the main before it and the cinerary urn in the main after it, the food-vessel in the Highland Zone and the megalithic west represents the coming of Bronze Age people bearing the British equivalent of the Tumulus cultures which the Single-grave or Corded-ware people gave to the Bronze Age of the Continent. And now emerges the importance of the idea put forward above (p. 322), that the Irish bowl type of food-vessel represents the rendering in Irish ceramic tradition of the vase type first engendered in Great Britain.

For it will mean that the spread of this food-vessel in Ireland, with its main strength in the north-east of the island over against the north of Great Britain, implies an immigration from thence of Bronze Age people taking over to Ireland their share in the great European entity of the Tumulus cultures—the entity that we have seen was the real making of the original Celts. If Ireland's Late Bronze Age or even later invaders played the most powerful part in making her an abode of Celtic language and culture, they surely arrived to find the ground already well prepared. It is the food-vessels of the Middle Bronze Age that really mark Ireland's first admission of a breach in the pure dominance of the megalithic religion: thereafter her culture became a balance between old and new, as in one form or another it ever afterwards remained. While in a continued multitude of secondary burials with food-vessels in megalithic tombs, in a continued memory of megalithic structural forms in the round cairns or barrows made for themselves by the Food-vessel people, and in a continued devotion to the cult of stone circles, the megalithic past of Ireland remained still essentially alive, yet the change had come; and in the imports of Baltic amber exchanged for Irish gold, the incoming of the cast-flanged axe-type across England from the Continent and of the socketed spearhead that England created in emulation of the Continental pattern, the introduction of the stone axe-hammer from Britain and its specialization in the region of the Bann—all these show in one aspect or another Ireland's participation in the main stream of European Bronze Age culture. And the active vitality of Irish civilization appears oversea in the strong reflex influence exerted by the Irish bowl food-vessel on the British vase type, manifest most notably in the spread of its favourite 'false-relief' ornament (p. 319), and still further afield in the fidelity to the same bowl model of the gold vessels of the later Bronze Age in the Germanic North. Without immigration Celtic or proto-Celtic—derived from the main ethnic continuum of the European peoples, this participation is, if not quite incredible, at least in strange contrast to the case of Spain, where this period shows no such immigration, and accordingly an isolated Bronze Age culture participating scarcely at all in the general march of Europe.

And we have not exhausted Ireland's share of the part played in Bronze Age Europe by the British Isles. While the Irish halberd, like the flat axe, goes back to an earlier stage of our story, its Continental derivatives lasted to the Middle Bronze Age, and we have seen it appearing at Mycenae itself; and the gold lunula was only one of the beginnings of the Irish goldsmith's contributions to prehistoric magnificence. The 'sheet' gold-work it represents was equally that employed for the gold ornaments that we have seen make the principal glory of Early Bronze Age Wessex, and before the supervening of the heavier 'bar' work, exported already to Central Europe in late Aunjetitz times but most typical of the Middle Bronze Age, it had made its mark as far away as the Aegean also. For the gold-mounted amber disc of the Wessex graves[1] reappears, with much other amber, in the Late Minoan Tomb of the Double-axes at Knossos; the gold pointillé technique of the Breton-Wessex dagger-haft is not unknown in Mycenean Greece; and that the influence was mutual is shown by the Mycenean reminiscences in much of the other finery of the

---

[1] Fig. 26, 18 ; Pl. XI, 1.

Wessex graves, in the similarity of the corrugated gold cup from Rillaton in Cornwall (Pl. XI, 7) to two from the Fourth Shaft-grave at Mycenae, and in the copying of segmented faience beads in Irish gold—these last appearing as far along the connecting trade-route as the Middle Rhineland. And the maintenance of these connexions in the Late Mycenean period, the Irish and European Middle Bronze Age, when the faience bead-trade still flourished, as we have seen, is further shown by the chiselled rendering of that period's soldered technique of multiple-ribbon gold-work, as seen on the ear-rings from Enkomi in Cyprus and Tell el-Ajjul in Palestine, by which the Irish smiths created not only ear-rings but the great four-leaved gold torcs which are among the acknowledged masterpieces of their craft. This is the witness of material archaeology, but it is the spirit that quickeneth, and if the boat-coffin burials on both sides of the North Sea were inspired from the Orient, the Minoan-Mycenean motives in the magical carvings on the famous chalk drums from the Early Bronze Age barrow at Folkton in East Yorkshire[1] show likewise that the spiritual potency of the Mediterranean in the far North-West was not exhausted with the inspiration of the old megalithic religion.

The North-West thus reached in the Middle Bronze Age a cultural balance consequent upon the immigrations in which we believe should be recognized the first forerunners of the Celts: we can call them proto-Celts if we will, but at least the Eastern groups of Beaker folk and the Wessex invaders from Brittany between them connected Britain indisputably with the peoples who in the Adlerberg, Rhône, and Breton cultures, and the whole nexus of Tumulus cultures from Bavaria and Switzerland to the Rhine mouth and the North Sea and westward over France, made the main Bronze Age foundation of the later Celtic world. And in the Food-vessel cultures that were thereupon set up in the north of Great Britain and, we believe after and in consequence of that, in Ireland, we have recognized an essential kinship, which in the Middle Bronze Age will thus cover nearly the whole of the British Isles, with the same complex of Celtic origins.

[1] Pl. X, 1.

Meanwhile, to the south-west, Spain remains comparatively aloof, and only not discordant, from the rest of Europe; and while in her Apennine and Terramara cultures Italy blends the Mediterranean with the trans-Alpine, the complicated range of cultures in Central Europe becomes poised in a Middle Bronze Age civilization with a unity of its own in the Hungarian Urnfield territories, and another in the great province of which Aunjetitz Bohemia had been the first progressive centre. Out of these, if we allow also for the obscurer contributions from beyond their southern and south-eastern borders, will emerge the Thracian and Illyrian groups of peoples, through a later age of movement radiating from the more north-easterly focus of the vigorous Lausitz culture. In the North, the most compact of all the European culture-groups proclaims the now full achievement of Germanic solidarity. And while the East of Europe is still in comparative twilight, and the genesis of the Slavs has yet to be defined, the primacy of all European civilization is brilliantly held by the Mycenean culture of the Greeks— a primacy built up in the orbit of Minoan Crete, with the Orient behind it, but consummated with the downfall of a Cretan power turned Oriental despotism. So our survey of the Europe of 1400 B.C., the turning-point of the Fall of Knossos, brings us back whence we started.

The conception of the Mycenean achievement as a European primacy is no mere fancy. Right across Europe in the middle of this millennium run the signs of the same pattern of society, impoverished though it may most often seem by comparison with Mycenean splendour. Power is in the hands of a chieftain class who have inherited the tradition of fighting strength and personal prowess built up by the hunters and pastoralists of their Stone Age ancestry, through Eastern contacts on the steppe-lands, in the warrior cultures we know from the kurgan, the barrow, the single-grave and the equipment typified by the battle-axe, and clothed it with the material wealth of the Bronze Age which by its economic, industrial, commercial connexions with the Orient the central core of Europe had created for itself. The artisans and craftsmen on whose work that material wealth was based are the indispensable technicians of the society, interconnected by a long-distance trade in both raw materials and finished goods, which is true commerce indeed, but is yet bound up with values not strictly economic only, but also social and religious. The pride of the chieftain demands costly finery and weapons of war and ceremonial, which will be interchanged as 'presents' even over great distances: this feature of Mycenean culture is constantly portrayed in the Homeric poems, and when the archaeologist speaks of such interchange as 'trade', he does well to remember it as a social as much as an economic phenomenon. Equally, he can recall that the long-distance dissemination of objects of all kinds seems (p. 85) to have started with the seeking out of things thought to be precious for some magic value, and this thought reveals the naïve superstition that we saw behind the early traffic in shells and bright stones as the true begetter of the most imposing trades of the Bronze Age—in the amber that explains Herodotus' tale of the straw-packed offerings of the Hyperboreans to the Delian shrine of Apollo, and the gold for which our culture still claims the worship of a 'standard'. And in religion itself, the Greek adjustment of Olympian deities, headed by the sky-god Zeus, over the earth-powers of older chthonic worship, seems typical of most of Europe, whether in the West and North, with their supernal divinities—the sun, the Hyperboreans' Apollo, in especial prominence—accommodated to a background of megalithic fertility-cult, or in Central Europe where the background was the same earth-religion, as shared with the early Aegean and the Orient by the basic element in the population, the Danubian peasant. With him we come back to the patient primary production at the root of all this growth, the tillage and stock of the Neolithic farmer, through whose labours Europe had followed the Ancient East in the revolution to food-producing economy from the food-gathering of the older Stone Age. The cultivator and the herdsman between them, for all the vitality of the hunter's far older skill, stand at the base of Europe's economic development and social structure, whether in Greek lands, the Danubian centre or Italy, the West or the North. As socially and economically, so also in language, this element, in all its diversity, is everywhere the substratum. From Greece to the British Isles, and from Italy to the Baltic, the tongues that dominated Bronze Age Europe were the languages of the Indo-European or Aryan family, the diffusion of which has on every count to be equated with the spread of our warrior-culture peoples. That spread was largely accomplished before and in the beginning of the Bronze Age; but the ethnic and cultural disharmony created by those centuries of migration, conflict, and change was not resolved until the Middle Bronze Age, and the even balance of cultures that it brought, whether Germanic or Illyrian, Celtic, Italic, or Mycenean Greek, into a coherent unity of European civilization. Thus the formation of European language, as of European religion, accompanied the moulding of European society and its material culture. In that process the great race-approximations of Mediterranean, Alpine, and Nordic stand indeed ever in the background; but already by the Middle Bronze Age, and indeed well before it, to say nothing of what followed in the next two thousand years, the diversities of human movement and mingling complicated the ethnic realities in every culture in some degree, though within the Nordic sphere the cultural compactness of the Germanic grouping answered to a greater degree of ethnic solidarity than is to be expected over the Alpine or Mediterranean substratum-elements encountered in so much of the rest of Europe. What is characteristic of Europe is not its internal complexities of race so much as its attainment already by the Middle Bronze Age of so large a measure of a cultural unity and coherence absolutely distinctive of itself. Therein lie the prehistoric foundations of European history.

We have repeatedly spoken of this as a cultural balance, and the metaphor applied to our foundations is just, for equilibrium is never far from instability, and instability and movement, elasticity and change, have been of the essence of the European endeavour to 'live well'. We have long ago seen that the dawn of civilization broke in the East, and that from the earliest Neolithic onwards its spread westward over Europe was an affair of Oriental influence, the West receiving, tardily and in comparative poverty, what the East was only giving after long familiarity within its own borders. But we have never found it possible to call this reception merely passive. The peoples of Europe already had developed cultural traditions within the limits imposed by their Mesolithic economy, and the spontaneity and adaptive vigour with which they took to themselves the elements of Oriental culture that reached them typify not passive reception but positive reaction. From the Danubian Neolithic to the Mycenean Bronze Age, the result was characteristically not second-hand reflexion of Eastern achievement, but integration of Eastern with native elements in something essentially new. And the very remoteness and poverty that divided Europe from Mesopotamia or Egypt was a naturally imposed safeguard against Orientalization. For, above all, it kept most of Europe for thousands of years free of the 'urban revolution' which set in so early in the history of the Near East and set its magnificent achievement of initial civilization in a rigid framework of conservatism under the absolute rule of priest and king. Writing and numeration, astronomy and mathematics, were all invented in the East to be pinned to the service of a static civilization dominated by the temple and the court, and it was the hard mould of urban culture that kept that civilization static. When the culture of cities came to Europe, it was taken into a social tradition already matured on other lines, and the ancient inventions and discoveries of Sumer, Babylon, and Egypt were vitalized by the Greeks, in whom the European dawn of civilization passed into bright morning. The culture of the Greek city-states absorbed what it drew from the Orient only to withstand and finally to transform the mass of what the Orient retained, and the tradition of the Greek people went back far beyond their Orientalizing period to the Mycenean Bronze Age of which we have here written, in the literature of their mythology and above all in the unique possession of the Homeric poems. It is in Homer that the citizens of ancient and modern Europe alike come closest to their culture's prehistoric foundations, and the moderns have what the ancients had not, the clue of archaeology not only to the Cretan labyrinth of the Aegean world of which Homer kept the memory, but to the whole maze of prehistoric civilization in Europe. In this book we have tried to follow that clue through the many meanderings that have led to the point at which the Minotaur was slain, and with the Fall of Knossos the culture of the European Bronze Age stands free of the Oriental debt whence for two thousand years its independence had been slowly matured.

Its foundations were formed of a balance of cultures, in which Mediterranean and Western, Alpine and Danubian, Nordic and East European elements of Stone Age inheritance were poised against the civilizing influence of the Orient, in an equilibrium dominated by the peoples of Aryan speech and warrior tradition, who from the years before and after 2000 B.C. onwards have given so much to the moving pattern of European achievement. The movement of the pattern, the instability of the balance, seem throughout characteristic of historic process in Europe, as against the 'changeless East', which invented civilization only to stagnate in it. In particular, our balance of 1400 B.C. proved as unstable as the balance of the Antonine Age from which Gibbon traced the Decline and Fall that was the counterpart of the rise of mediaeval and modern Europe. For the Mycenean supremacy, spreading out to its share in the great age of land-raids and sea-raids, the Trojan War, and the whole turmoil in which the Bronze Age of the Near East during the next three centuries or so sank to its end, collapsed in exhaustion, and its seats of power in the Peloponnese fell before the Dorian invasion from the hinterland of North Greece where Mycenean culture had stopped short, leaving the fatal blank we marked at the beginning of this chapter. And the Oriental reaction to its downfall brought the Phoenicians on to the seas, to reach as far west as Carthage and Spain, and in due course the Etruscans from Asia Minor to Italy, while the Greek world emerged from this Dark Age with the walled cities and the alphabetic writing of the Near East, painfully rebuilding a new cultural poise of its own, in which Hellenism set its citizens in antithesis to the 'barbarians' of Europe, even while colonizing their shores. And from that antithesis sprang the division of Europe between the Graeco-Roman world and the peoples beyond, whom it could never conquer, so that it was not till the centuries of its Decline and Fall, of the Germanic migrations, and of the rise of Christendom, that a balance of cultures could again be struck, in which European civilization could again be at one. And thereafter the balance has changed into a Balance of Power. Yet the instability of Europe's equilibrium has been not its weakness but its strength: its safeguard against Oriental stagnation, and perhaps of an inner virtue of its own which possesses absolute value for human progress. For we saw in our prologue that change and adaptiveness seemed the grand biological condition of survival in evolution, and suspected that of human progress the same was true. And the Europeans, who from their Palaeolithic past made a Mesolithic background ready for civilization, and thereon fashioned civilization into a thing of their own, have throughout our story kept that adaptiveness alive, and so have built on foundations whose instability of balance has been the measure of their success under the law of all life.

BIBLIOGRAPHICAL NOTES

In the space available these notes cannot be exhaustive. They aim only at giving a selection of (normally) the most recent literature suitable for further reading. The citation of any work does not imply that its author's views are those adopted in the text : though this may often be the case, the selection has been made rather on the strength of material evidence presented than of interpretation offered. Works useful for their own bibliographies or citations of earlier literature are marked with an asterisk.*

A. NOTE ON BOOKS OF GENERAL REFERENCE

The most ambitious essay in the documentation of European Prehistory is the *Reallexikon der Vorgeschichte** edited by Max Ebert (Berlin, 1924-32 ; 15 vols.). This is only cited below where more recent accessible works do not cover some particular ground, but it remains generally indispensable, though of course not of uniformly equal value throughout. N. Åberg's *Bronzezeitliche und Früheisenzeitliche Chronologie* (Stockholm, 1930-35 ; 5 vols.), being bound up with the advocacy of a chronological system which has not found very wide acceptance, is only cited in certain special places, but as a descriptive survey it may often be found of use. The *Manuel d'Archéologie (Préhistorique, Protohistorique)** of Joseph Déchelette (Paris, 1908-14 ; 2nd ed., 1924-27 ; 4 vols.) aimed at presenting the prehistory of France in its general European setting, and need by no means be considered superseded. Professor V. Gordon Childe's *Dawn of European Civilization** (London, 1925) proceeds from Mesolithic to Bronze Age cultures in each of the main European regions successively, and was the first work of its kind to be written ; while this book was in proof (1939), the author published a new edition, enlarged and re-written, here referred to below as *Dawn²*.

It remains to notice certain works of importance dealing with particular regions or periods, with the abbreviations for them used below.

Palaeolithic. See below under Chs. I and II.

Northern Europe, Mesolithic. Clark, *Meso. Settlement*. J. G. D. Clark, *The Mesolithic Settlement of Northern Europe** (1936).

Northern Europe, general. Shetelig, Falk, and Gordon, *Scand. Arch.* H. Shetelig and Hj. Falk (translated by E. V. Gordon), *Scandinavian Archaeology** (1937).

Northern and Central Europe. Forssander, *Ostskand. Norden*. J. E. Forssander, *Der Ostskandinavische Norden während der ältesten Metallzeit Europas** (K.H.V.Lund, Skrifter XXII, 1936).

Central Europe. Childe, *Danube*. V. Gordon Childe, *The Danube in Prehistory** (1929).

Italy, Sicily. Peet, *Italy*. T. E. Peet, *The Stone and Bronze Ages in Italy and Sicily* (1909)*.

Spain, Portugal. Åberg, *Civ. Pén. Ib.* N. Åberg, *La Civilisation Énéolithique dans la Péninsule Ibérique* (Uppsala, 1921). Bosch Gimpera, *Etnologia*. P. Bosch Gimpera, *Etnologia de la Península Ibérica** (Barcelona, 1932).

British Isles. K. & H., *Arch. E.W.* T. D. Kendrick and C. F. C. Hawkes,

2 B

386   *The Prehistoric Foundations of Europe*

*Archaeology in England and Wales 1914-1931** (1932). Hawkes, Pr. Br.
C. F. C. and J. Hawkes, *Prehistoric Britain in 1931-32*, ... *1933*, ... *1934*,
... *1935*: a Review of Periodical Publications, in *Archaeological Journal* 89-92
(1933-36). Since 1935 a full annual survey of excavation-results for the
British Isles and bibliography appears in the *Proceedings of the Prehistoric
Society*.
British Isles, Wales. Grimes, *Pr. Wales*. W. F. Grimes, *Guide to the
collections illustrating the Prehistory of Wales*, National Museum of Wales
(Cardiff, 1939).
British Isles, Scotland. Childe, *Scotland*. V. Gordon Childe, *The Pre-
history of Scotland** (1935).
British Isles, Ireland. Mahr, *P.P.S. III*. A. Mahr, 'New Aspects and
Problems in Irish Prehistory,' in *Proceedings of the Prehistoric Society* III
(1937), 262-436*.
British Isles, prehistory as geography. Fox, *Personality*³. Cyril Fox,
The Personality of Britain, 3rd ed., National Museum of Wales (Cardiff,
1938).

B. KEY TO ABBREVIATIONS USED BELOW IN CITING PERIODICALS

Aarbøger	.	Aarbøger for nordisk Oldkyndighed og Historie (Copenhagen).
Acta Arch.	.	Acta Archaeologica (Copenhagen).
L'Anthr.	.	L'Anthropologie (Paris).
Antiq. Journ.		Antiquaries Journal (Society of Antiquaries of London).
A.S.A.	.	Anzeiger für schweizerische Altertumskunde (Zürich).
Arch. Journ.	.	Archaeological Journal (R. Arch. Institute, London).
Arch. I.P.H.	.	Archives de l'Institut de Paléontologie Humaine (Paris).
A.F.A.S.	.	Association française pour l'avancement des Sciences (Paris).
B.R.G.K.	.	Berichte der Römisch-Germanischen Kommission (Frankfurt a. M.).
B.S.A.	.	Annual of the British School at Athens (London).
B.A.S.P.R.	.	Bulletin of the American School of Prehistoric Research (New Haven).
B.S.P.F.	.	Bulletin de la Société Préhistorique Française (Paris).
B.P.I.	.	Bulletino di Paletnologia Italiana (Rome).
C.I.A.A.P.	.	Congrès International d'Anthropologie et d'Archéologie Préhistorique.
C.I.S.P.P.	.	Congrès International des Sciences Préhistoriques et Protohistoriques.
E.S.A.	.	Eurasia Septentrionalis Antiqua (Helsinki).
Geol. Mag.	.	Geological Magazine (London).
INQUA	.	International Congress for the Study of the Quaternary Period.
I.P.E.K.	.	Jahrbuch für Prähistorische und Ethnographische Kunst (Köln).
J.R.A.I.	.	Journal of the Royal Anthropological Institute (London).
J.R.S.A.I.	.	Journal of the Royal Society of Antiquaries of Ireland (Dublin).
J.H.S.	.	Journal of Hellenic Studies (London).
K.H.V.Lund.		K. Humanistiska Vetenskapssamfundets i Lund (*Årsberattelse*).
M.A.G.W.	.	Mitteilungen der anthropologischen Gesellschaft in Wien (Vienna).
P.P.S.	.	Proceedings of the Prehistoric Society (London).
P.R.I.A.	.	Proceedings of the Royal Irish Academy (Dublin).
P.S.A.Scot.	.	Proceedings of the Society of Antiquaries of Scotland (Edinburgh).

P.S.E.A. . Proceedings of the Prehistoric Society of East Anglia (London).
P.Z. . . Prähistorische Zeitschrift (Berlin).
R.G.Ph.G.D. Revue de géographie physique et de géologie dynamique (Paris).
S.M.Y.A. . Suomen Muinaismuistoyhdistyksen Aikakauskirja (Helsinki).

C. BIBLIOGRAPHY BY CHAPTERS

Chapter I

Methods and aims of Prehistory : Clark, *Archaeology and Society* (1939) ; Childe, *P.P.S.* I (1935), 1 ; Crawford, *Man and his Past* (1921).

Early Man and Evolution, recent surveys : von Eickstedt, *Rassenkunde und Rassengeschichte der Menschheit** (1933–4) ; Weinert, *Enstehung der Menschenrassen** (1937) ; various authors, *Early Man* (Symposium held by Philadelphia Academy of Natural Sciences, ed. MacCurdy, 1937) ; Moir, *The Earliest Men* (Imperial College of Science Huxley Memorial Lecture, 1939) ; and see under Ch. II.

Evolution and Progress : Childe, *Man Makes Himself* (1936) ; cf. Toynbee, *A Study of History* I (1934).

Physical and Human Geography : Myres, *The Dawn of History* (Home University Library, no. 29).

Chapter II

1. Ice Age Geology : *INQUA Reports* I–III ; Wright, *The Quaternary Ice Age** (2nd ed., 1937), and *Tools and the Man** (1939) ; Soergel, *Das Eiszeitalter** (1937) ; chapters in Burkitt, *The Old Stone Age** (1933), and Leakey, *Adam's Ancestors* (1933) ; Blanc, *L'Anthr.* 48, 261 ; (solifluxion) Breuil, *R.G.Ph.G.D.* VII, 4, 269.

Astronomical Chronology : Zeuner, *Geol. Mag.* lxxii, 350*.

Early Man : see under Ch. I and below ; Swanscombe skull, *J.R.A.I.* LXVIII, 17 (with LXVII, 339).

2. Palaeolithic, general : see Wright, Soergel, Burkitt, Leakey under 1 above ; lists of sites : MacCurdy, *Human Origins** (1924).

Technology : the same ; Pei, *R.G.Ph.G.D.* IX, 4 ; (bone, early) Breuil, *Antiquity* XII, 56 ; (flake-tools in Acheulian) Kelley, *P.P.S.* III, 13 ; (Mousterian gravers) Peyrony and others, *C.I.A.A.P.*, Portugal 1930, 310.

Africa : Leakey, *Stone Age Africa** (1937).

Palestine : Garrod and Bate, *The Stone Age of Mount Carmel* (1937).

Eoliths and Pre-Crag Industries : to 1931, summarized by Kendrick, *Arch. E.W.*, ch. I* ; Moir, *J.R.A.I.* LXV, 343 ; (Darmsden) *P.P.S.* I, 93 ; (attack on Moir's position) Barnes, *L'Anthr.* 48, 217.

Western Europe, Abbevillian, Acheulian, Clactonian, Levallois, Mousterian : Breuil, *B.S.P.F.* XXIX, 570 ; and on Abbevillian, *L'Anthr.* 49, 13 (cf. on Chelles, *Quartär* 2, 1) ; on Clactonian and Tayacian, *Préhistoire* I, 125.

Somme : Breuil and Koslowski, *L'Anthr.* 41, 449 ; 42, 27 ; 42, 291 ; Bowler Kelley, *Lower and Middle Palaeolithic Facies in Europe and Africa** (1937) ; Breuil (latest), *P.P.S.* V, 33.

Thames : King and Oakley, *P.P.S.* II, 51* ; Bowler Kelley, *op. cit.** ; (Clacton) Oakley and M. Leakey, *P.P.S.* III, 217 ; (Swanscombe) *J.R.A.I.* LXVIII, 17 ; (Ponder's End) *P.P.S.* IV, 328.

East Anglia : to 1931, summarized by Kendrick, *Arch. E.W.*, chs. II–III* ; 1931-35, by Hawkes, *Pr. Br.** ; Boswell, *P.P.S.* II, 149 ; Zeuner, *P.P.S.* III, 136 ; Paterson, *Nature* 143, 822, with fuller publications* forthcoming ; (Cromer) Moir, *B.A.S.P.R.* 1936, 141 ; (Barnham) Paterson, *P.P.S.* III, 87 ; (Brundon) Moir and Hopwood, *P.P.S.* V, 1.

Belgium : Breuil and Koslowski, *L'Anthr.* 44, 249*.

388   *The Prehistoric Foundations of Europe*

Germany and Central Europe : Andree, *Der eiszeitliche Mensch in Deutschland und seine Kulturen* (1939)* ; Woldstedt, *Mannus* 27, 275 ; Zeuner, *Geol. Mag.* lxxii, 350*, and *P.P.S.* III, 136* ; (Markkleeberg) Grahmann, *L'Anthr.* 45, 257 ; and E. Europe : Woldstedt, *Jahrbuch der preussischen geologischen Landesanstalt* 54, 371. Austria : Pittioni, *Urgeschichte Österreichs*, 127, 132 (in *Allgemeine Urgeschichte*, Vienna, 1937).
Alpine Caves : Kyrle, *Quartär* 2, 22.
South French Caves : older documentation in MacCurdy, *Human Origins* (1924)* ; Burkitt, *Prehistory* (2nd ed., 1925)*, and *The Old Stone Age* (1933) ; survey of excavation 1914-30 : Lantier, *B.R.G.K.* XX, 78* ; (La Micoque) Peyrony, *C.I.A.A.P.*, Paris 1931, 435 ; (Le Moustier) Peyrony, *Revue anthropologique* 1930, 48 ; (La Quina, latest summary) Martin, *Préhistoire* V, 7 ; (Périgord Aurignacian question) Peyrony, *B.S.P.F* XXX, 543, with Breuil, *L'Anthr.* 45, 114 ; (Laugerie Haute, for Solutrian) Peyrony, *Arch. I.P.H.*, Mémoire 19 (1938) ; (Solutrian sculptures of Le Roc) Martin, *Antiquity* III, 45 ; (La Madeleine) Capitan and Peyrony, *Publ. de l'Institut International d'Anthropologie*, no. 2 (1928) ; and see 'Art ' under 3 below.
Spain : Obermaier, *Fossil Man in Spain*, and art. in *Reallexikon* X ('Pyrenäenhalbinsel : A'*, esp. 340-2) ; (Gibraltar) Garrod, *J.R.A.I.* LVIII, 33 ; (Parpalló) Pericot in *Investigación y Progreso* VII (1933).
Italy : Vaufrey, *Arch. I.P.H.*, Mémoire 3 (1928)* ; Blanc, works reviewed in *L'Anthr.* 48, 94 ; 49, 376 ; *Quartär* 1, 1 ; Rellini, *B.P.I.* n.s. I, 5.
Moravia : Breuil, *L'Anthr.* 34, 515 ; 35, 131 (caves, and on Pekárna cave Absolon and Czižek, *Acta Musei Moraviensis* (Brno), 1926, 1927, 1932) ; (Vistonice) Absolon, *Die Erforschung der Mammutjäger-Station von Unter-Wisternitz* (1937), and in *Revue anthropologique* 1927.
Hungary : Breuil, *L'Anthr.* 33, 323 ; Hillebrand, *B.R.G.K.* XXIV-V, 16* (esp. for Solutrian : for S. German Solutrian cf. *Germania* 22, 147).
S.E. Europe : Breuil, *L'Anthr.* 35, 131 ; Moroşan in *XVIth International Geological Congress*, Washington 1933 ; Nestor, *B.R.G.K.* XXII, 13* ; Jaranoff, *Quartär* 1, 103 ; Brodar, *ibid.* 140 ; Plopsor, *Dacia* V-VI, 41 (cf. I, 23) ; Garrod, *B.Á.S.P.R.* 1939, 46.
Poland (Upper Palaeolithic, latest article) : Jura, *Quartär* 1, 54.
Russia (Middle and Upper Palaeolithic) : U.S.S.R. contributions to *INQUA Reports* II and III ; Childe, *P.P.S.* I, 151* ; Hančar, *Urgeschichte Kaukasiens* (1937)* ; Golomshtok, *The Old Stone Age in European Russia* (Transactions American Philosophical Society, new ser., 39, II, 1938)*.
Hamburg culture : Rust, *Das altsteinzeitliche Renntierjägerlager Meiendorf* (1937) ; Clark, *Antiquity* 1938, 154 ; cf. *Offa* 2, 1 ; *Quartär* 1, 75.
Creswellian : Armstrong, *J.R.A.I.* LV, 146 ; *P.S.E.A.* VI, 4, 330.
Upper Palaeolithic, general : Breuil, *Les Subdivisions du Paléolithique Supérieur et leur Signification* (1937) ; Garrod, *P.P.S.* IV, 1 *(Presidential Address, British Association, section H, 1936).
3. Palaeolithic Life and Art : many general works, *e.g.* Kühn, *Kunst und Kultur der Vorzeit Europas: das Paläolithikum* (1929) ; Burkitt, *The Old Stone Age* (1933)*. Length of Life : Vallois, *L'Anthr.* 47, 499.
Hunting : Sollas, *Ancient Hunters* (3rd ed., 1924*) ; Lindner, *Die Jagd der Vorzeit* (1937). Dwellings : Clark, *P.P.S.* V, 98*. Psychology, Magic : Schmidt, *The Dawn of the Human Mind* (1936)*. ' Venuses ' : Burkitt, *E.S.A.* IX, 113 ; Passemard, *Les Statuettes féminines dites Vénus Stéatopyges* (1938). West European Cave Art : main publications in *Arch. I.P.H.* ; also Bégouen, *Les Grottes de Montesquieu-Avantès* (1936) ; many papers in *L'Anthr.* and *I.P.E.K.* (*e.g.* Breuil on Magdalenian art, *I.P.E.K.* 1936-37, I) ; Baldwin Brown, *The Art of the Cave-Dweller* (1928)* ; more recently, Leason, *P.P.S.* V, 51 (an important original study by a professional artist, showing the models used were dead animals). East Spanish Art, latest studies : Obermaier, *L'Anthr.* 47, 477, and *Quartär* 1, 111.

Chapter III

1 and 2. Mesolithic: summary, Childe, *Dawn*[2], ch. I (previously: Menghin, *B.R.G.K.* XVII, 154). Technology (microliths, microburins): Clark, *Mesolithic Age in Britain*, xix, 97* ; Vaufrey, *L'Anthr.* 41, 432. N. Africa, Capsian: Vaufrey, *Swiatowit* xvi, 15 ; *L'Anthr.* 43, 457 ; Oranian: Vaufrey, *L'Anthr.* 42, 449 ; and Spain: the same ; Obermaier, *Germania* 18, 165.

Climate-history, shore-levels, fauna, pollen-analysis, geochronology: Brooks, *Antiquity* I, 412 (Britain)* ; *Quarterly Journ. R. Meteorological Soc.* 60, 377 ; Bertsch, *B.R.G.K.* XVIII, 1 ; Dubois, *L'Anthr.* 42, 269 ; De Geer, in *Geografisk Annalen* xvi (1934) ; Clark, *Meso. Settlement*, ch. I ; and see under Scandinavia below.

Spain and Portugal, Azilian: Obermaier, *Fossil Man in Spain*, 340* ; Asturian: *ibid.*, 349 ; de la Vega, *El Asturiense* (Comisión de Investigaciones . . . Prehistóricas, Madrid, Memoria 32 (1923). Jalhay, *C.I.S.P.P.*, London 1932, 95* ; Mugem: Mendes Correa, *C.I.A.A.P.*, Paris 1931, 362. France, Azilian, Sauveterrian, Tardenoisian, 'Campignian': Octobon, *C.I.A.A.P.*, Portugal 1930, 326 ; Pyrenean caves: Tréat and Couturier (Trou-Violet), *L'Anthr.* 38, 235 ; Narbonne caves: Héléna, *Les Origines de Narbonne* (1937), 52, 57, and in *A.F.A.S.* 1923 ; Sauveterre: Coulonges, *Arch. I.P.H.*, Mémoire 14 (1935), and cf. *L'Anthr.* 38, 495 ; 43, 196 ; (Le Cuzoul), *ibid.* 427 ; Tardenoisian: Daniel in *B.S.P.F.* 1932-33-34; Montbani: Octobon, *Revue anthropologique* 1920, 107 ; Piscop: Giraud, Vaché, Vignard, *L'Anthr.* 48 1 ; Téviec: Péquart (with Boule and Vallois, whom see here too on Mesolithic human types generally), *Arch. I.P.H.*, Mémoire 18 (1937) ; cf. *L'Anthr.* 38, 479 (similar site at Hoédic: *L'Anthr.* 44, 1).

Italy: Vaufrey, *Arch. I.P.H.*, Mémoire 3 (1928)*.

Switzerland: Keller-Tarnuzzer, *C.I.S.P.P.*, London 1932, 83.

S. Germany: Peters, *Nachrichtenblatt für deutsche Vorzeit* 1932, 52 ; Peters, *Germania* 18, 81 (Falkenstein) ; Gumpert, *Fränkisches Mesolithikum* (Mannusbibliothek 40) ; Peters, *Germania* 19, 98, and (Rappenfels) 281 ; Clark, *Meso. Settlement*, ch. V (covering Federsee, Ensdorf, etc.)*.

Central and S.E. Europe: Childe, *Danube*, ch. II* ; Hillebrand, *B.R.G.K.* XXIV-V, 25.

Russia: as under Ch. II, 2 above ; Joukov, *L'Anthr.* 49, 1 ; Childe, *Early Man* (see under ch. I above), 233.

N. Germany (with E. Germany and Poland) and Scandinavia: Clark, *Meso. Settlement** ; Schwantes, *Geschichte Schleswig-Holsteins* I, pts. 1-2 ; Shetelig, Falk, and Gordon, *Scand. Arch.* 12 ; Brøndsted, *Danmarks Oldtid I, Stenålderen* (1938), 13 ; Nordman, *Danmarks GeologiskeUndersøgelse*, 3rd ser., 27, 248 ; Rydbeck, *K.H.V.Lund Årsberättelse* 1927-28, I, 1, 99 ; *Acta Arch.* I, 55 ; and (criticizing Brøndsted and Nordman) *ibid.* 1937-38, VI, 1 ; cf. Bagge, *Fornvännen* 1937, 357 ; Tanner, *S.M.Y.A.* XXXIX, 1. Pollen-analysis: Jessen, *Acta Arch.* V, 185 ; *Quartär* 1, 124 ; Ahrensburg-Stellmoor, Lyngby: *Offa* 1, 2 ; cf. *Antiquity* 1938, 165 ; *Mannus* 29, 109 ; Swiderian (Poland): Sawicki, *Festschrift . . . des Museums Vorgeschichtlicher Altertümer in Kiel* 1937, 18 ; (Silesia) Rothert, *Die Mittlere Steinzeit in Schlesien* (1936) ; Klosterlund, Gudenaa: Mathiassen, *Aarbøger* 1937. Arctic Stone Age and Rock-engravings: see under Ch. VI, 1 below. Finnmark: Bøe and Nummedal, *Le Finnmarkien* (Inst. for Sammenlignende Kulturforskning, B, XXXII, Oslo 1936).

Holland, Hengelo skull: Florschütz, Van der Vlerk, Van den Broek, Bursch, in *Koninkl. Akademie van Wetenschappen te Amsterdam* (Proceedings) XXXIX, 1 (1936).

Belgium: Clark, *Meso. Settlement**.

Britain : Clark, *The Mesolithic Age in Britain* (1932)* and *Meso. Settlement**; (separation from Continent) *P.P.S.* II, 36, 169, 239 ; Fox, *Personality*³, 23 ; (Broxbourne) *J.R.A.I.* LXIV, 101 ; (Horsham culture) Clark, *Arch. Journ.* XC, 52 ; (Farnham) *P.P.S.* V, 61. Scotland : Childe, *Scotland*, ch. II*.

N. Ireland : Whelan, *P.R.I.A.* XLIV, C, 115 ; *Irish Naturalist* (Quaternary Research no.), 1934 ; (Glenarm) Movius, *J.R.S.A.I.* LXVII, 181.

3. Near Eastern Civilization, general : Childe, *New Light on the Most Ancient East* (1934)* ; *Man Makes Himself* (1936) ; principal periodicals : *Iraq, Syria, American Journal of Archaeology, Liverpool Annals of Archaeology and Anthropology* ; monographs : *Mitteilungen der deutschen Orient-Gesellschaft, Oriental Institue of Chicago Studies.* Palestine : *Revue Biblique* 1934, 237 ; *Liverpool Annals* XXII, 174 ; XXIII, 67 ; *Syria*, XVI, 353. Cyprus : *Syria*, XVII, 356. Cilicia : *Liverpool Annals* XXIV, 62 ; XXV. Anatolia : Bittel, *Prähistorische Forschungen in Kleinasien** (Istanbuler Forschungen, 1934) ; von der Osten, *The Alishar Hüyük* (Or. Inst. Chicago Publications XXVIII-XXX, 1937) ; Troy, Thermi : see under ch. IV, 2 below ; Kum Tepe, *American Journ. of Arch.* XXXIX, 33 ; and Mesopotamia : *Iraq* II, 211. Greece, Thessaly, Macedonia, Crete : see under ch. IV, 1 below. Egypt, climate-changes (with rest of Old World) : Huzayyin, *Man* 1936, 20 ; Merimde : see Childe, *New Light* . . ., 59* ; Fayûm : Caton-Thompson and Gardner, *The Desert Fayûm* (1935) ; Tasian : Brunton, *Mostagedda and the Tasian Culture* (1937) ; Badarian : Brunton and Caton-Thompson, *The Badarian Civilization* (1928) ; and North African rock-paintings : Vaufrey, *B.S.P.F.* 1936, 624 ; North Africa and Spain : Bosch Gimpera, *Etnologia*, ch. III.

Pottery-making : Childe, *Man* 1937, 55.

Agriculture, grains : Peake, *Man* 1939, 36* ; Netolitzky, *B.R.G.K.* XX, 14 ; Bertsch, *Mannus* 31, 171.

Domestic animals : (dogs) *Lunds Universitets Aarskrifter*, new ser., 32 (1937) ; *Antiquity* 1932, 411 ; (sheep) *ibid.* 1936, 194 ; (cattle) Peake and Fleure, *Peasants and Potters* (Corridors of Time, III, 1927), ch. 3.

Shells : cowrie represents not vulva, but eye (charm against Evil Eye), M. A. Murray, *Man* 1939, 165.

Chapter IV

1. Aegean cultures, general : documented survey of research to 1933 : Myres, ' The Cretan Labyrinth,' *J.R.A.I.* LXIII, 269* ; summaries : Myres, *Who were the Greeks?* (1930), ch. V ; Childe, *Dawn²*, chs. II-V* ; annual reviews in *J.H.S.* Pottery : Forsdyke, British Museum *Catalogue of Vases* I, 1 (1925).

Crete: Evans, *The Palace of Minos* (1921-28) ; Pendlebury, *The Archaeology of Crete* (1939)*.

Cyclades : (summary) Childe, *Dawn²*, ch. IV*.

Mainland Greece, Neolithic : Mylonas, 'Η νεολιθικὴ ἐποχή ἐν Ἑλλάδι (1928)* ; Kunze, *Orchomenos II* (Bayerische Akademie, Phil.-hist. Klasse, new ser., V, 1931) ; Blegen, *Prosymna* (1937) ; *Hesperia* VI, 490. Thessaly : Tsountas, Αἱ προϊστορικαὶ ἀκροπόλεις Διμηνίου καὶ Σέσκλου (1908) ; Wace and Thompson, *Prehistoric Thessaly* (1912) ; Hanson, *Early Civilization in Thessaly* (1933).

Helladic : Blegen and Wace, *B.S.A.* XXII, 189 ; Blegen, *Korakou* (1921) ; Goldman, *Excavations at Eutresis in Boeotia* (1931) ; Kunze, *Orchomenos III* (Bayerische Akademie, Phil.-hist. Klasse, new ser., VIII, 1934) ; Frödin and Persson, *Asine* (1938).

Macedonia : Mylonas, *Excavations at Olynthus* I (Johns Hopkins Univ. Studies in Archaeology, 6) ; Heurtley, *Prehistoric Macedonia* (1939) ; cf. *Antiq. Journ.* XII, 227.

Bibliographical Notes

391

Troy, Thermi : see under 2 below.
2. Vinča, Starčevo, Morava (-Vardar) : Fewkes, *B.A.S.P.R.* 1933, 33 ;
1934, 29 ; 1936, 5* ; Childe, *Dawn²*, ch. VI* ; English version of Vassits'
Preistorijskaya Vinča forthcoming.
Körös group : Tompa, *B.R.G.K.* XXIV-V, 46* ; Childe, *Dawn²*, 92*.
Tordos (Turdas), W. Rumanian : Nestor, *B.R.G.K.* XXII, 51*.
Boian A, Vodastra, Gumelnitza, Erösd (Ariuşd), Cucuteni : Nestor,
B.R.G.K. XXII, 31* (cf. *P.Z.* XIX, 110) ; Dumitrescu, *L'Art préhistorique
en Roumanie* (1937) ; Childe, *Dawn²*, ch. VIII*. Erösd : Childe, *Danube*,
98* ; (pottery) *Dacia* I, 1. Izvoare : Vulpe, *E.S.A.* XI, 135. Cucuteni :
Schmidt, *Cucuteni in der oberen Moldau* (1932).
Tripolye culture : Childe, *Dawn²*, 135* ; Passek, *La Céramique tripolienne*
(1935) ; Kandyba, *Schipenitz : Kunst und Kultur eines neolithischen Dorfes*
(1936) ; (Niezwiska) Hutchinson, *Liverpool Annals of Arch. and Anthr.*
XVII, 19.
Macedonian B and Dimini : Wace, *E.S.A.* IX, 123 ; Nestor, *B.R.G.K.*
XXII, 47 ; Heurtley, *Antiq. Journ.* XII, 227 (cf. *Prehistoric Macedonia*,
109, 113).
Troy, Thermi : Childe, *Dawn²*, ch. III* ; Lamb, *Excavations at Thermi in
Lesbos* (1936) ; chronology, 210-11 ; Troy, recent excavations : Blegen in
American Journ. of Arch. XXXVIII onwards ; chronology, XLI, 563, 595 ;
see previously Dörpfeld, *Troja und Ilion* (1902) ; Schmidt, *Schliemann-
Sammlung* (1902) ; also 'Anatolia ' under ch. III, 3 above.
3. Danubian Civilization, general : Childe, *Danube*, chs. IV-V* ; *Dawn²*,
ch. VI*. Hungary (Bükk, Theiss (Tisza), etc.) : Tompa, *Die Bandkeramik
in Ungarn* (1929) ; *B.R.G.K.* XXIV-V, 28*. Bohemia : Stocky, *La
Bohème préhistorique* (1929)*. Austria ; Pittioni, *Urgeschichte Österreichs*,
140 (in *Allgemeine Urgeschichte*, Vienna, 1937). Germany (all Danubian
cultures, with Rössen, Hinkelstein, Münchshöfen, Jordansmühl, etc.) :
Buttler, *Der donauländische und der westische Kulturkreis der jüngeren
Steinzeit* (Handbuch der Urgeschichte Deutschlands 2, 1938)* ; cf. *B.R.G.K.*
XIX, 146 (N.W. area) ; Rössen at Goldberg : Bersu, *Germania* 20, 229 ;
Aichbühl : Schmidt, *Jungsteinzeit-Siedlungen im Federseemoor* (1937) ;
Köln-Lindenthal : Buttler and Haberey, *Das bandkeramische Dorf Köln-
Lindenthal* (Röm.-Germanische Forschungen 11, 1936). Alsace : Forrer,
Bauernfarmen der Steinzeit von Achenheim und Stützheim (1903) ; *Nouvelles
Découvertes et Acquisitions du Musée Préhistorique* ... *de Strasbourg* (1924) ;
Bulletin archéologique 1921, 11. France, Ante : *B.R.G.K.* XX, 101 (cf.
Childe, *Dawn²*, 296*). Belgium, Omalian : Hamal-Nandrin, Servais,
Louis, in *Bulletin de la Soc. royale belge d'Anthropologie et de Préhistoire*
1936 ; Buttler, *Revue belge d'Archéologie et d'Histoire de l'Art* VI, 351 ;
cf. Buttler, *B.R.G.K.* XIX as above. Holland (Caberg, Stein) : Buttler,
ibid. ; (Geleen) Bursch, *Germania* 21, 5 (claiming survival till Beaker times).
Trade (general) : Buttler, *Marburger Studien* (1938), 26.

Chapter V

1. Neolithic Sicily, S. Italy, Sardinia : Childe, *Dawn²*, 220, 242* ; arts.
in *B.P.I.* XLI ff., *Monumenti Antichi* XX ff. ; Mayer, *Molfetta und Matera*
(1924) ; Rellini, *La più antica ceramica dipinta in Italia* (1935) ; *C.I.S.P.P.*,
London 1932, 220; *B.P.I.* n.s. II, 83.
S. Spanish Caves : Bosch Gimpera, *Etnologia*, 63* ; Childe, *Dawn²*, 253.
Rock-paintings : Breuil, *Les Peintures rupestres schématiques de la Peninsule
ibérique* (1933-35). Almerian : Siret, *Les Premiers âges du métal dans le
Sud-Est de l'Espagne* (1888) ; Bosch Gimpera, *Etnologia*, 145* ; Childe,
Dawn², 251* ; arts. in *Archivo de Prehistoria Levantina* I (Valencia 1928),
and J. Martinez Santa Olalla in *Universidad* (Zaragoza), 1930.
Ligurian Caves, N. Italy : Morelli, *Iconografia della Preistoria Ligustica*

(1901). France (S., C., and E.) : Héléna, *Les Origines de Narbonne* (1937), ch. II ; Delort, *Dix Années de Fouilles en Auvergne* (1901), 10 ; J. Hawkes, *Antiquity* VIII, 24*.

Swiss Cortaillod culture : J. Hawkes, *op. cit.** ; Vouga, *Le Néolithique lacustre ancien* (1934), and in *A.S.A.* 1929, nos. 2-3 ; Vogt, *Germania* 18, 89. Michelsberg culture : J. Hawkes, Vogt, *opp. citt.** ; Buttler, *Der donauländische und der Westische Kulturkreis* (see under Ch. IV, 3), 69, 82* ; Childe, *Arch. Journ.* LXXXVIII, 37* ; (Altenburg) Kraft, *P.Z.* XX, 167. Belgium (Spiennes, etc.) : De Loë, *La Belgique ancienne* I, 184. ' Campignian ' : Schwantes, *Germania* 16, 177*.

Britain : Flint Mines : Piggott and Clark, *Antiquity* VII, 166* ; Curwen, *Arch. of Sussex* (1937), 104. Neolithic A and Camps : Curwen, *Antiquity* IV, 22* ; Keiller, *C.I.S.P.P.*, London 1932, 135 ; Curwen, *Archaeology of Sussex*, 64* ; Liddell, *Proceedings Devon Arch. Exploration Society* I, 180 ; II, 161 ; (Haldon) *ibid.* II, 244, and *P.P.S.* IV, 222. Neolithic A and B : Piggott, *Arch. Journ.* LXXXVIII, 83* ; *P.S.E.A.* VII, 373 (cf. J. Hawkes, *P.P.S.* I, 127) ; presumed prototypes of B at Ebbsfleet, N. Kent : Burchell and Piggott, *Antiq. Journ.* XIX, 405. Yorkshire : Newbigin, *P.P.S.* III, 189*. Fens, Essex Coast : see under Ch. VI, 3 below. Long Barrows (unchambered) : Piggott, *P.P.S.* I, 115* (cf. II, 77 ; III, 1) ; from Brittany : *Antiquity* XI, 441*.

2. Mediterranean-Atlantic-Baltic, tombs and connexions (general) : Peake, *Memoirs and Proceedings Manchester Literary and Philosoph. Soc.* 8 (1937), 37*. Minoan, Cycladic, Helladic : Childe, *Dawn*², chs. II, IV, V*, and see under Ch. IV, 1. S. Italy, Siculan I : Childe, *Dawn*², 220, 223, 228*, and see under 1 above ; bossed bone ornaments (Siculan I, Malta, Troy) : *B.P.I.* XLVI, 13, with warning as to date by Bittel, *Marburger Studien* (1938), 9.

Malta : Zammit, *Prehistoric Malta* (1930) ; Ugolini, *Malta : Origini della Civiltà Mediterranea* (1934 : valuable chiefly for illustrations) ; M. Murray, *Excavations in Malta* (for Borg-en-Nadur), I-III (1923-25-29) ; (rocktombs) Zammit, *Antiq. Journ.* VIII, 481 ; latest summaries : E. de Manneville, *Commission Internat. Préhist. Médit. Occidentale* (Barcelona, 1935), 36* ; Childe, *Dawn*², 237*.

C. and N. Italy : Childe, *Dawn*², 229, 231* (cf. *B.P.I.* III, 1 (Reggio), and (Vibrata) XXXII, 181 ; XXXIII, 100, 193) ; Liguria : see under 1 above and *B.P.I.* XIX, 1, 57 ; Gargano : Baumgärtel, *B.P.I.* L-LI, 119. Sardinia : Childe, *Dawn*², 242* ; Bosch Gimpera, *Commission Internat. Préhist. Médit. Occidentale* (Barcelona, 1935), 29*.

Almerian and S. Iberian tombs and culture : Bosch Gimpera, *Etnologia*, 145, 175*, and see under 1 above, with Siret, *C.I.S.P.P.*, London 1932, 250 ; Obermaier, *M.A.G.W.* L, 107* ; Leisner, *Marburger Studien* (1938), 147 ; Forde, *American Anthropologist* XXXIII, 33* (the guiding authority here followed) ; Childe, *Dawn*², 255* (these last two also* for Portugal).

Rise of Bell-beaker culture : Castillo, *La ceramica incisa* (1922) and *La Cultura del Vaso Campaniforme* (1928)* ; Bosch Gimpera, *Etnologia*, 163* ; J. Martinez Santa Olalla, *Anuario de Prehistoria Madrileña* I (1930), 97.

Catalonia and N. Spanish Caves : see under 3 below.

Channelled Pottery and its significance : J. Hawkes, *Arch. Journ.* XCV, 126*.

3. Catalonia, tombs and caves ; ' Pyrenean culture ' : Pericot, *La Civilización Megalitica Catalana y la Cultura Pirenaica* (1925) ; Serra Vilaró, *Civilitzacio Megalitica a Catalunya* (Solsona, 1927).

France, S. and S.W. : Bosch Gimpera and Serra Ráfols in *Revue anthropologique* 1927, nos. 7-9 ; Héléna, *Les Origines de Narbonne* (1937), ch. II ; J. Hawkes, *Antiquity* VIII, 30, and on Channelled Ware *Arch. Journ.* XCV, 126* ; Childe, *Dawn*², 285, 289* ; Daniel, *Antiq. Journ.*

Bibliographical Notes 393

XIX, 157, assigning a position not here endorsed to 'long barrows' in Aveyron; tombs in W.: Déchelette, *Manuel* I, 461 (cists)*, 373 (megaliths)*; Poitou : De Longuemar, *Les Dolmens du Haut-Poitou* (Soc. des Antiquaires de l'Ouest, 1866), where the Maranzais tomb of Fig. 18 c is described p. 11 (with n. 2) and planned (very possibly not with modern accuracy) Pl. IV, centre top, of separate album of plates; Chassey : Thomasset, *L'Anthr.* 37, 45, with J. Hawkes *opp. citt.* and Childe, *Arch. Journ.* LXXXVIII, 37*; Fort-Harrouard : Philippe, *Cinq Années de Fouilles au F.-H.* (Soc. normande d'études prehist. XXV *bis*, 1927) and *L'Anthr.* 46, 257, 541 ; 47, 253, with J. Hawkes, Childe, *opp. citt.**; Campigny : *Revue mensuelle de l'École d'Anthropologie de Paris* 1898, with the same. Breton and W. French transeptal gallery-graves : Daniel, *P.P.S.* V, 143*.

Brittany : Marsille, *Le Morbihan préhistorique* (1931); Le Rouzic, *L'Anthr.* 43, 233 (tombs) ; 44, 485 (material) ; Le Rouzic and Péquart, the series *Carnac: Fouilles faites dans la région* (Carnac Museum) ; S. Finistère : Forde, *Antiq. Journ.* VII, 6*; (general) J. Hawkes, Childe, *opp. citt.**; Childe, *Dawn²*, 297*; Forde, *American Anthropologist* XXXIII, 33*.

Channel Islands : *The Archaeology of the Channel Islands* I, T. D. Kendrick, *Guernsey* (1928) ; II, J. Hawkes, *Jersey* (1939 : also general)*. Fontenay-le-Marmion : *B.S.P.F.* 1918, 65. Breton Megalithic Art : Péquart and Le Rouzic, *Corpus des Signes Gravés* (1927); cf. *Préhistoire* VI, 1. On S.O.M. in Brittany see below.

S. Britain : 'Dolmens': Daniel, *Antiquity* XI, 183*; Long Barrows, Severn-Cotswold : Daniel, *P.P.S.* III, 71* (cf. V, 119, 143); Clifford, (Notgrove) *Archaeologia* 86, 119 ; (Nympsfield) *P.P.S.* IV, 188 (cf. IV, 122, Lanhill). Wales : Grimes, *P.P.S.* II, 106*.

Ibero-Irish relations : Bosch Gimpera, *Préhistoire* II, 195. Ireland : Mahr, *P.P.S.* III, 332*; Passage-graves : Powell, *P.P.S.* IV, 239*; N. Irish tombs, esp. Horned Cairns : Evans, *Ulster Journal of Archaeology³* I, 7*; *P.P.S.* III, 166*; and see recent vols. of *Ulster Journ. of Arch.* Ballynamona : *J.R.S.A.I.* LXVIII, 260.

Isle of Man : Clark, *P.P.S.* I, 70 (general) ; Fleure and Neeley, *Antiq. Journ.* XVI, 373.

Scotland, S.W., N.W., Caithness, Orkney, Clava : Childe, *Prehistory of Scotland**, ch. III, 25, 40, 32, 44, 51 ; (material culture) ch. IV ; and see recent vols. of *P.S.A.Scot.*

Seine-Oise-Marne culture : Childe, *Arch. Journ.* 88, 49*; in Brittany : Forde, *Man* 1929, 80 (cf. J. Hawkes, *Archaeology of Jersey* (1939), 7) ; and Horgen culture : Vogt, *A.S.A.* XL, 1*.

N. European Megaliths, general : Nordman, *The Megalithic Culture of N. Europe* (*S.M.Y.A.* XXXIX, 3, 1935) ; and see under Ch. VI below.

Chapter VI

1. Northern cultures, general : Shetelig, Falk, and Gordon, *Scand. Arch.* (1937)*; Childe, *Dawn²*, ch. X*. Rock-engravings : Clark, *Antiquity* XI, 56*, with *I.P.E.K.* 1936-37, 50, and Gjessing, *Nordenfjelske Ristninger og Malinger av den Arktiske Gruppe* (1936). Garnes : Clark, *Meso. Settlement*, 70*. Eastern Comb-ware province : Childe, *Dawn²*, ch. XI*; Rosenberg, *Kulturströmungen in Europa zur Steinzeit* (1931) ; in Silesia : Richthofen in *Aus Oberschlesiens Urzeit* 4 (1929) ; and British Neolithic B : Childe, *Arch. Journ.* 88, 58*. Baltic Dwelling-places and shore-lines : Tanner, *S.M.Y.A.* XXXIX, no. 1 ; Ayräpää, *Acta Arch.* I, 165 ; Bagge, *Fornvännen* 1927, 357. Denmark (general) : Bröndsted, *Danmarks Oldtid I, Stenålderen* (1938)*; (Havnelev) Nordman, *Finskt Museum* 1929, 4; (Strandegaard) *Acta Arch.* II, 265 ; (criticizing these) Rydbeck, *K.H.V.Lund Årsberättelse* 1937-38, VI, 1. Schleswig-Holstein : Schwantes, *Geschichte Schleswig-Holsteins* I, ch. V. Funnel-beaker cultures :

Jazdzewski, *P.Z.* XXIII, 77 ; in Poland, his *Kultura Puharów Lejkowatych w Polsce* (Bibl. Prehist. 2, 1936, with German summary) ; in C. Europe : Childe, *Danube*, ch. VII* ; Baalberg culture : Grimm, *Mannus* 29, 155. Elbe-Weser culture and Northern Passage-grave pottery : Jazdzewski, *op. cit.* ; Forssander, *K.H.V.Lund. Årsberättelse* 1935-36, VI, 1. Northern Megalithic : Nordman, *The Megalithic Culture of N. Europe (S.M.Y.A.* XXXIX, 3, 1935) ; Germany : Sprockhoff, *Die nordische Megalith-Kultur* (Handbuch der Urgeschichte Deutschlands 3, 1938* : includes Walternienburg, etc.) ; Schleswig-Holstein : Langenheim, *Tonware der Riesensteingräber in Schleswig-Holstein* (1935) ; Troldebjerg : Winther, *Troldebjerg* (1935). Kujavian graves : Jazdzewski, *opp. citt.** Holland : van Giffen, *De Hunnebedden in den Nederlanden* (1925-28) ; and Kentish megaliths : Piggott, *P.P.S.* I, 122. Megalithic and invading Single-Grave cultures : Sprockhoff, in *Germanen und Indogermanen* (Hirt-Festschrift, 1936), 255 ; Tode, *Mannus* 27, 19. Saxo-Thuringian Corded-Ware culture : Childe, *Danube*, ch. VIII* ; Agde, Nowothnig, *Mannus* 28, 361, 423 ; Seger, in *Germanen und Indogermanen* (Hirt-Festschrift, 1936), 17.

Warrior cultures in E., Battle-axes, Caucasus, S. Russia : Childe, *Dawn²*, ch. IX* ; Hančar, *Urgeschichte Kaukasiens* (1937)* ; (Mariupol) *E.S.A.* IX, 140 ; Sumerian types, Battle-axe typology : Childe, *M.A.G.W.* LXIII, 217, *Liverpool Annals of Arch. and Anthr.* XXIII, 114, and *E.S.A.* IX, 157 ; Alaca Höyük : *Turk Tarih Kurumu* I, 210, 222 ; Remzi Oguz Arik, *Alaca Höyük* (Istanbul, 1937) ; Hammer-head pin at Frejlev : Rosenberg, *Aarbøger* 1929, 204 ; *Mém. Soc. Ant. du Nord* 1932-33, 433. Russian Battle-axe cultures : Äyräpää, *E.S.A.* VIII, 1 ; and Globeamphora, Zlota, Swedish and Finnish Boat-axe cultures : Forssander, *Die schwedische Bootaxt-Kultur* (1933)*. Finnish animal sculpture, axes : Nordman, *I.P.E.K.* 1936-37, 36.

2. Warrior cultures and archaeology of ' Indogermanic ' question : Seger, in *Germanen und Indogermanen* (Hirt-Festschrift, 1936) 1 ; Childe, *Dawn²*, 166. Tripolye B, Cucuteni B, Gumelnitza B, Schipenitz B, Koszylowce : see Tripolye under Ch. IV, 2 above. Coţofeni, Schneckenberg : Nestor, *B.R.G.K.* XXII, 61, 69*.

Troy II, Early Macedonian, Middle Helladic : see under Ch. IV, 1, above ; Childe, *Dawn²*, 39, 68* ; Fuchs, *Die griechische Fundgruppen der frühen Bronzezeit* (1937) ; Corded ware at Eutresis : Ünze, in *Festgabe aus Athen Th. Wiegand dargebracht* (1936), 43.

Crete, Middle Minoan : Pendlebury, *Archaeology of Crete* (1939), 94*.

Danubian Copper Age, Bodrogkeresztur, Baden, E. Alps : Tompa, *B.R.G.K.* XXIV-V, 50* ; Patay, *Frühbronzezeitliche Kulturen in Ungarn* (1938)* ; Willvonseder, *Die Mittlere Bronzezeit in Österreich* (1937) I, 23, 32 ; Forssander, *Ostskand. Norden*, ch. I* ; Childe, *Dawn²*, 109, 282*. Horgen, Altheim : Vogt, *A.S.A.* XL, 1* ; (Goldberg) Bersu, *Germania* 21, 149. Italy, Remedello ; Sicily, Villafrati ; Sardinia ; Tuscany : Childe, *Dawn²*, 232, 227, 242* ; Forssander, *Ostskand. Norden.* 42 ; Åberg, *Bronzezeitliche und früheisenzeitliche Chronologie* III, 82 ; Colini, *B.P.I.* XXVI, 196.

Bell-Beakers : Castillo, *La Cultura del Vaso Campaniforme* (1928)* ; Childe, *Dawn²*, 213* ; Neumann, *P.Z.* XX, 3 (for C. Germany).

3. Rhineland Beaker cultures : Castillo, Childe, *opp. citt.* ; Stampfuss, *Die jungneolithische Kulturen in Westdeutschland* (1929) ; Lower Rhine native culture and Bell-urns : Kersten, *Germania* 22, 71 ; Nähermemmingen : Frickhinger, *Germania* 21, 6. Holland, Beaker cultures : Bursch, *Die Becherkulturen in den Niederlanden* (*Oudheidkundige Mededeelingen* xiv, 1933, 39)* ; barrows : van Giffen, *Die Bauart der Einzelgräber* (Mannusbibl. 44-5, 1930), with *P.P.S.* IV, 252. Beaker outliers in N. : Forssander, *Ostskand. Norden.* 57. Western Cists, Germany : Sprockhoff, *Die nordische Megalithkultur*, 59 ; Balearic and Arles tombs, Seine-Oise-Marne cists and grottoes : Hemp, *Archaeologia*, 76, 121* ; *Antiq. Journ.* XIII, 33, and

Bibliographical Notes 395

(suggesting relations with Britain not here endorsed) *P.P.S.* I, 108;
E. Provence, *Antiq. Journ.* XIV, 277; Bosch Gimpera, *Etnologia*, 187*;
Commission Internat. Préhist. Médit. *Occidentale* (Barcelona, 1935), 17, 25*.
Seine-Oise-Marne and Horgen; and Brittany : see under Ch. V, 3 above.
Double-axes, metal (ingots) and stone : Hawkes, *B.S.A.* XXXVII, 141*.
Brittany (Bell-beakers, etc.) : see under Ch. V, 2 above; Er-Lannic Circles :
Le Rouzic, *Les Cromlechs de Er-Lannic* (1930); and British B 1 Beakers :
Piggott, *P.P.S.* IV, 55. Graig Lwyd axes : *Archaeologia Cambrensis* XC,
189.
British Beakers, general : Abercromby, *Bronze Age Pottery of Great
Britain* I (1912), with Clark, *Antiquity* V, 415.
Essex Coast, subsidence and Neolithic, Beakers, Grooved ware : *P.P.S.*
III, 178. Fens : Godwin, *Philosoph. Trans. Royal Soc.* 229, B, 323;
Neolithic and A Beaker cultures : Clark and others (Fenland Research
Cttee.), *Antiq. Journ.* XIII, 266; XV, 284. Lincs, A Beakers : Phillips,
Arch. Journ. XC, 123; Skendleby Long Barrow : *Archaeologia* 85, 37.
'Henge' Monuments : Clark, *P.P.S.* II, 1*; Avebury : (W. Kennet
Avenue) Keiller and Piggott, *Antiquity* X, 417; (Circles) Keiller, *ibid.* XIII,
223.
Scotland : Beakers : Childe, *Scotland*, ch. V*; Skara Brae : Childe,
Skara Brae (1931), with Rinyo, *P.S.A.Scot.* 73, 6.
Flint Daggers : (Britain) Grimes, *P.S.E.A.* VI, iv, 340; (Continent)
Forssander, *Ostskand. Norden.* 121*; cf. *Mannus* 27, 199. Marschwitz,
Lower Oder, German Stone Cists : Forssander, *op. cit.* 57*; Britz :
Umbreit, *Ausgrabung des steinzeitl. Dorfes Berlin-Britz* (Mannusbüch. 56,
1937). Danish Islands, Single-graves and Stone Cists : Becker, *Aarbøger*
1936, 145; Jutland, W. Swedish Cists : Forssander, *op. cit.* 106*; and
Seine-Oise-Marne : Vogt, *A.S.A.* XL, 1*.

Chapter VII

1. Bronze Age general and bronze metallurgy : Childe, *The Bronze Age*
(1930); Witter, *Die älteste Erzgewinnung im Nordisch-Germanischen
Lebenskreis*, Bde I, II (Mannusbüch. 60, 63, 1938)*; Coghlan, *Man* 1939, 92.
Climate : Childe, *op. cit.*, 48; Brooks, *Quarterly Journ. R. Meteorological
Soc.* LX, 377. Tin at Crisa (Greece) : Davies, *J.H.S.* 49, 89. Distribution
of ores, S., C., and W. Europe : Davies, *Roman Mines in Europe* (1935)*;
C. Europe : Childe, *Danube*, ch. I; in C. Germany : Witter, *Die älteste
Erzgewinnung* (*op. cit.*), Bd. I, and in *Mannus* 28, Heft 4. 'Cypriote'
daggers : Childe, *Danube*, 218, but Reinecke, *Germania* 17, 256 : cf. *B.S.A.*
XXXVII, 158.
Danubian Early Bronze Age cultures : Childe, *Danube*, chs. XI-XII*;
Dawn², 113. Rumania : Nestor, *B.R.G.K.* XXII, 79*; Hungary : Tompa,
B.R.G.K. XXIV-V, 61*; Patay, *Frühbronzezeitliche Kulturen in Ungarn*
(1938); Austria : Willvonseder, *Die Mittlere Bronzezeit in Österreich*
(1937), I, ch. I*; Bohemia, Moravia : Schránil, *Vorgeschichte Böhmens u.
Mährens*, and Stócky, *La Bohème préhistorique* (1929); C. Germany :
Neumann, *P.Z.* XX, 70; Childe, *Dawn²*, 189*; Adlerberg : Childe,
Danube, 245*; Switzerland (pottery) : Vogt, *45 Jahresbericht des Schweiz.
Landesmuseums*, 1936, 76. Chronology : (old standard) Montelius, *Archiv.
f. Anthropologie* 25, 443; 26, 1, 905; (new) Reinecke, *Germania* 17, 11;
Bittel, *ibid.* 91 and *Marburger Studien* (1938), 13; Ünze, *ibid.* 243*;
Forssander, *Ostskand. Norden.* 256*.
2. Spain, transitional and El Argar cultures : Bosch Gimpera, *Etnologia*
164, 175*; *Investigación y Progreso* VI, 145; metallurgy (Portugal) :
Serpa Pinto, *C.I.S.P.P.*, London 1932, 253, and in *Arrais de la Faculdade
de Ciéncias do Porto* 18 (1933); (Catalonia) Serra Vilaró, *De Metallurgia
prehistorica a Catalunya* (Solsona, 1924). S. France : Héléna, *Les Origines*

de Narbonne (1937), ch. II ; Childe, *Dawn*², 290*. N. Italian bronzes : Åberg, *Bronzezeitliche u. Früheisenzeitliche Chronologie* III, 92* ; daggers, N. Italian, Aunjetitz, Northern, and Rhône culture : Ünze, *Die frühbronzezeitlichen triangulären Vollgriffdolche* (1937). France, Singleyrac, St. Menoux : Déchelette, *Manuel* II, 142, 147, 314, 317, 320 ; Brittany, Early Bronze Age : Piggott, *P.P.S.* IV, 64* ; V, 193. Britain, Wessex culture : Piggott, *ibid.* IV, 52* (Welsh barrows : Grimes, *ibid.* 107 ; Fox, *Archaeologia* 87, 129). Stonehenge : Clark, *P.P.S.* II, 23, 44*. British Bronze Age, general : Childe, *American Anthropologist* XXXIX, 1. Yorkshire (Neolithic, Beakers, and) Food-vessels : M. Kitson Clark, *Arch. Journ.* XCIV, 43*. Scotland : Childe, *Scotland*, ch. V*. Ireland, Beakers and Food-vessels : Abercromby, *Bronze Age Pottery of Great Britain* I (1912), 38, 116 ; Mahr, *P.P.S.* III, 364* ; arts. in *Ulster Journ. of Arch.*³, esp. 1, ii, 164, and 2, ii, 254 (surely really Early not Late Bronze Age) ; *P.P.S.* III, 29. Flat axes, British Isles and N. Europe : Megaw and Hardy, *P.P.S.* IV, 272* ; Forssander, *Ostskand. Norden.* 163*. Halberds : O'Riórdáin, *Archaeologia* 86, 195*.

3. Italy : Lake-dwellings, Hut-villages, Caves, Apennine culture, Terremare : Messerschmidt, *Bronzezeit u. frühe Eisenzeit in Italien* (1935) ; *B.P.I.* XLVI, 18 (Calvatone : cf. *ibid.* 34, 81 ; *Notizie degli Scavi* 1923, 117) ; *B.P.I.* XLVII, 58 (Cetona) ; XLIX, 46 (Garda) ; XLIX, 19 ; L-LI, 148 ; LV, 87 ; (Terramara origins and material) Rellini, *C.I.S.P.P.*, London 1932, 229, and *B.P.I.* LIII, 63 ; LIV, 65 (N. Italian and Apennine cultures in relation to Terremare : cf. *Rivista di Antropologia* XXXI (Barocelli) on Castellaro di Gottolengo). Säflund's large monograph *Le Terremare* (Svenska Institut Rom, 1939)* has appeared too late for a criticism of his high chronology and other findings, but cf. now Forssander, *K.H.V.Lund. Årsberättelse* 1938-39, III, 79 ff., and Rellini, *B.P.I.* new ser., III (1939), 114 ff. Hungary, Toszeg periods B and C : Tompa, *B.R.G.K.* XXIV-V, 74, 83 ; Patay, *Frühbronzezeitliche Kulturen in Ungarn* (1938), with new, expanded classification. Faience Beads : Beck and Stone, *Archaeologia* 85, 203 (N.B. 252)* ; Childe, *American Journal of Archaeology* 44, 23-4 ; *Dawn*², 114, 120, 317 ; cf. Blegen, *Prosymna* (1937), 306-12. Crete, Middle Minoan : Pendlebury, *Arch. of Crete* (1939), 94* ; Late Minoan, 180* (cf. Ch. V). Mycenean Greece : Karo in *Reallexikon* VIII, 389* ; Nilsson, *Homer and Mycenae* (1933)*, with Pendlebury, *op. cit.*, 225 ; Mycenae : Wace, *Antiquity* X, 405, and in Persson, *The Royal Tombs at Dendra* (K.H.V.Lund Skrifter, 1931) ; Shaft-graves : Karo, *Die Schachtgräber von Mykenä* (1930). Further bibliography : Childe, *Dawn*², 77-8 ; and see under Ch. IV. 1, above. Fall of Knossos : Pendlebury, *op. cit.*, 228.

Chapter VIII

Troy VI : Childe, *Dawn*², 45* ; and see under Ch. IV, 2, above. Russia: Childe, *Dawn*², 201*. Danubian countries : see under Ch. VII, with Willvonseder, *Die Mittlere Bronzezeit in Österreich* (1937)* ; J. Böhm, *Základy Hallstattské Periody v Čechách* (1937)*, for rise of Tumulus cultures (cf. Childe, *Danube*, ch. XV*). C., E. Germany, Lausitz, Poland : W. Böhm, *Die ältere Bronzezeit in der Mark Brandenburg* (1935) ; Richthofen, *Die ältere Bronzezeit in Schlesien* (1926) ; (Poland) *Reallexikon* X, 191. Northern Early Bronze Age : Forssander, *Ostskand. Norden*, ch. III* ; Kersten, *Zur älteren nordischen Bronzezeit* (1936) ; Schwantes, in *Geschichte Schleswig-Holsteins* I ; Brøndsted, *Danmarks Oldtid* II, *Bronzeälder* (1939) ; Šturms, *Die Bronzezeit im Ostbaltikum* (1936). British boat-coffin burials : Loose Howe to be published by Dr. and Mrs. Elgee in *Antiquity* shortly. W. Germany, latest contribution : Holste, *Die Bronzezeit im nordmainischen Hessen* (1939). France, Tumulus culture : (Alsace) Schaeffer, *Les Tertres funéraires préhistoriques de la Forêt de Haguenau* I (1926) ; (Vosges) *B.S.P.F.*

XXXV, 426; (Lorraine), Beaupré, *Études préhist. en Lorraine* (1902), 29; (Jura) Piroutet, *Congrès Préhist. de France*, Lons-le-Saunier 1913, 375; (Burgundy) F. Henry, *Les Tumulus du Dépt. de la Côte d'Or* (1933), 22, 26; (bronze types and distributions) M. Dunlop, *L'Anthr.* 48, 457* ; 49, 35*. Dawn of British Middle Bronze Age : Piggott, *P.P.S.* IV, 60, 90. Ireland, metallurgy ; Maryon, *P.R.I.A.* XLIV, C, 181. Irish Sea in relation to Bronze Age culture : Lily F. Chitty in *Archaeologia Cambrensis* (forthcoming)*. Most recent general survey of European Bronze Age : Forssander, *K.H.V.Lund Årsberättelse* 1938-39, III, 38-111.

INDEX

Abbeville 14
Abbevillian culture 14-15, 18
Abingdon 144
Abri Audi 27
Abydos 348
Acheulian culture 12, 15-18, 19-24, 26-7
Acton 19, 26
Addington 213
Adlerberg culture 302-3, 311, 314, 367, 378
adzes 77, 80-1, 94, 110, 116, 123, 163
Aegean 76-7, 80-1, 86-90, 94, 114-15, 149 ff., 222-5, 238 ff., 246, 291, 304-5, 348 ff., *and see* Crete, Cyclades, Greece
Aegina 349, 354
Aesch 198
Africa 4-6, 10-11, 15, 17, 24-7, 35, 43-7, 51, 71-2, 77-9, 81-4, 86-7, 125-131
agriculture, 70 ff., 80 ff., 87, 91-2, 94, 98-9, 102, 110, 112, 117-23, 127, 129, 134, 136, 141-2, 148, 163, 174, 177-8, 197, 199, 205-6, 208-9, 216, 236, 255, 272, 289-90, 296-301, 306, 327, 332, 335-6, 338-40, 374, 380
Ahrensburg culture 49, 52-4, 56
Aichbühl 112, 119-21, 134, 137-8, 244-5
Alaca Höyük 222
Alcalá 161, 192, 216, 248
Aldbourne 315, 331, 346
Alishar 107
Allerød climate-phase 52, 56
Almeria 83, 128-31, 148, 160 ff., 251-2, 262, 279, 303-4, 306-8, 313, 346, 368
Almizaraque 160-1, 183
Alpine race 32-3, 51, 381
Alps 6, 7-8, 15, 35, 69, 119, 128, 133-7, 244 ff., 278, 292, 294, 303-4, 309-10, 333 ff., 350, 359
Alsace 117, 119, 123, 137, 158-9, 257, 311, 367
Alsfeld 257, 272

Alt R. 102-3, 108, 235, 296
Altamira 40
Altenburg 136
Altheim culture 245-7, 249, 360
Al 'Ubaid 73, 75
amber 163, 181, 205, 212, 215, 217-18, 255, 264, 323 ff., 331, 338, 346, 350, 353, 376-7, 380
Amber Route 327-8, 330, 345, 349, 361, 366
Amenhotep III 348, 356
Amorgos 165
Amratian culture 78
amulets 85, 134
Anatolia 4, 28, 51, 75-7, 80-1, 86, 88-91, 93-4, 96-7, 103-4, 107, 115-16, 150, 222-3, 226, 238-42, 291, 296, 349
Ancylus Lake 56, 59
Angelu Ruju 155, 157, 171, 194, 252, 262
Ante 123
Antequera 161, 168, 192
antler implements, reindeer 30, 33, 41, 49, 53-4 ; red deer 48-9, 59-65, 93, 101, 103, 116, 133, 136, 142, 235, 246, 304-5, 364, 374, *and see* axes, axe-sleeves, picks
Apennine culture 334 ff., 347, 359, 379
Apennines 334 ff.
Arbor Low 321
Arctic culture 62, 69, 200, 205, 231, *and see* Finland, Norway, Sweden
Aristotle 1
Arles tombs 198, 262-3, 275
Arminghall 274
Arnstadt 302
Arpachiyah 73, 149, 153
Arquà 250, 334
Arraiolos 162
Arreton Down 374
arrowheads 119, 125, 130, 136, 221, 254, 278, 307, 310 ; barbed and tanged 130-2, 161, 165, 252, 263, 267-8, 277, 279, 312-15 ; hollow-based 77, 130, 161, 165, 184 ; leaf-shaped 78, 130-2, 142-3, 161,

398

165, 213, 263 ; tanged 204, 215, 247, 309 ; transverse 61, 62, 66, 68, 142-4, 215, 260-1, 272, 374 ; triangular 134, 247

arrow-points, copper 'Palmella' 163, 165, 267

arrowshaft-smoothers 347, 350

Aryan languages 64, 232-3, 239-40, 370, 375, 381-3

Arzabal 172

Asia 4-6, 10-11, 24-5, 27-8, 30-1, 39, 51-2, 64, 70, 86

Asia Minor, *see* Anatolia

Assyria 73, 75-6, 149

Asturian culture 63, 68-9

Aterian culture 45

Athens 354

Atlantic climate-phase 57, 60, 64, 66-8, 71, 117, 132-3, 141-2, 144, 200, 269, 288-90

Atlantic sea-route 169, 173 ff., 211-213, 216, 266, 288, 305-8, 324, 369

Atlas 4, 45, 82, 125, 127

Attersee 245-6

Aunjetitz culture 256, 293-303, 305, 308-11, 314, 316, 325 ff., 330-3, 340, 344 ff., 364, 366, 370-1, 377, 379

Aurignacian cultures 12, 25 ; Lower 26, *and see* Châtelperron ; Middle 27-32, 39 ; Upper 27-8, 45, *and see* Gravette

Austria, palaeolithic 28, 30, 39 ; mesolithic 65 ; neolithic 111, 116, 234, 244-6, 249 ; bronze age 298 ff., 330, 333, 342, 345-6, 359-60

Availles 173

Avas culture 65

Avebury 267-8, 272, 276, 316

Avila 165

axe-adzes 104, 150, 221, 225, 234, 238, 242-3

axe-hammers 223-5, 242-3, 277, 279, 296, 377, *and see* battle-axes, knob-hammer axes

axes, antler (and hafts) 49, 53-4, 61, 63, 223-5 ; bronze 150, 279, 296, 301, 307, 310, 312-15, 325 ff., 328 ff., 334-5, 338, 340, 361, 377 ; copper 73, 88-9, 92, 104-5, 150, 161, 165, 184, 190, 210-11, 215, 219, 232, 242-3, 246-8, 290, 307, 310, 325 ff., *and see* axes, shaft-hole, axe-adzes, battle-axes, double-axes ; shaft-hole, 73, 150, 211-12, 215, 217, 218 ff., 223 ff., 239, 264-5, 305, 358, *and see* axe-adzes, axe-hammers, battle-axes, chopper-

axes, double-axes, knob-hammer axes ; stone, flint 49, 53-4, 58-9, 61-2, 63, 65, 66-7, 68-9, 73, 77-8, 80, 81-4, 88, 92, 105, 125, 127, 129, 131-6, 140, 142-3, 146-7, 184, 188, 204-5, 210-17, 213, 218-19, 220, 228, 231, 234, 236, 248, 256, 258-61, 263-4, 267-8, 280-1, 310, 312, 324, 334

axe-sleeves, antler 49, 59, 63, 65, 133-6, 142, 244-5, 263

Azilian culture 41, 47-8, 49, 50-1, 64-8

Azov, Sea of 220

Baalberg barrow 228, 302

Baalberg culture 208, 214, 219, 227, 249, 281, 301

Badarian culture 78-9, 85

Baden culture 209, 234, 237, 241, 243, 299-300, 333, 342, 345, 360

Baker's Hole 18, 19

Balearic Is. 262-3, 305

Ballyalton 196

Ballynagard 197

Ballynamona 194

Baltic end-moraine 54

Baltinglass 190

Banat 95, 292

Bandkeramik, *see* pottery, Danubian Neolithic

Bann River culture 197 ; axe-hammers 377

barley 71-2

Barnham gravels 17

barns 117-18, 120-3

Barroso 168

barrows, long 145-8, 174-6, 179-82, 184, 187, 193-5, 212, 259, 264-5, 270, *and see* burials, cairns, megaliths

barrows, round 145, 166, 218, 225, 228, 233-4, 238-9, 241, 249, 258-9, 266 ff., 274 ff., 282, 296, 299-302, 311 ff., 315 ff., 322, 328, 333, 342, 357-63, 365 ff., 373 ff., 379, *and see* burials, cairns, kurgans, single-graves

basketry 74-5, 77, 80, 82, 84, 127, 134, 204, 214, 217, 219

Basques 368

battle-axes 218-19, 220 ff., 223 ff., 250, 258, 277, 279, 281, 336, 358, 364, 379, *and see* boat-axes

Bavaria 48, 51, 65, 111, 116, 118-19, 245 ff., 254, 301, 360, 367, 371

Baven 365

Beacharra 176-80, 190-6

beads, amber 212, 215, 217, 323-4,

328, 346, 350; bronze 348; copper 94, 104, 222, 263; faience 308, 345-50, 353, 361, 369, 375, 378; glass 346; gold 263, 348, 378; tin, 346, 348
Beaker people 164-7, 244, 250 ff., 257 ff., 265-6, 287-8, 299-302, 304, 306; in Britain 266 ff., 316 ff., 332-45, 367, 369 ff., and see pottery, (Bell-) Beaker
Belgium, palaeolithic 17, 23, 34; mesolithic 50, 52, 63, 65, 67-8; neolithic 121-2, 132, 137-8, 144-5, 261; brcnze age 324
Bernburg, see Walternienburg
Bigum 255, 280
Bijelo Brdo 34⁻
Bilce 236
Birseck 253
bison 37, 40-2
bits 341
Bize 131, 158
black earth 81, 98-9, 109-10, 203
Blackpatch 140
blade cultures, industries 12, 20-1, 25-8, 29, 30-5
blades, palaeolithic 20, 24, 26, 28-30, 32, 34; mesolithic 46-7, 50, 58, 61-2; neolithic 73, 77-8, 93, 116, 127
Bloksbjerg 64
boat-axes 227-31, 282
Bodrogkeresztur culture 108, 241-3, 246
Böheimkirchen culture 300, 333, 342, 360
Bohemia, mesolithic 65
neolithic 111 ff., 118 ff., 137, 208-9, 230, 234, 244, 246-7, 249 and chalcolithic 254-7, 278
bronze age 256, 293 ff., 326-7, 332, 346, 360-1, 379
Bohuslän 171, 214
Boian A culture 97-8, 102-3, 108
Boitsfort 137-8
bone implements 28 ff., 48 ff., 77, 101, 111, 113, 116, 126-7, 131, 134, 140, 142, 174, 198, 204, 235-6, 246, 296, 301, 364
Boquique 128, 164, 191
Boreal climate-phase 57-60, 71, 141
Borg-en-Nadur 154-5
Bornholm 201, 206, 231
Borodino 226, 358
Bottendorf 248
boulder-clays 7 ff.; E. Anglian lower 15; middle 15-16, 20; upper 20; brown 33
Bounias 263, 275

Boun-Marcou 251
bows 42-3, 136, 254, 277
Brabrand 205
bracers 165, 252, 254, 256, 267-8, 277, 281, 296, 307
Bramford 13
Brassempouy 39
Breach Farm 318
Breckland (Clactonian) 17
Brenner Pass 253, 289, 327
brick-earth 9 ff., 15-16, 20
Britain, palaeolithic 12 ff., 19-22, 24, 26, 29, 31-4, 38, 41-2, 50
mesolithic 49-50, 56, 59, 63, 66-67, 69-70
neolithic A 132, 138-48, 175 ff., 202, 213, 267, 269-70, 316, 372-3
neolithic B 140-4, 190, 201-2, 204, 213, 267, 269, 271-2, 276, 316-20
bronze age 266 ff., 303, 315 ff., 346-8, 363, 366-7, 369 ff., 372-4, 378
Brittany 68-9, 146-8, 173 ff., 264 ff., 291, 303, 311-16, 324, 346, 368, 371-3, 378
Britz 281
Brodgar 275, 321
Bronegger 271
bronze 130, 215, 223, 239, 241, 264, 279, 284, 290 ff., 304, 307 ff., 323 ff., 332 ff., 361, 364, 374
Bronze Age defined 284 ff.
brooches 339
Browndod 196
Broxbourne 59
Brundon 22
Bruniquel 41-2
Brünn 30; 'race' 31-2
Bryn Celli Ddu 188
Bryn yr Hen Bobl 267
Bükk culture 112-16
Bulgaria, palaeolithic 28; neolithic 97, 103, 108; and chalcolithic 235-8, 358
burials, palaeolithic 38; mesolithic 68-9, 174-5, 186
neolithic, chalcolithic: Beaker 166, 190, 252 ff., 257 ff., 266 ff., 320 ff., and see bronze age, British; British 145; cave 126, 130, 172-3, 261, 309; collective 130, 146-8, 149 ff., 170 ff., 211 ff., 263 ff., 306, 309, 322, 376; Danubian 124, 242; French 173; Iberian 130-1; Italian 126, 130, 250-4; Michelsberg 138; Northern 206 ff., 217 ff; ochre-graves 38, 220 ff., 225, 234

bronze age : British 266 ff., 315 ff., 371 ff. ; Danubian 293 ff., 328 ff., 357 ff. ; French 310 ff., 367-8, 371-2 ; Iberian 306-8 ; Italian 335 ff ; Mycenean 350 ff. ; Northern 362 ff., *and see* barrows, cairns, catacomb-graves, cists, coffins, cremation, dolmens, gallery-graves, inhumation, kurgans, megaliths, passage-graves, shaft-graves, single-graves, tombs, urnfields
Butmir 114, 151, 157-8
Butterwick 279
Byblos 294
Bygholm 215, 248

Cabecinha 171
Caberg 121-2
Caddington 19-20
Ca' di Marco 253
Cairnholy 176
cairns, horned 180, 187, 193-7, 263, 276 ; long 179-80, 193-8, 212-13 ; round 130, 160, 167, 170, 175-6, 182, 188-90, 192, 194, 212, 312, 315, 320, 322, 376, *and see* barrows
Calais Wold 274
callais 163, 165, 181, 263-4, 308
Calvatone 334
Camerton 331
'Campignian' culture 67, 133, 138, 140, 197
Campos 129-30
Camster 192
Canyaret 131
Capsa 45
Capsian culture 25, 35, 44-7, 51, 71, 127
Carlingford Lough 196
Carmona 163-4
Carnac 264-5, 346
Carnanmore 191
Carn Ban 193, 195
Carn Brea 146
Carrowkeel 189-90
Carrowmore 189
Cashtal yn Ard 195-6
Castellaro di Gottolengo 339
Castellazzo di Fontanellato 338-9
Castellet 263
Castelluccio 152, 154
Castione dei Marchese 339
Castro-Marim 307
catacomb-graves 222 ff., 255
Catalonia 32, 128, 130-1, 166-7, 169-73, 251, 304, 307, 319
Cataragna 334

Catenoy 159, 185
cattle 72-3, 77-8, 99, 110, 127, 134, 142, 201, 237, 335, *and see* pastoralism
Caucasus 220-7, 230-1
caves, palaeolithic 21 ff., 25 ff., 36 ff. ; mesolithic 46-8, 50-2, 64-6, 68 ; neolithic, chalcolithic 82-4, 112, 125-8, 130-2, 156-8, 163-7, 191, 244, 251-2, 254, 261, 309, 311, 335, 368
bronze age 335, 359, 368
Cella Dati 334
Celts 363, 369 ff., 376-8
cemeteries, *see* burials, urnfields
Chaeronea 79
Chalain 133-5
Chalcis 354
Chalcolithic defined 76, 152, 250
Chambéry 133
Chamblandes culture 253, 310
Charente R. 173, 368
chariots 237, 352
Chassey 132-5, 158, 167, 185, 261, 314
Châtelperron, Chatelperronian culture 27-8, 29-31, 40, 43, 45
Chelles 14
'Chellian' culture 12, 14
Chilham 213
Chilterns 20
chisels 215
Chodoun-Zeleny 361
chopper-axes 223-4, 242
Christchurch 266
Ciempozuelos 165-6 ; dagger-type 164-5, 252-4, 263, 267-8, 278, 281
Cilicia 73, 77, 80
circles, stone 160, 186-7, 193-4, 265, 267, 275-6, 316-17, 321-2, 375-6
wood 274-6, 316-17
Cissbury 138
cists, stone 130-1, 147, 148-9, 167, 169-70, 172-6, 179-82, 184, 190-1, 195-9, 212 ff., 217, 221-3, 228, 234, 239, 253, 257, 262-4, 270, 282-3, 306-8, 310, 320, 325-7, 333, 351, 365
segmented 172-3, 176-7, 179-81, 192-6
Clachaig 176, 195
Clacton 16, 141-2, 272
Clactonian culture 16-21
Clandon 324
Clapton, Lower 19
Clava 321
Clettraval 192
climate, glacial and inter-glacial 5, 7-11, 12-13, 20-8, 30-5, 41, 44-6, 71

post-glacial 44 ff., 54 ff., 200 ff.,
  and see Atlantic, Boreal, Sub-
  Boreal
Clonlum 196
coffins 237, 351, 365-6, 378
Coldrum 213
Cologne 117, 123, 137, *and see*
  Köln-Lindenthal
Combe-Capelle 21-2, 31-2
combs 134, 145
Conguel 181, 183
Constance, L. 136-7, 245
Coombe Hill 139, 142
Coombe Rock 18
Coppa della Nevigata 336
copper 73, 76, 78, 85, 87-9, 92, 94,
  98, 104, 115, 128-9, 136-7, 150-1,
  155, 161, 163-5, 184, 190, 210-11,
  215, 220 ff., 232 ff., 246 ff., 252 ff.,
  263-5, 267-8, 278-80, 285 ff.,
  303 ff., 310 ff., 318, 323 ff., 351,
  358
core cultures, industries 12-13, 14 ff.,
  19-25, 27
Cornwall 146, 176, 178, 291, 318,
  323-4, 378
Cortaillod culture 134-6, 244-5, 249
Coţofeni culture 234-5, 237-8
Cotswolds, *see* Severn-Cotswold
Cotte de St. Brelade 22
Cova d'en Daina 170-1
crag deposits 13-14
Cranves 257, 262
Crayford 20
Creevykeel 195, 197
cremation 124, 138, 145, 196, 312,
  315, 338, 340, 342 ff., 357 ff., 362,
  373 ff.
Cressingham 318
Creswell Crags 22, 29, 31, 34, 41-2,
  50, 63
Creswellian culture 34-5, 50, 63
Crete 77, 80, 84, 86-7, 89, 125
  Early Minoan 79, 87-8, 90, 107,
  115-16, 129-30, 148-50, 156, 222-
  223, 225, 292
  Middle Minoan 152, 240-1, 291,
  304, 348 ff.
  Late Minoan 152, 240, 351 ff.,
  377, 382-3
Crimea 28, 30, 64, 221
Crisa 291, 351
Croh-collé 186
Crô-magnon skull-type 24-5, 28, 31,
  124
Cromer 14-16
Crucuny 175
Crufensee 249
Csoka 224

Cucuteni 100-8, 113-15, 225, 235-7,
  242, 297
culture (general) : beginning of 3-4 ;
  and evolution 4, 6, 10-11, 384 ;
  dawn of civilization 70 ff.
Cyclades, Cycladic culture 79, 88-90,
  149-51, 153-6, 160, 165, 167,
  222-3, 238-40, 291, 349
Cyprus 80-1, 165, 246, 294-5, 355,
  378

daggers, bronze 150, 241, 279, 296,
  301, 307, 309, 310-15, 318, 325 ff.,
  328 ff., 331, 334-5, 338, 340, 352,
  361, 377
  copper 88-9, 150, 161, 164-6,
  184, 215-16, 221, 237, 242-3,
  246-8, 252-4, 263, 267-8, 278-80,
  295, 307, 309-10
  flint 161, 189, 247, 273-83, 309,
  324-6
  silver 358
Daniglacial 54
' Danordic ' 209
Danube R. 80, 92, 94-7, 99, 103-6,
  108 ff., 293 ff., 327, 330, 333, 359
Danubian cultures, neolithic 109 ff.,
  136-7, 205, 208-11, 214, 227, 233
  copper age 108, 209, 224, 230,
  234, 241 ff., 278, 281, 291 ff.
  bronze age 293 ff., 332-3, 341 ff.,
  357 ff.
Danubian glaciations 7
Darmsden pebble-implements 13
Decia 234
Deerpark 197
Delphi 291
Dendra 353-4
Denmark, mesolithic 49, 53-64, 66-7,
  76, 200-1
  neolithic 200 ff., 213 ff., 223,
  229-31, 252, 255, 258, 279, 281-3,
  320
  and bronze age 324 ff., 329,
  364-6, *and see* Jutland, Zealand
De Soto 168, 183
Devil's Tower 21, 26, 29
Dieskau 328, 330
Dietzenley 258
Dikilitash 103
Dimini 101, 105-8, 126, 151, 239
Dinaric 101
Doberschau 248
Dogger Bank 56
dogs 59, 134, 142
dolmens 169-70, 171, 172-4, 176,
  178-81, 187-8, 190-1, 195, 200,
  206, 211-13, 251, 262-3, 277, 309,
  329, 337

domestication, *see* pastoralism
Don R. 221-2, 230, 255
Donetz R. 222, 226, 230, 255
Dordogne R. 21, 25, 29, 42, 314
Dorians 383
double-axes, bronze 215, 265, 328
copper 150, 215, 223, 265
stone 215, 217, 264-5
symbol 150, 188, 215, 377
Doune 191, 320
Drachmani 238
Drave R. 114, 298, 333, 342
Drenthe 213, 216-17, 259, 271, 345, 367
Dryas flora 56
Dullenried 245
Durfort 311
Duvensee 58, 60

East Anglia, palaeolithic 13-17, 19-20, 22, 23, *otherwise see* Britain
Easton Down 138-40, 267
Ebbsfleet 22
Egypt, prehistoric, predynastic 45, 70-2, 75, 77-9, 82-3, 85, 125, 127, 129, 136, 148
dynastic 86-7, 129-30, 149, 240-1, 294, 345-9, 355-6, 366, 382
Ehenside Tarn 143, 196
Ehringsdorf 23
Eilean na Tighe 191
Elam 73, 75-6
El Argar culture 307-9, 313, 329, 346, 368
Elbe R. 117, 137, 208, 210, 214, 217-19, 227, 230, 248, 255-6, 258-9, 280-2, 298, 326, 364-7
Elbe-Weser culture 214-17, 219
El Garcel 69, 83-4, 128-9, 131
Ellerbek 206
El Oficio 307, 313
El Sotillo 24
Elster glaciation 8
Emmen 195
Ems-land 213, 216-17, 259 ff., 367
Enkomi 378
Ensdorf 65
eoliths 12-13
Erd 243
Er Lannic 183, 186, 265
Erösd 102-8, 113, 115-16, 225, 235, 239
Ertebølle culture 60-4, 66, 68, 76, 133, 178, 200-7, 211, 271
Essex coast 141-2, 269-73
Esthonia 59, 62
Etruscans 359, 383
Euboea 149-51, 171
Eutresis 238, 240

evolution 2-4, 10, 12, 384
Exloo 345

faience 308, 345-50, 361, 369, 375
Falaise 251
Falkenstein 48, 63, 65
Falkenwalde 279, 325-6
Farnham 67
Fatyanovo culture 224, 228-31, 358
fauna (wild), pleistocene 13-16, 18, 20, 23, 32, 34, 36-7, 39
in mesolithic 48, 53, 55-7, 59-61, 62, 68-9
Fayûm 77-9, 82, 129
Fedeleseni 102
Federsee 65, 119
Felanitx 262
Feldkirch 257
Fenno-Scandian moraines 54-5, 58
Fens 141-2, 144, 269-70, 320
Feuersbrunn 330
figurines, *see* statuettes
Filottrano 336, 347
Fimon 250, 334
Finiglacial 54, 56-7
Finland, mesolithic 55, 62, 200
neolithic 202-4, 228, 231, 359, 364
Finmark 57-8
Finno-Ugrian 364
Fjaelkinge 326
flake-cultures, industries 12-13, 16-19, 20-4, 26-7
Flandrian sea-transgression 56, 68
flax 134
flint implements, palaeolithic, meso-lithic, Chs. I-III *passim.*; later: 93-4, 98, 101, 111, 113, 127, 131, 133-4, 138, 142, 161, 163, 174, 198, 201, 204, 223, 235-6, 242, 244, 246, 254, 263, 278-80, 296, 304, 309, 329, 334, 364, 374, *and see* arrowheads, axes, blades, core, eoliths, flake, gravers, halberds, hand-axes, laurel-leaf, microliths, microburins, picks, rostro-carin-ates, scrapers, sickles, shouldered, tanged points, tortoise-cores, wil-low-leaf; Grand Pressigny 186, 263-4, 278, 311-12
flint-mines 138-40, 142, 267
Flomborn 118
Folkton drums 378
Fontaine-le-Puits 310
Font-de-Gaume 40
Font del Roure 170-1
Fontenay-le-Marmion 185
Font-Robert 29, 31-2

forecourts (tomb-) 160, 171, 186-7, 193-7, 321, *and see* circles, stone
forest 41, 48, 52-4, 56-7, 60-2, 64, 69-70, 76, 117, 119, 133, 141, 200-1, 203-4, 231, 261, 273, 288 ff., 343, 358-9
Forest Cultures (N. Europe) 54, 58-64, 65, 67, 69-70, 76, 132-3, 200 ff.
Fort-Harrouard 159, 185-6, 261
fortification 102, 105, 118, 120-2, 126, 129, 132, 136-7, 142-6, 150, 173-4, 186, 235, 246, 258, 306-7, 338-9, 356, 358
Fosna culture 57, 204
Foxhall 13
France, palaeolithic 14-21, 21-5, 25-34, 39-41, 42
  mesolithic 47-8, 49-51, 59, 65-7, 68-70
  neolithic 122-3, 128, 130, 131 ff., 158-9, 165, 167, 169-70
  and chalcolithic 172 ff., 250 ff., 257, 260 ff., 264-6, 275, 283, 303-304, 308-12, 333
  bronze age 303, 310-14, 324, 328, 330, 367-8, 370 ff., 378
Frankenthal 257
Frejlev 223, 229
Frosinone 305
Fuente Alamo 307, 346, 369
Fuente Vermeja 307
Fulda 258

Gafsa 45
Gagarino 29-30, 37
Galich 358
Galicia 99, 111, 203, 208-9, 225-6, 228, 230, 234, 236-7
Galicia (Spain) 166, 169, 182, 188, 307
gallery-graves 170, 172-5, 182, 184, 187, 193-4, 195, 196, 212, 259-60, 263-4, 308-9
Garda L. 334, 339
Garnes 204
Garton Slack 145
Gata 299
Gavr'inis 188-9
Geleen 121
geochronology 55 ff.
Germans 364-7, 371, 379, 381
Germany, palaeolithic 14-15, 17-18, 22-3, 34-5
Germany, Central, mesolithic 64
  neolithic 111-12, 116-19, 137, 205 ff., 218-19, 227 ff., 256-8, 274, 280-1
  bronze age 292 ff., 301-2, 328-330, 361-4, 370-1, 379

Germany, East, mesolithic 64-5
  neolithic, 111-12, 116 ff., 205 ff., 219, 227 ff., 255, 280-2
  bronze age 301-2, 330, 362-4, 379
Germany, North, mesolithic, 49, 52-4, 58, 60
  neolithic 117, 205 ff., 217-19, 227 ff., 258 ff., 270, 274, 277-83
  and bronze age 324 ff., 329, 362-7, 370 ff., 379
Germany, Rhineland, neolithic 111 ff., 117 ff., 136-8, 249, 257 ff., 270-2, 277-8
  bronze age 302-3, 367 ff., 378
Germany, South, mesolithic 48, 51, 63, 64-5
  neolithic 116 ff., 136-8, 144, 244-9, 254, 257-8
  bronze age 301-2, 360, 367, 370-1, 378
Gerzean culture 78-9, 127
Get 171
Gibraltar 22-3, 26, 29, 79, 127, 130 ; Straits of 24, 45, 125-6
Gigantea 153
Gingst 208
glaciations 5, 7 ff.
Glina 97-8, 235
Globe-amphora (-flask) people 213, 226-30, 232, 249, 281-2, 301-2, 364
gold 85, 88, 94, 104, 106, 150, 161, 163, 184, 190, 221-2, 226, 255, 286, 292, 294-7, 304, 311, 314-16, 323-4, 326, 330-1, 345, 347, 350, 352 ff., 358, 377-8, 380
Goldberg 119, 137-8, 245, 249
Gor 161, 168, 171
Gotiglacial 54-5
Gottorf 365
gouges 215
gourd 74-5
Gournia 355
Goward 196
Gozo 153
Graig Lwyd 267
Gramat 66
gravels 7 ff.
gravers (burins), palaeolithic 20, 24, 26, 28-30, 33
  mesolithic 46-9, 52, 58-9, 63
  neolithic 133
graves, *see* burials
Gravette, Gravettian culture 29, 30-5, 39-40, 50-1, 54, *and see* Creswellian, Font-Robert, Grimaldian ; East-Gravettian, 31-5, 52, 54, 64, 105, 233 ; West-Gravettian 31-3

Greece, Early Helladic 89-90, 149-151, 238-9
  Middle Helladic 239-41, 250, 288, 291, 350-1
  Mycenean 349 ff., 357-8, 377 ff., 382-3, *and see* Thessaly
Greeks 240, 356, 379, 382-3 ; Greek colonization 359, 383
Griesheim 257
Grimaldi caves 38, 50, 69
Grimaldian culture 34, 69
Grime's Graves 140, 143
grinding-stones 72, 123, 127, 133, 136, 142, 174, 177, 220
Gristhorpe 366
Grotte des Fées 263
Grovehurst 213, 271-2
Grünhof 365
Guardistallo 243, 250
Guadix 168
Gudenaa culture 60-1, 64, 218
Guernsey 198, 264
Gumelnitza culture 103-5, 108, 225, 235, 238, 358
Günz glaciation 7, 14

Hagia Marina 238
Hagia Triada 354
Hagiar Kim 153
Haguenau 367
halberds 304-5, 307-8, 313, 329-32, 347, 350, 352, 361, 377
Haldon 146
Haldorf 248
Halstow, Lower 63, 67, 133, 140, 202
Hal Saflieni 153-4
Hal Tarxien 153-4, 194
Hamburg culture 34-5, 49, 52
Hammeldon Down 315
hand-axes 13, 14 ff., 19, 20, 21-5, 27
Hanging Grimston 145
Harageh 348
Harlyn Bay 324
harpoons 29, 33, 35, 48, 49, 59, 65, 77, 93, 103
Harrow Hill 138-9
Harz 208, 214, 217, 227, 302
Havel, *see* Walternienburg
Havnelev 206
Hayland House 144
Hebrides 191-2
Heidelberg man 10, 14
Helmsdorf 328, 365
Helperthorpe 279
Hembury 146
Hengelo skull 54
Herkheim 122
Herodotus 380

Hessen 256-7, 260, 367
High Lodge industry 16, 19
Hinkelstein 112, 121, 124, 137
Hissarlik 76, *and see* Troy
Hittites 239, 352
Hjelm 171
hoes 73, 80, 94, 99, 110, 113, 116, 123, 136, 236
Hohle Stein 48, 52
Holdenhurst 146, 175
Holland, palaeolithic 54
  mesolithic 66
  neolithic 121-2, 213, 216-17, 258-9, 268, 270-8
  bronze age 345, 367, 369 ff.
Holmegaard 58-60
Homer 354, 358, 380, 382
homo sapiens 10-12, 17, 23-4, 27-8, 31-2
Homolka 246
Horgen culture 135, 198, 244-5, 249
Hornsea 49, 59
Horodnycja 236
horses 30, 32-3, 37, 99, 237, 341-3
Horsham culture 67
houses 37, 65, 67, 73, 80, 87, 94, 99, 102, 105, 110, 117-20, 122-4, 126, 133-4, 136, 138, 142, 145-6, 201, 205, 216, 236, 239, 241, 245, 248, 306, 320-1, 334-5, 338, 340-1, 354-6
  mortuary 365
Hove 318, 324, 366
Hoxne 19-20
Hoyo de la Mina 46, 127
Hungary, palaeolithic 27-8, 32
  mesolithic 65, 69
  neolithic 95 ff., 109 ff., 224, 233-5
  copper age 224-5, 234-5, 241 ff., 246 ff., 255, 291 ff.
  bronze age 256, 293 ff., 332-3, 341 ff., 347, 357-61, 366, 379
Huns'-beds 213, 216-17, 259-60, 271, 367
hunting 6, 12 ff., 35 ff., 44 ff., 57, 70 ff., 119, 127, 134, 141, 144, 200-5, 209, 272, 364, 374, 379-80
Hyksos 349
Hyperboreans, 380

Iberians 129-30, 368
' Ibero-Maurusian,' *see* Oranian
Ice Age 5, 7 ff.
Icklingham 373
idols, Cycladic, Anatolian 89, 94, 150, 156 ; Iberian 160-3, 183, 188, 324 ; *and see* statuettes
Île Longue 182

Illyrians 363-4, 379
India 25, 76
Indo-European, *see* Aryan
ingot torcs 294-7, 310, 325, 328
inhumation 124, 138, 145 ff., 148 ff.,
    166 ff., 170 ff., 211 ff., 218 ff.,
    233 ff., 239, 242, 252 ff., 257 ff.,
    264 ff., 281 ff., 293 ff., 306 ff.,
    310-16, 322, 337, 341, 345, 373 ff.,
    and see burials
Ipswich 13, 22
Iran 25, 28, 73
Ireland, mesolithic 34, 67-8, 177,
    190, 329
    neolithic, chalcolithic 176 ff.,
    263, 276-7, 322-3
    bronze age 279, 322 ff., 328-32,
    347, 350, 371 ff., 376 ff.
Isopata 353
Italy, palaeolithic 23, 34, 39, 50
    mesolithic 50, 68-70, 84
Italy, North, neolithic 128, 131-2,
    136, 156-8
    chalcolithic 157, 159, 165, 215,
    243, 247, 250-4, 278, 292, 303, 334
    bronze age 303-5, 309-11, 326-
    327, 330, 333 ff., 350, 359, 368,
    370, 379
Italy, South, neolithic 84, 125-6,
    152, 155-7
    chalcolithic 135-7, 167
    bronze age 334 ff., 355, 359
Izvoare 98, 100, 104

Jackovica 230
Jäkärlä 203
Jära Bank 270
Jersey 22, 185, 264
jet 163 ; necklaces 323-4
Jirikovice 345
Jordansmühl 112, 116, 118, 122, 124,
    137, 209-10, 213, 215, 224, 242,
    244, 246-7, 281
Jura 122, 133, 311, 367
Jutland, mesolithic 53-4, 57, 58, 60-1
    neolithic 201, 205, 215-16, 217-
    218, 228, 230, 255, 258, 274, 281-2
    and bronze age 365-6 ; *and see*
    Denmark

Kahun 348
Kakovatos 353
Kanam, Kanjera 11
Karelia 58, 232
Kemp Howe 145
Kenezlö 114
Kenny's Cairn 171, 192
Kenya 45

Kercado 171, 182, 187, 195
Kerlagard 182
Kerlescant 198, 265
Kermarquer 182
Kervilor 183
Kharga Oasis 45
Kharkov 229
Kielce 230
Kiev 99, 230
kilns 75, 162
Kish 73
Kiskörös 243
kitchen-middens, *see* shell-mounds
Kiukais 231
Klampenborg 64
Kličevac 343
Klosterlund 49, 58
knives, bronze 239 ; copper 88,
    242-3
knob-hammer axes, 211-12, 215,
    224-9, 234, 246, 264
Knocknarea 189
Knossos 241, 349, 353-6, 377, 379,
    383
Kökenydomb 98
Köln-Lindenthal 112, 117-18, 120-
    123, 137
Konyar 242
Korakou 89, 240
Körartorp 202
Körös culture-group 95 ff., 109, 113,
    115-16, 234
Košir 246
Kostienki 30, 39
Koszyłowce 236-7
Krapina 23
Krtenov-Smedrova 360
Kuban, Kuban-Terek 220-6, 228
Kujavian graves 212, 228
Kum Tepe 76
Kunda 59
kurgans 220-30, 237, 274, 343, 358,
    379

Labbacallee 194
La Chapelle aux Saintes 23
La Ferrassie 23
Lagazzi 334
La Gerundia 129
La Guillotière 313
La Halliade 174, 309
La Hougue Bie 185, 189
Laibach Moor 245-6, 249, 299, 333,
    342
lake-dwellings 133-7, 243-7, 249-50,
    310, 333-6, 339-40, 359
Lambourn 279
La Micoque 21
La Mujer 127

land- and sea-levels 8 ff., 55 ff., 60 ff., 66 ff., 68-9, 141-2, 145, 200-1, 269-73, 278, 280
Langedijk 275
language 3-4, 70, 232-3, 239-40, 339, 364, 370, 381
Languedoc 172-4, 188, 198, 251, 263, 311
La Pernera 130-1
La Pileta 127
Lapps 51, 365
La Quina 23
Larne 177
Las Carolinas 183
laurel-leaf implements 27, 29, 32, 45, 78
Lausitz 302, 362
Lausitz culture 302, 362-5, 367, 369, 371, 379
Laussel 40
leather vessels 74-5, 77-8, 156, 206
Le Campigny 67, 133, 158, *and see* Campignian
Le Castellic 175
Le Couperon 198
Le Cuzoul 66
Le Grand Pressigny 86, *and see* flint
leister-prongs 59
Le Martinet 50, 66
Le Moustier 19, 21-2
Lengyel 115, 124, 242
Leporano 336
Le Roc 40
Le Rocher (Plougoumelen) 182
Les Buissières 311
Les Eyzies 29
Les Mureaux 135, 261
Lesniczovka 212
Les Pierres Plates 188
Les Trois Frères 41
Leubingen 328, 365
Leukas 151
Levallois, Levalloisian culture 17-18, 19, 20-3, 26 ; technique 18
Liège 50, 67, 121, 138
Liguria 131-2, 156-7, 252-3, 335-6, 359, 368
Ligurians 368
Lihult axe 61, 204
Limhamn 61
Lithuania 330, 362
Litorina sea, transgression 56 ff., 200, 270
Lizo 186
Lloyd's skull (London) 24
Llucmajor 262
Loch Crew 189-90
lock-rings 295, 297, 326, 345
Locmariaquer 165

Locras 247, 265
loess 8 ff., 18, 22, 30, 33, 37, 81, 92, 99, 110, 111, 116-17, 121-2, 203, 208-9, 298, 332, 360
Longhouse 187, 212
long mounds, barrows, *see* barrows, cairns, Huns'-beds, Kujavian graves, megaliths
Loose Howe 366
Los Millares 160-4, 171, 183, 186, 192, 251, 262, 306
Los Murcielagos 127
Los Tollos 129
Lovasberény 342
Lucska 224
Lugansk 226
Lugarico Viejo 279, 307
lunulae 323-4, 347, 377
Lyngby 53, 57 ; axes 49, 53-4

Maastricht 121
Macedonia 80, 90-1, 93, 96, 102-9, 111, 114, 150-1, 234, 238-40, 355, 357-8
mace-heads 61, 63, 212, 213, 218, 234
Mad'arovce culture 299-300, 333, 342, 360
Madrid 24, 166, 183
Maes Howe 192
Magdalenian culture 12, 29, 33-5, 40-1, 42, 43, 46-9, 53, 64
magic 38-43, 84-5, 127, 160, 163, 166, 173, 181, 183, 185-6, 188, 215, 306, 311, 316, 378, 380, *and see* religion
Maglemose culture 49, 58-61, 64, 67, 74
Maiden Bower 144
Maiden Castle 146
Maikop 221-2, 225, 237
Main R. 117, 258
Mainz 121, 137, 257
Majorca 262-3
Malchin 326
Malinmore 197
Malta 84, 153-6, 158-9, 171, 188, 194
Malta (Siberia) 39
mammoth 30, 37 ; ivory 30, 39, 105
Man, I. of 195-7
Mané-Bras 184
Mané-er-Hroëk 188
Mané-Lavarec 182
Mané-Lud 182
Mané-Roullarde 182
Manio 147, 174-5, 186, 195, 265
Manton 331
Maranzais 174, 195
Marendole 337

Mariupol 220-2
Maros R. 95, 234, 292-3
Marschwitz culture 255, 281, 293, 301-2
Mas bou Serenys 170
Mas d'Azil 47
Matarrubilla 161
Matera 126, 336-7
Matrensa 84, 125
Mauer Sands 10, 14-15
Mayen 137-8
Mecklenburg 207-8, 212-13, 216, 326, 364
Mediterranean race 32, 83, 124, 126, 136, 145, 252-3, 381
Mediterranean Sea 4-5, 46, 68-9, 76-7, 83-4, 88, 148 ff., 252 ff., 304-5, 359
Medway R. 213
megaliths, general 168-70 :
　Balearic 262-3
　British 175-80, 184, 187-8, 190-6, 212-13, 263, 276, 316-17, 321, 376
　Danish 169-71, 178-81, 195, 200, 206, 211 ff., 282-3, 365, 376
　Dutch 195, 213, 217, 259, 271, 367
　French, S. and S.W. 167, 169, 172-4, 251, 257, 261-4, 308-9, 311, 368
　　Seine-Oise-Marne 198-9, 260-261, 263
　W. and Breton 169-71, 173-6, 179-89, 193-5, 264-6, 309, 311-14
　German, N. 212 ff., 260, 282-3, 365, 367 ; W. 259-61, 283
　Iberian 167-74, 176, 179-83, 187-9, 192-3, 195-6, 251, 262, 304, 306-7
　Irish 176-8, 188-92, 194-8, 263, 276-7, 322-3, 376
　Sardinian and Corsican 167, 194, 260, 263
　Siculan and S. Italian 152, 167, 337
　Swedish 169-71, 212, 216, 282-283, *and see* barrows, cairns, cists, dolmens, gallery-graves, passage-graves, circles
megaron 102, 105, 119, 239, 341, 354
Meiendorf 34, 52
Melk 346
Melos 77, 79, 88, 240, 349
Mere 267
Merimde 77-9, 129
Mersin 73, 77
Mesolithic cultures 44 ff., 91, 93, 100, 103, 105, 110, 113, 118-19,
121, 126-7, 129, 132-4, 137-8, 141, 144, 147-8, 164, 198, 200-8, 210, 214, 233, 244, 271, 284, 329, 367, 370, 372, 374, 382, 384
　metallurgy 73-4, 78, 85, 91-2, 104-5, 128-9, 148, 150, 160, 178, 184, 199, 221, 224-6, 241-2, 244, 246-7, 284 ff., 290 ff., 302-4, 307-11, 317-18, 323, 325 ff., 329-33, 334-5, 339, 361, 374, 377-80
Mézine 105
Michelsberg culture 136-8, 142, 144-5, 158-9, 244-5, 258, 261, 370
microburins 47-8, 49, 50-1, 59, 68
microliths 46-8, 49, 50-4, 58, 61, 63, 64-9, 73, 83, 127, 129-30, 134, 147, 374
Midhowe 193
Mindel glaciation 7, 15-16
Minorca 263
Miskolcz 65
Mnaidra 153, 171, 194
Mochlos 222
Mola Alta de Serelles 130
Molfetta 126, 336-7
Mondsee 243, 245-6, 249, 299, 333
Montale 339
Montbani 66
Monte Bego 305, 335
Monte Castellaccio 334
Monte Cetona 335-6
Monte Gargano 157
Monteoru 296-8, 333, 343, 358
Monte Racello 152
Montières 20
moraines 7 ff., 14 ff., 46, 54 ff.
Morava R. 94-6, 106
Morava-Vardar 106-9, 111, 114, 150-1
Moravia, palaeolithic 27, 30, 37, 39
　mesolithic 65
　neolithic 109 ff., 208-9, 230, 234, 244, 246, 249
　and chalcolithic 254, 278
　bronze age 293 ff., 327, 332, 345, 360-1
Morges 310
Mother Grundy's Parlour 50, 63
Moulin des Oies 181
Mousterian culture 12, 19, 21-7, 29, 45
Moustoir 184
Moytirra 191
Mugem 69
Mullerup 58
Münchshöfen 112, 116, 118-19, 121
Münzingen 111
Mycenae 347, 350 ff., 377-8

Nagy Rev 293, 296-7
Nagyteteny 113
Nähermemmingen 257, 274
Nalčik 220, 222
Narbonne caves 68, 131, 172, 251
Natufian culture 72
navetas 263
navigation 60, 66, 378, *and see* paddles, ships
Neanderthal man 10, 22-31
Near Eastern civilization 70 ff., 220 ff., 284 ff., 348 ff., 381-4
Neckar R. 117, 121, 137, 244, 258
needles 29, 34
Nemcice 345
neolithic defined 91-2
Nermont 132
Nether Largie 176
Neuchâtel, L. 134-5, 229, 244, 249
Neuenheiligen 328
Neusetz 248
New Grange 171, 183, 189
Niederwil 247, 249
Niezwiska 99, 111
Nordic race 32, 51, 64, 124, 232-3, 381
Normanton 315
Northfleet (Baker's Hole) 18-19
North Sea 15, 56, 59, 67, 141-2, 202, 323, 328, 330, 366, 378
North Sea Drift 15
Norway, mesolithic 57-8, 61-2, 63, 204-5
    neolithic 204-5
    bronze age 364
Nosswitz 208, 214, 219, 227, 249, 281
Nøstvet axe 61, 63, 204
Notgrove 175, 184, 195
Novy Mlyn 52
Nympsfield 184

Ó Beba 294
Obourg 138
obsidian 73, 77, 85, 87, 113, 116, 126, 150, 154, 220, 242
Oder R. 117, 302, 326, 362, 364
Oder culture 255, 281-2, 301-2, 362
Oelsnitz 293
Ofnet 51
Olynthus 102
Omalian 121-2, 132, 137
Opatovice 293
Opfikon 253
Oranian culture 45, 47, 71
Orca dos Juncaes 183
Orchomenos 239-40, 351, 354
Orkney 180, 191-3, 320-1
Ostuni 126

Oszentivan 293, 297, 345
Otomani culture 297-8, 300, 333, 343
Ottitz 116
Oussatova 203, 237
Overton Hill Sanctuary 275-6, 316

paddles, paddle-rudders, 60, 211, 272
Pair-non-pair 40
Palaces 130-1
Palaeolithic 12-43, 384
    Lower 12-18, 19, 36
    Middle 17, 19, 20-5, 29, 36
    Upper 12, 20-1, 24-8, 29-35, 36-43, 233
Palestine 26, 28, 36, 72-3, 80, 378
Palmella 161-6, 183, 322
Parazuelos 129-30
Parc-Guren 182, 346
Parc le Breos Cwm 184
Paros 89
Parpalló 32, 43
passage-graves 160-2, 167-73, 178-182, 184-94, 196-7, 206-7, 212-218, 255, 264-5, 270, 282, 321-3, *and see* tombs
pastoralism 70 ff., 80 ff., 87, 92, 112-13, 118-23, 127, 134, 136, 141-2, 148, 163, 174, 197, 203, 205, 208-9, 216, 233, 236-7, 255, 289-90, 298, 301, 338, 374, 379-80
Paviland 38
Peacock's Farm 141, 269
peats 22, 56-9, 136, 141-2, 269, 289
pebbles, painted 41, 48, 49
Pecska 293
Penker-ar-bloa 174
Pentre Ifan 194
Périgord 28, 30-1, 50, 66, 68
Perjamos 235, 293-300, 332, 343-5, 357
Pernau 59
Pertosa 336
Peterborough 140, 202, *and see* Britain, neolithic B
Petreni 236
Peu-Richard 173-4
Phaestos 241, 354
Phoenicians 369, 383
Phrygians 363
Phylakopi 88, 240, 349
Pianello di Genga 335-6
picks, antler 134, 140, 143, 304-5
    flint, stone 63, 67, 68, 84, 133, 138, 161, 305
pigs 77, 99, 110, 134, 142, 237
Pile 279, 325
pile-dwellings, *see* lake-dwellings

Piltdown skull 11
Pin Hole cave 22, 29, 31, 36, 42
Pinnacle Rock 185
pins, bone 223, 247, 297, 326-7, 332
  bronze 223, 293-5, 297, 301,
  309-11, 314, 325-8, 331-2, 338,
  340
  copper 98, 104, 221-3
  silver 247, 358
'pintaderas' 116
Pjatigorsk 224, 227
Plaidt 120-1
Plas Newydd 188
Pleistocene 3, 5-6, 7 ff., 12 ff.
Pliocene 2-3, 13
ploshchadki 236-7
plough (-share) 123, 136, 205-6,
  335
pluvial periods 5, 9-10, 45-6, 71
Po R. 132, 251-3, 334 ff.
Polada 313, 334
Poland, mesolithic 52, 64-5, 204
  neolithic 203-4, 205-11, 219,
  228, 230-1, 249, 255, 280-1
  bronze age 330, 362-3; *and see*
  Galicia
Polep 346
Polgar 114-15
pollen-analysis 57-9, 141, 200-1
Pomerania 117, 205, 208, 212
Pomeranian glaciation 54
Ponder's End 22
Port-Conty 134
Portugal, mesolithic 69
  neolithic,   chalcolithic   128,
  161 ff., 179 ff., 304, 329
  bronze age 304, 307
pottery, general 74 ff.
  (Bell-) Beaker 164-7, 170, 181-2,
  185-6, 190-1, 243, 250 ff., 257 ff.,
  265-6, 307, 309; British 266 ff.,
  318 ff., 373
  bell-urns 270-3, 277
  binocular vases 101, 236
  braided ware 299-300, 360
  channelled 158-9, 172-4, 177,
  183, 185-6, 188, 251
  cinerary urn 346, 373 ff., *and
  see* urnfields
  comb-ornamented 62, 99, 105,
  202 ff., 231, 233, 237, 358, 362,
  364
  cord-impressed 140, 191, 201 ff.,
  214, 216, 219, 220 ff., 234, 237,
  271, 320, 373; Corded Ware
  218-19, 227 ff., 233-5, 238, 248-50,
  253, 256, 257 ff., 274, 280-2,
  298 ff., 311, 332-3, 342, 360, 367,
  370 ff.

crusted 106, 108, 114-15, 234,
  238
  Cycladic 88-90, 151, 153-5,
  238-40
  Danubian neolithic 80, 95,
  109 ff., 116 ff., 151, 157; copper
  age 242 ff., 254 ff.; bronze age
  293 ff., 341 ff.
  early plain and incised, Eastern
  75-84, 129, 151, 153, 220 ff.;
  Western 82-4, 125 ff., 151 ff.,
  164-6, 170 ff.
  finger-tip 128, 136, 156-7, 170,
  244-6, 251, 254, 257-8, 260, 266,
  270-3, 276-7, 307, 309, 321,
  371
  food-vessels 309, 319 ff., 372 ff.
  grooved ware 271-3, 276, 316,
  318 ff., 373
  Helladic 89-90, 151, 238-40;
  Minyan 234, 239-40, 242-3, 250,
  296, 351; Mycenean 351 ff., 358
  mesolithic 61-2, 76, 201-2, 207
  Minoan 87-8, 156-7, 222, 241,
  348 ff.
  Northern neolithic 178, 181,
  201 ff., 234, 245, 248-9, 260, 264,
  281 ff.
  painted 75-6, 78-80, 88, 90,
  95 ff., 113-15, 126, 151, 154, 209,
  225, 235-7, 238, 240-1, 297, 349,
  351, 355-6
  pygmy cups 315, 331, 346,
  373-4
  Western neolithic 69, 82-3,
  125 ff., 156 ff., 170 ff.; bronze
  age 308 ff.
Pre-Aunjetitz culture 293-5, 300-1
Pre-Crag flints 13-14
Předmost 30, 54
Presely 317
pressure-flaking 32, 254, 278-80
Prokuplje 96
Prossnitz 209
Prosymna 353
Proto-Solutrian culture 27-8, 29
Puerto Blanco 130
Puig Rodó 172, 195
Pusztaistvánháza 241-2
Pylos 353
Pyrenees 131, 169, 172, 251, 309
Pyrenean culture 170-4, 176, 179-80,
  182, 199, 251, 263, 304, 307-8,
  320, 368

Quaternary period 5
Quelvezin 165, 265
Quinta da Agua Branca 307
Quoyness 192

rapiers 241, 352
Rappenfels 65
Ras Shamra 348
Reggio Emilia 157, 334
reindeer 23, 32, 34, 37, 41-2, 48, 62
religion 37-9, 148 ff., 159 ff., 170 ff.,
  180 ff., 185 ff., 188 ff., 199, 211,
  215, 262, 264-6, 306, 311-14,
  316-17, 366, 372, 374-6, 378,
  380-1, *and see* magic
Remedello culture 157, 159, 165,
  215, 243, 247, 250, 253, 292,
  303-5, 334, 336
Remedon 313
Remouchamps 52
Rhine R. 117 ff., 252, 256, 257 ff.,
  328, 330, 333, 345, 367, 369 ff.,
  378, *and see* Germany, Rhineland,
  and Holland
Rhône, R. 131, 159, 251-2, 257, 304,
  309-10, 368
Rhône culture 310-14, 328, 330, 368,
  370-2, 378
Rijckholt Ste. Gertrude 67
Rillaton 378
Rinaldone 250
Riner 307
Rinyo 321
Riss glaciation 7, 15, 17-18, 20,
  23-4, 26
river-drift 7 ff., 14 ff.
Roca del Lladoner 42
rock-engravings, 62, 82, 188, 304-5,
  307, 321-2
rock-paintings 42-3, 48, 82, 127, 164,
  183
Romanelli 50
Rössen culture 118 ff., 124, 137, 214,
  217, 245
rostro-carinates 13
Rothesay 177
Roundway Down 267
Rudh'an Dunain 192
Rügen 208, 212, 326
Rumania, palaeolithic 28, 32
  mesolithic 65
  neolithic 95 ff., 224-6, 234-8, 242
  bronze age 296, 300, 333, 343,
  358, *and see* Transylvania
Russia, palaeolithic 29, 30, 37, 39, 58
  mesolithic 62, 64, 69, 203-4
Russia, N. and Central, neolithic
  105, 203, 224 ff.
  and chalcolithic 358-9
Russia, South, neolithic 98 ff., 203-4,
  221 ff., 232-3, 236-7
  bronze age 343, 358-9
Rüssingen 257
Rybno 212

Saale glaciation 8, 18
Saale R. 117, 136, 227, 248
Sahara 4, 71, 129
St. Acheul 15, 18, *and see* Acheulian
St. Antoine-du-Rocher 174
St. Menoux 314
St. Michel 184
St. Vellier 257
San Bartolomeo 126, 157, 252
Sandarna 62
Sandomierz 230, 255
San Michele Ozieri 158
San Pietro in Mendicate 334
Santa Caterina 339
Santa Cristina 253
San Vicente 262
Sardinia 83-4, 125-7, 155-60, 162,
  167, 171-3, 194, 251-2, 254, 261-2,
  304-5, 359
Šarka 115
Sarvaš 246
Säter 202
Sauveterre 50, 66
Sauveterrian culture 51, 65, 66
Save R. 114, 246, 298, 333, 342
Savignano 39
Savoie 133, 257, 310
Saxony 118, 208, 214, 256-7, 297,
  301, 362
Saxo-Thuringia 219, 227-30, 233,
  248, 256-8, 280-1, 302, 328-30,
  333, 361-2, 365
Scandinavia, mesolithic 49, 53-64,
  66-7, 69, 76, 200 ff., *otherwise
  see* Denmark, Finland, Norway,
  Sweden
Schafstedt 366
Scheldtiz 248
Schipenitz 99-100, 236-7
Schleswig-Holstein 49, 58, 206, 210,
  212, 215-18, 228, 230, 258,
  364-6
Schneckenberg culture 235, 237-8,
  241, 296
Schulzenberg 248
Schussenried 137, 244-5
Scoglio del Tonno 338-40
Scotland, mesolithic 67
  neolithic 176 ff.
  and bronze age 268, 273, 276,
  318 ff., 324-5, 329, 346, 375 ff.
sculpture, animal 40, 105, 153, 231,
  358-9
  megalithic 173, 188-9, 198
  Mycenean 352
scrapers 16, 19-20, 28-30, 34, 48-9,
  58, 63, 68, 129, 133-4, 278, 374
Scyths 359
sea-level, *see* land- and sea-levels

seals 85, 116, 241, 354
Sebilian culture 72
Seefin 190
Seima 358
Seine-Oise-Marne culture, 135, 198-199, 260-6, 283
Servia 80, 96
Sesklo 79-80, 90, 101, 105, 350
Settiponti 126
Severn-Cotswold tombs 175, 184, 187, 193, 270
shaft-graves 347, 350-3, 378
sheep 72-4, 77-8, 99, 110, 134, 142, 237, and see pastoralism
shells, shell ornaments 38, 51, 68, 84-5, 94, 104, 111, 116, 121, 130-1, 161, 253, 263, 294, 308, 345, 380
shell-mounds 60-4, 68-9, 200-1, 205, 211
ships 85, 156, 211, 355-6
shoe-last celts 94-5, 99, 110, 113, 116, 123, 205, 236, 296
shouldered points 29-32, and see tanged points
Siberia 25, 39
Sicily 83-4, 125-6, 128, 151-2, 154-160, 162-3, 167-8, 251-2, 336, 355, 359
sickles 72, 77, 83, 94, 123, 136, 142-3, 213, 272, 340
Siculan I culture, 152-7, 336
Sidestrand 15
Silesia 62, 112, 114, 116-18, 205, 208-9, 214, 230, 249, 255, 280-1, 301-2, 327, 362
silver 89, 150, 155, 161, 221, 237, 247, 286, 308, 358
single-graves 218 ff., 228-31, 232-3, 255, 258-9, 266, 274-5, 277-8, 280-2, 311, 322, 365-7, 371 ff., 376, 379
Singleyrac 314
Siphnos 89
Sipplingen 245
Sireuil 39
Sittingbourne 165
Skara Brae 321
Skendleby 270
Skogsbo 275, 282
skulls 10-11, 17, 22-3, 25, 28, 31-2, 33, 51-2, 54, 68-9, 124, 136, 145, 252-4, 263, 267, 301
slate implements 204, 364
Slavonian culture 243, 246, 298, 333, 337, 342-3, 345, 357
Slavs 363, 379
sleeves, see axe-sleeves
Slieve Gullion 190
Sligo 190-1, 197

Slovakia 110, 112, 246, 249, 255, 292, 294, 299-300, 360
Sølager 201, 205-6
solar radiation 9
solifluxion 7 ff., 14 ff.
Solutré 27, 32-3, 37, 51
Solutrian culture 12, 27-8, 29, 32-3, 40, 45
Somme R. 8, 14, 15-18, 20, 22
Spain, palaeolithic 17, 24, 32, 34, 35, 40 ; E. Spanish art 42-3
mesolithic 45-8, 63, 68-9, 83
neolithic 69, 79, 81-4, 125 ff., 148, 156-8
chalcolithic 160 ff., 170 ff., 247, 250-2, 262, 292, 303, 306
bronze age 303-9, 363, 368-9, 377, 379
spearheads 221, 326, 352-3, 358, 374, 377
Spiennes 138
spinning 74, 203, 205, 220, 239, 341
Spondylus 111, 121
spoons 77-9, 132, 134, 143-4
Spy 23
Stanton Drew 267
Starčevo 96-7, 99, 101, 104-6, 108
Stary Zámek 209, 234
state 1, 85, 382
statues 173, 188, 198
statuettes 38-9, 84, 89, 94-5, 98-9, 101-3, 105, 115, 153, 156, 220, 225, 235-6
Steinheim skull 17
Stennis 321
Stentinello 84, 125-6, 128, 154, 157-8
step-flaking 20-1
steppes, S. Russian 5, 25, 30, 37, 64, 203-4, 220 ff., 274, 343, 358-9
Stoke Down 138
stone-anvil technique 14-15
stone circles, see circles, stone
stone implements, Chs. I-III passim ; 98, 101, 110, 150, 161, 204, 235-6, 242, 246, 301, 364, and see adzes, axes, battle-axes, double-axes, flint, hoes, knob-hammer axes, maceheads, shoe-last celts
stone vessels 115, 271, 300
Stonehenge 276, 316-17, 374-5
Stoney Littleton 184
Strandegaard 201, 205-6, 216
Straubing 301, 360
Stretovka 230
Sub-Boreal climate-phase 201, 269, 288-90, 303, 305-6, 374
Südensee 206
Sumer, Sumerian(s) 73, 75, 86, 221-4, 232, 382

Suomusjärvi culture 62
Susa 73, 75
Sussex 138-40, 142-4, 268, 318, 324, 347
Sutton Courtenay 165
Svaerdborg 58
Svodobne Dvory 255
Swanscombe 16-17
Swanscombe skull, 11, 17
Sweden, mesolithic 49, 54-9, 61-2, 63
  neolithic 201 ff., 213 ff., 225, 228, 231, 275, 279, 282-3
  and bronze age 325-7, 329, 364-5
Swiderian culture 49, 52, 65
Swidry 52
Switzerland, palaeolithic 34
  mesolithic 65, 69
  neolithic 122, 133-6, 244-9, 253
  bronze age 310-11, 368
swords 307, 338
Syria 73, 75, 80, 241, 294, 348-9, 355
Szeleta cave 28-9
Szöreg 345, 347

tanged points 30-2, 49, 52-3, 58, 65, 67, 204, 215, *and see* shouldered points
Tannstock 65
Taplow 20, 26
Taranto 336, 338-9
Tardenoisian culture 50-1, 60-1, 63, 64-70, 132-3, 141, 200
Tasa, Tasian culture 78, 136
Taubach-Ehringsdorf 23
Taula dels Llades 172
Tayacian culture 17, 21
Tell Atchana 348
Tell Duweir 348
Tell el-Ajjul 378
Tell el-Amarna 348
Tell Halaf culture 73, 75-6, 80, 96-7, 153
Tell Ratcheff 235
Tepe Hissar 222
terraces, river 8 ff.
terremare 338, 343, 347, 359, 379
Tertiary period 2, 13
Téviec, Île 68-9, 147, 175, 186
Thames R. 16-18, 19-20, 22, 26, 266, 273, 276, 318, 320
Thayngen 136
Thebes 351, 354
Theiss R. 114, 224, 343
Theiss culture 98, 108, 112, 114 ff., 118, 124, 209-10, 234-5, 241-2, 292-3
Thermi 76, 90-1, 93, 107-8, 150, 154, 226

Theseus 356
Thessaly, Thessalian cultures 79-81, 90-1, 93-4, 96, 101, 104-9, 114, 116, 126, 150-1, 234, 238-40, 350, 354-5, 357
Thoricos 354
Thracians 363, 379
Thun, L. 136
Thuringia 118-19, 256-8, 292, 302, 371
tin 150, 290 ff., 303-4, 307, 309, 311-12, 318, 323, 346, 351
Tinsdahl 279, 325
Tiryns 351, 353-4
Tisza, *see* Theiss
Tiszaug 242
tombs, corbelled 148-9, 153, 160-2, 167-9, 171, 182, 184, 189, 191-2, 262, 306, 312, 353-4, 356
  Cycladic 88-9, 149-51, 153-6, 160, 167, 222
  Minoan 130, 148-50, 153-4, 160, 171, 353
  Mycenean 350-6
  rock-cut 130-1, 148-9, 151-3, 155-7, 160-4, 167, 171, 189, 194, 198, 222, 252, 262-3; 337, 353; chalk-cut 198, 263, *and see* burials, forecourts, megaliths
torcs 378, *and see* ingot torcs
Tordos 95-7, 106, 108, 114, 224
Torre del Moro 170, 195
tortoise-cores 18-19
Tószeg A 293 ff., 332-3, 357
  B 341 ff., 357
  C 344, 357
trade 70 ff., 84 ff., 87-8, 90-2, 94, 97, 104, 107, 115, 121, 123, 129, 148, 150-3, 154, 155-6, 157-63, 166, 173-5, 178, 199, 210-11, 215-16, 220 ff., 240-2, 247-8, 253 ff., 261-5, 268, 276 ff., 286 ff., 291 ff., 299 ff., 304 ff., 309 ff., 316 ff., 323 ff., 327 ff., 335, 345 ff., 349 ff., 358 ff., 366 ff., 377 ff.
Transylvania 94 ff., 246, 292, 297, 343, *and see* Rumania
Tres Cabezos 83, 128, 130
Tressé 198
Trieste 254
Tripolye culture 99-109, 203-4, 225
Trojan War 358, 383
Troldebjerg 216
Troy, Troad 90-1, 93, 103, 107-8, 116, 150-1, 154, 238, 241, 363
  Troy I 90
  Troy II 93, 107-8, 115, 116, 150, 152, 163, 222, 226, 238-9, 242, 291, 294, 358

Troy III, IV 107, 239-40
Troy V 358
Troy VI 358
Troy VIIa 359
Trundle 142, 144-5
Tsangli 79
Tumulus cultures 361, 367, 369 ff.
378
Tuscany 132, 156-7, 251-2, 305
Tzarevskaya 221, 228

Ukraine 52, 64, 98-109, 203-4, 221-3,
226, 229-30, 233, 236-7, 255
Ülde 260
Uley 184
Unstan 191-2
Unter-Wölbling 300
Urjala 203
Urmitz 137, 258
urn-burial, urnfields 338, 340, 342 ff.,
357 ff., 371 ff., 379
Utoquai 249

Valdygaard 195
Valla 171
Vapheio 353
Vardar R. 94-5, 106, and see
Morava-Vardar
Varese, L. 136, 250, 334
varves 55
vase-supports 183, 185, 314, 316
Västergötland 214, 275, 282-3
Vattina 298, 343
Vaucelles 261
Velefique 165
Velez Blanco 130-1
Velka Ves 293
Veluwe 271-4
Velvary 247
' Venuses,' see statuettes
Veselé 299
Vézère R. 21
Vibrata R. 157, 335-6
Vidra 97-8, 108, 225, 235
Villafranca 247
Villafrati 126, 252
Villers-St.-Sépulcre 275
Vinča 92-9, 104, 106, 109-10, 114-15,
234
Vinelz 247, 249, 278
Vistonice 30, 37, 39
Vistula glaciation, see Weichsel
Vodastra 103, 108
Vogtland 292-3, 302
Volo 354
Vozdivezenskaya 224
Vučedol 246

Wales 184, 187-8, 194, 267, 273,
317-18, 324, 330, 347
Walternienburg - Bernburg - Havel

cultures 207, 217, 219, 227-8, 260,
280, 301-2
' warrior cultures ' 217 ff., 232 ff.,
257 ff., 287, 296 ff., 311 ff., 332-3,
336, 342, 357 ff., 367, 370 ff.,
379 ff.
Warthe glaciation 8
Wash 145, 273, 277
Waterford 176, 194
weaving 74, 134
Weichsel glaciation 8, 33, 35
Weiher 136
Weimar culture 23
Weissensee 297
Weser R. 117, and see Elbe-Weser
Wessex 138 ff., 266 ff., 315 ff., 324,
330-2, 346-8, 366, 372 ff., 378
Wessinghuizen 275
West Kennet Avenue 267-8, 272, 276
Westleton beds 15
Wetterau 119, 137
wheat 71-2, 77-8, 110, 123, 136,
205-6
Whitehawk 143-4, 202, 268
Wieselburg culture 299, 345, 360
Willendorf 30, 39
Willerby 279, 325
willow-leaf implements 32
Windmill Hill 132, 137, 142-4,
267-8, and see Britain, neolithic A
Winterbourne Dauntsey 267
Winterslow 267
Wiorek 208
Witenberg culture 297, 333
Wolfsbach 116
wood-bar technique 16-17, 20, 26
Woodhenge 276, 316-17, 373
Wor Barrow 175, 195
Worms 112, 120, 137, 302
writing 85, 241, 354-5, 382-3
Würm glaciation 7, 45
Würm 1 20-3, 26-7, 31
Würm 2 31, 33, 35, 54
Wurm 3 35, 46, 54, 71

Yarrows 193
Yoldia Sea 55-6
Yorkshire 145, 196, 268-70, 276,
279, 318 ff., 329, 366, 373, 378
Yverdon 229

Zalisčyky 99-100, 236
Zarrenthin 206
Zealand 58-9, 201, 206, and see
Denmark
zemljanki 236
Złota culture 230, 280-1
Zseliz 111, 113
Zürich 134-5, 244
Züschen 260

MAPS AND TABLES

MAP I. LOWER AND MIDDLE PALAEOLITHIC

A very simplified sketch of the relative distribution of the Hand-axe and Flake Cultures, with that of the Mousterian 'complex' of the Middle Palaeolithic roughly indicated in addition. (P.=Palestine.) See pp. 12-24.

Glaciations	HAND AXE CULTURES	FLAKE CULTURES
	P R E - C R A G	
Günz	ABBEVILLIAN	CROMER
Mindel		CLAC-
	EARLY & MIDDLE ACHEULIAN	-TON-
Riss		LE-
Würm 1	LATE⎤ACHEULIAN	-VALL- -IAN
	FINAL⎦	MOUST--OIS-ERIAN

TABLE I. LOWER AND MIDDLE PALAEOLITHIC

MAP II. UPPER PALAEOLITHIC AND MESOLITHIC

Upper Palaeolithic Cultures in Capitals. CH.=Châtelperron ; C.=Creswell ;
H.=Hamburg ; P.=Palestine.
Stipple shows extent of Magdalenian. See pp. 24-43.

Mesolithic Sites : M.=Mugem ; Ast.=Asturian coast; Az.=Mas d'Azil ; S.=Sau-
veterre ; T.=Téviec ; FT.=Fère-en-Tardenois ; H.=Horsham ; P.=Pennines ;
G.=Glenarm ; Z.=Zonhoven ; A.=Ahrensburg ; D.=Duvensee ; K.=Kloster-
lund ; L.=Lyngby ; K.=Kunda ; Sw.=Swidry. See pp. 44-70.

Glaciations	UPPER PALAEOLITHIC CULTURES					
Würm 1	S	CHÂTELPERRON				
	P	**AURIGNAC**-SOL- **-IAN**				
Würm 2	A	WEST-GRAV-		EAST-) -UTR-(-GRAV-		
	N	-ETTIAN			-IAN	-ETT-
	I					
	S	MAGDALEN- GRIMALD- CRES-				-I-
Würm 3	H	-IAN	-IAN	-WELLIAN	HAMBURG -AN	
Climate-phases	MESOLITHIC CULTURES					
Late Glacial and Pre-Boreal	S	AZ-	AHRENSBURG, LYNGBY		SWID-	
	P	-ILIAN	**TARD-**	KLOSTERLUND	-ERIAN	
	A	SAUVE-		GUD- **MAGLE-**		
Boreal	N	-TERRIAN	**-EN-**	-EN- **-MOSE**		
	I					
Atlantic	S	AST-	**-OISIAN**	-AA **ERTEBØLLE,**ETC.		
	H	-URIAN				

TABLE II. UPPER PALAEOLITHIC AND MESOLITHIC

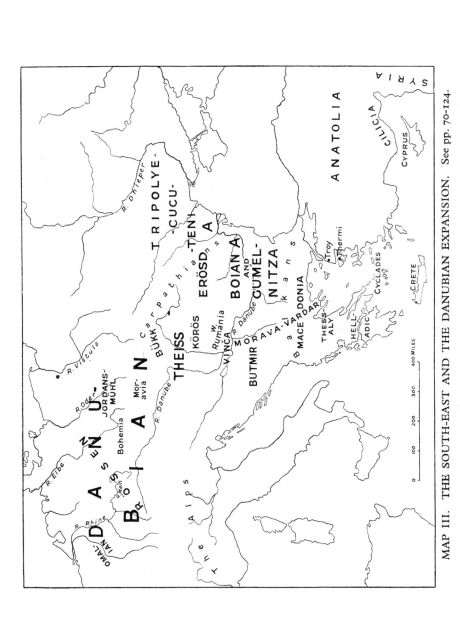

MAP III. THE SOUTH-EAST AND THE DANUBIAN EXPANSION. See pp. 70-124.

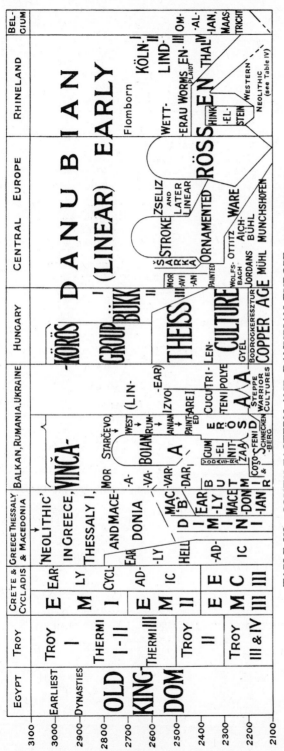

TABLE III. SOUTH-EASTERN AND DANUBIAN EUROPE, 3100–2100 B.C.

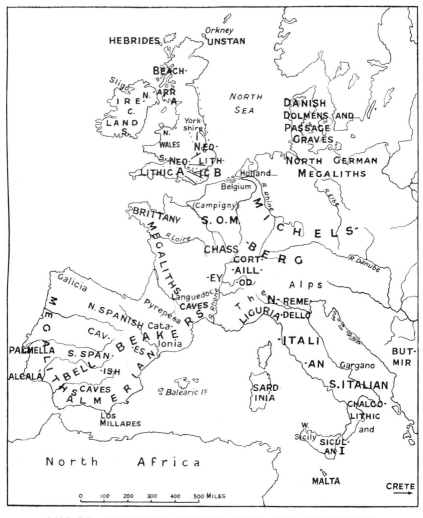

MAP IV. THE WEST, THE SEA-WAYS, AND THE NORTH.
See pp. 125-199.

TABLE IV. MEDITERRANEAN, WESTERN, AND NORTHERN EUROPE, 3100–1900 B.C.

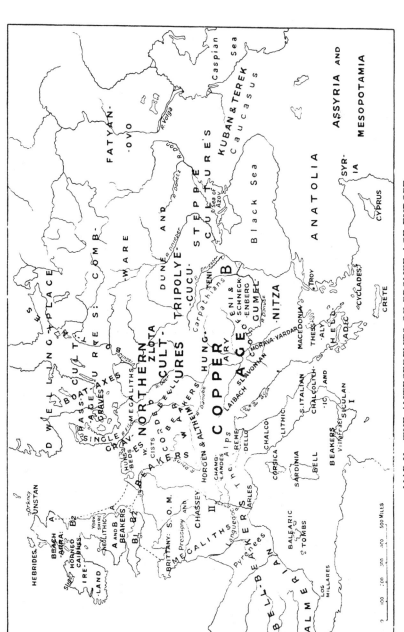

MAP V. THE ANTECEDENTS OF BRONZE AGE EUROPE.

See pp. 189-281.

TABLE V. THE CHANGING PATTERN OF EUROPEAN CULTURES, 2300-1700 B.C.

MAP VI. EARLY BRONZE AGE EUROPE.
See pp. 281-384.

TABLE VI. THE ACHIEVEMENT OF THE EUROPEAN BRONZE AGE,
1800–1400 B.C.